11/12

Also by Thomas Keller

Ad Hoc at Home
with Dave Cruz,
along with Susie Heller, Michael Ruhlman, and Amy Vogler

Under Pressure
with Jonathan Benno, Corey Lee, and Sebastien Rouxel,
along with Susie Heller, Michael Ruhlman, and Amy Vogler

Bouchon
with Jeffrey Cerciello,
along with Susie Heller and Michael Ruhlman

The French Laundry Cookbook
with Susie Heller and Michael Ruhlman

BOUCHON BAKERY

Thomas Keller and Sebastien Rouxel

With Susie Heller, Matthew McDonald, Michael Ruhlman, and Amy Vogler

Photographs by Deborah Jones

ARTISAN

Copyright © 2012 by Thomas Keller

Photographs copyright © 2012 by Deborah Jones

Published by Artisan

A division of Workman Publishing Company, Inc.

225 Varick Street

New York, NY 10014-4381

artisanbooks.com

Published simultaneously in Canada by

Thomas Allen & Son, Limited

Keller, Thomas

Bouchon Bakery / Thomas Keller and Sebastien Rouxel ; with Susie Heller, Matthew

McDonald, Michael Ruhlman, and Amy Vogler ; photographs by Deborah Jones.

p. cm.

Includes index.

ISBN 978-1-57965-435-1

1. Baking. 2. Bouchon Bakery. I. Rouxel, Sebastien. II. McDonald, Matthew.

III. Title.

TX719.K345 2012

641.5944—dc23   2012000695

Design by Level, Calistoga, California

Printed in China

First printing, September 2012

1 3 5 7 9 10 8 6 4 2

Contents

92

158 **186**

30 **126**

To the world of pastry chefs and bread bakers who delight us every day
with the simplicity of their craft and the wonders they produce.
And to my brothers James, Robert, and Joseph; my sister, Judith; and my late brother, Michael.
—Thomas Keller

To past, present, and future pâtissiers and to the chefs who inspired me in my career.
And to my dear family—my wife, Andrea; our daughters, Ava and Grace; my in-laws, Rob and
Naomi Brantjes; and my parents, Henri and Hélène—for their endless support and love.
—Sebastien Rouxel

To my wife, Kristina, whose love and support make my work worthwhile.
—Matthew McDonald

66   **336**

252

212

Every Morning in Paris

When I was twenty-eight, I lived on the top floor of 15, rue de Vouille. On the ground floor was a tiny *boulangerie*. Every morning I woke to the smell of baking bread. But before I got to Paris, my time in France hadn't gone well. It took me several years of building up contacts to find a *stage* there. At last I did, at a Michelin-starred restaurant in Arbois, a small city near the Swiss border. My traveling friends dropped me off at the hotel where I was to work. The gruff matron

showed me to my cell-like room, which was barely big enough for the bed. Strangely, the single window was almost completely black. When I was taken to the basement kitchen, I realized why: the kitchen still relied on a coal-burning stove, and my room was right above the chimney.

It wasn't just the kitchen stove that evoked a past era of cooking—everything was antiquated. I had come from working at The Polo Lounge, where young chefs Patrice Boely and Daniel Boulud were preparing really forward-thinking cooking. I had spent three years searching for a *stage* only to learn how to cook on a coal-burning stove? In desperation, I called Serge Raoul, a New York restaurateur for whom I'd worked and whom I considered a friend.

He told me to take the next train to Paris, where he had an apartment. I could stay there while I regrouped. Rue de Vouille was in the fifteenth arrondissement, a lovely middle-class neighborhood, with small shops and bars and brasseries. My bedroom window framed the Eiffel Tower. A good sign.

In a short time, I had my first Parisian *stage*, one of seven. For fifteen months, I immersed myself in the cuisine of France, working at different restaurants, ending at the Michelin three-star Taillevent. It was here that I witnessed the structure and organization, the attention to detail and consistency that made one of the world's great restaurants what it was.

Open five days a week, Taillevent served lunch and dinner, so I had a great schedule. I arrived in the morning and helped to prepare the *mise en place* for lunch service. When lunch was done and the kitchen cleaned, by 3:30 or so, we'd have a break when I could hang out with my fellow cooks, walk in a park, or take a French lesson. We had to be back at 5:30 (dinner didn't begin until 8:00 or so), and one of my afternoon jobs was to make the *marquise au chocolat*, one of the restaurant's signature desserts, for the next day. It was a very rich confection, kind of a cross between mousse and ganache. It was sliced and served with a pistachio sauce. I love chocolate, so I loved making it. It became one of the highlights of my day and of my time in France.

I learned so much during those months in France in 1983 and 1984. It was where I first worked with foie gras, and with more obscure cuts we weren't used to in the United States, like lamb breast. It's where I had my first *macaron*, that most extraordinary of cookies. And where I tasted my first real croissant and mille-feuille (I was in heaven when I was eating one of those). Three days a week, a wonderful, noisy food market set up on my street selling fresh chickens, cheeses I'd never heard of, *saucissons secs*, and *jambon cru*, then unavailable back home. I was living at the heart of a thoroughly food-centric culture.

But looking back on it now, from an emotional standpoint, my most enduring memory is of waking up every morning to that smell of baking bread. The central staircase of our old building had been renovated to contain a tiny elevator, and I'd take this downstairs, pay a franc fifty for a demi-baguette (I had little money), and head back up. I'd share the bread with my housemate— we cooked at the same restaurant—with butter and jam and coffee.

It had quickly become clear to me how central bread was to life in Paris. The *boulangerie* in my building was maybe 100 square feet of retail space; the ovens were in the back. I was fascinated by the man who baked the bread. I saw that a man could devote his life to baking bread, and that it was a good life, a worthy profession and one to be revered. That was very powerful for me.

On our way to the metro I'd pass at least three *boulangeries*, of all different calibers. The one in my building made bread and rustic little apple tarts. A second one sold large, garish meringues. The finest one made the most beautiful mille-feuilles and tarts. I'd never seen apple tarts like theirs, slices of apple, each one perfect, in concentric rings, with a glossy sheen of a glaze. I couldn't afford them, but they were beautiful to behold, and they taught me about the level of excellence a bakery might strive for.

I also learned that a bakery is an anchor— it draws a community around it. People would sit in the bakeries to eat their croissants;

they would gather in the morning, and in the afternoon. People come together at and around bakeries. Baking is a unifying force.

The smell of baking bread is universally adored for a reason: it appeals to us at the core of our humanness. It's the smell of sustenance and security. To enjoy that aroma even before I was conscious of the new day had a great impact on me—one I didn't truly realize until, well, now, trying to understand why on earth I have five bakeries. I'm a restaurant chef, a savory cook—what am I doing with five bakeries?

The reason is bread, and croissants, macarons, puff pastry, apple tarts, and mille-feuilles.

Per se and The French Laundry, highly refined restaurants, speak to only a small segment of the population. Even our bistro, Bouchon, and our family-style restaurant, Ad Hoc, have specific, somewhat narrow, audiences. Bread does not. Pastries do not. They are universal. And that is one source of my desire to offer baked goods to as many people as possible, and why I'm so excited to be sharing the craft in this book.

Pecan Sandies for My Mom

My mom, Betty Keller, was a creature of habit. She worked very hard at her job managing restaurants while raising five boys and a daughter as a single mother. She loved to have cookies on hand at the end of the day, and she especially loved the Keebler pecan sandie. It was part of my childhood, and it's a flavor combination, vanilla and pecan, that I associate with her. It was an adult cookie to me. There was always a bag of them in the cupboard.

Or almost always. We *were* six kids, and we were voracious. That was a problem when it came to my mother's cookies. We had our own cookies, Oreos and Nutter Butters, but when we'd dispatched those, there would be that bag of Mom's pecan sandies, daring us. It was really hard. Those cookies were sacrosanct, but sometimes, guiltily, we ate her cookies, one by one, until they were gone.

Mom had very few things she could call her own. She had no real luxuries. We didn't have winter family vacations; we didn't go to a cabin by a lake in the summer. She worked, and she gave us everything we wanted and needed. But we didn't appreciate it then. How could we know? How could I, youngest of the boys, know?

But I do now. Day after day, year after year, Mom set an extraordinary example for me. An example of hard work, attention to detail, and an all-consuming love for our family that I still have today.

Food is a powerful connecter of who we are to who we were, to our past, to our memories, and, for me, to a different and simpler time. Even the smallest thing—a cookie—can help us understand what we feel now while reminding us of what we once felt and who we've become versus who we were then. So much of who I am today is tied to who my mom was, the choices she made, the way she worked, and how she lived her life. What success I have today, I owe to her.

All of which is why the pecan sandie is so important to me.

All-purpose flour	250 grams	1¾ cups + 1½ teaspoons
Coarsely chopped pecans	80 grams	¾ cup
Unsalted butter, at room temperature	170 grams	6 ounces
Powdered sugar	90 grams	¾ cup + 1¾ teaspoons

Additional powdered sugar
for dusting (optional)

Position the racks in the upper and lower thirds of the oven and preheat the oven to 325°F (convection) or 350°F (standard). Line two sheet pans with Silpats or parchment paper.

Toss the flour and pecans together in a medium bowl.

Place the butter in the bowl of a stand mixer fitted with the paddle attachment and mix on medium-low speed until smooth. Add the 90 grams/¾ cup plus 1¾ teaspoons powdered sugar and mix for about 2 minutes, until fluffy. Scrape down the sides and bottom of the bowl. Add the flour mixture and mix on low speed for about 30 seconds, until just combined. Scrape the bottom of the bowl to incorporate any dry ingredients that have settled there.

Divide the dough into 30-gram/1½-tablespoon portions, roll into balls, and arrange on the sheet pans, leaving about 1½ inches between them. Press the cookies into 2-inch disks.

Bake until pale golden brown, 15 to 18 minutes if using a convection oven, 22 to 25 minutes if using a standard oven, reversing the positions of the pans halfway through. (Sandies baked in a convection oven will not spread as much as those baked in a standard oven and will have a more even color.)

Set the pans on a cooling rack and cool for 5 to 10 minutes. Using a metal spatula, transfer the cookies to the rack to cool completely.

If desired, dust with powdered sugar.

The cookies can be stored in a covered container for up to 3 days.

MAKES 1½ DOZEN COOKIES

The Road to Bouchon Bakery

I try to get better each day, to do my job just a little better every day. Not a lot, but a little. Every day. That's what we try to do at Bouchon Bakery and at all our restaurants. When I opened The French Laundry in 1994, our bread was brought over from Petaluma by Kathleen Weber, a former nurse who had started a small bakery with her husband, Ed, and their children. Their bakery, Della Fattoria, continues to grow and thrive, and we love the Webers' bread, but when you run a restaurant and are always striving to improve, you ask yourself, How can we give our guests a better experience? Once we got the essentials right and The French Laundry had a number of years under its belt, we decided that one of the ways we could make the restaurant a better experience would be to bake our own bread. We wanted specific sizes and shapes, bread very precisely tailored to the food we were serving, types of bread that weren't feasible for Della Fattoria—or any of the great artisanal bakeries that were opening in increasing numbers in Northern California—to create on our scale.

We needed our own bakery. We'd opened Bouchon, a bistro, in 1998, so our own bakery could not only make bread for The French Laundry, it could also provide baguettes and épis to serve at the bistro.

Once again, we were lucky. Bouchon Bakery is in the space where I used to get my hair cut: it was a salon. But the owners wanted to take some time off and travel, so I bought their lease.

Once the bakery got under way, and we had that space right next to the bistro, we wondered if we might do more. Couldn't we also open a small *boulangerie* in front, a little retail shop like the kind I'd loved so much in Paris? We could offer croissants and *pains aux raisins* in the morning, cookies and macarons in the afternoon, and sell baguettes and *pains de campagne* right next to Bouchon, with a European-style courtyard out front that might become a kind of community center.

Bouchon Bakery opened in July 2003, making items in three categories: bread for The French Laundry, French-style breads for the bistro, and retail bakery products. But while the bread we made was excellent, it's very difficult to make money baking bread, and the bakery struggled. It was really frustrating. A number of times I came close to shutting it down and opening a sushi restaurant on the site. Honestly.

Then Matthew McDonald arrived, and that was the turning point. The bakery was getting there—we were learning, chipping away at the obstacles. But Matthew, who had trained at one of the most prominent baking programs in the country, and with some of the world's best bakers, and who had run his own bakery on the East Coast, brought an understanding of wholesale baking, the organization and production schedules required to make it work. And he brought a deep love and knowledge of bread itself.

Being a baker requires uncommon commitment and work. As with any kitchen job, it's physically grueling and requires long hours. But they are odd hours. A baker who is expected to have fresh bread in the morning has to begin baking in the middle of the night.

And the product is incredibly fragile: it has no shelf life. You've got to sell it right away or it's no good—and you've got to have more on the way for when you do sell it all.

Also, it's such an inexpensive product, you've got to sell an awful lot of it just to make a little bit of money.

After Matthew arrived, all our previous efforts came together with a click. He was able to teach the pastry chef of Bouchon Bakery about production schedules for pastry, so that we wouldn't run out of macarons in two hours but have twenty éclairs left at the end of the day. Matthew made sure there was always product in the case, and he came up with ways to use anything that was left over.

Today the bakery is not just a success, it outpaces all the restaurants in terms of number of guests served. We may serve three hundred at Bouchon, but Bouchon Bakery will serve up to a thousand people on a good day—more than all our Yountville restaurants combined.

Sebastien Rouxel was executive pastry chef at The French Laundry for four years before we opened the bakery. He worked with Matthew to bring consistency to the pastry end of the business—the laminated doughs used for croissants and puff pastry, and the confections.

It was almost accidental, though, that Sebastien, the man who leads the five Bouchon Bakeries today, was even there, as he hadn't wanted to be a part of my restaurant in the first place. He hadn't even applied for the pastry chef job. He was living and working in New York City, but his wife wanted the sun and dry air of California. So when she read an ad I'd placed for a pastry chef for the restaurant, she secretly sent me Sebastien's résumé.

I am very lucky he accepted the tryout. Sebastien is one of the leading pastry chefs in America. He has embraced every challenge I've put before him, and he has proven to be an extraordinary teacher as well as chef, making an impact throughout the industry as his disciples spread out to restaurants around the country.

When per se opened in 2004, Sebastien got his wish to return to New York, becoming its pastry chef. As the New York Bouchon Bakery grew and we discussed expanding in Yountville, Las Vegas, and Los Angeles, I asked Sebastien to oversee the entire program.

The operation has now found its fullest realization as a stand-alone bakery at Rockefeller Center. I took extraordinary pleasure in being able to build a proper bakery for Sebastien and the team, a place to display the results of their remarkable efforts.

I'm honored to work with Sebastien and Matthew. Sebastien has amassed a huge body of knowledge and experience over almost two decades as a pastry chef at some of the finest restaurants in France and America, though he's not yet forty. Matthew is one of the best and most knowledgeable bread bakers in the country.

And now we have put all this knowledge and experience between covers, in *Bouchon Bakery*.

Enter Sebastien BY MICHAEL RUHLMAN

"I don't think I can teach pâtisserie to anyone who hasn't first learned to work clean," Sebastien Rouxel says. Andrea, Sebastien's wife, is seated beside him on the couch. "Drives me crazy," she says. Andrea is a pastry chef as well. In fact, she learned much of what she knows from Sebastien, for whom she worked at L'Orangerie after graduating from the Culinary Institute of America in 1996.

"I have my own way of working," she explains. She nods to the small open kitchen of their house in Garrison, New York, where she does all her baking. "When I know I'm going to be using something again, I'll leave it out," she continues. "So I'll be making a cake, and I'll go back to use the stand mixer, and he'll have already cleaned it and put it back in the cupboard!"

Sebastien chuckles in acknowledgment. "I can't help it," he says. "I'm maybe set in my ways."

"*Maybe?!*" Andrea echoes.

She should know. For her eighteen months at L'Orangerie in Los Angeles, a Relais & Châteaux, he was relentlessly difficult, stubborn, and demanding, a perfectionist who knew only one way—his way—and who spoke little English. He was twenty-two.

Sebastien had been trained in the traditional apprentice fashion, and by the time he left France, he was one of the youngest, if not the youngest, executive pastry chefs of a Michelin-starred restaurant. He had also run the pastry team within the Elysée Palace in Paris, the seat of the Republic of France and the official residence of the French president.

But when his friend Ludo Lefebvre took a job as the chef of L'Orangerie, he called Sebastien, then at the two-star Le Grand Véfour, and offered him the position of executive pastry chef. Sebastien, eager to see America, accepted. There he met Andrea, and while he was a tough boss, he couldn't deny his attraction to her. Nor could she deny hers to him.

"What made him irritating as a boss," she said, looking first at him, then at me, "I found endearing in a friend. He was so passionate and focused and talented. He knew how to do *everything*. And he could fix *anything*."

"What did you see in him?" I asked.

She paused, thinking. "His *care*."

I knew what she meant. I'd been working with Sebastien for more than a year, and his care was evident everywhere. In the way he made sure I had what I wanted when we sat to talk about this book. He was quick to smile and to laugh. I saw it in the way he dressed, his chef coat always crisp and white. He was casual and at ease, but elegant in his movements. I saw it in the commitment to the product his team presents. A few days after I sat with him and Andrea in their house, he was off to Los Angeles to make sure the product at the newest bakery was exactly as it was in New York (he spent his first eighteen hours there tweaking a dozen preparations).

"He's one of the best pastry chefs in America," said Thomas Keller, who hired him in 1998 as head pastry chef of The French Laundry. Stand with Keller at one of the bakery's cases, and you'll see this four-star chef marvel: "Look at those éclairs! See how perfect they are? Look at that glaze—so often at bakeries the glaze will be rough or dull or cracked. But *look* at that!" He becomes as giddy as a boy. Keller is no pastry chef; he knows exactly how good Sebastien makes him look. It's why he's so grateful to have Sebastien run the bakeries, and why he wanted to do this book.

Finally, you see Sebastien's care in his relationships with his staff. After a long day at the bakery at Rockefeller Center, Sebastien and I were heading out. It was after six, and he was eager to catch the train home to Andrea and their daughters, Ava and Grace. But one of his newer staff members stopped him on the way out to ask a question. His puff pastry just wasn't working. Sebastien asked him what the problem was. The new chef said he wasn't sure because he hadn't really made puff pastry before.

Sebastien said, "So we'll make some now. I'll show you." He removed his overcoat, put his chef coat back on, and went to work.

From the Loire Valley to Napa Valley

BY SEBASTIEN ROUXEL In 1997, I got a voice mail from Thomas Keller, saying he'd received my résumé and would like to meet with me. This was surprising, because I hadn't sent him a résumé. When I told my wife, Andrea, she confessed that she'd sent it without telling me. Soon I was trying out at The French Laundry, which had just been described as the most exciting restaurant in America by *The New York Times*. And I've been with Thomas happily ever since.

But my path to The French Laundry began decades before, during the Wednesdays of my childhood. In France, kids don't go to school on Wednesdays. And while I loved not having to go to school, the best part was the morning, when my brothers and sister and I would open the kitchen shutters to find beside the flowerpots wonderful *viennoiserie*, fresh from the bakery, waiting for us to devour with a cup of hot chocolate. Every Wednesday, my grandmother walked to the bakery and then all the way to our house (she didn't drive) to leave the pastries on the window ledge while we were still in bed. It was a long walk, but we adored *viennoiserie* and she knew it, and so I forever associate them with childhood delight and my grandmother's love.

Then in the afternoon, my mother often dropped us off at my grandmother's house for the rest of the day. My grandmother's sister ran a small restaurant, Café des Tonnelles, which served lunch on weekdays and dinner on weekends, one menu. Workers from the town would come there for lunch or a drink or to play *pétanque* out back. The café served platters of food family-style. A typical meal would begin with *céleri rémoulade*, followed by *blanquette de veau* or *bavette de bœuf* with haricots verts, and, for dessert, clafoutis or floating islands—traditional French dishes. I began working there on Wednesdays at a young age, and as I got older, I helped clear tables, wash dishes, and tend bar. Eventually I was buying, prepping, and serving food. I was very happy there.

When I was fifteen, my father took us all to the best restaurant in our area, the Michelin-starred Les Jardins de la Forge. I'd never had service or food like this; I didn't know such elegance and refinement existed. I immediately wanted to work there.

My father spoke with the chef-owner, Paul Pauvert, and there I began my apprenticeship. I was a cook; I worked the line. I loved working in a restaurant—the camaraderie, the discipline required to be ready on time, and the service itself. One day the chef asked me to help the pastry department. He was opening a retail pastry shop and a *salon de thé*, and the pastry chef needed assistance. Chef Pauvert had brought down a consulting chef from Gaston Lenôtre in Paris, considered the finest pâtisserie in the country, to help create the pastries.

I found the complex world of pastry and baking far more interesting than the world of savory cooking, with its hours of cleaning shellfish and peeling vegetables and the like. Pastry intertwined science, craftsmanship, and precision in ways that made savory cooking seem almost primitive by comparison.

So I took the next step and went to work at the pâtisserie Le Péché Mignon under Daniel Durand, one of the best pâtissiers in the country. It was under his wing that I became a true pastry chef. The work was hard and often tedious. Lining hundreds of tart shells, laminating doughs, or filling and glazing thousands of cream puffs for croquembouche was not something that engaged the imagination, but it taught me that consistency, repetition, finesse, and organization are key in becoming a great pastry chef.

My two years at Le Péché Mignon were the hardest of my life. But just when I thought I couldn't continue, Chef Durand sent me to a class given by Pierre Hermé, who was revitalizing and modernizing French pâtisserie, and I was mesmerized and rejuvenated. I went on to work at the Elysée Palace in Paris and then at Le Grand Véfour, the two-star landmark restaurant across from the Louvre. And then, as Michael describes on page 16, to Los Angeles as executive pastry chef at L'Orangerie. But I longed for New York City, so my wife and I found work there. We stayed until that call came from Thomas. After I spent several years as executive pastry chef of The French Laundry and working with the burgeoning bakery in Yountville, my situation changed. Thomas's business was continuing to expand, and he asked me to return to New York. I got my dream, a permanent post in the most remarkable restaurant city in the world.

A Bread Baker's Journey: *From doughnuts and fry oil to brioche and baguettes*

BY MATTHEW MCDONALD For most of my life, I resisted becoming what I am. My parents split up when I was young, and because my older brother and sister were unreliable caretakers for a nine-year-old (as they were teenagers in the late 1970s, I can hardly blame them), I would go to work with Mom. She worked in a doughnut shop, making America's favorite pastry. And, since doughnuts are

a breakfast food, the job required her to keep baker's hours. There was a clock on the wall and, under it, a beat-up radio cranking out rock and roll. Those were the sights, sounds, and smells of my childhood: a clock reading three a.m., Heart wailing "Barracuda" on FM, and the smell of fry oil and sweet doughnuts.

After high school, unable to commit to any one subject—math, physics, foreign languages?—I enrolled in junior college in Diamond Bar, California, because it was an affordable way to keep moving ahead in school while I figured out what I wanted to do. To support myself, I worked in pizzerias in Los Angeles. There were all kinds of things I could do at these places, from serving to working the pasta station, but everywhere I worked, I gravitated toward the oven. I was the oven guy, the dough guy. Yet while I loved to make pizza, I didn't want to spend my life making pizza. So I kept going to school.

Eventually I headed north to Eureka, California, where my mom, stepdad, and little sister had moved, and I got a job at one of the Safeways in town, in the bakery. Today grocery store bakeries tend to use bake-off operations or heat-and-serve operations, or a combination of the two. But in 1993, that Safeway still baked from scratch every day.

I was the guy who, yep, made the doughnuts. I hadn't been able to eat a doughnut for years, having overdosed on them as a child, but as I made them and gained some skill, I was able to enjoy them again. It was at this point, with one credit left to go for my degree, that I had an epiphany: heading into work, driving to a grocery store to make the day's doughnuts, I realized *I was really happy to be going to work.* I liked to make things. And I liked dough. I'd resisted a life of baking since I was nine years old: I saw how

hard my mom worked for almost no money, and I didn't want to do that; I didn't want to be frying doughnuts, listening to "Barracuda" at three in the morning for the rest of my life—but I finally realized that maybe I did.

So when my mom bought a bakery in Eureka with her husband and a business partner, I went to work for her. She sold mainly pastries and cakes, but I wanted to do bread. I worked fast alongside Kent, my mom's partner, making doughnuts, croissants, cookies, and pies, and doing anything else that needed to be done, so that there would be time to make six loaves of a new bread we hadn't made before. American bread baking was on the move, and I tried recipes from magazines, books, and friends in the industry. I had heard about people who could make up a bread recipe on the spot, and I wanted to learn how to do that. I worked hard to introduce breads into Mom's bakery.

I took a continuing education course at the Culinary Institute of America in St. Helena. I learned how to start a sourdough culture and to use baker's percentages. I learned that I had to have a deck oven—a special oven for breads with narrow openings and long, deep hearths—and what kind of ingredients worked best. I learned about pre-ferments—levain and poolish—and other techniques for the slow creation of flavor critical to great bread. I was on fire.

I earned an internship at the National Baking Center, and that is where I changed. I entered as a young badass baker who thought he knew something, and I emerged, as I see it now, a professional. The NBC exposed me to whole new levels of quality, discipline, presentation, and attention to detail. I learned proper baking *mise en place*. What I'd been doing wasn't bad—we put out really good products at Mom's Cherry Blossom bakery, bread I'm still proud of. But the NBC was the hub of baking education at the time, with bakers from all over the world coming to share the experience offered at the school, and you were expected to live up to a certain standard. I trained under the superheroes of traditional European bread baking: Didier Rosada, Philippe LeCorre, and, briefly, Raymond Calvel, the godfather of modern bread baking.

And I was quickly and painfully made aware of my ignorance and insignificance. Going from a small family bakery to an international educational facility was a giant leap for me. The experience changed my identity. I was trained, and I was one of those guys who could make up a recipe from nothing. I'd become what I wanted to be.

I returned to Napa, and the CIA, to reenter the industry. I met and married my wife, Kristina. I took the test for Certified Master Baker and passed. I owned a bakery in New Jersey for a while that didn't take off, but it taught me about production schedules—and humility. There I made bread for a Manhattan restaurant, The Tonic, headed by chef Chris Gesualdi, who had worked with Kristina at Thomas Keller's Rakel. Chris loved my bread, and ultimately, in 2001, I decided to leave my bakery to work with him at Drew Nieporent's Tribakery, in lower Manhattan.

In September, I stood out on the street with Chris and watched the towers go down. Chris knew people in the buildings, and I baked bread for Windows on the World. Our delivery guy was there delivering the day's bread. He and so many others never made it out.

Kristina and I continued to move around the country. Angling to get back to the Napa Valley, she called her old boss, Thomas Keller, and told him I was available. As it happened, he was looking for a head baker. He brought me up for a tryout. It was this experience that taught me the importance of green tape—the green painter's tape used in all Thomas's restaurants to label food containers. I got everything set up the night before. I made my pre-ferments, which had to sit at room temperature overnight. I worked with the staff and set my *mise en place* in a corner by itself. I was totally prepared.

When I returned the next morning, all my food was gone—everything. I hadn't labeled it, and the cleaning crew knew that unlabeled food was food that could be discarded. Faced with a tasting later that afternoon with Chef Keller and French Laundry chef de cuisine Corey Lee, I had to improvise. I borrowed some levain and poolish and made the necessary adjustments in my recipes. I had to work with what was available. I pulled it off. Both chefs liked the breads. (The multigrain I made that day was soon on the menu at The French Laundry.)

And here I am, amazed and lucky.

Throw Out Your Measuring Cups—*and other notes on using this book*

BY SUSIE HELLER AND AMY VOGLER The recipes in this book are the same ones, though scaled down, that Bouchon Bakery uses daily, along with many tips to make them easier to prepare at home. We tested them all multiple times, and we think your results will be as stunning as ours were. • We have learned so much working with Thomas; Sebastien, Bouchon Bakery's executive pastry

chef; and Matthew, Bouchon's head baker, over many months, primarily in our Napa development kitchen but also in the Bouchon Bakery kitchens in Yountville and in New York City. As they baked, we weighed, measured, took notes, and asked questions. Then the testing began. More questions, more revisions, and, finally, the recipe! Then on to editing, and many more rounds of questions and answers. It was a remarkable process.

Sebastien and Matthew have wildly different personalities—Sebastien has the cool, precise nature required for pastry; Matthew is a rogue baker obsessed with bread—but at their core, they are more similar than they might appear. Both respect tradition and are influenced by classic techniques, but they reach beyond what has come before to develop their own unique techniques. For instance, when Sebastien makes cream puffs, he pipes the pâte à choux into silicone molds, freezes them, and then tops each cream puff with a thin cookie before baking to ensure a crunch when you bite. Matthew developed

an unusual steam-generating system using a water gun, chains, and rocks to achieve the ultimate crust when baking bread at home. It's the first time we've seen truly effective steam in a home oven.

The techniques that we learned during the writing of this book have changed our own approaches in many ways. We would like to share some of the insights.

WEIGHING VERSUS MEASURING

For years, chefs, professional bakers, and cookbook authors alike have urged home cooks to become comfortable with a scale, but habits are hard to change. Your mother and grandmother probably didn't use scales, and you may even have their measuring cups in your kitchen drawer. But using a scale will change the way you cook and bake for the better in many ways.

And the merits of weighing are not only about accuracy: weighing is also more convenient. Weighing is a much easier and cleaner way to measure peanut butter,

molasses, or corn syrup, for example—you simply set the mixing bowl on the scale, tare the scale (set it to zero), and measure the ingredient into the bowl, rather than having to scrape it into and out of a measuring cup. And, of course, there is the additional bonus that more than one ingredient can be measured into that same bowl.

Precision matters more in baking than in savory cooking, which is why Sebastien and Matthew provided exact weights, for optimum results. You'll see that most of these recipes have what may seem crazily specific weights: 519 grams of flour, for instance, or 234 grams of sugar. This is because we converted these recipes from the larger-scale recipes used by the bakery. (This is another benefit of using weights—all recipes can easily be halved, doubled, or tripled, and so on, and they will work.) Do not be intimidated by these specific amounts— when you use a scale, it's easy to measure 234 grams. However, when converting those weights to volume, we often had to round

{ Weighing }

them off (despite Sebastien and Matthew's preference that we not). In a short time it should become readily clear why weighing is the preferable route.

We strongly recommend using digital scales, either a bigger one that weighs to the tenth of a gram, or a basic kitchen scale for larger quantities and a palm scale that weighs smaller quantities.

We encourage you to measure out all your ingredients before you begin, so you can mix and bake without interruption. You'll notice that when an ingredient, such as sugar, is used more than once in a recipe, we split the measurements accordingly.

EQUIPMENT

Many home kitchens are now equipped with convection ovens. All the recipes in this book work well in a standard oven, but we give temperatures and times for convection baking as well when it yields a better result—and we explain why.

There are so many variables present every time you begin a recipe: the heat of the kitchen, the ingredients, the calibration of your oven, to name just a few. Weighing rather than measuring by volume is a simple way of eliminating one big variable. It no longer matters whether the flour is lightly scooped into a measuring cup or packed into it, or whether it comes slightly over the rim or under it. When you measure by volume, the weight of an ingredient can differ each time. Once you get a scale, you can see for yourself how wide a range of weights a cup of flour can be, depending on how it is spooned or scooped or packed; it can vary in volume by as much as 50 percent depending on who's doing the measuring, how the flour was stored and measured, and the humidity.

Another example is salt—different salts are not equal in weight when measured by volume. A tablespoon of Diamond Crystal kosher salt (used in these recipes), for example, weighs only 60 percent of what a tablespoon of Morton kosher salt weighs. So if you measure Morton kosher salt by volume, you will be adding far too much salt to your recipe.

Likewise, eggs vary slightly in weight from one to another; measuring eggs by weight ensures great accuracy. "Large" eggs are 56 grams/2 ounces by definition, but they vary in weight by 10 or more grams, so calling for eggs by weight, as we do in these recipes, guarantees more consistent results. And weighing allows you to use any size egg you have access to, which is especially helpful if you use farm-raised eggs, which are often not graded by size.

Weighing ingredients is also cleaner, faster, and more efficient. Digital scales have a "tare" button, a zeroing button, which allows you to measure a number of ingredients into the same bowl. You can, say, measure 500 grams of flour into the bowl, then hit the tare button, which will return the scale to zero so that you can add 100 grams of sugar, or whatever the recipe calls for.

Believe us, getting on the scale wave will change your life.

If your range hasn't been calibrated for years, it would be wise to have it checked. A few degrees off in either direction can affect baking times. Maintaining a consistent temperature is also important. For that reason, it's good to get into the habit of checking on what you are baking by turning on the oven light rather than opening the oven door, which will lower the temperature significantly.

We developed and tested the recipes in a Viking dual-fuel convection range.

KNOW YOUR HOT SPOTS

All ovens, even convection ovens, have hot spots, and it's useful to know where your oven's hot spots are. There's an easy way (a trick we learned from Viking) to check for both hot spots and temperature accuracy: Buy a tube of refrigerated or ready-to-bake biscuits. Preheat your oven to the temperature given on the package, with a rack in the center. Bake the biscuits for the time the package recommends. These doughs have been rigorously tested, and the time and temperature guidelines are accurate. If the biscuits are overdone at the minimum recommended time, your oven is running hot; if they are underdone even after the maximum recommended time, your oven is running cool. Then evaluate the biscuits: some will be darker than others; this will show you your hot spots.

OVEN CYCLING

All ovens cycle, meaning they heat up to over the designated temperature and stop heating, then start heating up again when the temperature drops below what is set. An oven will bake or cook food most evenly if it has cycled three times (watch for the light to go on and then off each time). If you would rather not bother to check for cycling, preheat the oven for a minimum of 45 minutes.

STAND MIXER

Any dough or batter requires some kind of mixing. A stand mixer does that work with paddle, whisk, or dough hook. The recipes in this book were tested with a KitchenAid 5-quart Artisan mixer. Whatever type you use, learn its behavior: Does the mixing attachment hit all surfaces of the bowl, incorporating ingredients evenly? How fast does it run? How powerful is it? Once you've made a stand mixer a part of your kitchen, it's hard to imagine doing without one.

The following are the terms we use to describe mixing speeds and their corresponding number on the 5-quart Artisan model:

low = 2
medium-low = 4
medium = 6
medium-high = 8
high = 10

The KitchenAid Artisan manual specifies that all yeasted doughs be mixed on low, which has an rpm (revolutions per minute) of 95. If you have a very powerful professional mixer, as we do at the bakery, you'll be able to mix on medium speed (180 rpm) for half the time.

INGREDIENTS

Having worked with Thomas for many years, we are astounded by the number of products previously available only to chefs that can now be purchased in grocery or specialty stores or through the Internet. Perhaps this is nowhere more evident than in the candy chapter, which will have you making, among other confections, peppermint patties that give the original a run for its money. If an ingredient is not easily available in your neighborhood, turn to Sources, on page 382, where you'll find purveyors for every specialty item used in the book. Following the headnote in many recipes, we give the particular brands that we used—for various chocolates or food coloring, for instance—but of course other brands can almost always be substituted.

WORK CLEAN

Thomas always emphasizes the importance of working cleanly and efficiently. It begins simply with a clean work surface and tools, continues with his (and Sebastien's) preference for using disposable pastry bags

(it's difficult to clean other pastry bags and keep them fresh), and ends with labeling all containers for storing doughs, batters, and any food. Working clean also refers to keeping batters and doughs "clean": that is, preventing them from absorbing odors by double-wrapping them in plastic wrap before storing them in airtight containers.

Rolling out dough between sheets of parchment paper or plastic wrap allows you to roll them out without adding extra flour and, of course, keeps the work surface clean. And always clean as you go! Each time you finish a recipe or a component of a recipe, put away what you don't need and wipe the counter down.

Equally important, *read each recipe before you dive in.* Read the recipe at least once from beginning to end, so that you understand the process. Picture yourself doing each step. In some cases, you'll see a timeline alongside the recipe to help you gauge the time needed on longer recipes. Read the recipe notes. The captions to the photographs, and the essays that appear throughout the book, offer additional information.

THE DANCE OF CHILL

Sometimes a dough that has been chilled in the refrigerator may be too firm and cold to roll out with ease. So, you pound the dough with a rolling pin to flatten it somewhat and warm it to a temperature where it can be rolled out. Then you roll the dough slowly and see how it reacts. If it is difficult to roll or begins to crack, it's too cold and should rest at room temperature a bit longer. (You may wonder why it was refrigerated in the first place, if it now needs to warm up, but the chilling is essential to relax the dough.) Then, depending on your level of experience and the temperature of the room, the dough may soften too much during rolling and need to be chilled again before it can be cut into shapes. This is part of why the refrigerator and freezer are such important tools in the baker's kitchen. There's nuance in knowing when a dough is at the right temperature to be worked, and an instinct for this comes with practice and experience.

Thomas has plaques in his restaurant kitchens that read "It's all about finesse." Nowhere is this more true than in baking. It's all in the details!

WEIGHING EGGS

Before weighing eggs, crack the eggs into a bowl and beat them with a fork to combine the yolks and whites. Strain the eggs; this will remove the chalazae (white spiral bands attaching the yolk to the membrane) and any small bits of shell and allow the eggs to flow freely when you weigh them.

The Eternal Question: *What Are Your Favorite Recipes?* BY SUSIE HELLER AND AMY VOGLER

What are your favorite recipes? We're asked this all the time. Of course, these recipes are all favorites, as they've been chosen for Bouchon Bakery's pastry cases and are devoured by thousands of people every day. You'll also find some of the bakery's seasonal hits, such as Marshmallow Eggs (page 356), Pumpkin Muffins (page 86), and Witches' Hats (page 352). Plus there are some bonuses,

such as the Pithiviers (page 223), available only to readers who bake from this book. But here are our very favorite recipes that we find ourselves coming back to again and again.

SUSIE: I love the cookies, all of them—a love Thomas shares. They're delicious and versatile. You can make them large or small. You can bake them soon after mixing the dough, or freeze it to bake later. Recently a large group of us rented a house in Santa Barbara for a weekend-long celebration. I traveled there with dozens and dozens of frozen cookie dough balls. We baked them fresh each day, and as many as we baked, they were gone in seconds.

A small bite doesn't have to be a cookie—it can be a little cake. When you need to bake something in a hurry, you can't beat the Financiers (page 98). I love both the traditional brown-butter and the chocolate versions, with their soft centers and crisp edges, but if I had to choose just one, I'd go with the traditional.

My first Bacon Cheddar Scone (page 72) was a revelation. They're perfect with eggs for breakfast, or with soup for lunch or dinner. They also make wonderful croutons on a salad (if you have any left over). And I never tire of the Chocolate Cherry Scones (page 69)—there is something about that combination of sweet and tart, chocolate and cherry, that makes them irresistible to me.

Then there are the tarts! Each one is unique, and although I normally choose fruit tarts (try the Rhubarb Tart, page 148, and Plum Tart with Almond Cream, page 150) over chocolate, our Chocolate, Praline, and Cocoa Nib Tart (page 134) is the best I've ever eaten. It has four distinct textures: a pâte sucrée crust, a praline layer, a chocolate ganache, and a crisp chocolate dentelle on top. It may seem like a lot of work, but you won't regret spending the time.

One of the first desserts that Sebastien made for us was his version of a palmier, which bears little resemblance to the small rolled palmier cookies you may be picturing. It's a showstopper (see the photo on page 219)—crunchy puff pastry filled with homemade raspberry jam and dusted with powdered sugar. (Warning: Once you make your own puff pastry, you'll never be able to go back to store-bought frozen dough.)

Although I have made more traditional candies in the past, much of the confections chapter came as a complete surprise. I was like a kid in a candy shop, learning about new ingredients and techniques. Didn't you love Cracker Jack, Peppermint Patties, and marshmallows as a kid? But could you have ever imagined making them—in fact, making versions far better than the originals?

And if you want to see your dog smile, make the Dog Treats (page 52). I have three dogs, and they've made it very clear that this is their favorite recipe in the book. (My husband's is the Oatmeal Raisin Cookies, page 32.)

AMY: My first baking job was making sticky buns, when I was a teenager on Long Beach Island, New Jersey. For years after, I couldn't even think about eating one. But when it came time to test the brioche recipes, the familiarity of working with the "schmear" and the dough came rushing back. I made multiple batches to find the perfect amount of schmear coverage and "bubble over," and in the process got reacquainted with an old favorite. Like so many of Sebastien's pastries, the taste may be familiar and takes you back to a certain time and place, but the reality is far better than any recollection.

Often during the recipe testing, I found myself with a countertop covered by dozens of pastries at the end of the day. I tested batch after batch of Hot Cross Buns (page 192), with the terrific icing touched by a hint of cinnamon and cardamom, just the right counterpoint to the cranberries and currants in the buns. I sent my husband out late one afternoon with trays of the buns and a mission: give them all away to the neighbors. He came home with empty trays and a big

smile, and he spent the rest of the evening answering calls of thanks.

The croissant was the most challenging recipe for me. Weighing the ingredients rather than measuring them helped shorten my learning curve. My advice to you is to be patient: although a block of butter encased in a simple yeasted dough seems fairly straightforward, much can change based on room temperature, time in the freezer, pressure of the rolling pin, etc. With each batch, you will have your own "aha" moment and an increasingly elevated level of satisfaction.

Overall, I'm most drawn to the breads, particularly the Pain de Campagne (page 290), the Multigrain Bread (page 296), and the Pain Rustique (page 307). As Thomas says, bread is the simplest of foods, but it can be fantastically nuanced: elemental ingredients transformed into a dough that you feel changing and strengthening with every fold and shaping. And then comes the wholesome, comforting smell as it bakes. Nothing tops that for me.

For the past two years, our houses have been filled with the wonderful aromas of pastries and breads baking in our ovens. We hope you will experience the same sense of pride that we do as you pull these beautiful products from your oven and share them with the people you love.

When I was growing up in Maryland and Southern Florida, our house always had cookies: pecan sandies, Nutter Butters, and Oreos. Who doesn't like Oreos? I've never met anyone who doesn't. Sometimes a cook would bring a bag of Oreos into the kitchen at The French Laundry. I'd set them on the shelf above the stoves so that their centers would get hot and creamy, and I'd devour them when there was a break in the action. Cookies incorporate the textures and flavors that we love best: crispness, chewiness, chocolate, caramel, vanilla, cream—all those different components that are so adored, all wrapped up in a little package that fits in your hand. The macaron is the most special cookie of all. When you eat a macaron for the first time, the world changes. I had my first macaron in France, in my late twenties—and wow! I didn't know such a thing was possible: the delicate shell, the chewiness that followed, the sweet, creamy filling. What's most important in making cookies is to master the basic techniques involved for each of them. For the chocolate chunk and chip cookies, the consistency of the butter before you add the sugar is important, as is how much to mix the eggs when you add them and then how long to mix in the flour. It's a lesson in mixing. Shortbread, with only three basic ingredients, is all about the proportion of fat that a dough can hold and about how to maintain the shape of cookies with so much fat in them. Cookies are something that you can play around with; they allow you freedom and creativity. Once you understand the basic techniques, you will be limited only by your imagination.

Oatmeal Raisin Cookies

All-purpose flour	144 grams	1 cup + 1 teaspoon
Ground cinnamon	7.7 grams	1 tablespoon
Baking soda	7.4 grams	1½ teaspoons
Kosher salt	3.6 grams	1¼ teaspoons
Light brown sugar	140 grams	½ cup + 3½ tablespoons (lightly packed)
Granulated sugar	69 grams	¼ cup + 1½ tablespoons
Unsalted butter, at room temperature	155 grams	5.5 ounces
Eggs	62 grams	¼ cup
Vanilla paste	7.7 grams	1¼ teaspoons
Old-fashioned oats	155 grams	2 cups
Mixed raisins	156 grams	1 cup

We think that an outstanding oatmeal raisin cookie is crunchy on the outside and chewy on the inside, and that's how these bake. We source a mixture of raisins; if a high-quality mixture is not available, use half dark and half golden raisins. If the raisins are not plump, pour hot water over them and let them sit for about 30 minutes before making the cookies, then drain and pat thoroughly dry.

You'll need a 2½-inch (#10) ice cream scoop. ● *Cookies baked in a convection oven will have a more even color and will not spread as much as those baked in a standard oven.*

Place the flour in a medium bowl. Sift in the cinnamon and baking soda, add the salt, and whisk together. Whisk together the sugars in a small bowl, breaking up any lumps.

Place the butter in the bowl of a stand mixer fitted with the paddle attachment. Turn to medium-low speed and cream the butter, warming the bowl if needed (see Pommade, page 190), until it is the consistency of mayonnaise and holds a peak when the paddle is lifted. Add the sugars and mix for 3 to 4 minutes, until fluffy. Scrape down the sides and bottom of the bowl. Add the eggs and vanilla paste and mix on low speed for 15 to 30 seconds, until just combined. Scrape down the bowl again. The mixture may look broken, but that is fine (overwhipping the eggs could cause the cookies to expand too much during baking and then deflate).

Add the combined dry ingredients in 2 additions, mixing on low speed for 15 to 30 seconds after each, until just combined. Scrape the bottom of the bowl to incorporate any dry ingredients that have settled there. Add the oats and pulse on low about 10 times to combine. Pulse in the raisins. Refrigerate the dough for 30 minutes.

Position the racks in the upper and lower thirds of the oven and preheat the oven to 325°F (convection or standard). Line two sheet pans with Silpats or parchment paper.

Using the ice cream scoop, divide the dough into 6 equal portions, 145 grams each. Roll each one into a ball between the palms of your hands. (The dough can be shaped in advance; see Note, page 35.)

The cookies are very large; bake only 3 on each pan. With a short end of the pan toward you, place one cookie in the upper left corner, one in the lower left corner, and the third one in the center, toward the right side of the pan. Bring the dough to room temperature before baking.

Bake the cookies until golden brown, 15 to 17 minutes in a convection oven, 21 to 23 minutes in a standard oven, reversing the positions of the pans halfway through baking. Set the pans on a cooling rack and cool for 5 to 10 minutes, then transfer the cookies to the rack to cool completely.

The cookies are best the day they are baked, but they can be stored in a covered container for up to 3 days.

PHOTOGRAPH ON PAGE 35   MAKES SIX 4-INCH COOKIES

FOR SMALLER COOKIES: Divide the dough into 12 equal portions (72 grams each). Bake for 14 to 16 minutes in a convection oven, 18 to 20 minutes in a standard oven.

TLCs

All-purpose flour	153 grams	1 cup + 1½ tablespoons
Baking soda	2.3 grams	½ teaspoon
Ground cinnamon	1 gram	⅜ teaspoon
Granulated sugar	138 grams	½ cup + 3½ tablespoons
Dark brown sugar	75 grams	¼ cup + 1½ tablespoons (lightly packed)
Unsalted butter, at room temperature	212 grams	7.5 ounces
½ vanilla bean, split lengthwise		
Eggs	52 grams	3 tablespoons + 1 teaspoon
Old-fashioned oats	134 grams	1¾ cups
Coarsely chopped pecans	134 grams	1 cup + 2 tablespoons

Some inventions happen just because we're having fun. When Sebastien discovered that my partner, Laura Cunningham, liked oatmeal cookies but had been picking out the raisins (she doesn't like dried fruit), he decided to make a cookie in her honor, replacing the fruit with nuts. Thus The Laura Cunningham, aka TLC, was born.

You'll need a 2½-inch (#10) ice cream scoop. • *Cookies baked in a convection oven will have a more even color and will not spread as much as those baked in a standard oven.*

Place the flour in a medium bowl, sift in the baking soda and cinnamon, and whisk together. Whisk together the sugars in a small bowl, breaking up any lumps.

Place the butter in the bowl of a stand mixer fitted with the paddle attachment. Turn to medium-low speed and cream the butter, warming the bowl if needed (see Pommade, page 190), until it has the consistency of mayonnaise and holds a peak when the paddle is lifted. Add the sugars and mix for 3 to 4 minutes, until fluffy. Scrape down the sides and bottom of the bowl. Scrape the seeds from the vanilla bean, add them to the butter mixture, and mix on low speed for about 30 seconds to distribute the seeds evenly, stopping to break up any larger pieces.

Add the eggs and mix on low speed for 15 to 30 seconds, until just combined. Scrape down the bowl again. The mixture may look broken, but that is fine (overwhipping the eggs could cause the cookies to expand too much during baking and then deflate).

Add the combined dry ingredients in 2 additions, mixing on low speed for 15 to 30 seconds after each, or until just combined. Scrape the bottom of the bowl to incorporate any dry ingredients that have settled there. Add the oats and pulse on low about 10 times to combine. Pulse in the pecans. Refrigerate the dough for 30 minutes.

Position the racks in the upper and lower thirds of the oven and preheat the oven to 325°F (convection or standard). Line two sheet pans with Silpats or parchment paper.

Using the ice cream scoop, divide the dough into 6 equal portions, 145 grams each. Roll each one into a ball between the palms of your hands. (The dough can be shaped in advance; see Note, page 35.)

The cookies are very large; bake only 3 on each pan. With a short end of the pan toward you, place one cookie in the upper left corner, one in the lower left corner, and the third one in the center toward the right side of the pan. Bring the dough to room temperature before baking.

Bake until golden brown, 14 to 16 minutes in a convection oven, 18 to 20 minutes in a standard oven, reversing the positions of the pans halfway through baking. Set the pans on a cooling rack and cool for 5 to 10 minutes, then transfer the cookies to the rack to cool completely.

The cookies are best the day they are baked, but they can be stored in a covered container for up to 3 days.

PHOTOGRAPH ON PAGE 35   **MAKES SIX 4-INCH COOKIES**

FOR SMALLER COOKIES: Divide the dough into 12 equal portions (72 grams each). Bake for 13 to 15 minutes in a convection oven, 17 to 19 minutes in a standard oven.

Chocolate Chunk and Chip Cookies

All-purpose flour	238 grams	1½ cups + 3 tablespoons
Baking soda	2.3 grams	½ teaspoon
Kosher salt	3 grams	1 teaspoon
Dark brown sugar	134 grams	½ cup + 2 tablespoons (lightly packed)
Unsulfured blackstrap molasses	12 grams	1¾ teaspoons
Granulated sugar	104 grams	½ cup + 1 teaspoon
⅜-inch chunks 70% to 72% chocolate	107 grams	⅔ cup
Chocolate chips	107 grams	scant ½ cup
Unsalted butter, at room temperature	167 grams	5.9 ounces
Eggs	60 grams	3 tablespoons + 2½ teaspoons

Bouchon Bakery is well known for its cookies. We love our cookies, and we make them big. The chocolate chunk and chip recipe was one of our first. In most cooking or baking, varying textures is important, and cookies are no different. This is why we use both chocolate chunks and chocolate chips, which behave differently in the dough. The chunks melt, but the chips don't.

I've always believed that when you have a special, expensive ingredient—truffles, for instance, or foie gras—it's important to offer it in abundance so that people know what the fuss is about. Chocolate falls into that category here—these cookies are packed with chocolate. (When we want even more chocolate flavor, as in our Double Chocolate Chunk and Chip Cookies—see the variation—we replace about 25 percent of the flour with cocoa powder.) We use plenty of brown sugar as well as molasses for a deep, rich flavor. If you like nuts in your cookies, feel free to add them instead of either the chocolate chunks or the chocolate chips.

You'll need a 2½-inch (#10) ice cream scoop. • *For this recipe, we use Valrhona Guanaja 70% or Guittard 72% chocolate.* • *Cookies baked in a convection oven will have a more even color and will not spread as much as those baked in a standard oven.*

Place the flour in a medium bowl. Sift in the baking soda. Add the salt and whisk together. Place the dark brown sugar in a small bowl and stir in the molasses and granulated sugar, breaking up any lumps; the mixture will not be completely smooth.

Place the chocolate chunks in a strainer and tap the side to remove any powdered chocolate, which would cloud the cookies. Mix with the chocolate chips.

Place the butter in the bowl of a stand mixer fitted with the paddle attachment. Turn to medium-low speed and cream the butter, warming the bowl if needed (see Pommade, page 190), until it is the consistency of mayonnaise and holds a peak when the paddle is lifted. Add the molasses mixture and mix for 3 to 4 minutes, until fluffy. Scrape down the sides and bottom of the bowl. Add the eggs and mix on low speed for 15 to 30 seconds, until just combined. Scrape the bowl again. The mixture may look broken, but that is fine (overwhipping the eggs could cause the cookies to expand too much during baking and then deflate).

Add the dry ingredients in 2 additions, mixing on low speed for 15 to 30 seconds after each, or until just combined. Scrape the bottom of the bowl to incorporate any dry ingredients that have settled there. Add the chocolates and pulse on low speed about 10 times to combine. Refrigerate the dough for 30 minutes.

Position the racks in the upper and lower thirds of the oven and preheat the oven to 325°F (convection or standard). Line two sheet pans with Silpats or parchment paper.

Using the ice cream scoop, divide the dough into 6 equal portions, 150 grams each. Roll each one into a ball between the palms of your hands. (The dough can be shaped in advance; see Note.)

The cookies are very large; bake only 3 on each pan. With a short end of the pan toward you, place one cookie in the upper left corner, one in the lower left corner, and the third one in the center, toward the right side of the pan. Bring the dough to room temperature before baking.

Bake until golden brown, 14 to 16 minutes in a convection oven, 18 to 20 minutes in a standard oven, reversing the positions of the pans halfway through baking. Set the pans on a cooling rack and cool for 5 to 10 minutes, then transfer the cookies to the rack to cool completely.

The cookies are best the day they are baked, but they can be stored in a covered container for up to 3 days.

MAKES SIX 4-INCH COOKIES

NOTE ON ADVANCE PREPARATION: The shaped dough can be refrigerated for up to 2 days before baking. For longer storage, freeze the dough in a covered container or a plastic bag for up to 1 month; the day before baking, place the cookies on a lined baking sheet and defrost in the refrigerator overnight. Bring to room temperature before baking.

FOR SMALLER COOKIES: Divide the dough into 12 equal portions (75 grams each). Bake for 12 to 14 minutes in a convection oven, 16 to 18 minutes in a standard oven.

Double Chocolate Chunk and Chip Cookies

Reduce the flour to 190 grams/1¼ cups plus 1½ tablespoons and use 48 grams/½ cup plus 1½ tablespoons unsweetened alkalized cocoa powder, preferably Guittard Cocoa Rouge.

Place the flour in the medium bowl and sift in the cocoa. Continue with the recipe as written. Because the cocoa is dark, it is tricky to tell when the cookies are done, but all areas should look baked, and you should smell their aroma.

MAKES SIX 4-INCH COOKIES

NOTES ON COCOA POWDER: Cocoa powder tends to compact and be difficult to measure accurately using spoons or cups. If you do not have a scale, transfer the cocoa to a canister or other container and stir to aerate it before measuring. Break up any lumps of cocoa with a small whisk or a fork.

There are two types of cocoa powder. Natural, or nonalkalized, cocoa is pure ground cocoa powder. It's paler in color and is often somewhat more bitter than alkalized, or Dutched, cocoa, which has been treated with a mild alkali solution to raise the pH level. The process deepens the color (making it dark brown to red-brown) and improves the flavor of the cocoa. Alkalized cocoa is our preferred cocoa powder.

DOUBLE CHOCOLATE CHUNK AND CHIP

CHOCOLATE CHUNK AND CHIP

OATMEAL RAISIN

TLC

Better Nutters

COOKIES

Unsalted peanut halves	30 grams	¼ cup
All-purpose flour	198 grams	1¼ cups + 2½ tablespoons
Baking soda	9.1 grams	1¾ teaspoons + ⅛ teaspoon
Baking powder	3.8 grams	¾ teaspoon
Unsalted butter, at room temperature	210 grams	7.4 ounces
Creamy peanut butter	86 grams	⅓ cup
Light brown sugar	106 grams	½ cup + 1 tablespoon (lightly packed)
Eggs	54 grams	3 tablespoons + 1 teaspoon
Vanilla paste	8.5 grams	1½ teaspoons
Old-fashioned oats	106 grams	1⅓ cups

PEANUT BUTTER FILLING

Basic Buttercream (page 375)	175 grams	1 cup + 3 tablespoons
Creamy peanut butter	175 grams	½ cup + 3 tablespoons
Kosher salt	0.2 gram	¹⁄₁₆ teaspoon

The Nutter Butter was my favorite cookie when I was a kid, so it was obvious that we had to come up with our own version. Because there is a high proportion of fat—in the form of butter *and* peanut butter—in these cookies, they are best when frozen before baking, which makes them hold their shape better and spread less. So they're a terrific cookie to make ahead of time: simply pop the frozen cookies into the oven whenever you have a craving for them.

You'll need a 3¼-inch round cutter and a pastry bag with an Ateco #867 French star tip. ● *For this recipe, we use Virginia jumbo peanut halves and Skippy natural peanut butter.* ● *Cookies baked in a convection oven will have a more even color and will not spread as much as those baked in a standard oven.*

TO TOAST THE PEANUTS: Preheat the oven to 325°F (standard).

Spread the peanuts on a small tray and toast in the oven, stirring often, for 16 to 18 minutes, until a light golden brown. Let cool, then coarsely chop.

FOR THE COOKIES: Place the flour in a medium bowl, sift in the baking soda and baking powder, and whisk together.

Place the butter and peanut butter in the bowl of a stand mixer fitted with the paddle attachment. Turn to medium-low speed and cream the butter, warming the bowl if needed (see Pommade, page 190), until it has the consistency of mayonnaise and holds a peak when the paddle is lifted. Add the sugar and mix for about 2 minutes, until fluffy. Scrape down the sides and bottom of the bowl. Add the eggs and vanilla paste and mix on low speed for 15 to 30 seconds, until just combined. Scrape down the bowl again. The mixture may look broken, but that is fine (overwhipping the eggs could cause the cookies to expand too much during baking and then deflate).

Add the combined dry ingredients in 2 additions, mixing on low speed for 15 to 30 seconds after each, or until just combined. Scrape the bottom of the bowl to incorporate any dry ingredients that have settled there. Add the oats and pulse on low about 10 times to combine. Add the chopped peanuts and pulse to combine.

Mound the dough on a large piece of plastic wrap and, using a pastry scraper, push it together into a 5-by-7-inch block. Wrap in plastic wrap and refrigerate for at least 2 hours, or until firm. (The dough can be refrigerated for up to 2 days or frozen for up to 1 month.)

Unwrap the dough, place it between two pieces of parchment paper or plastic wrap, and roll it out to a ¼-inch-thick sheet. If the dough has softened, slide it (in the parchment) onto the back of a sheet pan and refrigerate until firm enough to cut.

Using the round cutter, cut 8 cookies from the dough. (If the dough softens, return it to the refrigerator until the cookies are firm enough to transfer to a sheet pan.) Arrange the rounds on a lined sheet pan.

Push the trimmings together and refrigerate until the dough is firm enough to roll, then roll out and cut into 4 more rounds. Add them to the sheet pan. Wrap the sheet in plastic wrap and freeze the dough for at least 2 hours, or until firm. (For longer storage, remove the frozen rounds from the sheet pan and freeze in a covered container or a plastic bag for up to 1 month.)

Position the racks in the upper and lower thirds of the oven and preheat the oven to 325°F (convection or standard). Line two sheet pans with Silpats or parchment paper.

Arrange the frozen cookies on the sheet pans, leaving about 2 inches between them. Bake the cookies until golden brown, 12 to 14 minutes in a convection oven, 16 to 18 minutes in a standard oven, reversing the positions of the pans halfway through baking. Set the pans on a cooling rack and cool for 5 to 10 minutes, then transfer the cookies to the rack to cool completely.

TO ASSEMBLE THE COOKIES: Combine the buttercream, peanut butter, and salt in the bowl of the mixer, fitted with the paddle attachment, and mix for 2 minutes on medium-low speed, until combined and smooth. Transfer the mixture to the pastry bag.

Turn half of the cookies over. Beginning in the center, pipe a spiral of peanut butter filling (55 grams) on each one, to within ¼ inch of the edges. Top each with a second cookie and press gently to sandwich the cookies.

The cookies are best the day they are baked, but they can be stored in a covered container, at room temperature if unfilled, refrigerated if filled, for up to 3 days.

PHOTOGRAPH ON PAGE 38   **MAKES 6 SANDWICH COOKIES**

NOTE ON ROLLING OUT THE DOUGH: At the bakery, we use a commercial sheeter to roll out the dough quickly and evenly. At home, the dough must be refrigerated as necessary during the rolling and cutting process.

TKOs

WHITE CHOCOLATE FILLING

35% white chocolate, chopped	125 grams	4.4 ounces
Unsalted butter	15 grams	0.5 ounce
Heavy cream	125 grams	½ cup + 1 teaspoon

CHOCOLATE SHORTBREAD

All-purpose flour	259 grams	1¾ cups + 1½ tablespoons
Unsweetened alkalized cocoa powder	87 grams	1 cup + 1½ tablespoons
Baking soda	1.6 grams	⅜ teaspoon
Unsalted butter	227 grams	8 ounces
Kosher salt	6 grams	2 teaspoons
Granulated sugar	161 grams	¾ cup + 1 tablespoon

Again playing with the American cookie idiom, Sebastien, well aware of my love for Oreos, devised this cookie in my honor. It uses a special cocoa powder, Guittard Cocoa Noir, which results in a very, very dark dough. The white chocolate filling is piped onto each bottom cookie in teardrop shapes, rather than simply spread, and these become an elegant pearled border when the cookie is topped with a second one. The chocolate wafers are excellent cookies even without the filling, by the way. They can be cut into seasonal shapes, like bats for Halloween, or they can be pulverized and used to make a chocolate cookie crust, just as you'd use graham crackers.

You'll need a Matfer #75 3-inch fluted cutter and a pastry bag with a 3/16-inch plain tip. • For this recipe, we use Valrhona Ivoire 35% white chocolate and Guittard Cocoa Noir.

FOR THE FILLING: Melt the chocolate and butter together, stirring constantly. Meanwhile, bring the cream to just under a simmer.

Pour the cream over the melted chocolate and whisk to combine. Pour into a container and refrigerate for at least 4 hours, or up to 1 day, until completely chilled.

MEANWHILE, FOR THE SHORTBREAD: Place the flour in a medium bowl, sift in the cocoa and baking soda, and whisk to combine.

Place the butter in the bowl of a stand mixer fitted with the paddle attachment. Turn to medium-low speed and mix until smooth. Add the salt and mix for another 15 to 30 seconds. Add the sugar and mix for about 2 minutes, until fluffy. Scrape down the sides and bottom of the bowl.

Add the dry ingredients in 2 additions, mixing on low speed for 15 to 30 seconds after each, or until just combined, then mix until the dough begins to come together.

Mound the dough on the work surface and, using the heel of your hand or a pastry scraper, push it together into a 6-inch-square block. Wrap in plastic wrap and refrigerate for at least 1 hour, until firm. (The dough can be refrigerated for up to 2 days or frozen for up to 1 month.)

Position the racks in the upper and lower thirds of the oven and preheat the oven to 325°F (standard). Line two sheet pans with Silpats or parchment paper.

Unwrap the dough and place it between two pieces of parchment paper or plastic wrap. With a rolling pin, pound the top of the dough, working from left to right, to begin to flatten it, then turn the dough 90 degrees and repeat (this will help prevent the dough from cracking as it is rolled). Roll out to a ⅛-inch-thick sheet. If the dough has softened, slide it (in the parchment) onto the back of a sheet pan and refrigerate until firm enough to cut.

Using the fluted cutter, cut rounds from the dough. If necessary, push the trimmings together, refrigerate until firm, and reroll for a total of 16 rounds. (Any trimmings can be baked as is, cooled, and ground in the food processor to use as cookie crumbs over ice cream.) If the dough softens, return to the refrigerator until the cookies are firm enough to transfer to a sheet pan. Arrange the rounds on the sheet pans, leaving about ¾ inch between them. (The dough can be shaped in advance; see Note.)

Bake for 15 to 17 minutes, turning the pans around halfway through baking, until the cookies are fragrant, with small cracks on the surface. (Because the cookies are so dark, it can be difficult to tell when they are done.) Set the pans on a cooling rack and cool for 5 to 10 minutes, then transfer the cookies to the rack to cool completely.

TO ASSEMBLE THE COOKIES: Place the filling in the bowl of the mixer, fitted with the paddle attachment, and beat until smooth. Transfer to the pastry bag.

Turn half of the cookies over. Pipe ½-inch-long teardrops in a ring on each one, beginning ⅛ inch from the edges of the cookie, and then, working toward the center, pipe concentric rings of teardrops to cover the cookie (use 18 grams of filling per cookie). Top each with a second cookie and press gently to sandwich the cookies.

The cookies are best the day they are baked, but they can be stored in a covered container, at room temperature if unfilled, or refrigerated if filled, for up to 3 days.

PHOTOGRAPHS ON PAGES 39, 42, AND 43　　　　MAKES 8 SANDWICH COOKIES

NOTE ON ADVANCE PREPARATION: The shaped dough can be frozen on the sheet pan—wrapped in a few layers of plastic wrap—for up to 1 month. Transfer to a lined room-temperature sheet pan, and bake from frozen.

Note to Professionals: At the bakery, we use a commercial sheeter to roll out the dough quickly and evenly.

TO MAKE BITE-SIZE COOKIES

The cookies in the Bouchon Bakery case are large. That's how we like them in this country: we're big on cookies! In Sebastien's country, France, cookies are much smaller as a rule. Most cookies can be made large or small, depending on your preference. We often make bite-size cookies for special events and catering orders, and nothing changes except for the baking times. The smaller the cookie, the shorter the time it needs to be in the oven. Pay attention and use common sense when baking a cookie in a new size.

For CHOCOLATE CHUNK AND CHIP, DOUBLE CHOCOLATE CHUNK AND CHIP, OATMEAL RAISIN, and TLC cookies: Using a small scoop (1½ inches in diameter), scoop the dough, level the top, and drop onto the sheet pan. Or roll the dough into small balls, using 15 grams/a scant 1 tablespoon per cookie. Bake the Chocolate Chunk and Chip Cookies for 7 to 9 minutes in a convection oven, 9 to 11 minutes in a standard oven, and Oatmeal Raisin Cookies and TLCs for 6 to 8 minutes (convection) or 8 to 10 minutes (standard). Each recipe will make about 4 dozen bite-size cookies.

For BETTER NUTTERS: Roll out the dough and cut into 1½-inch rounds. Freeze the dough as directed before baking. Bake the cookies for 5 to 7 minutes in a convection oven, 8 to 10 minutes in a standard oven. The recipe will make about 2 dozen bite-size sandwich cookies.

For TKOs: Roll out the dough and cut using a Matfer #45 1-inch fluted cutter. Bake the cookies for 9 to 11 minutes. The recipe will make about 2 dozen bite-size sandwich cookies.

Shortbread

Unsalted butter, at room temperature	180 grams	6.3 ounces
Granulated sugar	90 grams	½ cup
Kosher salt	2 grams	½ + ⅛ teaspoon
Vanilla paste	5.9 grams	1 teaspoon
All-purpose flour	270 grams	1¾ cups + 3 tablespoons
Granulated sugar for dusting	24 grams	2 tablespoons

Traditional shortbread is a rich, crumbly, buttery cookie made with nothing more than flour, butter, and sugar. It delights me that these most basic staple ingredients become so special in your hands when you treat them well and use them in the right proportions.

Shortbread is traditionally baked in a round or square pan, then cut into wedges or rectangles. Sebastien likes to cut the dough first, sprinkle it with sugar, and then bake it, for a more beautiful cookie with a sugary crust. Because of the large amount of butter, the dough should be well chilled before you roll it out; keeping the dough cold will also help the cut cookies retain their shape when baked.

This is a wonderfully versatile dough. For instance, you can roll out the dough, cut out shapes, bake them, and fill them to make sandwich cookies. Or make chocolate shortbread by replacing a quarter of the flour with unsweetened alkalized cocoa powder.

These are also good cookies to frost and decorate for the holidays (see page 51).

Shortbread will maintain straight edges better if baked in a convection oven rather than in a standard oven.

Place the butter in the bowl of a stand mixer fitted with the paddle attachment. Turn to medium-low speed and cream until smooth. Add the 90 grams/½ cup sugar and the salt and mix on medium-low speed for about 2 minutes, until fluffy. Scrape down the sides and bottom of the bowl. Add the vanilla paste and mix on low speed for about 30 seconds to distribute it evenly.

Add the flour in 2 additions, mixing on low speed for 15 to 30 seconds after each, or until just combined. Scrape the bottom of the bowl to incorporate any flour that may have settled there.

Mound the dough on the work surface and, using the heel of your hand or a pastry scraper, push it together into a 5-inch-square block. Wrap in plastic wrap and refrigerate for at least 2 hours, until firm. (The dough can be refrigerated for up to 2 days or frozen for up to 1 month.)

Position the racks in the upper and lower thirds of the oven and preheat the oven to 325°F (convection or standard). Line two sheet pans with Silpats or parchment paper.

Unwrap the dough and place it between two pieces of parchment paper or plastic wrap. With a rolling pin, pound the top of the dough, working from left to right, to begin to flatten it, then turn the dough 90 degrees and repeat. (This will help prevent the dough from cracking as it is rolled.) Roll out to a 9-inch square. If the dough has softened, slide it (in the parchment) onto the back of a sheet pan and refrigerate it until it is firm enough to score. (See Note to Professionals.)

Using a chef's knife and a ruler, score the dough horizontally 3 times to mark four 2¼-inch-wide strips. Then score it vertically 5 times at 1½-inch intervals (for a total of 24 sections). If the dough is not cool to the touch, refrigerate it. Once it is firm, cut through the markings. (The dough can be shaped in advance; see Note, page 41).

Dust the tops of the shortbread with the 24 grams/2 tablespoons granulated sugar and arrange on the prepared sheet pans, leaving about ¾ inch between them. Bake until pale golden brown, 13 to 15 minutes in a convection oven, 17 to 19 minutes in a standard oven, reversing the positions of the pans halfway through baking. Set the pans on a cooling rack and cool for 5 to 10 minutes, then transfer the cookies to the rack to cool completely.

The shortbread can be stored in a covered container for up to 3 days.

PHOTOGRAPH ON PAGE 46　　　　　　　　　　　　　　　　MAKES 24 COOKIES

Note to Professionals: To ensure a perfectly shaped block of dough, with no waste, we continue to shape the dough as it firms in the refrigerator. We smooth the top with a rolling pin and then push a straightedge against each side of the dough.

THE SHORT OF IT

When using butter to make a firm tart dough or an elastic brioche dough, you are literally shortening the long strands of gluten, the protein network that makes dough elastic. This is why we call shortening "shortening," and why a cookie dough with lots of butter and sugar is called "shortbread."

When water and flour are mixed together, long strands of proteins are released, but they're all in a clump, a big mass. Think of them as like those old coiled telephone cords, in a pile. The more you work the dough, however, the more the strands line up in a row, get connected, and become parallel. They can stretch, and the dough becomes elastic. This is why a pasta or bread dough can go from a shaggy mass, one that would fall apart if you tried to stretch it, to a smooth, elastic ball, perfect for rolling or shaping.

When you add fat, however, you weaken the bonds of those long gluten strands, separating them, preventing them from hooking up and making the dough strong and elastic. You keep those cords short and disconnected. We want a strong dough for pasta and bread, but for brioche, tarts, or cookies, we want a tender one.

Raspberry Macarons (page 63)

Speculoos

All-purpose flour	104 grams	¾ cup
Cake flour	74 grams	½ cup + 1½ tablespoons
Whole wheat flour	74 grams	½ cup + 2 tablespoons
Baking soda	1.3 grams	¼ teaspoon
Ground cinnamon	1.3 grams	½ teaspoon
Kosher salt	1.3 grams	⅜ teaspoon
Dark brown sugar	74 grams	⅓ cup (lightly packed)
Granulated sugar	59 grams	¼ cup + 2¼ teaspoons
Clover honey	8 grams	1⅛ teaspoons
Unsalted butter, at room temperature	177 grams	6.2 ounces
Powdered sugar for dusting		

This delicious, simple spice cookie is a specialty of the Netherlands and Belgium. Because of its high butter content, the dough needs to be well chilled before you roll it out and then, if necessary, chilled again before you cut out the cookies. We sprinkle the baked cookies with powdered sugar, but feel free to dust them with crystal or turbinado sugar before baking, for a sugary topping, or ice and decorate them if you like (see page 51). This is the dough we use to create our Witches' Hats (page 352).

You'll need a 4- to 5-inch decorative cookie cutter.

Place the all-purpose flour in a medium bowl and sift in the cake and whole wheat flours. Break up any lumps of flour remaining in the sieve and add them to the bowl. Sift in the baking soda and cinnamon. Add the salt and whisk together.

Combine both sugars in a small bowl and whisk to break up any lumps. Using a fork, stir in the honey.

Place the butter in the bowl of a stand mixer fitted with the paddle attachment. Turn to medium-low speed and cream the butter until smooth. Add the sugar mixture and mix for about 2 minutes, until fluffy. Scrape down the sides and bottom of the bowl. Add the dry ingredients in 2 additions, mixing on low speed for 15 to 30 seconds after each, or until just combined. Scrape the bottom of the bowl to incorporate any dry ingredients that have settled there.

Mound the dough on the work surface and, using the heel of your hand or a pastry scraper, push it together into a 4-by-6-inch block. Wrap in plastic wrap and refrigerate for at least 2 hours, or, preferably, overnight.

Position the racks in the upper and lower thirds of the oven and preheat the oven to 325°F (standard). Line two sheet pans with Silpats or parchment paper.

Unwrap the dough and place it between two pieces of parchment paper or plastic wrap. With a rolling pin, pound the top of the dough, working from left to right, to begin to flatten it, then turn the dough 90 degrees and repeat. (This will help prevent the dough from cracking as it is rolled.) Roll out to just under ⅛ inch thick. If the dough has softened, slide it (in the parchment) onto the back of a sheet pan and refrigerate until firm enough to cut into cookies.

Using the decorative cutter, cut out the cookies and arrange them on the prepared sheet pans, leaving about ¾ inch between them. If necessary, push the trimmings together, refrigerate until firm, and reroll for a total of 8 cookies. If the dough softens, return it to the refrigerator until the cookies are firm enough to transfer to the sheet pans. (The dough can be shaped in advance; see Note, page 41.)

Bake the cookies until golden brown, 13 to 15 minutes, reversing the positions of the pans halfway through baking. Set the pans on a cooling rack and cool for 5 to 10 minutes, then transfer the cookies to the rack to cool completely.

The cookies can be stored in a covered container for up to 3 days. Just before serving, sift powdered sugar over the cookies.

MAKES 8 COOKIES

This is our holiday seasonal cookie.
Cut them into snowflakes to celebrate winter.

COOKIES, AN APPRECIATION

I love a simple cookie for dessert. In fact, I love the whole notion of single servings: cookies, éclairs, cream puffs. We tend to think of desserts as cakes, tarts, and pies that we cut and serve, but sometimes a cookie is all you need for a dessert. And what could be more appreciated or easier to end a meal with than warm cookies and ice cream?

What's neat about cookies, of course, is that they can also be a great component of a dessert. Freeze a small pan of ice cream and cut into disks to make easy ice cream sandwiches with large cookies. Serve small cookies with a pudding or pot de crème.

Crumbled cookies add crunch to almost any soft or creamy dessert. Savory chefs are always conscious of crunch, making sure that texture is included in a dish. So, too, should you be when composing a dessert.

Decorated Cookies

There's nothing better than being in the kitchen with family, and decorating cookies is one of the best ways to engage children in the kitchen. Be on the lookout for interesting cutters; we have found some beauties in antique stores. We use all kinds of different colored glazes, then sprinkle the iced cookies with a variety of garnishes. At the bakery, we make decorated cookies using speculoos and shortbread doughs (pages 48 and 44), as well as pâte sucrée (see page 129).

TO GLAZE AND GARNISH COOKIES: Preheat the oven as directed in the individual recipe, and line sheet pans with Silpats or parchment paper. Roll out the dough for the speculoos or the pâte sucrée to ⅛ inch thick. Roll out the shortbread dough to about ¼ inch thick. Use decorative cutters to cut out the cookies, and arrange them on the sheet pans, leaving space between them.

Bake the cookies as the recipe specifies, but keep a watchful eye on them, as baking times will vary based on the shape and size of the cookies. Cool the cookies.

Line a sheet pan with parchment and position a cooling rack on it. Arrange the cookies on the rack, leaving space between them.

Warm the desired amount of pâte à glacer (see Note) to 130°F/54.4°C. Mix in the yogurt powder and drops of colored cocoa butter until you reach the desired color. Strain the mixture and pour it into a disposable pastry bag. Cut ½ inch from the tip of the bag.

Pipe the icing generously over the cookies, letting the excess drip down the sides. Tap the pan against the work surface to smooth the glaze and burst any air bubbles. Using the tip of a paring knife, move each cookie a couple of inches, so the rack knocks off any glaze dripping from the bottoms of the cookies. Sprinkle any garnish or decoration you like over the cookies, and refrigerate for a few minutes to set the icing. The cookies can be stored in a covered container for up to 3 days.

NOTE: Pâte à glacer is a coating chocolate that doesn't require tempering. Here we use Cacao Barry's Ivoire white chocolate. Because it's so sweet, we like to add yogurt powder (dehydrated yogurt) to it, which balances the sweetness with acidity; add it in the proportion of 10 percent of the weight of the pâte à glacer. Because pâte à glacer is fat-based, it requires a fat-based medium to color it; we use drops of Artisanal Colorants colored cocoa butter.

FAVORITE COMBINATIONS

GLAZE	GARNISH
GREEN ICING	pistachio flour
WHITE ICING	large-crystal sparkling sugar
RED ICING	raspberry powder
LEMON ICING	leave plain

Dog Treats

TREATS

Sliced bacon, cut into 1-inch-wide pieces	453 grams	1 pound
Chicken livers, cut into ½-inch pieces	370 grams	13 ounces
Fine cornmeal	130 grams	¾ cup + 1 tablespoon
All-purpose flour	450 grams	3 cups + 3 tablespoons
Chicken stock	235 grams	1 cup

KETCHUP GLAZE

Ketchup	50 grams	3 tablespoons
Egg whites	13 grams	1 tablespoon

We love dogs at Bouchon, and we even have a special watering area for them in the courtyard. A lot of the chefs have dogs too, and they'd talk about their dogs, so it was a natural progression—chefs who like to come up with ideas to please customers also wanted to create something for their beloved pooches. The Bouchon dog treats originally included leftover foie gras trimmings from The French Laundry, but we make so many of these now that we have replaced it with chicken liver. This is a popular item at all the bakeries; your pet may never go back to Milk-Bones again.

You'll need a 2⅝-inch-long dog bone cookie cutter. ● *The baking time is halved in a convection oven.*

Position the racks in the upper and lower thirds of the oven and preheat the oven to 250°F (convection or standard). Line two sheet pans with Silpats or parchment paper.

FOR THE TREATS: Heat a large nonstick frying pan over medium-high heat. Add the bacon and cook for 4 to 5 minutes, until it has rendered its fat and is a rich golden brown. Remove from the pan and drain on paper towels.

Pour off all but a generous film of bacon fat. Add the chicken livers to the pan and sauté, turning them frequently and smashing them slightly, for about 5 minutes, until broken down to a paste. Remove from the heat.

Place the bacon in a food processor and pulse a few times to grind it. Add the chicken livers and process to combine, then add the cornmeal and process until you have a coarse mixture.

Transfer the mixture to the bowl of a stand mixer fitted with the paddle attachment. Add the flour and mix to combine. Slowly pour in the chicken stock and mix until the dough begins to gather around the paddle and feels moist to the touch. Remove the dough from the mixer and knead it just enough to combine.

Place the dough between two pieces of parchment paper or plastic wrap and roll it out to a ⅜-inch-thick sheet. Using the dog bone cutter, cut out the treats and arrange them on the prepared sheet pans. Knead the trimmings together, roll out, and cut out additional treats.

Bake until the treats are completely dry, about 1½ hours in a convection oven, 3 hours in a standard oven. Remove from the oven and lower the oven temperature to 200°F.

FOR THE GLAZE: Combine the ketchup and egg whites; the glaze will be very thick. Brush it over the top of the warm treats. Return the pans to the oven and bake for 20 to 30 minutes, or until the glaze has set. Place the pans on a cooling rack and cool for 5 to 10 minutes, then transfer the treats to the rack to cool completely.

The treats can be stored in a covered container for up to 1 month.

MAKES 45 TREATS

Note to Professionals: At the bakery, we used to use foie gras trimmings from our restaurants in the dog treats, substituting foie gras for one-third of the liver amount. We rendered the foie gras and then sautéed the chicken livers in the fat. If we had enough foie gras, we also added a dice of it to the dough along with the flour. If foie gras is added, you'll need less chicken stock.

Florentines
FLORENTINS

Pâte Sucrée (page 129), cold	325 grams	11.5 ounces

NUT AND FRUIT LAYER

Whole milk	52 grams	3 tablespoons + ¾ teaspoon
Granulated sugar	79 grams	¼ cup + 2½ tablespoons
Glucose (see Note)	42 grams	2 tablespoons
Clover honey	42 grams	2 tablespoons
Unsalted butter, cut into ½-inch pieces, at room temperature	105 grams	3.7 ounces
Kosher salt	a pinch	
Sliced blanched almonds	126 grams	1½ cups
Shelled raw unsalted pistachios	42 grams	¼ cup + 1 tablespoon
⅛-inch dice Candied Orange Peel (page 379)	42 grams	3 tablespoons
Brune pâte à glacer (see Note, page 120) or 64% chocolate, melted (see Note to Professionals)	200 grams	7 ounces

Florentines, one of my favorite treats when I go to France, are great cookies composed of caramelized nuts and dried fruit and chocolate. I kept asking Sebastien to do a Florentine, and when I brought in a traditional Florentine mold, which gives the chocolate a wavy texture, he finally got the picture and caved. Of course, we make so many now that my little mold is impractical, so we use a plastic comb from a specialty store or the kind sold in the tile section of Home Depot and other stores for spreading adhesive. Buy one with rectangular, not triangular, teeth. (If you don't have a comb, simply spread enough melted chocolate on the pâte sucrée to make a thick layer.)

Traditionally Florentines are just a fruit and nut layer spread with chocolate, but we added a base of pâte sucrée, which makes the cookies much easier to pick up and eat, and makes them more substantial too. The crust also cuts the sweetness of the traditional version.

You'll need a quarter sheet pan, a Thermapen or other candy thermometer, and a plastic tile comb. ● *For this recipe, we use Sicilian pistachios and Cacao Barry pâte à glacer. If using chocolate, we recommend Valrhona Manjari 64% chocolate.*

Preheat the oven to 350°F (standard). Line a quarter sheet pan with parchment paper.

Unwrap the dough and place between two pieces of parchment paper or plastic wrap. With a rolling pin, pound the top of the dough, working from left to right, to begin to flatten it, then turn the dough 90 degrees and repeat. (This will help prevent the dough from cracking as it is rolled.) Roll out to a 10-by-14-inch rectangle.

Remove the top piece of parchment and invert the dough into the prepared pan, pressing it gently against the bottom and into the corners. Run your hands over the parchment to smooth the dough and force out any air bubbles. (Any dough extending up the sides will be trimmed later.) Repair any cracks in the dough. Freeze the dough for 10 minutes or refrigerate for 30 minutes, or until firm.

Trim the edges of the dough if necessary so that only the bottom of the pan is covered with dough. Line the pan with a piece of parchment paper (covering the dough) and fill with ½ inch of raw rice. Bake for about 12 minutes, or until the dough is a pale golden brown around the edges. Transfer the pan to a cooling rack, remove the paper and rice, and lower the oven temperature to 325°F.

FOR THE NUT AND FRUIT LAYER: Combine the milk, sugar, glucose, and honey in a medium saucepan and cook over medium heat, stirring, to dissolve the sugar. Then cook for about 8 minutes, until the temperature reaches 248°F/120°C. Remove from the heat and stir in the butter and salt. Stir in the almonds, pistachios, and orange peel.

Pour the mixture into the crust and, using an offset spatula, spread it evenly, reaching into the corners. Bake for 25 to 30 minutes, turning the pan around halfway through. To check for doneness, remove the pan

from the oven and let the bubbles subside (see Notes to Professionals). The nut mixture should be a rich golden brown, with no undercooked areas, or the cookies will be chewy; on the other hand, overcooked cookies may be too crisp—it is a balancing act. Don't worry if there are dark edges, as they will be trimmed later. If the nut mixture isn't level, push it into place with a small offset spatula. Set the pan on a cooling rack and cool completely.

Line a cutting board with parchment paper. Run a paring knife around the edges of the Florentine to loosen it from the pan, and invert it onto the parchment.

Pour 70 grams/¼ cup of the chocolate over the crust and, using an offset spatula, spread it into a thin, even layer, working it for about 30 seconds, or until it begins to thicken (this will temper the chocolate). The layer should be just thick enough to cover the crust. Use the comb to create waves in the chocolate. If some of the crust is visible through the chocolate, spread on more chocolate and comb again. (You may not use all of the chocolate.) Let stand at room temperature until the chocolate is completely set.

Using a serrated knife, trim the edges to straighten them and remove any dark parts. Cut the Florentine into six 3½-by-2½-inch rectangles.

The Florentines are best the day they are made, but they can be wrapped individually in plastic wrap and stored for up to 3 days.

PHOTOGRAPHS ON PAGES 56 AND 57 **MAKES 6 COOKIES**

NOTE ON GLUCOSE: Glucose is a common sugar that we buy in a clear syrup form. Used for part of the sugar in a recipe, it smooths the texture and helps prevent crystallization. Glucose is very viscous at room temperature and so can be quite messy to work with. Stored in the refrigerator it becomes easier to work with. To measure a small portion, moisten your fingers and pinch out what you need—the cold glucose won't drip and it won't stick to wet fingers.

Notes to Professionals: At the bakery, we use brune pâte à glacer rather than melted chocolate; it spreads easily, and the more you work it, the thicker it will become.

We make large batches of the Florentines on full sheet pans. Because of the large surface area, we know they are done when they stop bubbling in the oven. However, with a small batch, the nut layer would become too crisp if baked until the bubbling stops.

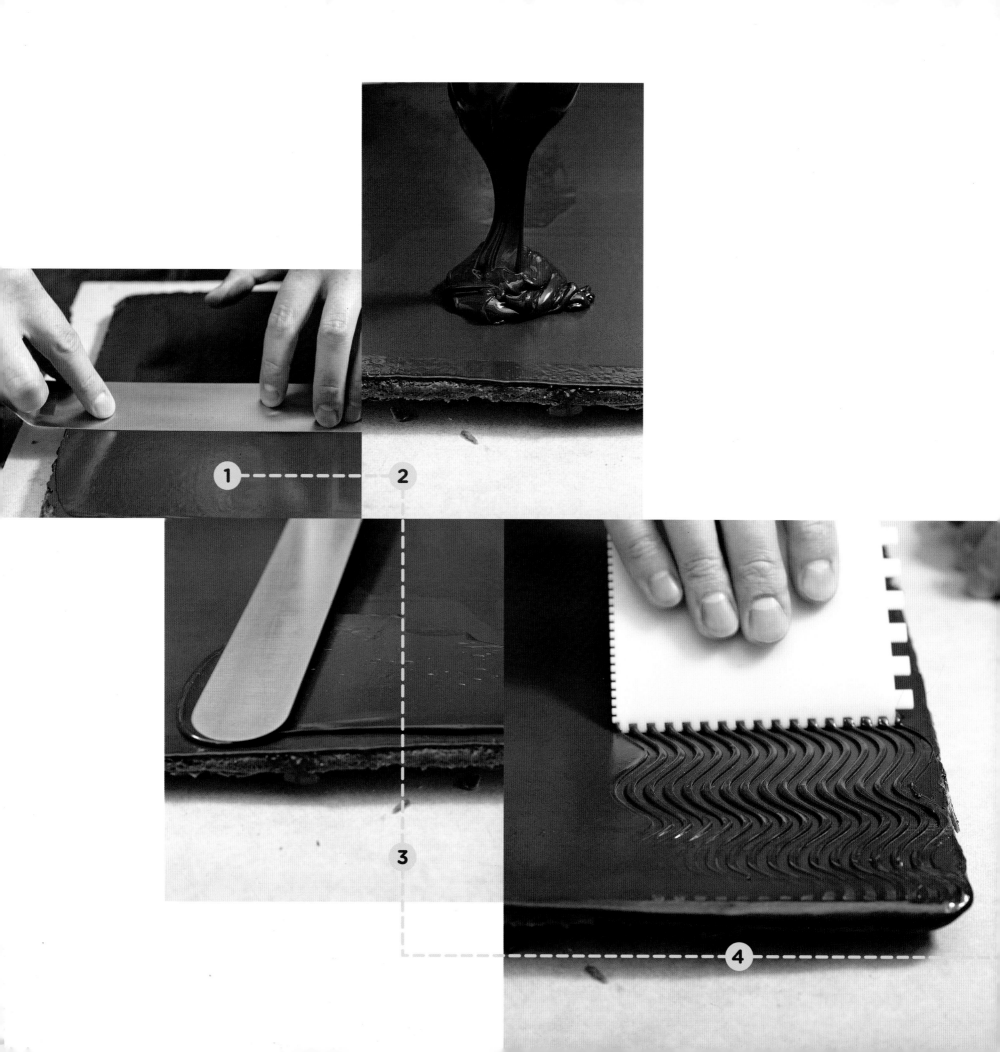

Macarons

The macaron is a magical cookie. Two meringue shells sandwiching a filling, it satisfies on so many different levels it's no wonder Americans have gone crazy for them, and no wonder they're Bouchon Bakery's biggest seller. The shells are crisp and fragile on the outside, chewy on the inside, and the filling is sweet and creamy. And their beautiful pastel colors attract your eye.

Bouchon makes both traditional macarons—chocolate and vanilla, lemon and raspberry—and playful macarons, ice-cream-filled or enrobed in chocolate. Sometimes we put two batters in one bag to pipe the shells, so that their appearance is marbled. There's no end to the creativity you can bring to the macaron.

The macaron shell isn't difficult to make, but it can be a little tricky. You have to get the consistency of the batter just right—not too thick, not too thin, just so that it settles gently.

There are a few cooking notes to consider. High humidity can affect the shells, causing the meringue to weep; macarons are best made on dry days. A convection oven works a little better than a standard oven, though either can be used. Macarons are best baked on the middle rack and left undisturbed (opening the door and turning the sheet pan can cause them to deflate). So, yes, they can be temperamental, but they're well worth the effort. With a little patience and care, you can make great macarons at home.

The flavor of the macarons develops as they stand. In fact, macarons are actually best individually wrapped in a few layers of plastic wrap and frozen for 24 hours (or for up to 2 weeks); transfer to the refrigerator for 3 hours or so, then return to room temperature.

Vanilla Macarons

MACARONS

Almond flour/meal	212 grams	1¾ cups + 2½ tablespoons
Powdered sugar	212 grams	1¾ cups + 1 tablespoon + 2 teaspoons
Egg whites (see Easier with the Freezer, page 108)	82 grams	¼ cup + 1½ tablespoons
	90 grams	¼ cup + 2 tablespoons
1 vanilla bean, split lengthwise		
Granulated sugar, plus a pinch for the egg whites	236 grams	1 cup + 3 tablespoons
Water	158 grams	⅔ cup

VANILLA BUTTERCREAM FILLING

French Buttercream (page 375)	250 grams	1 cup + 2 tablespoons
½ vanilla bean, split lengthwise		

You'll need a Thermapen or other candy thermometer, a pastry bag with a ½-inch plain tip, and a pastry bag with a ⅜-inch plain tip. ● *Baking in a convection oven is preferable; the tops of macarons baked in a standard oven often develop small speckles, which can affect the texture (though not the flavor).*

FOR THE MACARONS: Because the cookies will be sandwiched, it is important that they be as close in size as possible. Even if you are proficient with a pastry bag, we suggest making a template, as we do. Use a compass or a cookie cutter as a guide and a dark marking pen, such as a fine-tip Sharpie.

Lay a sheet of parchment paper (see Note to Professionals, page 63) on the work surface with a long side closest to you. Trace 4 evenly spaced 2¼-inch circles along the top long edge, leaving 1 inch of space around them. Trace 3 circles below them, spacing them between the first circles. Continue with another row of 4, followed by another row of 3. Turn the parchment over and lay it on a sheet pan. Lift up each corner of the parchment and spray the underside with nonstick spray

to keep it from blowing up while the cookies are baking. Repeat with a second sheet pan and piece of parchment paper.

Preheat the oven to 350°F (convection) or 400°F (standard).

Place the almond flour in a food processor and pulse to grind it as fine as possible.

Sift the almond flour and powdered sugar into a large bowl and whisk together. Mound the almond flour mixture, then make a 4-inch well in the center, leaving a layer of the flour at the bottom. Pour in the 82 grams/¼ cup plus 1½ tablespoons egg whites and combine with a spatula. Scrape the seeds from the vanilla bean and add them to the mixture, stirring until evenly distributed. Set aside.

Place the remaining 90 grams/¼ cup plus 2 tablespoons egg whites in the bowl of a stand mixer fitted with the whisk attachment. Combine the 236 grams/1 cup plus 3 tablespoons granulated sugar and the water in a small saucepan and heat over medium-high heat until the syrup reaches 203°F/110°C.

Letting the syrup continue to cook, add the pinch of sugar to the egg whites, turn the mixer to medium speed, and whip to soft peaks. If the whites reach soft peaks before the syrup reaches 248°F/120°C, reduce the speed to the lowest setting, just to keep them moving.

When the syrup reaches 248°F/120°C, remove the pan from the heat. Turn the mixer to medium-low speed, and slowly add the syrup, pouring it between the side of the bowl and the whisk; the meringue will deflate. Increase the speed to medium and whip for 5 minutes, or until the whites hold stiff, glossy peaks. Although the bowl will still be warm to the touch, the meringue should have cooled; if not, continue to whip until it is cool.

Fold one-third of the meringue into the almond mixture, then continue adding the whites a little at a time (you may not use them all) until when you fold a portion of the batter over on itself, the "ribbon" slowly moves. The mixture shouldn't be so stiff that it holds its shape without moving at all, but it shouldn't be so loose that it dissolves into itself and does not maintain the ribbon; it is better for the mixture to be slightly stiff than too loose.

Continued on page 62

WARMING UP EGGS

For meringues, we like to "warm up" the egg whites with a small amount of sugar, usually just a pinch or so (if you're working with large quantities, add about 5 percent of the sugar at this point). Cold whites can break down when overwhipped, the water separating from the protein; adding sugar to the whites before you start whisking them will prevent this.

PARCHMENT PAPER

We use lots and lots of parchment paper. We line any sheet pan we use with parchment or a Silpat. It's about both working clean and not allowing what we are baking or have baked to come in direct contact with the metal.

We also use parchment paper for making templates, and we roll dough between sheets of it. Rather than rolls of parchment, look for precut sheets, which are available at restaurant supply stores; these will lie flat on the pan or work surface without curling and provide the best results.

FLAVOR MATURATION

That's what we call it in the bakery, but what we really mean is that flavors are alive, always changing, traveling a bell curve as they transform. Once a macaron is finished, its flavor is good, but it will get better. This is why we freeze the macarons (it also makes them chewier and more fun to eat). After a stint in the cold, their flavor will be at its peak. But if you let the macarons sit and sit and sit, their flavor will evolve past its peak. So our goal is to grab our creations at the height of their flavor.

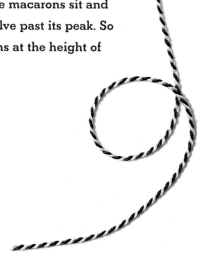

Transfer the mixture to the pastry bag with the ½-inch tip. Hold the bag upright ½ inch above the center of one of the traced circles and pipe out enough of the mixture to fill in the circle. Lift away the pastry bag and fill the remaining circles on the first pan. Lift up the sheet pan and tap the bottom of the pan to spread the batter evenly and smooth any peaks left by the pastry bag.

If using a convection oven, bake for 8 to 10 minutes, until the tops are shiny and crisp. If using a standard oven, place the sheet pan in the oven, immediately lower the oven temperature to 325°F, and bake for 9 to 12 minutes, until the tops are shiny and crisp. Set the pan on a cooling rack and cool completely. If using a standard oven, preheat it to 350°F again.

Pipe the remaining meringue mixture into the circles on the second sheet pan and bake as directed above. Let cool completely.

FOR THE FILLING: Place the buttercream in the bowl of a stand mixer fitted with the paddle attachment and mix on medium-low speed until smooth and fluffy. Scrape the seeds from the vanilla bean, add them to the buttercream, and mix on low for about 30 seconds to distribute the seeds evenly.

TO FILL THE COOKIES: Transfer the buttercream to the pastry bag with the ⅜-inch tip.

Remove the macarons from the parchment paper. Turn half of them over. Starting in the center, pipe 15 grams/1 tablespoon of the buttercream in a spiral pattern on one upside-down macaron, not quite reaching the edges. Top with a second macaron and press gently to spread the buttercream to the edges. Repeat with the remaining macarons and filling.

The macarons are best if wrapped individually in a few layers of plastic wrap and frozen for at least 24 hours or up to 2 weeks. Defrost in the refrigerator for 3 hours, then bring to room temperature before serving. They can be served the day they are made or stored in a covered container in the refrigerator for up to 2 days.

MAKES 14 MACARONS

Lemon Macarons

For this recipe, we use Chefmaster Liqua-Gel Lemon Yellow food coloring.

For the macarons, omit the vanilla bean and fold 3 or 4 drops lemon food coloring into the finished meringue mixture. For the filling, substitute 200 grams/1⅓ cups Basic Buttercream (page 375) for the French Buttercream and omit the vanilla bean. Beat the buttercream as directed, then add 50 grams/3½ tablespoons Lemon Curd (page 377) and mix for 1 minute, or until evenly combined. If adding a curd center (see Note), use 80 grams/¼ cup plus 2 tablespoons additional Lemon Curd.

Raspberry Macarons

For this recipe, we use Chefmaster Liqua-Gel Rose Pink food coloring.

For the macarons, omit the vanilla bean and fold 3 or 4 drops pink food coloring into the finished meringue mixture. For the filling, substitute 200 grams/1⅓ cups Basic Buttercream (page 375) for the French Buttercream and omit the vanilla bean. Beat the buttercream as directed, then add 50 grams/2 tablespoons Raspberry Jam (page 379) and mix for 1 minute, or until evenly combined. If adding a jam center (see Note), use 80 grams/3½ tablespoons additional Raspberry Jam.

PHOTOGRAPHS ON PAGES 47, 64, AND 65

NOTE: At the bakery, we sometimes fill the macarons with "bull's-eyes" (see following page). Pipe buttercream around the edge of each bottom macaron and then place a small amount of curd or jam in the center of each.

Be creative with buttercream and flavor centers. For example, we like to make a peanut butter and jelly macaron. Peanut butter buttercream is piped around the edge and the center is filled with jam.

We color the shells with a combination of Chefmaster Buckeye Brown, Violet, and Red-Red.

Hazelnut Macarons

For the macarons, substitute hazelnut flour for the almond meal and omit the vanilla bean. Omit the buttercream filling and use the ganache recipe below—note that the filling must be made a day ahead.

CARAMELIA GANACHE

Trimoline (invert sugar)	27 grams	1 tablespoon
Heavy cream	90 grams	¼ cup + 2 tablespoons
Fleur de sel	1.5 grams	⅜ teaspoon
34% Caramélia chocolate, melted	225 grams	7.9 ounces

For this recipe, we use Erstein Trimoline and Valrhona Caramélia 34% chocolate.

Combine the trimoline, cream, and salt in a small saucepan and heat over medium heat, stirring, until the trimoline melts and the mixture comes to a boil. Stir the cream mixture into the melted chocolate. Let sit in a cool spot overnight to set up.

PHOTOGRAPH ON PAGE 58

Note to Professionals: When piping macarons by hand, we always use templates that we make by tracing circles onto large sheets of plastic. That way, no matter who makes the macarons, they are the same size. We place a template on a sheet pan, cover it with parchment paper, and pipe the macarons onto the parchment. Then we simply slide the guide out without disturbing the cookies. Don't be tempted to try this by using a second sheet of parchment paper; it is not sturdy enough and could disturb the cookies and alter their shape when pulled out.

Avoid a blowout! Keep the filling below the level of the buttercream.

①

②

③

KEEP YOUR BUBBLE WRAP

When we box up macarons for gifts, we stack them between layers of bubble wrap so their delicate shells won't shatter. All delicate dry items can be protected with bubble wrap.

Making "bull's-eyes" with Raspberry Macarons (page 63)

4

My first experience with scones, the very simple quick bread that has been a breakfast staple for ages, was through my stepmother, who was Scottish. (Hers were more like drop biscuits, and I recall that they were studded with currants.) Thus I have an emotional connection to them, but I feel that they are too often dry. And the same goes for muffins. So the excitement in making scones and muffins is in finding different ways to get moisture into them (even by adding bacon). Scones couldn't be easier to make, and this reflects the humble nature of the scone itself. ⊘ The keys to good scones are to avoid overworking the dough, to use just the right amount of butter relative to the flour, and to make sure that the flour and butter are thoroughly combined. (Sebastien doesn't leave chunks of butter in the dough, as many recipes instruct. The butter gets thoroughly incorporated; this helps keep the scones moist as well.) ⊘ I didn't eat many muffins growing up. My mom sometimes made corn-bread muffins, and they were fine, but my brothers and sister and I were too busy eating Pillsbury cinnamon buns, with their ready-made frosting. There was never enough frosting! I do like muffins now, but they need a judicious amount of fat or an ingredient such as fruit to keep them from being dry. My favorite muffin is blueberry, because it's so moist and flavorful.

SCONES &

MUFFINS

Plain Scones

All-purpose flour	152 grams	1 cup + 1½ tablespoons
Cake flour	304 grams	2¼ cups + 2 tablespoons
Baking powder	12.5 grams	2½ teaspoons
Baking soda	2.5 grams	½ teaspoon
Granulated sugar	91 grams	¼ cup + 3½ tablespoons
Cold unsalted butter, cut into ¼-inch pieces	227 grams	8 ounces
Heavy cream, plus additional for brushing	135 grams	½ cup + 1½ tablespoons
Crème fraîche	135 grams	½ cup + 2 tablespoons
Large-crystal sparkling sugar	6 grams	1 teaspoon

This is a great basic scone. It uses both butter and crème fraîche for a rich dough that also has some acidity and, therefore, some complexity. As with any dough, the more you work this, the tougher it will become, so mix only until all the ingredients are incorporated. We use cake flour in addition to all-purpose for a more tender crumb. We finish the scones by brushing them with cream and sprinkling them with coarse sugar.

This dough also makes a good shortcake.

Scones baked in a convection oven will have a slightly higher rise and more even color.

Place the all-purpose flour in the bowl of a stand mixer and sift in the cake flour, baking powder, baking soda, and granulated sugar. Fit the mixer with the paddle attachment and mix on the lowest setting for about 15 seconds to combine. Stop the mixer, add the butter, and, on the lowest setting (to keep the flour from flying out of the bowl), pulse to begin incorporating the butter. Increase the speed to low and mix for about 3 minutes to break up the butter and incorporate it into the dry mixture. If any large pieces of butter remain, stop the mixer, break them up by hand, and mix just until incorporated.

With the mixer running, slowly pour in the cream. Add the crème fraîche and mix for about 30 seconds, until all of the dry ingredients are moistened and the dough comes together around the paddle. Scrape down the sides and bottom of the bowl and the paddle and pulse again to combine. (If making Cinnamon Honey Scones, mix in the cinnamon honey cubes at this point; see page 70.)

Mound the dough on the work surface and, using the heel of your hand or a pastry scraper, push it together. Place the dough between two pieces of plastic wrap and, using your hands, press it into a 6-by-9-inch block, smoothing the top. Press the sides of your hands against the sides of the dough to straighten them. Wrap the dough in plastic wrap and refrigerate for about 2 hours, until firm. (See Note to Professionals, page 45.)

Line a sheet pan with a Silpat or parchment paper. Using a chef's knife, cut the block of dough lengthwise into thirds and then crosswise in half. Cut each rectangle in half on the diagonal to make a total of 12 triangles. Arrange them on the prepared sheet pan, leaving space between them. Cover with plastic wrap and freeze until solid, at least 2 hours, but preferably overnight. (The scones can remain in the freezer for up to 1 month.)

Preheat the oven to 325°F (convection) or 350°F (standard). Line a sheet pan with a Silpat or parchment paper.

Arrange the frozen scones 1 inch apart on the sheet pan and brush the tops with cream. Sprinkle the top of each scone with a generous pinch of sparkling sugar. Bake for 15 to 18 minutes in a convection oven, 25 to 28 minutes in a standard oven, until golden brown. Set the sheet on a cooling rack and cool completely.

The scones are best the day they are baked, but they can be stored in a covered container for 1 day.

MAKES 12 SCONES

Chocolate Cherry Scones

MACERATED CHERRIES

Water	118 grams	½ cup
Granulated sugar	105 grams	½ cup + 1¼ teaspoons
Kirsch (optional)	20 grams	1 tablespoon + 2 teaspoons
¼ vanilla bean, split lengthwise		
Dried tart cherries	105 grams	¾ cup + 2 tablespoons

SCONES

All-purpose flour	332 grams	2¼ cups + 2 tablespoons
Baking powder	6.5 grams	1⅜ teaspoons
Baking soda	4.5 grams	¾ + ⅛ teaspoon
Kosher salt	2.2 grams	¾ teaspoon
Cold unsalted butter, cut into ¼-inch pieces	133 grams	4.7 ounces
Heavy cream	178 grams	¾ cup
Chocolate chips	105 grams	½ cup

CHERRY GLAZE

Powdered sugar	100 grams	¾ cup + 2 tablespoons
Reserved strained cherry syrup	45 to 50 grams	2½ to 3 tablespoons
Heavy cream	30 grams	2 tablespoons

Loaded with macerated dried cherries and chocolate chips, this scone is finished with a simple glaze of powdered sugar and the cherry soaking liquid. These scones are so delicious they could almost be served as dessert.

You'll need a 2½-inch (#10) ice cream scoop. ● *Scones baked in a convection oven will have a slightly higher rise and more even color.*

FOR THE MACERATED CHERRIES: Combine the water, sugar, and kirsch, if using, in a small saucepan. Scrape the seeds from the vanilla bean and add the seeds and pod to the pan. Bring to a simmer over medium-high heat, stirring to dissolve the sugar. Stir in the cherries and return to a simmer, then remove from the heat and let cool.

Transfer the cherries and their liquid to a covered container and refrigerate overnight.

FOR THE SCONES: Set a fine-mesh strainer over a measuring cup and drain the cherries. Reserve 50 grams/3 tablespoons of the liquid for the glaze.

Place the flour in the bowl of a stand mixer and sift in the baking powder and baking soda. Fit the mixer with the paddle attachment, add the salt, and mix on the lowest setting for about 15 seconds to combine. Stop the mixer, add the butter, and pulse on the lowest setting to begin incorporating the butter. Increase the speed to low and mix for about 3 minutes to break up and incorporate the butter. If any large pieces of butter remain, stop the mixer, break them up by hand, and mix until just incorporated.

With the mixer running, slowly pour in the cream and mix for about 30 seconds, until all of the dry ingredients are moistened and the dough comes together around the paddle. Scrape down the bottom and sides of the bowl and the paddle. Add the drained cherries and the chocolate chips and pulse on low speed to incorporate. Transfer the dough to a covered container and refrigerate for about 2 hours, until firm.

Line a sheet pan with a Silpat or parchment paper. Using the ice cream scoop, divide the dough into 12 equal portions (72 grams each) and arrange on the sheet pan, leaving space between them. Cover with plastic wrap and freeze until solid, at least 2 hours, but preferably overnight. (The scones can remain in the freezer for up to 1 month.)

Preheat the oven to 325°F (convection) or 350°F (standard). Line a sheet pan with a Silpat or parchment paper.

Arrange the frozen scones 1 inch apart on the sheet pan. Bake for 20 to 23 minutes in a convection oven, 32 to 35 minutes in a standard oven, until golden brown.

MEANWHILE, MAKE THE GLAZE: Whisk together the powdered sugar and 45 grams/2½ tablespoons of the reserved cherry syrup in a small bowl. Slowly whisk in the cream. Add additional syrup if needed to maintain the consistency of a glaze. When the scones are baked, set the sheet pan on a cooling rack and immediately brush them with the glaze. Cool completely.

The scones are best the day they are baked, but they can be stored in a covered container for 1 day.

MAKES 12 SCONES

Cinnamon Honey Scones

CINNAMON HONEY CUBES

All-purpose flour	30 grams	3 tablespoons
Granulated sugar	30 grams	2½ tablespoons
Ground cinnamon	4 grams	1½ teaspoons
Cold unsalted butter, cut into ¼-inch cubes	30 grams	1 ounce
Clover honey	20 grams	1 tablespoon
Plain Scone dough (page 68; see method below)		

HONEY BUTTER GLAZE

Clarified Butter (page 381)	45 grams	3 tablespoons + 2 teaspoons
Clover honey	20 grams	1 tablespoon

For this variation on the plain scone, we make a cinnamon honey butter that we chill, then dice and mix into the dough, almost as if it were currants or nuts. The butter pieces both flavor and enrich the dough and give it some visually appealing streaks. We finish the scones with a honey butter glaze.

You may want to use a bicycle cutter to cut the dough. ● *Scones baked in a convection oven will have a slightly higher rise and more even color.*

FOR THE CINNAMON HONEY CUBES: Place the flour in a medium bowl. Sift in the sugar and cinnamon and whisk to combine. Toss in the butter cubes, coating them in the dry mixture. Using your fingertips, break up the butter until there are no large visible pieces. Using a spatula, mix in the honey to form a smooth paste.

Press the paste into a 4-inch square on a sheet of plastic wrap. Wrap tightly and freeze until solid, about 2 hours (the paste can be frozen for up to 1 week).

FOR THE SCONES: Cut the butter paste into ¼-inch cubes. Once the dough is mixed, remove the bowl from the mixer and mix in the cubes by hand. (See Note to Professionals.) They may begin to break up a bit in the dough; that's okay. Mound the dough on the work surface and, using the heel of your hand or a pastry scraper, push it together. Place the dough between two pieces of plastic wrap and, using your hands, press it into a 7½-by-10-inch block, smoothing the top. Press the sides of your hands against the sides of the dough to straighten the edges. Wrap the dough in plastic wrap and refrigerate for about 2 hours, until firm. (See Note to Professionals, page 45.)

Line a baking sheet with a Silpat or parchment paper. Using a chef's knife or a bicycle cutter, cut the block of dough lengthwise into thirds and then crosswise into quarters. Arrange the scones on the prepared sheet pan, leaving space between them. Cover with plastic wrap and freeze until frozen solid, at least 2 hours, but preferably overnight. (The scones can remain in the freezer for up to 1 month.)

Preheat the oven to 325°F (convection) or 350°F (standard). Line a sheet pan with a Silpat or parchment paper.

Arrange the frozen scones 1 inch apart on the sheet pan. Bake for 20 to 23 minutes in a convection oven, 28 to 30 minutes in a standard oven, until golden brown.

FOR THE GLAZE: Stir the butter and honey together in a butter warmer or a small saucepan over medium-low heat until the butter has melted and combined with the honey.

As soon as you remove the scones from the oven, brush the tops with the glaze. Set the sheet pan on a cooling rack and cool completely.

The scones are best the day they are baked, but they can be stored in a covered container for 1 day.

MAKES 12 SCONES

Note to Professionals: You can use a commercial mixer to combine the dough and the cubes.

BICYCLES

Adjustable strip cutters, which chefs refer to as bicycles, are essentially sets of pastry wheels mounted on an expandable frame that you roll over a sheet of dough to cut it with precision. Most often we use one with five straight-edged wheels to cut dough into strips. But for tarts and pastries with a lattice top, we use a special strip cutter that makes a series of cuts that opens out into a lattice when it is stretched; see the Pear Feuilletés on page 226.

Bacon Cheddar Scones

All-purpose flour	107 grams	¾ cup + 1 teaspoon
Cake flour	196 grams	1½ cups + ½ tablespoon
Baking powder	8.1 grams	1½ + ⅛ teaspoons
Baking soda	1.6 grams	⅜ teaspoon
Granulated sugar	27 grams	2 tablespoons + ¾ teaspoon
Kosher salt	3.6 grams	1¼ teaspoons
Cold unsalted butter, cut into ¼-inch pieces	132 grams	4.7 ounces
Heavy cream, plus additional for brushing	71 grams	¼ cup + 1 tablespoon
Crème fraîche	89 grams	¼ cup + 2½ tablespoons
Hobbs applewood-smoked bacon, cooked, drained, and cut into ⅛-inch pieces (77 grams cooked weight)	340 grams	12 ounces
Grated white cheddar cheese	144 grams	2 cups
	36 grams	½ cup
Minced chives	10 grams	¼ cup
Freshly ground black pepper		

We wanted a savory scone in our repertoire, and because scones are traditionally eaten at breakfast, adding bacon—with its great flavor and power to enrich—was a natural. We incorporated another flavorful fat in the form of cheddar cheese, as well as chives for their oniony note and vivid color. No surprise that this is our most popular scone.

Leftover scones, traditional or savory, can be frozen, then pulverized and used as a crunchy topping for other foods. For instance, the bacon cheddar scone would be great on Corn Muffins (page 74). And don't think of these only as a breakfast treat: they are terrific for dinner. I could make a meal of a good salad and a couple of these scones.

Scones baked in a convection oven will have a slightly higher rise and more even color.

Place the all-purpose flour in the bowl of a stand mixer fitted with the paddle attachment. Sift in the cake flour, baking powder, baking soda, and sugar and mix on the lowest setting for about 15 seconds to combine. Add the salt and mix to combine. Stop the mixer, add the butter, and, on the lowest setting (to keep the flour from flying out of the bowl), pulse to begin incorporating the butter. Increase the speed to low and mix for about 3 minutes to break up the butter and incorporate it into the dry mixture. If any large pieces of butter remain, stop the mixer, break them up by hand, and mix until just incorporated.

With the mixer running, slowly pour in the cream. Add the crème fraîche and mix on low speed for about 30 seconds, until all of the dry ingredients are moistened and the dough comes together around the paddle. Scrape down the sides and bottom of the bowl and paddle and pulse again to combine. Add the bacon, the 144 grams/2 cups cheese, and the chives and pulse to incorporate.

Mound the dough on the work surface and, using the heel of your hand or a pastry scraper, push it together. Place the dough between two pieces of plastic wrap and, using your hands, press it into a 7-by-9-inch block, smoothing the top. Press the sides of your hands against the sides of the dough to straighten them. Wrap the dough in plastic wrap and refrigerate for about 2 hours, until firm. (See Note to Professionals, page 45.)

Line a sheet pan with a Silpat or parchment paper. Cut the block of dough lengthwise in half and then cut each half crosswise into 6 rectangles (70 grams each). Arrange them on the prepared sheet pan, leaving space between them. Cover with plastic wrap and freeze until frozen solid, at least 2 hours, but preferably overnight. (The scones can remain in the freezer for up to 1 month.)

Preheat the oven to 325°F (convection) or 350°F (standard). Line a sheet pan with a Silpat or parchment paper.

Arrange the frozen scones 1 inch apart on the sheet pan. Brush the tops with cream and sprinkle with the remaining 36 grams/½ cup cheese and black pepper. Bake for 24 to 27 minutes in a convection oven, 33 to 36 minutes in a standard oven, until golden brown. Set the sheet on a cooling rack and cool completely.

The scones are best the day they are baked, but they can be stored in a covered container for 1 day.

MAKES 12 SCONES

Corn Muffins

All-purpose flour	201 grams	1¼ cups + 3 tablespoons
Fine cornmeal	51 grams	⅓ cup
Baking powder	12 grams	2½ teaspoons
Granulated sugar	135 grams	½ cup + 3 tablespoons
Kosher salt	7.2 grams	2½ teaspoons
Whole milk	168 grams	⅔ cup
Eggs	90 grams	¼ cup + 2 tablespoons
Canola oil	90 grams	¼ cup + 2½ tablespoons
Frozen corn kernels	72 grams	½ cup + 2 tablespoons

The batter we use for our corn muffins is slightly sweet and includes corn kernels, which add both flavor and texture. These are great in the morning, but, like corn bread, they can accompany savory dishes. Pulverize leftover muffins in a food processor to use as a topping on sweet or savory dishes, or even as a topping for your next batch of corn muffins.

You'll need a 6-cup jumbo muffin pan, muffin papers, and a pastry bag with a ½-inch plain tip (optional).

Place the flour in the bowl of a stand mixer fitted with the whisk. Sift in the cornmeal and baking powder. Rub any lumps of cornmeal left in the strainer to break them up and add to the bowl. Add the sugar and salt and mix on the lowest setting for about 15 seconds to combine. Add the milk and eggs and mix on low speed for about 30 seconds, until just combined (see Note on Mixing Muffin Batter). With the mixer running, slowly pour in the oil, then increase the speed to medium-low and mix for about 30 seconds to combine.

Remove the bowl from the mixer stand and scrape the bottom of the bowl to incorporate any dry ingredients that have settled there. Fold in the corn. Transfer the batter to a covered container and refrigerate overnight, or for up to 36 hours.

Preheat the oven to 425°F (standard). Line the muffin pan with muffin papers and spray the papers with nonstick spray.

Transfer the batter to a pastry bag fitted with a ½-inch plain tip, or use a large spoon. Pipe or spoon the batter into the muffin papers, stopping ½ inch from the top (135 grams each).

Place the pan in the oven, lower the oven temperature to 325°F, and bake for 28 to 30 minutes, or until the muffins are golden brown and a skewer inserted in the center comes out clean. Set the pan on a cooling rack and cool completely.

The muffins are best the day they are baked, but they can be wrapped individually in a few layers of plastic wrap or stored in a single layer in a covered container at room temperature for up to 3 days or frozen for up to 1 week. (See Note on Defrosting Frozen Baked Muffins.)

MAKES 6 MUFFINS

NOTE ON MIXING MUFFIN BATTER: When mixing a muffin batter, it is important not to overwhip the eggs, as that could cause the muffins to expand too much during baking and then deflate. The mixture may look broken after you whip in the eggs, but that is fine.

NOTE ON DEFROSTING FROZEN BAKED MUFFINS: Defrost the muffins still in the container so any condensation will form on the outside of the container, and not on the muffins. Place on a sheet pan and refresh in a 325°F oven (standard) for about 5 minutes, if desired.

Bran Muffins

BATTER

Ingredient	Grams	Volume
All-purpose flour	110 grams	¾ cup + 2 teaspoons
Toasted wheat bran	74 grams	1 cup + 2½ tablespoons
Toasted wheat germ	16 grams	2½ tablespoons
Baking soda	6.6 grams	1⅜ teaspoons
Baking powder	5.5 grams	1⅛ teaspoons
Buttermilk	149 grams	½ cup + 2 teaspoons
Half-and-half	58 grams	3 tablespoons + 2 teaspoons
Water	55 grams	¼ cup
Unsalted butter, at room temperature	46 grams	1.6 ounces
Granulated sugar	82 grams	¼ cup + 3 tablespoons
¼ vanilla bean, split lengthwise		
Eggs	55 grams	3½ tablespoons
Clover honey	46 grams	2 tablespoons + ½ teaspoon
Unsulfured blackstrap molasses	46 grams	2 tablespoons + 1 teaspoon
Diced Poached Pears (page 227)	28 grams	1½ tablespoons
Golden raisins	28 grams	3 tablespoons
Pumpkin seeds	55 grams	¼ cup + 2 tablespoons
Whole flaxseeds for sprinkling	5 grams	2 teaspoons

Bran muffins are tricky, because the added fiber from the bran and wheat germ can make them dry and flavorless if you're not careful. The key is to fill them with all kinds of other delicious ingredients, here honey and molasses, pumpkin seeds, and fruit.

The diced poached pears make a unique addition to the muffins, but since it's only a small amount, feel free to substitute high-quality canned pears if you wish. Dried cranberries can be used instead of the raisins.

You'll need a 6-cup jumbo muffin pan and muffin papers.

FOR THE BATTER: Combine the flour, bran, and wheat germ in a medium bowl. Sift in the baking soda and baking powder and whisk together. Combine the buttermilk, half-and-half, and water in a large spouted measuring cup.

Place the butter in the bowl of a stand mixer fitted with the paddle attachment, turn to medium-low speed, and cream the butter, warming the bowl as needed (see Pommade, page 190), until it has the consistency of mayonnaise.

Add the sugar and mix on medium-low speed for 1 to 2 minutes, until the mixture is fluffy. Scrape down the sides and bottom of the bowl. Scrape the seeds from the vanilla bean, add them to the butter mixture, and mix on low speed for about 30 seconds to distribute the seeds evenly; stop as necessary to break up any larger pieces.

Add the eggs, honey, and molasses and mix on low speed for about 30 seconds, until just combined (see Note on Mixing Muffin Batter, page 74). Add half the flour mixture and mix on low speed for 15 seconds, or until just combined. With the mixer running, add half the buttermilk mixture and mix for 15 to 30 seconds, until just combined. Repeat with the remaining dry ingredients, followed by the remaining buttermilk mixture.

Remove the bowl from the mixer stand and scrape the bottom of the bowl to incorporate any dry ingredients that have settled there. Fold in the pears, raisins, and pumpkin seeds. Transfer the batter to a covered container and refrigerate overnight, or for up to 36 hours.

TO BAKE THE MUFFINS: Preheat the oven to 425°F (standard). Line the muffin pan with the muffin papers and spray the papers with nonstick spray.

Spoon the batter evenly into the muffin papers, stopping ⅜ inch from the top (140 grams each). Sprinkle the flaxseeds on top of the muffins.

Place the pan in the oven, lower the oven temperature to 325°F, and bake for 30 to 33 minutes, until a skewer inserted in the center comes out clean. Set the pan on a cooling rack and cool completely.

The muffins are best the day they are baked, but they can be wrapped individually in a few layers of plastic wrap or stored in a single layer in a covered container at room temperature for up to 3 days or frozen for up to 1 week. (See Note on Defrosting Frozen Baked Muffins, page 74.)

MAKES 6 MUFFINS

Blueberry Muffins

BATTER

Frozen wild blueberries	180 grams	¾ cup + 3 tablespoons
All-purpose flour	10 grams	1 tablespoon
	86 grams	½ cup + 2 tablespoons
Cake flour	109 grams	¾ cup + 1½ tablespoons
Baking powder	2.8 grams	½ + ⅛ teaspoon
Baking soda	2.8 grams	½ + ⅛ teaspoon
Salt	2.4 grams	¾ teaspoon
Unsalted butter	96 grams	3.4 ounces
Granulated sugar	96 grams	½ cup
Unsulfured blackstrap molasses	40 grams	2 tablespoons
Clover honey	54 grams	2½ tablespoons
Eggs	72 grams	¼ cup + 1½ teaspoons
Vanilla paste	1.2 grams	¼ teaspoon
Buttermilk	57 grams	¼ cup
Almond Streusel (recipe follows)	150 grams	¾ cup + 1 tablespoon
Powdered sugar for dusting (optional)		

Blueberry muffins are my favorite muffin, and this is a straightforward recipe except for the fact that we add molasses and use wild blueberries; we like the lower water content of the wild ones. Blueberries freeze well and are available in most grocery stores; look for frozen wild berries at Whole Foods and similar markets. We toss the berries with a little flour and keep them frozen until we're ready to add them to the batter; coating them with flour helps keep them uniformly suspended throughout the mixture. And their low water content and the fact that they are added to the batter frozen prevent them from bleeding too much into the batter as they bake, so they are a little more clear and distinct in the crumb. The muffins are topped with an almond streusel, for more flavor and texture.

You'll need a 6-cup jumbo muffin pan and muffin papers.

FOR THE BATTER: Toss the blueberries with the 10 grams/1 tablespoon all-purpose flour in a small bowl, and place in the freezer.

Place the remaining 86 grams/½ cup plus 2 tablespoons all-purpose flour in a medium bowl. Sift in the cake flour, baking powder, and baking soda. Add the salt and whisk together.

Place the butter in the bowl of a stand mixer fitted with the paddle attachment, turn to medium-low speed, and cream the butter, warming the bowl as needed (see Pommade, page 190), until it is the consistency of mayonnaise.

Add the sugar and mix on medium-low speed for about 1 minute, until the mixture is fluffy. Scrape down the sides and bottom of the bowl. Add the molasses and honey and mix on low speed for about 1 minute to incorporate.

Add the eggs and vanilla paste and mix on low speed for about 30 seconds, until just combined. Add half the flour mixture and mix on low speed for 15 seconds, or until just combined. Add half the buttermilk and mix for 15 to 30 seconds to combine. Repeat with the remaining dry ingredients, followed by the remaining buttermilk.

Remove the bowl from the mixer stand and scrape the bottom of the bowl to incorporate any dry ingredients that have settled there. Transfer the batter to a covered container and refrigerate overnight, or for up to 36 hours.

TO BAKE THE MUFFINS: Preheat the oven to 425°F (standard). Line the muffin pan with the muffin papers and spray the papers with nonstick cooking spray. Remove the batter from the refrigerator and let it sit at room temperature for 5 minutes to begin to soften.

Stir the blueberries into the batter and spoon the batter evenly into the muffin papers, stopping about ⅜ inch from the top (about 140 grams each). Sprinkle 30 grams/a generous 3 tablespoons of the streusel on top of each muffin.

Place the pan in the oven, lower the oven temperature to 325°F, and bake for 36 to 40 minutes, or until the topping is golden brown and a skewer inserted in the center comes out clean. Set the pan on a cooling rack and cool completely. Dust with powdered sugar if desired.

The muffins are best the day they are baked, but they can be wrapped individually in a few layers of plastic wrap or stored in a single layer in a covered container at room temperature for up to 3 days or frozen for up to 1 week. (See Note on Defrosting Frozen Baked Muffins, page 74.)

PHOTOGRAPH ON PAGE 78   MAKES 6 MUFFINS

Almond Streusel Topping

All-purpose flour	120 grams	¾ cup + 2 tablespoons
Almond flour/meal	120 grams	1 cup + 1 tablespoon
Granulated sugar	120 grams	½ cup + 1½ tablespoons
Kosher salt	0.6 gram	¼ teaspoon
Cold unsalted butter, cut into ¼-inch pieces	120 grams	4.2 ounces

Combine the all-purpose flour, almond flour, sugar, and salt in a bowl and whisk to break up any lumps.

Add the butter and toss to coat the pieces. Work the mixture with your fingertips, breaking the butter into pieces no larger than ⅛ inch and combining it with the flour mixture. Do not overwork the mixture or allow the butter to become soft; if it does, place the bowl in the refrigerator to harden the butter before continuing.

Transfer the streusel to a covered container or resealable plastic bag. Refrigerate for at least 2 hours, or up to 2 days, or freeze for up to 1 month. Use the streusel while it is cold.

MAKES 480 GRAMS/3¾ CUPS

RESTING BATTER

The key to making a great muffin is letting the batter rest, to allow the flour to hydrate (absorb liquid). We rest our batters overnight, or for as long as 36 hours, which results in a very moist muffin. Resting the batter also enhances the flavor and gives a better crumb. As an added benefit, when you make the batter a day ahead, it's ready to pour into the muffin pan in the morning so you can have fresh-baked muffins for breakfast.

Lemon–Poppy Seed Muffins

Cake flour	161 grams	1¼ cups
Baking powder	3.4 grams	½ + ⅛ teaspoon
Kosher salt	1.7 grams	½ teaspoon
Granulated sugar	234 grams	1 cup + 3 tablespoons
Eggs	170 grams	½ cup + 3 tablespoons
Vanilla paste	4.5 grams	¾ teaspoon
Unsalted butter, melted and still warm	194 grams	6.8 ounces
Fresh lemon juice	60 grams	¼ cup
Grated lemon zest	6 grams	generous 1 tablespoon
Poppy seeds	4 grams	1½ teaspoons

Lemon and poppy seeds are a popular pairing. This batter is much looser than the batters for the other muffins in this chapter and so results in a very light, lemony muffin. It's best to use an immersion blender to emulsify the melted butter into the batter.

You'll need a 6-cup jumbo muffin pan, muffin papers, and a pastry bag with a ¾-inch plain tip (optional).

FOR THE BATTER: Sift the cake flour and baking powder into a medium bowl. Add the salt and whisk to combine.

Combine the sugar, eggs, and vanilla paste in a deep medium bowl and mix with an immersion blender. Add the dry ingredients in 2 additions, mixing until just combined. With the blender running, pour in the butter in a steady stream, and continue to mix until the batter is smooth. Add the lemon juice and blend again to combine.

Fold in the lemon zest and poppy seeds (see Note). Transfer the batter to a covered container and refrigerate overnight, or for up to 36 hours.

TO BAKE THE MUFFINS: Preheat the oven to 425°F (standard). Line the muffin pan with the muffin papers and spray the papers with nonstick spray.

Transfer the batter to the pastry bag, or use a large spoon, and pipe or spoon the batter evenly into the papers, stopping ⅜ inch from the top (135 grams each).

Place the pan in the oven, lower the oven temperature to 325°F, and bake for 34 to 37 minutes, or until the muffins are golden brown and a skewer inserted in the center comes out clean. Set the pan on a cooling rack and cool completely.

The muffins are best the day they are baked, but they can be wrapped individually in a few layers of plastic wrap or stored in a single layer in a covered container at room temperature for up to 3 days or frozen for up to 1 week. (See Note on Defrosting Frozen Baked Muffins, page 74.)

MAKES 6 MUFFINS

NOTE ON FOLDING: Folding one ingredient into another—flour into beaten eggs for a cake, for instance—is so common an instruction that we scarcely think to define it, but there is a best way to do it. The method we teach our chefs for folding is to use a double action: spin the bowl gently counterclockwise with your left hand as you draw your spatula from the back of the bowl toward you, scraping the bottom of the bowl, lifting and folding the batter. (If you're a lefty, do the reverse, spinning the bowl clockwise with your right hand as you fold with your left.) The idea is to incorporate the dry and the wet ingredients uniformly but as quickly as possible to avoid smashing the air bubbles out of your batter.

Banana Muffins

BATTER

Cake flour	168 grams	1¼ cups + 1 tablespoon
Baking soda	3.6 grams	¾ teaspoon
Baking powder	2.4 grams	½ teaspoon
Kosher salt	4.4 grams	1½ teaspoons
Unsalted butter, at room temperature	120 grams	4.2 ounces
Light brown sugar	144 grams	¾ cup (lightly packed)
Eggs	80 grams	¼ cup + 1 tablespoon
Vanilla paste	7 grams	1⅛ teaspoons
Crème fraîche	24 grams	1 tablespoon + 2 teaspoons
Mashed banana	256 grams	1 cup (2 large bananas)
Walnut Streusel Topping (recipe follows)	180 grams	generous 1⅓ cups

Banana quick breads are often heavy and dense. To make our muffins light and fluffy, we use a little less banana than most recipes and add crème fraîche. It's also important not to overmix the batter, to keep the muffins light. The walnut streusel gives them a nutty flavor and crunch.

You'll need a 6-cup jumbo muffin pan and muffin papers.

FOR THE BATTER: Sift the cake flour, baking soda, and baking powder into a medium bowl. Add the salt and whisk together.

Place the butter in the bowl of a stand mixer fitted with the paddle attachment, turn to medium-low speed, and cream the butter, warming the bowl as needed (see Pommade, page 190), until it has the consistency of mayonnaise. Add the sugar and mix for 1 to 2 minutes, until fluffy. Scrape down the sides and bottom of the bowl, add the eggs and vanilla paste, and mix for 15 to 30 seconds on low speed, until just combined (see Note on Mixing Muffin Batter, page 74).

Add the dry ingredients in 2 additions, mixing on low speed for 15 seconds after each, or until just combined. Scrape the bottom of the bowl to incorporate any dry ingredients that have settled there. Add the crème fraîche and banana and mix on low speed for about 30 seconds, until just combined. Transfer the batter to a covered container and refrigerate overnight, or for up to 36 hours.

TO BAKE THE MUFFINS: Preheat the oven to 425°F (standard). Line the muffin pan with the muffin papers and spray the papers with nonstick spray.

Spoon the batter evenly into the papers, stopping ½ inch from the top (133 grams each). Sprinkle 30 grams/3 tablespoons of the streusel on top of each muffin.

Place the pan in the oven, lower the oven temperature to 325°F, and bake for 35 to 38 minutes, until the muffins are golden brown and a skewer inserted in the center comes out clean. Set the pan on a cooling rack and cool completely.

The muffins are best the day they are baked, but they can be wrapped individually in a few layers of plastic wrap or stored in a single layer in a covered container at room temperature for up to 3 days or frozen for up to 1 week. (See Note on Defrosting Frozen Baked Muffins, page 74.)

MAKES 6 MUFFINS

Walnut Streusel Topping

All-purpose flour	100 grams	½ cup + 3 tablespoons
Granulated sugar	100 grams	½ cup
Walnuts, very finely chopped	100 grams	¾ cup
Kosher salt	0.4 gram	⅛ teaspoon
Cold unsalted butter, cut into ¼-inch pieces	100 grams	3.5 ounces

Combine all of the ingredients except the butter in the bowl of a stand mixer fitted with a paddle attachment and mix on the lowest setting. Toss in the butter and mix on low speed for about 1 minute, or until the butter is incorporated, with no large chunks remaining.

Transfer the streusel to a covered container or a resealable plastic bag. Refrigerate for at least 2 hours, or up to 2 days, or freeze for up to 1 month. Use the streusel while it is cold.

MAKES 400 GRAMS/3 CUPS

BAKING MUFFINS IN FREESTANDING PAPER PANETTONE MOLDS

Spray 2¾-inch paper panettone molds with nonstick spray, set them on a sheet pan, and place the pan on a scale before weighing.

CORN Pipe or spoon 130 grams of batter into each paper mold, stopping ⅞ inch from the top. Bake for 30 to 33 minutes, or until golden brown and a skewer inserted in the center comes out clean.

BRAN Spoon 135 grams of batter into each paper mold, stopping ⅞ inch from the top, and sprinkle the flaxseed mixture on top of the muffins. Bake for 24 to 27 minutes, or until a skewer inserted in the center comes out clean.

BLUEBERRY Spoon 125 grams of batter into each paper mold, stopping ½ inch from the top. Sprinkle 15 grams/1½ tablespoons of the streusel on top of each muffin and press gently into the batter. Bake for 27 to 30 minutes, or until golden brown and a skewer inserted in the center comes out clean.

LEMON-POPPY SEED Pipe or spoon 130 grams of batter into each paper mold, stopping ⅞ inch from the top. Bake for 30 to 33 minutes, or until golden brown and a skewer inserted in the center comes out clean.

BANANA Spoon 115 grams of batter into each paper mold, stopping 1 inch from the top. Sprinkle 15 grams/1½ tablespoons of the streusel on top of the muffins and press gently into the batter. Bake for 28 to 31 minutes, or until golden brown and a skewer inserted in the center comes out clean.

CARROT Spoon 130 grams of batter into each paper mold, stopping ½ inch from the top. Sprinkle 15 grams/1½ tablespoons of the streusel on top of the muffins and press gently into the batter. Bake for 35 to 38 minutes, or until golden brown and a skewer inserted in the center comes out clean.

PUMPKIN Pipe or spoon 135 grams of batter into each paper mold, stopping 1 inch from the top. Bake for 40 to 43 minutes, or until golden brown and a skewer inserted in the center comes out clean.

Carrot Muffins (page 84) in muffin papers (left) and in freestanding paper molds (right)

Carrot Muffins

BATTER

All-purpose flour	180 grams	1¼ cups + 2 teaspoons
Baking soda	3.1 grams	½ + ⅛ teaspoon
Baking powder	1 gram	¼ teaspoon
Ground cinnamon	2.3 grams	¾ + ⅛ teaspoon
Kosher salt	2 grams	½ + ⅛ teaspoon
Granulated sugar	207 grams	1 cup + 2 teaspoons
Canola oil	142 grams	½ cup + 2 tablespoons
¼ vanilla bean, split lengthwise		
Eggs	80 grams	⅓ cup
Shredded carrots	212 grams	1¾ cups
Oat Streusel Topping (recipe follows)	180 grams	generous 1¼ cups

This is a good basic carrot muffin, and we sprinkle it with a great oat streusel for even more flavor and texture.

Carrots—and other vegetables, such as zucchini—add moisture to muffin and cake batters. Carrots are so plentiful that we often take them for granted, but all carrots are not alike. I hope you'll pay a little extra for bunch carrots, carrots still with their tops, rather than the ones in plastic bags. The quality makes a big difference when they're a major part of the recipe.

This recipe uses vegetable oil, not butter, and if you omit the streusel, it is dairy free.

You'll need a 6-cup jumbo muffin pan and muffin papers.

FOR THE BATTER: Place the flour in a medium bowl. Sift in the baking soda, baking powder, and cinnamon. Add the salt and whisk together.

Combine the sugar and oil in the bowl of a stand mixer fitted with the whisk attachment and mix on low speed for about 1 minute. Scrape the seeds from the vanilla bean, add them to the sugar mixture, and mix for 30 seconds to distribute the seeds evenly. Scrape down the sides and bottom of the bowl, add the eggs, and mix on low speed for about 1 minute, until just incorporated (see Note on Mixing Muffin Batter, page 74). Add the dry ingredients in 2 additions, mixing on low speed for 15 seconds after each, or until just combined.

Remove the bowl from the mixer stand and scrape the bottom of the bowl to incorporate any dry ingredients that may have settled there. Stir in the carrots. Transfer the batter to a covered container and refrigerate overnight, or for up to 36 hours.

TO BAKE THE MUFFINS: Preheat the oven to 425°F (standard). Line the muffin pan with the muffin papers and spray the papers with nonstick spray.

Spoon the batter evenly into the papers, stopping ⅜ inch from the top (135 grams each). Sprinkle 30 grams/3 tablespoons of the streusel on top of each muffin and press gently into the batter. Place the pan in the oven, lower the oven temperature to 325°F, and bake for 40 to 43 minutes, or until the muffins are golden brown and a skewer inserted in the center comes out clean. Set the pan on a cooling rack and cool completely.

The muffins are best the day they are baked, but they can be wrapped individually in a few layers of plastic wrap or stored in a single layer in a covered container at room temperature for up to 3 days or frozen for up to 1 week. (See Note on Defrosting Frozen Baked Muffins, page 74.)

PHOTOGRAPH ON PAGE 83 **MAKES 6 MUFFINS**

Oat Streusel Topping

Ingredient	Weight	Volume
All-purpose flour	142 grams	1 cup
Old-fashioned oats	107 grams	1¼ cups + 1 tablespoon
Toasted wheat germ	106 grams	¼ cup + 3½ tablespoons
Light brown sugar	50 grams	½ cup + 2½ teaspoons (lightly packed)
Granulated sugar	29 grams	2 tablespoons + 1¼ teaspoons
Ground cinnamon	1.2 grams	½ teaspoon
Freshly grated nutmeg	0.5 gram	½ teaspoon
Kosher salt	0.4 gram	⅛ teaspoon
¼ vanilla bean, split lengthwise		
Cold unsalted butter, cut into ¼-inch pieces	113 grams	4 ounces

Combine all of the ingredients except the vanilla bean and butter in the bowl of a stand mixer fitted with the paddle attachment and mix on low speed to combine. Scrape the seeds from the vanilla bean, add them to the dry mixture, and mix until evenly distributed. Toss in the butter and mix for about 1 minute, or until the butter is incorporated, with no large chunks remaining.

Transfer to a covered container or a resealable plastic bag. Refrigerate for at least 2 hours, or up to 2 days, or freeze for up to 1 month. Use the streusel while it is cold.

MAKES 544 GRAMS/4 CUPS

SEBASTIEN ON

SIFTING AND STRAINING

I don't find it necessary to sift all-purpose flour. I do think it's important to sift most other dry ingredients, though—cake flour, nut flours, baking powder and baking soda, cocoa powder. These items tend to clump and form "pebbles," and you need to break them up. Be sure to press all the pebbles through the sifter rather than discard them. Especially with chemical leaveners, which are used in small quantities, tossing out pebbles may result in not having enough of the leavener in your dough or batter.

Likewise, strain liquid ingredients if there's any chance of clumps. Clumps can form when you're working with gelatin, if it doesn't all dissolve. When you're working with eggs, the chalazae (the cords of protein that suspend the yolk within the white) should be strained out. Always lightly whip your eggs before passing them through a chinois. Straining eggs also makes them easier to measure when weighing out specific quantities, because you're breaking up the viscous, cohesive egg whites. If I'm using yolks only, I add whatever liquid is included in the recipe, mix them, and then strain them. Or if I'm making a custard, which requires that sugar be mixed with the yolks, I strain the finished custard.

Pumpkin Muffins

BATTER

All-purpose flour	200 grams	1¼ cups + 3 tablespoons
Baking soda	2.3 grams	½ teaspoon
Ground cinnamon	2.2 grams	¾ + ⅛ teaspoon
Ground cloves	0.6 gram	¼ teaspoon
Freshly grated nutmeg	0.5 gram	½ teaspoon
Ground allspice	0.1 gram	pinch
Kosher salt	1 gram	½ teaspoon
Granulated sugar	222 grams	1 cup + 2 teaspoons
Canola oil	100 grams	¼ cup + 3 tablespoons
Pure canned pumpkin puree or fresh pumpkin puree	210 grams	¾ cup + 2 tablespoons
Eggs	100 grams	¼ cup + 2½ tablespoons
Golden raisins (optional)	80 grams	½ cup + ½ tablespoon
Cream Cheese Frosting (page 378)	286 grams	1¼ cups

These are great simply frosted with cream cheese frosting, but we pipe some frosting inside the muffins as well.

For Halloween, these muffins dressed up as pumpkins. See the recipe and instructions for decorating the muffins on page 87.

You'll need a 6-cup jumbo muffin pan, muffin papers, a disposable pastry bag, a pastry bag with an Ateco #865 French star tip (optional), and a 1⅜-inch round cutter (optional).

FOR THE BATTER: Place the flour in a medium bowl. Sift in the baking soda, cinnamon, cloves, nutmeg, and allspice. Add the salt and whisk to combine.

Combine the sugar and oil in the bowl of a stand mixer fitted with the whisk attachment and mix on low speed for about 1 minute. Add the pumpkin, increase the speed to medium-low, and mix for about 1 minute, until smooth. Reduce the speed to low and add the eggs in 2 additions, mixing for about 15 seconds after each, or until just combined (see Note on Mixing Muffin Batter, page 74).

Add the dry ingredients in 2 additions, mixing on low speed for about 15 seconds after each, or until just combined.

Remove the bowl from the mixer stand and scrape the bottom of the bowl to incorporate any dry ingredients that may have settled there. Fold in the raisins, if using. Transfer the batter to a covered container and refrigerate overnight, or for up to 36 hours.

TO BAKE THE MUFFINS: Preheat the oven to 425°F (standard). Line the muffin pan with muffin papers and spray the papers with nonstick spray.

Transfer the batter to the disposable pastry bag and cut ½ inch of the tip from the bag; or use a large spoon. Pipe or spoon the batter into the papers, stopping ½ inch from the top (140 grams each).

Place the pan in the oven, lower the oven temperature to 325°F, and bake for 45 to 48 minutes, or until the muffins are golden brown and a skewer inserted in the center comes out clean. Set the pan on a cooling rack and cool completely.

TO FILL THE MUFFINS: Using the round cutter, cut through the top of each muffin, stopping ½ inch from the bottom, and carefully remove the center (or use a paring knife to remove the centers).

Transfer the frosting to the pastry bag with the star tip and fill the cavity of each muffin with 35 grams/2½ tablespoons of the frosting. Then pipe a rosette in the center of each muffin. Refrigerate uncovered for about 30 minutes to firm.

The muffins are best the day they are completed, but they can be refrigerated in a covered container for up to 3 days. Unfilled muffins can be wrapped individually in a few layers of plastic wrap or stored in a single layer in a covered container at room temperature for up to 3 days or frozen for up to 1 week. (See Note on Defrosting Frozen Baked Muffins, page 74.)

MAKES 6 MUFFINS

Decorated Pumpkin Muffins

Powdered sugar for dusting

PUMPKIN FONDANT

White rolling fondant	900 to 1000 grams	2 to 2.2 pounds
Yellow food coloring		5 to 6 drops
Orange food coloring		8 to 15 drops
Red food coloring		1 to 1½ drops
Cream Cheese Frosting (page 378)	450 grams	2 cups
6 Pumpkin Muffins (page 86)		
6 cinnamon sticks or licorice sticks		

You'll need a traditional or fondant rolling pin, six 3-inch cardboard rounds (optional), and a gum paste/fondant tool kit (optional). ● For this recipe, we use Carma white rolling fondant and Chefmaster Liqua-Gel Lemon Yellow, Sunset Orange, and Christmas Red food coloring.

FOR THE PUMPKIN FONDANT: Dust the work surface lightly with powdered sugar. Flatten 900 grams/2 pounds fondant on the surface and squeeze 5 drops of yellow food coloring, 8 drops orange, and 1 drop red onto it. Fold the fondant over and press down on the edges to seal, then begin pulling the ends of the fondant to stretch it (like taffy). Twist the fondant, then roll it into a log under your palms. Repeat the steps until the color is solid with no streaks. If you would like a different shade of orange, add another drop of yellow food coloring, up to 7 more drops of orange, or another ½ drop of red. If the color becomes too dark, knead in additional fondant to lighten it.

Wrap tightly in plastic wrap and let rest at room temperature for at least 2 hours, but preferably overnight.

TO COMPLETE: Dust the work surface lightly with powdered sugar. Divide the fondant into 6 portions (150 grams each). Roll 1 piece into an 8-inch round, just under ⅛ inch thick. Center the round of fondant over a muffin, letting it drape over the sides. Press your fingertip gently into the center of the muffin to form an indentation for the stem.

If any of the fondant is overlapping at the base of the muffin, lift it to remove the overlap. Cup your hands around the muffin. Gently press the fondant against the muffin, turning the muffin to encase it in the fondant. The fondant should extend about ¾ inch below the bottom of the muffin, but the underside of the muffin should not be covered. With your hands still cupped, apply more pressure around the bottom of the muffin and continue turning to form a pumpkin shape. Using a paring knife, trim away the fondant from the bottom of the muffin. If you have the 3-inch cardboard rounds, place the muffin on a round. Use the heel of your hand to smooth the bottom of the pumpkin as needed. Using a gum paste/fondant tool, the edge of a Popsicle stick, or a chopstick, press 7 equidistant vertical lines around the pumpkin, working from the stem end to the center and then from the center to the base, to resemble the natural lines on a pumpkin.

Repeat with the remaining fondant and muffins. Push a cinnamon or licorice stick into the top of each muffin. The muffins can be stored in a covered container in the refrigerator for up to 3 days.

PHOTOGRAPHS ON PAGES 88 AND 89   **MAKES 6 MUFFINS**

Note to Professionals: We also decorate these with acorns made from gum paste and with additional licorice sticks.

FONDANT

THE PASTRY CHEF'S PLAY-DOH

We use fondant to have fun, to be creative, to add color and "decor" to everything from cakes to pâte à choux to muffins. We use two colors: off-white and white. We use the off-white, which contains white chocolate, as is, but we usually add coloring to the white fondant (orange for the pumpkin muffins, for instance).

Like Play-Doh, fondant is very easy to use. You simply knead it until it's pliable and roll it out or shape it. There are special tools for working with fondant, but they aren't essential. Store it in an airtight container so it won't dry out. If your fondant does dry out, remove it from the container and slice off the dried layer; it can't be incorporated back into the fondant. (Fondant can be moistened by rubbing a small amount of glycerin or vegetable shortening on your hands before you knead it;

glycerin will also help you roll it out more smoothly.) The more you knead it, the more pliable the fondant will become and the easier it will be to work with. When rolling out fondant, dust your work surface with powdered sugar, not cornstarch or flour, which would make the fondant dry out and change color.

We use the brands Chefmaster and AmeriColor (see Sources, page 382) for coloring fondant. Choose a brand you like and use it consistently so that you become familiar with the particular qualities of its coloring. You will want to wear gloves when you work with food coloring. It's best to color fondant at least 2 hours before you intend to use it, preferably the day before you need it. The kneading stresses the fondant, and it will become too soft to use right away. Wrap it well in plastic wrap and set aside at room temperature until it firms up or you are ready to use it.

4

5

6

7

{ Working Clean }

I get asked by a lot of young chefs just starting out in a kitchen, "Hey, Chef, how do I become a great chef?"

This is what I tell them: "Make sure your workstation is clean and organized at the end of the night."

They wait. They look at me and say, "And?"

I say, "And: translate that into everything you do."

Working clean isn't a skill. It's not really even an act. It's a philosophy. And it's probably the most important thing a young chef can learn. It's what allows Sebastien to be as good as he is. It's the reason for the success of the chefs in all my restaurants and for the success of those restaurants. And working clean also enhances your ability to be efficient.

The thing is, I'm not sure this idea, this ethos, can be taught. More to the point, as Sebastien has said, he doesn't know whether he can teach a young pastry chef anything if that young chef doesn't already have the attitude, the philosophy, the desire to work clean.

Working clean means being organized. It means looking sharp. It means always wiping down your station, because that's just what you do, same as breathing. It means cleaning the mixer when you've finished with it, wrapping up the cord, and storing it. It means sweeping the floor regularly. It means making sure your oil bottles don't have oil on them. It means having your *mise en place* in place. At your station, and in your mind, and in your hands.

It means making sure your counter is clean when you go home at the end of the day. This is important in all kitchens—at home, in a hot kitchen or a cold kitchen, or at a bakery.

Working clean doesn't begin when you get to work. It begins when you wake up.

If you go to Bouchon Bakery in Yountville when Matthew is scoring the baguettes, notice his posture. He's at a near right angle, bent at the waist to make that careful cut, nearly parallel to the loader's surface, his torso mirroring the angle of the score itself, his left hand elegantly behind his back (a habit from his days in competitive baking). This is part of working clean. It's all one thing. It's all part of the end product.

Watch Sebastien cut a thin cake, with a single stroke. Watch the way he smooths chocolate between confectionary guides or ices a cake with his offset spatula, pressing his fingers against the end of the spatula so that the pressure along the spatula is uniform and the icing is therefore uniformly smooth. This is part of working clean.

You can see clean in the photographs in this book. The surfaces are clean not because Deborah was there with her camera. They're clean because that's how we work. You can't be sloppy in the beginning and then precise at the end. You can't say, "I'm going to have a bad habit now, but later I'll have a good one."

This ethos is at the root of how any good kitchen runs. It's a fundamental part of our commitment to our craft and our commitment to our guests. I understand that my saying this can put pressure on the home cook. I don't want you to have expectations that are unrealistic given your situation. This is what we do. More important than working clean at home is awareness and desire. Always cook with awareness and desire.

In order to achieve what we do, we work clean. It's a way of being. And if you strive to work this way too, not only will your food be better, the cooking will also be easier, less stressful.

It's not difficult. You just have to be aware of it and make sure your counter is clean when you leave the kitchen for the night.

CAKES

I first made cake at my mother's side. It was a Duncan Hines cake mix, but the frosting was homemade. Just to be with my mother in the kitchen was special, since she worked long hours to support us. I loved licking the beaters to get every bit of frosting. Those moments were precious. At the bakery, cake is so much more than a batter baked in a pan and iced. It's a tool; it's a vehicle; it's a textural device; it's a building block. We make thin cakes and thick cakes; we layer them with icing or cream; we cut them into shapes; we put them in glasses as a component of a more elaborate dessert. In classic French pâtisserie, there are two basic types of cake: one that uses whole eggs, *génoise,* and one that uses yolks and whites whipped separately, *biscuit.* The génoise is denser, with slightly smaller bubbles. It's used to make the Madeleine Cake on page 115. The *biscuit* is lighter, with larger bubbles, so you get a slightly more open crumb. It's more pliable, which makes it easy to roll, which is what we do for the Oh Ohs on page 122. Neither cake is difficult. Don't let cakes from scratch become a lost art. Do try some of the extraordinary preparations in this chapter.

Madeleines

I often talk about how food can transport us back to our past. It's a pleasure available to all of us. The pecan sandies that take me back to my mom. The ratatouille that takes food critic Anton Ego back to his childhood in the movie *Ratatouille*. Perhaps the most famous of such moments is described in Marcel Proust's *Remembrance of Things Past:* the madeleine that returns the narrator to his childhood. This effect typically involves simple food, and these little cakes are indeed simple: butter, flour, eggs, and sugar. We add pistachio paste for a variation on the traditional madeleine; both recipes follow.

I love watching madeleines bake, the batter rising with the characteristic little bump, pregnant with flavor (see the photographs on pages 96 and 97). It's important not to overbake madeleines; they must be moist. We found when testing these at home that the best way of preventing them from sticking is to thoroughly butter the mold and then refrigerate or freeze the pan to harden the butter before adding the batter. And if your madeleine mold is very old, consider buying a new nonstick one.

Traditional Madeleines

All-purpose flour	68 grams	¼ cup + 3½ tablespoons
Baking powder	2.2 grams	½ teaspoon
Kosher salt	0.6 gram	¼ teaspoon
Eggs	83 grams	¼ cup + 1 tablespoon
Granulated sugar	55 grams	¼ cup + 1¼ teaspoons
Unsalted butter, at room temperature, plus additional for the pan	66 grams	2.3 ounces
Dark brown sugar	9 grams	2 teaspoons
Clover honey	9 grams	1¼ teaspoons
Lemon oil (optional)		1 to 2 drops

You'll need a 12-mold madeleine pan and a pastry bag with a ½-inch plain tip (optional). ● *To get the classic bubble on the madeleines, baking in a convection oven is preferable.*

Place the flour in a medium bowl and sift in the baking powder. Add the salt and whisk together.

Combine the eggs and granulated sugar in the bowl of a stand mixer fitted with the whisk attachment and mix on medium-high speed for about 1 minute, warming the bowl gently as needed (see Pommade, page 190) to dissolve the sugar. Increase the speed to high and whip for about 4 minutes, until the color lightens and the batter doubles in volume.

Meanwhile, heat the butter, brown sugar, and honey in a small saucepan over medium-high heat, whisking, to dissolve the sugar, about 1 minute. Remove from the heat.

Remove the bowl from the mixer stand and fold in half the dry ingredients, then fold in the remaining dry ingredients until just combined. Scrape the bottom of the bowl to incorporate any dry ingredients that may have settled there. Pour the warm butter mixture over the batter, add the lemon oil, if using, and fold until the mixture is incorporated and the batter is smooth. Place the batter in a covered container and refrigerate overnight.

Preheat the oven to 350°F (convection or standard). Brush the madeleine pan with butter. Refrigerate or freeze the pan to harden the butter.

Transfer the batter to the pastry bag, or use a spoon. Pipe or spoon the batter into the molds (20 grams/1 generous tablespoon each). Tap the bottom of the pan against the work surface to smooth the top of the batter.

Bake for 7 to 8 minutes in a convection oven, 8 to 9 minutes in a standard oven, until the tops are lightly browned and a skewer inserted in the center comes out clean. (The bottoms of the madeleines will brown more quickly than the tops, so keep the tops on the lighter side.) Immediately unmold the madeleines and cool on a cooling rack.

The madeleines are best the day they are baked, but they can be stored in a covered container for up to 1 day.

PHOTOGRAPHS ON PAGES 96 AND 97   **MAKES 12 MADELEINES**

Pistachio Madeleines
MADELEINES A LA PISTACHE

Make the batter as directed, using the following proportions and adding the pistachio paste to the finished batter.

All-purpose flour	57 grams	¼ cup + 2½ tablespoons
Baking powder	1.9 grams	⅜ teaspoon
Kosher salt	0.5 gram	⅛ teaspoon
Eggs	69 grams	¼ cup + 1 teaspoon
Granulated sugar	46 grams	3 tablespoons + 2 teaspoons
Unsalted butter, at room temperature, plus additional for the pan	55 grams	1.9 ounces
Dark brown sugar	8 grams	2 teaspoons
Clover honey	8 grams	1⅛ teaspoons
Pistachio paste (see Note)	46 grams	3 tablespoons

Place the pistachio paste in a medium bowl (microwave-safe if necessary). If the pistachio paste is very stiff, warm it in the microwave for about 20 seconds to soften it. Using a spatula, stir one-quarter of the batter into the pistachio paste to lighten it, then fold in the remaining batter.

NOTE ON PISTACHIO PASTE: At the bakery, we use Fabbri brand, but it is only available for purchase in large quantities. Look for a brand that has a vivid green color, such as Trablit.

Financiers

Financiers, with their moist center and crisp edges, are my favorite of the classic petit-four cakes. It's all about the brown butter, which gives them their flavor. You'll love the flavor the almond flour brings too, but it's the nutty brown butter that makes these irresistible. The temperature of the butter is key here, so it's best to make the brown butter just before you begin this recipe. It needs to be very warm when added to the flour mixture; if it is too cool, the batter will not emulsify.

If you like, add a few finely chopped lightly toasted nuts or one or two whole raspberries, a cherry, or a blueberry to each mold before filling them with batter. The traditional version of these little cakes is made using individual financier molds. The chocolate financiers are baked in mini-muffin pans.

Traditional Financiers

Butter for the molds, at room temperature		
Granulated sugar	120 grams	½ cup + 1½ tablespoons
All-purpose flour	40 grams	¼ cup + 1 tablespoon
Almond flour/meal	60 grams	½ cup + 2 teaspoons
Egg whites	100 grams	¼ cup + 2½ tablespoons
Brown Butter (page 380), still hot	100 grams	½ cup

You'll need twelve 3¼-by-1¾-inch financier molds and a pastry bag with a ⅜-inch plain tip (optional).

Preheat the oven to 425°F (standard). Brush the financier molds with butter and place on a sheet pan. Refrigerate or freeze the molds to harden the butter.

Place the sugar in a large bowl and whisk to break up any lumps. Add the all-purpose flour. Sift in the almond flour; break up any lumps remaining in the sieve, add them to the bowl, and whisk to combine.

Make a well in the center of the dry ingredients. Pour in the egg whites and whisk them, gradually incorporating the dry mixture, until all the ingredients are well combined. Scrape down the sides and bottom of the bowl and whisk again. Whisk in the brown butter in 2 additions. Transfer the batter to the pastry bag, or use a spoon. Pipe or spoon the batter into the financier molds, stopping ⅛ inch from the top (27 grams/1½ tablespoons per mold). Tap the bottom of each mold against the work surface to smooth the top of the batter. Arrange the molds on a sheet pan.

Place the pan in the oven, lower the oven temperature to 350°F, and bake for 20 minutes, or until the tops are golden brown and a skewer inserted in the center comes out clean.

Immediately unmold the financiers and cool on a cooling rack.

The financiers are best the day they are baked, but they can be stored in a covered container for 1 day.

MAKES 12 FINANCIERS

Chocolate Financiers

Granulated sugar	120 grams	½ cup + 1½ tablespoons
All-purpose flour	20 grams	2 tablespoons + 1 teaspoon
Almond flour/meal	60 grams	½ cup + 1½ teaspoons
Unsweetened alkalized cocoa powder	20 grams	¼ cup
Egg whites	100 grams	¼ cup + 2½ tablespoons
Brown Butter (page 380), still hot	100 grams	½ cup
70% chocolate, chopped	20 grams	0.7 ounce
100% unsweetened chocolate, chopped	10 grams	0.4 ounce

You'll need two 12-mini-muffin pans (see Note) and a pastry bag with a ⅜-inch tip. ● For this recipe, we use Valrhona Guanaja 70% chocolate, Valrhona 100% Pure Pâte de Cacao, and Guittard Cocoa Rouge.

Preheat the oven to 425°F (standard). Spray 16 mini-muffin cups with nonstick spray.

Place the sugar in a large bowl and whisk to break up any lumps. Add the all-purpose flour. Sift in the almond flour; break up any lumps of almond flour remaining in the sieve and add them to the bowl. Sift in the cocoa powder and whisk to combine.

Make a well in the center of the dry ingredients. Pour in the egg whites and whisk them, gradually incorporating the dry mixture, until all the ingredients are well combined. Scrape down the sides and bottom of the bowl and whisk again. Place the brown butter and the chocolates in a small saucepan over medium heat, stirring to melt the chocolate and heat the butter. When the mixture is very hot, just below a simmer, whisk it into the flour mixture.

Immediately transfer the batter to the pastry bag. Pipe the batter into the muffin cups, stopping just short of the rim (25 grams/1½ tablespoons each).

Place the pans in the oven, lower the oven temperature to 350°F, and bake for 12 minutes, or until a skewer inserted in the center comes out clean. Immediately unmold the financiers and cool on a cooling rack.

The financiers are best the day they are baked, but they can be stored in a covered container for 1 day.

MAKES 16 FINANCIERS

NOTE: If you have only one pan, bake the financiers in batches; set the extra batter aside at room temperature while you bake the first batch.

Bouchons

Unsalted butter, cut into chunks	141 grams	5 ounces
All-purpose flour	50 grams	¼ cup + 1½ tablespoons
Unsweetened alkalized cocoa powder	50 grams	½ cup + 2 tablespoons
Kosher salt	0.4 gram	⅛ teaspoon
Eggs	75 grams	¼ cup + 2 teaspoons
Granulated sugar	162 grams	¾ cup + 1 tablespoon
Vanilla paste	1.5 grams	¼ teaspoon
Chocolate chips	112 grams	½ cup
Powdered sugar for dusting		

This is our take on arguably the most loved little cake in America, the brownie. We've tweaked the recipe since we first began offering them at their namesake restaurant, reducing the amount of fat and sugar. They're so good we can never make enough of them. The silicone mold we use is one created specifically for this purpose, sold by Williams-Sonoma.

You'll need a pastry bag with a ½-inch plain tip (optional) and a bouchon mold. ● *For this recipe, we use Valrhona cocoa powder.* ● *Convection baking is faster and will keep the interior of the bouchons moister.*

Place half the butter in a medium bowl. Melt the remaining butter in a small saucepan over medium heat, stirring occasionally. Stir the melted butter into the bowl; all the butter will come to room temperature and become creamy looking, with small bits of unmelted butter. Set aside.

Place the flour in a bowl and sift in the cocoa powder. Add the salt and whisk together.

Combine the eggs, sugar, and vanilla paste in the bowl of a stand mixer fitted with the whisk attachment and mix on medium-low speed. Scrape down the sides and bottom of the bowl. With the mixer running, alternating between the two, add the butter and flour mixtures in 3 additions each. Then mix to combine well, scraping the bowl as necessary.

Remove the bowl from the mixer stand and fold in the chocolate chips. Set aside in a cool spot (not the refrigerator) for 2 hours. The batter can be refrigerated for up to 2 days but should be returned to room temperature before filling the molds.

Preheat the oven to 350°F (convection or standard).

Transfer the batter to the pastry bag, or use a spoon. Pipe or spoon the batter evenly into the molds, stopping just below the top rim.

Bake for 12 minutes in a convection oven, 16 minutes in a standard oven. Test a bouchon with a cake tester, making certain not to hit a chocolate chip; the tester should come out clean (if it comes out with chocolate on it, try again). Remove the mold from the oven and let the bouchons rest for 10 minutes (so that they will hold their shape), then unmold the bouchons onto a cooling rack, turn right side up, and cool completely.

The bouchons can be kept in a covered container for up to 3 days. Just before serving, dust the tops with powdered sugar.

PHOTOGRAPHS ON PAGES 100 AND 101　　　　　　　　　　**MAKES 12 BOUCHONS**

Gingerbread

PAIN D'EPICES

All-purpose flour	340 grams	2¼ cups + 2 teaspoons
Baking soda	8 grams	1½ teaspoons
Ground ginger	7 grams	1 tablespoon + 1 teaspoon
Ground cinnamon	4 grams	1½ teaspoons
Ground cloves	1 gram	⅜ teaspoon
Kosher salt	2 grams	½ + ⅛ teaspoon
Dark brown sugar	220 grams	1 cup + 1½ teaspoons (lightly packed)
Unsulfured blackstrap molasses	340 grams	1 cup + 2¼ teaspoons
Canola oil	214 grams	¾ cup + 3½ tablespoons
Eggs	100 grams	¼ cup + 2½ tablespoons
Boiling water	336 grams	1¼ cups + 2½ tablespoons
Grated lemon zest	8 grams	1 tablespoon + 1 teaspoon

Royal Icing
(page 378; optional)

French gingerbread, known as *pain d'épices,* or spice bread, was a favorite afternoon snack of Sebastien's when he was a schoolboy. It has more molasses and is moister, darker, and denser than the American gingerbread most of us know, which is lighter and more airy.

This cake is best made a day ahead to allow the flavors to develop and deepen.

You'll need two 8½-by-4½-by-2¾-inch loaf pans.

Preheat the oven to 350°F (standard). Spray the loaf pans with nonstick spray. Line the bottom of each pan with parchment paper, then spray the parchment.

Place the flour in a medium bowl. Sift in the baking soda, ginger, cinnamon, and cloves. Add the salt and whisk together.

Place the brown sugar in the bowl of a stand mixer fitted with the paddle attachment and mix on low speed to break up any lumps. Add the molasses and mix for about 1 minute, or until smooth. With the mixer running, add the oil in a slow, steady stream and continue to mix for about 1½ minutes, until completely combined. Scrape down the sides and bottom of the bowl. With the mixer on low speed, add the eggs and mix for 1 minute, or until the mixture is smooth.

Scrape down the sides and bottom of the bowl. Add the dry mixture in 2 additions, mixing on low speed for 15 to 30 seconds after each. With the mixer running, add the water 60 grams/¼ cup at a time, incorporating each addition before adding the next. Scrape down the bowl again. Fold in the lemon zest.

Divide the batter between the two pans. Bake for 1 hour, or until a skewer inserted in the center comes out clean. Set the pans on a cooling rack and cool for 10 minutes. Turn the cakes out onto the rack, remove the pans, and cool completely upside down.

The cakes are best if made 1 day ahead; wrap uniced in plastic wrap and store at room temperature.

Turn the gingerbread over. If desired, brush the tops of the cakes generously with the royal icing, letting it run down the sides (the cakes will not be iced if freezing). You may not need all of the icing.

The cakes can be wrapped in plastic wrap and frozen for up to 1 week; defrost in the refrigerator and rewarm if desired.

MAKES 2 LOAF CAKES

Coffee Cakes

BATTER

All-purpose flour	203 grams	1¼ cups + 3 tablespoons
Baking powder	5.5 grams	1⅛ teaspoons
Baking soda	1.7 grams	⅜ teaspoon
Kosher salt	1.7 grams	½ teaspoon
Unsalted butter, at room temperature	75 grams	2.6 ounces
Granulated sugar	210 grams	1 cup + 2½ teaspoons
Eggs	75 grams	¼ cup + 2 teaspoons
Vanilla paste	20 grams	1 tablespoon + ¼ teaspoon
Crème fraîche or sour cream	225 grams	1 cup + 1 teaspoon

TOPPING

Light brown sugar	15 grams	1 tablespoon + ¾ teaspoon
Unsweetened alkalized cocoa powder	15 grams	3 tablespoons
Almond Streusel Topping (page 77)	180 grams	generous 1⅓ cups

TO FINISH

Powdered sugar

Cocoa powder

Ground cinnamon

I n France, Parisians like pound cake with their morning coffee. Here we love coffee cake. These individual coffee cakes are richly flavored but light, so that they almost melt in your mouth. There's a crunch on the outside from the almond streusel topping and a soft interior crumb. The cakes are finished with a dusting of cocoa powder, powdered sugar, and cinnamon, just a hint, so there are all kinds of flavors intermingling here.

These are baked at a lower temperature than most cakes. Don't be tempted to increase the temperature to 350°F, or the coffee cakes will get too dark too fast.

You'll need six 4¼-inch round paper baking molds or six 4½-inch mini springform pans and a pastry bag with a ⅜-inch plain tip. ● *For this recipe, we use Guittard Cocoa Rouge.* ● *Coffee cakes baked in a convection oven will have a more domed top.*

FOR THE BATTER: Place the flour in a medium bowl. Sift in the baking powder and baking soda, then add the salt and whisk together.

Place the butter in the bowl of a stand mixer fitted with the paddle attachment. Turn to medium-low speed and cream the butter, warming the bowl if needed (see Pommade, page 190), until it has the consistency of mayonnaise and holds a peak when the paddle is lifted. Add the sugar and mix on medium-low speed for 1 to 2 minutes, until the mixture is fluffy. Scrape down the sides and bottom of the bowl. Add the eggs and vanilla paste and mix for 15 to 30 seconds on low speed, until just combined. (Overwhipping the eggs could cause the cakes to expand too much during baking and then deflate.)

Add the flour mixture and crème fraîche alternately in the following amounts, beating on low speed for about 15 seconds after each addition: one-third of the flour mixture, one-third of the crème fraîche, one-third of the flour mixture, one-third of the crème fraîche, the remaining flour mixture, and the remaining crème fraîche. Cover the batter and refrigerate for about 20 minutes to firm.

Preheat the oven to 325°F (convection or standard). Spray the paper molds or springform pans with nonstick spray and set them on a sheet pan.

FOR THE TOPPING: Whisk together the brown sugar and cocoa in a small bowl, breaking up any lumps.

Transfer the batter to the pastry bag and pipe a ¼-inch-deep spiral (60 grams) in the bottom of each mold. Dust the top of each with 5 grams/2 teaspoons of the cocoa mixture. Pipe a second spiral of batter over the cocoa, stopping at least ¼ inch from the top of the mold. Sprinkle the tops with streusel: 30 grams/3 tablespoons each. (The cakes can be refrigerated for up to 3 days before baking.)

Bake for 25 to 30 minutes in a convection oven, 35 to 40 minutes in a standard oven, or until the tops are golden brown and a skewer inserted in the center comes out clean. (If the cakes have been refrigerated, the baking time will be slightly longer.) Set the sheet pan on a cooling rack and cool completely.

The coffee cakes are best the day they are baked, but they can be wrapped individually in plastic wrap and frozen. Defrost frozen cakes at room temperature, and rewarm if desired.

Just before serving, dust the tops with powdered sugar and then a very light dusting of cocoa and cinnamon.

MAKES 6 INDIVIDUAL CAKES

Note to Professionals: When making these coffee cakes in larger batches, we add more crème fraîche to keep the batter from getting too stiff.

Rum Cake

Unsalted butter, at room temperature, plus additional for the pan	468 grams	16.5 ounces
Granulated sugar, plus additional for the pan	562 grams	2¾ cups + 1 tablespoon
Almond flour/meal	468 grams	4 cups + 3 tablespoons
All-purpose flour	150 grams	1 cup + 1 tablespoon
Eggs	562 grams	2 cups + 3 tablespoons
Myers's dark rum	75 grams	⅓ cup
	50 grams	3 tablespoons
Simple Syrup (page 378)	50 grams	3 tablespoons
Rum Icing (recipe follows)		

If you have a traditional cast-iron Bundt pan, this is the time to use it. These older pans, as well as newer pans marked "Original Bundt" or "Anniversary Bundt," with a 15-cup capacity, are what this recipe is made for. However, if you only have a smaller Bundt pan, it will work; just leave a ½-inch space at the top of the pan when filling it with batter, and bake the cake for slightly less time (if you like, you can bake the excess batter in a muffin pan, checking for doneness after 30 minutes or so).

This is one of Sebastien's favorite treats: a cake he has during trips to the Cayman Islands, where it's called Tortuga cake.

You'll need a 15-cup (10½-inch) Bundt pan. ● *Baking in a convection oven gives the cake a better crumb (but a standard oven yields fantastic results as well).*

Preheat the oven to 325°F (convection) or 350°F (standard). Brush the Bundt pan with butter. Refrigerate or freeze the pan to harden the butter (this will make it much easier to coat the pan with an even layer of sugar).

Add a large spoonful of sugar to the pan and rotate and tap the pan to cover the surface evenly. Invert the pan and tap lightly to remove any excess sugar.

Place the almond flour in the bowl of a food processor and pulse about 10 times to break up any larger clumps. Pour the almond flour into a large bowl and run it through your fingers to be certain that there are no remaining lumps. Add the all-purpose flour and whisk to combine.

Place the butter in the bowl of a stand mixer fitted with the paddle attachment. Turn to medium-low speed and cream the butter, warming the bowl if needed (see Pommade, page 190), until it has the consistency of mayonnaise and holds a peak when the paddle is lifted. Add the sugar and mix, stopping to scrape down the sides and bottom of the bowl as needed, for about 7 minutes, until the mixture is fluffy.

Scrape down the sides and bottom of the bowl. Turn the mixer to low speed, slowly add about one-third of the eggs, and mix until just combined, about 30 seconds. Scrape down the bowl again. Add half the remaining eggs and mix to combine, then scrape the bowl again, add the remaining eggs, and mix for another 10 seconds. The mixture may look broken, which is fine (overwhipping the eggs could cause the cake to expand too much during baking and then deflate).

On low speed, add the flour mixture one-third at a time, mixing for about 15 seconds after each addition. Remove the bowl from the mixer stand and scrape the bottom of the bowl to incorporate any dry ingredients that may have settled there.

Transfer 1 cup of the batter to a small bowl and stir in the 75 grams/ ⅓ cup rum until combined. Fold into the remaining batter, combining it thoroughly (the texture of the batter may not be smooth).

With a spatula, gently scrape the batter into the prepared pan. Tap the bottom of the pan against the work surface and rotate it back and forth to distribute the batter evenly. Bake for 55 to 60 minutes in a convection oven, 65 to 70 minutes in a standard oven, until the cake is golden brown (the color may be somewhat darker if you're not using a cast-iron pan) and a skewer inserted in the center comes out clean. Set the pan on a cooling rack and cool for 10 minutes.

Mix the remaining 50 grams/3 tablespoons rum with the simple syrup. Set a cooling rack over a baking sheet and unmold the cake onto it. Cool for about 10 minutes, then brush the cake evenly with the rum mixture. Let cool completely.

TO GLAZE THE CAKE: Using a pastry brush, drizzle the rum icing over the top of the cake; or spoon it over the cake for more coverage, letting it run down the sides. (You may not use all of the icing.)

The cake is best made a day ahead (store in a covered container at room temperature); it will keep well for up to 3 days.

SERVES 10 TO 12

Rum Icing

Powdered sugar	180 grams	1½ cups + 1 tablespoon
Myers's dark rum	15 grams	1 tablespoon
Water	15 grams	1 tablespoon

Sift the powdered sugar into a small bowl. Stir in the rum and water until smooth. The icing should be used immediately.

MAKES 200 GRAMS/⅔ CUP

PAN AND BAKING-MOLD PREP

Many baking molds are now nonstick, but if you have an older one, the best way to prepare it for baking is to brush it with very soft butter, freeze it, and then dust it with flour. Freezing the butter allows you to add the flour in a thin, even coating. For some recipes, like this rum cake, we dust the pans with sugar rather than flour, which gives the cake a delicate shell-like exterior.

WHAT FREEZES BEST?

- Cookie dough (to bake when needed)
- Scone dough (to bake when needed)
- Muffins, baked
- Cakes baked in sheet pans for ease of cutting
- Tart dough, unbaked, in the pan (bake straight from the freezer)
- Pâte à choux, unbaked or baked
- Brioche dough, raw (immediately after shaping) or baked (cool to room temperature; wrap individually)
- Puff pastry
- Croissants, baked

EASIER WITH THE FREEZER

- The Palet d'Or (page 117)
- The Oh Ohs (page 122)
- The mousseline cream for the Mille-feuille (page 230)
- Everything but the fruit for the chiboust tart on page 154, most notably the raw dough that gives the tart crust its texture
- Prepared metal baking pans, brushed with butter (see page 107)
- The Better Nutters dough (page 36)
- The egg whites used for macarons (pages 58–63) and meringue (page 152)
- The Croissant Dough (page 237) between turns

Chill out! In the pastry kitchen, the freezer is your friend.

SEBASTIEN ON
FREEZING

The most important kitchen tool for a pastry chef? The oven. What's the second? The freezer. By far. It's ironic to me that freezing food has a negative connotation—that people think food is invariably compromised when it's frozen. For me, a pastry chef, it actually makes my food better. It allows me more control over the food and my production schedule. When the kitchen is very hot and you are rolling out dough, the freezer can help you chill the dough quickly. It allows me great precision in shaping cakes by enabling me to slice perfect, clean right angles. When we were at Susie's making the cakes to photograph, Thomas marveled at my incredible slicing skills (I didn't tell him how easy it really was).

There are only two categories of items in the pastry kitchen that you cannot freeze: uncooked dairy products and something with a lot of gelatin in it. Freezing causes the water and fat to separate in dairy products like milk or yogurt (not butter, of course, which is so high in fat), and it breaks down gelatin.

Otherwise, everything freezes very well—cookie dough, scones, cakes, pâte à choux, brioche, puff pastry, and croissant dough. In many instances, such as with the macarons, the flavor will mature over the course of 24 hours in the freezer. And I believe cake that's been frozen actually tastes better, provided it's been well wrapped.

You can even slice creams when they're frozen; see the Caramel Chiboust (page 154).

In the savory kitchen, the freezer is a way to preserve raw and cooked food. In the pastry kitchen, the freezer is like a cherished colleague.

WRAPPING FOR THE FREEZER

Wrapping well is not only necessary for preserving flavor and freshness, it's also critical for keeping moisture off the product. The freezer is a humid environment; water in the form of frost or ice crystals can attach itself to the item. Also, when you take something out of the freezer, moisture tends to condense on it. Moisture is the enemy.

Store wrapped baked goods in an airtight container, and wrap that in plastic. (Just to be sure, Sebastien wraps the container twice.)

Olive Oil Cake

All-purpose flour	145 grams	1 cup + 1 teaspoon
Baking powder	3 grams	½ + ⅛ teaspoon
Kosher salt	2 grams	½ + ⅛ teaspoon
Eggs	50 grams	3 tablespoons
Granulated sugar	158 grams	¾ cup + 2 teaspoons
Whole milk	113 grams	¼ cup + 3 tablespoons
Extra virgin olive oil	79 grams	¼ cup + 2 tablespoons

By replacing butter with olive oil, we created a very flavorful cake with a light, delicious crumb. We use it for the Strawberry Parfait (page 111), but it's a wonderful all-purpose cake to have in your repertoire. Use a good olive oil; if your oil is very green, it may tint the cake slightly, an effect you may like.

You'll need a quarter sheet pan.

Preheat the oven to 350°F (standard). Line the sheet pan with a Silpat or spray lightly with nonstick spray, line with parchment paper, and spray the parchment.

Place the flour in a medium bowl. Sift in the baking powder and salt and whisk to combine.

Place the eggs and sugar in the bowl of a stand mixer fitted with the whisk attachment and mix on medium-low speed for about 1 minute to combine. Increase the speed to medium and whip for about 5 minutes, until the mixture is thick and pale yellow. Scrape down the sides and bottom of the bowl, then whip on medium-high speed for another 5 minutes, or until the mixture has thickened; when the whisk is lifted, the mixture should form a slowly dissolving ribbon.

Combine the milk and olive oil. With the mixer running on medium-low speed, add half the dry ingredients, then half the milk mixture, mixing until well combined. Repeat with the remaining dry ingredients, then the remaining milk mixture.

Pour the batter into the prepared pan and, using an offset spatula, spread it in an even layer, making sure that it reaches into the corners. Bake for about 15 minutes, until a skewer inserted in the center comes out clean and the cake springs back when you touch it lightly. Set on a cooling rack and cool completely.

Lay a piece of parchment paper on the back of a sheet pan. Run a knife around the edges to loosen the cake, and invert it onto the parchment. Remove the Silpat or parchment from the top of the cake.

Wrapped in a few layers of plastic wrap, the cake can be kept at room temperature for up to 4 hours, refrigerated for up to 3 days, or frozen for up to 2 weeks.

If you will be cutting the cake into shapes, the cake should be frozen before cutting. If frozen, and not being cut into shapes, the cake should be defrosted in the refrigerator still in the plastic wrap (this way, any condensation will form on the outside and not on the cake).

MAKES 1 QUARTER SHEET CAKE

Strawberry Parfait

FRAISIER

MOUSSELINE

Pastry Cream (page 373), cold	200 grams	¾ cup + 2½ tablespoons
Basic Buttercream (page 375), at room temperature	200 grams	1⅓ cups
Raspberry Jam (page 379), at room temperature	90 grams	¼ cup
Olive Oil Cake (page 110), frozen		
18 medium-large (about 1½ inches long) strawberries, halved lengthwise		
Crème fraîche	about 300 grams	1¼ cups
Strawberry powder (optional)		

This recipe is not simply a great dessert in itself, it's also a way of thinking about cakes and desserts generally. The idea is to take all the components you'd use for this final course and then build the dessert in a serving glass: soft, moist cake; sweet cream (here, pastry cream whipped with buttercream, technically called a mousseline) along with more acidic crème fraîche for balance; fresh fruit; and a little jam. Any composed dish like this is great for entertaining—it's impressive to serve, and you can make most of the components in advance. If you want to assemble the parfaits ahead of time, use the strawberries whole or replace them with raspberries, as the cut berries could bleed into the cream.

We use Kendall Farms crème fraîche, which is slightly looser than most, for this dessert. If your crème fraîche is very firm, you can loosen it with a little regular cream or milk.

You'll need a pastry bag with a ⅜-inch plain tip.

FOR THE MOUSSELINE: Place the pastry cream in the bowl of a stand mixer fitted with the whisk attachment and whip on medium speed until smooth. Add the buttercream and whip until well combined and smooth. Set aside.

TO ASSEMBLE THE PARFAIT: The jam should flow more like a puree than a jam; if it is too thick, stir in a little water to thin it. Spoon 15 grams (⅜ inch) of jam into the bottom of six clear glasses (about 12 ounces each).

Cut 6 rounds of cake large enough to cover the layer of jam and carefully place one in each glass. Lean 5 strawberry halves, cut side out, tips pointing up, against the sides of each glass. Cut the remaining pieces into a small dice, and arrange a few pieces in the center of the glass.

Spoon the mousseline into the pastry bag. Hold the bag vertically in the center of each ring of berries and pipe in enough mousseline to fill the gaps around the berries. Pipe a spiral over the top that extends a bit above the berries.

Cut 6 more pieces of cake to fit over the mousseline, and place one in each glass.

Gently stir the crème fraîche until it holds a soft shape. Spoon it over the shortcakes, sprinkle with strawberry powder, if desired, and the remaining diced strawberries, and serve.

PHOTOGRAPHS ON PAGES 112 AND 113   SERVES 6

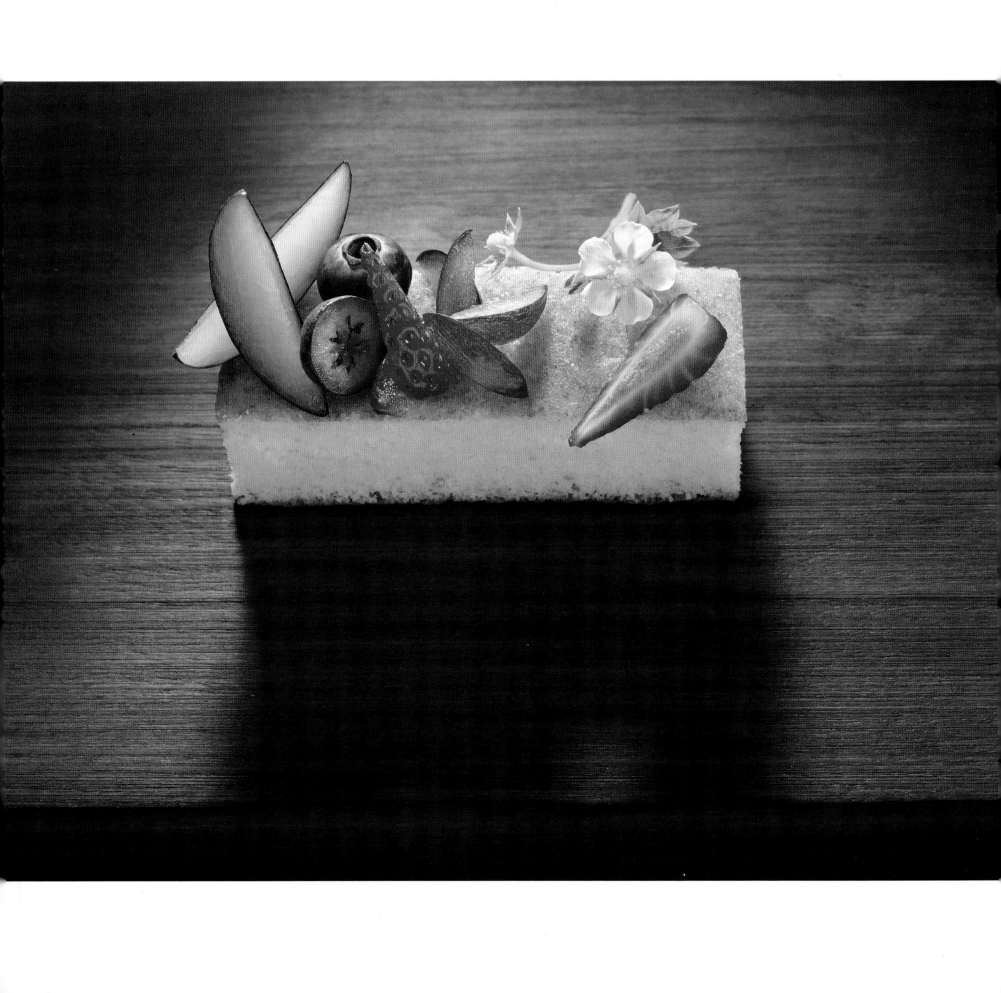

Madeleine Cake

All-purpose flour	188 grams	1¼ cups + 1½ tablespoons
Baking powder	6 grams	1¼ teaspoons
Eggs	200 grams	¾ cup + ½ tablespoon
Granulated sugar	180 grams	¾ cup + 2½ tablespoons
Glucose	112 grams	¼ cup + 1½ tablespoons
Unsalted butter	75 grams	2.6 ounces
Whole milk	38 grams	2 tablespoons + 1 teaspoon
Fresh lemon juice	75 grams	¼ cup + 1 tablespoon

Fresh fruit for garnishing

This cake can be served simply, with fresh fruit in season—blueberries or strawberries in spring, peaches in the summer, apples and pears in the fall. Although it's very delicate, it's versatile.

You'll need a quarter sheet pan.

Preheat the oven to 350°F (standard). Line the sheet pan with a Silpat or spray lightly with nonstick spray, line with parchment paper, and spray the parchment.

Sift the flour and baking powder into a medium bowl.

Place the eggs and sugar in the bowl of a stand mixer fitted with the whisk attachment and mix on medium-low speed for about 1 minute. Increase the speed to medium and whip for about 5 minutes, until the mixture is thick and pale yellow. Scrape down the sides and bottom of the bowl, then whip on medium-high speed for 5 minutes, or until the mixture has thickened but is still light and airy. Remove the bowl from the mixer stand.

Meanwhile, place the glucose and butter in a medium saucepan, set over medium heat, and whisk to combine as they melt. Remove from the heat and whisk in the milk, then pour into a bowl and let cool until just warm to the touch.

Whisk about one-quarter of the egg mixture into the glucose mixture. Whisk in the lemon juice. Fold the dry ingredients into the remaining egg mixture in 2 additions. Fold in the glucose mixture one-quarter at a time, completely incorporating each addition before adding the next.

Pour the batter into the prepared pan and, using an offset spatula, spread it in an even layer, making sure that it reaches into the corners. Bake for 22 to 24 minutes, until the top is golden brown, a skewer inserted in the center comes out clean, and the cake springs back when you touch it lightly. Set the cake on a cooling rack and cool completely.

Place a piece of parchment paper on the back of a sheet pan. Run a knife around the edges to loosen the cake and invert it onto the parchment. Remove the Silpat or parchment from the top of the cake.

Wrapped in a few layers of plastic wrap, the cake can be kept at room temperature for up to 4 hours, refrigerated for up to 3 days, or frozen for up to 2 weeks.

If you will be cutting the cake into shapes, the cake should be frozen before cutting. If frozen, and not being cut into shapes, the cakes should be defrosted in the refrigerator still in the plastic wrap (this way, any condensation will form on the outside and not on the cake).

TO SERVE: Place the cake on a cutting board. Trim the edges to straighten them, then cut the cake into 1-by-3¼-inch rectangles, or any size or shape you like. Garnish each piece with berries or slices of fresh fruit.

MAKES 1 QUARTER SHEET CAKE; SERVES 10

Madeleine Cake for Lemon Meringue Tarts

Using the following proportions, spread the batter in a thin layer and bake for 10 to 12 minutes; the layer should not take on any color. Let cool, then place the pan in the freezer until ready to use.

All-purpose flour	47 grams	¼ cup + 1½ tablespoons
Baking powder	1.5 grams	⅜ teaspoon
Eggs	50 grams	3 tablespoons + 1 teaspoon
Granulated sugar	45 grams	3 tablespoons + 2½ teaspoons
Glucose	28 grams	1 tablespoon + 1 teaspoon
Unsalted butter	19 grams	0.6 ounce
Whole milk	9 grams	2 teaspoons
Fresh lemon juice	19 grams	1 tablespoon + 1 teaspoon

Devil's Food Cake

All-purpose flour	101 grams	½ cup + 3½ tablespoons
Unsweetened alkalized cocoa powder	31 grams	¼ cup + 2 tablespoons
Baking soda	2.5 grams	½ teaspoon
Baking powder	0.5 gram	⅛ teaspoon
Kosher salt	1 gram	⅜ teaspoon
Eggs	56 grams	3½ tablespoons
Granulated sugar	126 grams	½ cup + 2 tablespoons
Vanilla paste	2 grams	⅜ teaspoon
Mayonnaise	86 grams	¼ cup + 2½ tablespoons
Water, at room temperature	105 grams	¼ cup + 3 tablespoons

This is the ultimate chocolate cake. We use it as the base for the Palet d'Or (page 117), but it's fabulous just by itself with some whipped cream or ice cream. Or use it as a component in a parfait (see the Strawberry Parfait on page 111). Or make cupcakes with the batter, piping it into regular liners or holiday cupcake papers.

Sebastien wanted the cake to be moist and rich, but not oily from too much butter. He decided to try mayonnaise instead, and the cake was superb. It was a brilliant revelation! Little did he know that chocolate mayonnaise cake was trendy in America, oh, some eighty years ago. It worked great then, and it works great now.

For this recipe, we use Valrhona cocoa powder.

Preheat the oven to 325°F (standard). Line a sheet pan with a Silpat or spray lightly with nonstick spray, line with parchment paper, and spray the parchment.

Sift the flour, cocoa powder, baking soda, and baking powder into a medium bowl. Add the salt and whisk to combine.

Place the eggs, sugar, and vanilla paste in the bowl of a stand mixer fitted with the whisk attachment and mix on medium-low speed for about 1 minute to combine. Increase the speed to medium and whip for about 5 minutes, until the mixture is thick and pale yellow. Scrape down the sides and bottom of the bowl, then whip on medium-high speed for another 5 minutes, or until the mixture has thickened. When the whisk is lifted, the mixture should form a slowly dissolving ribbon.

Add the mayonnaise and whip to combine. Remove the bowl from the mixer stand and fold in the dry ingredients and water in 2 additions each.

Pour the batter into the prepared pan and, using an offset spatula, spread it in an even layer, making sure that it reaches into the corners. Bake for 10 minutes, or until a skewer inserted in the center comes out clean and the cake springs back when lightly touched. Set on a cooling rack and cool completely.

Lay a piece of parchment paper on the back of a sheet pan. Run a knife around the edges of the cake to loosen it and invert it onto the parchment. Remove the Silpat or parchment from the top of the cake.

Wrapped in a few layers of plastic wrap, the cake can be kept at room temperature for up to 4 hours, refrigerated for up to 3 days, or frozen for up to 2 weeks.

If you will be cutting the cake into shapes, the cake should be frozen before cutting. If frozen, and not being cut into shapes, the cake should be defrosted in the refrigerator still in the plastic wrap (this way, any condensation will form on the outside and not on the cake).

MAKES 1 SHEET CAKE

Palet d'Or

Devil's Food Cake (page 116)

Brune pâte à glacer (see Note) or 55% to 70% chocolate, melted	25 grams	0.8 ounce

CHOCOLATE CREAM

Heavy cream	333 grams	1¼ cups + 3 tablespoons
64% chocolate, chopped	233 grams	8.2 ounces
Eggs	50 grams	3 tablespoons + 1 teaspoon
Egg yolks	100 grams	¼ cup + 3 tablespoons
Granulated sugar	83 grams	¼ cup + 3 tablespoons

CHOCOLATE GLAZE

Silver leaf gelatin (see Note)	7.2 grams	3 sheets
Heavy cream	150 grams	½ cup + 2 tablespoons
Granulated sugar	225 grams	1 cup + 2 tablespoons
Water	180 grams	¾ cup
Unsweetened alkalized cocoa powder, sifted	75 grams	¾ cup + 3 tablespoons

Gold leaf for garnishing

The palet d'or—literally, "gold disk"—conforms to my love of both simplicity and elegance. This beautiful cake looks as if it would be very difficult to make, like a cake you'd see in the fanciest pâtisserie, but it's actually quite simple: two thin layers of devil's food cake, chocolate cream, and a chocolate glaze. It's built within a cake ring, for perfectly straight, smooth, uniform sides.

This is a great example of how to make use of the freezer; the cake is essentially encased in cream, cream that would be impossible to glaze if it were not frozen. Once it's frozen, though, you remove the cake ring and pour the glaze over the cream-covered cake, and it sets up smooth and shiny. The cake can be refrigerated for up to a day and still retain the shine. It's garnished with a few flakes of gold leaf (be sure to use real gold leaf; imitation is not always edible).

You'll need an 8-by-1⅜-inch cake ring and a pastry bag with a ½-inch plain tip. ● *For this recipe, we use Cacao Barry brune pâte à glacer, Valhrona Manjari 64% chocolate, and Valhrona cocoa powder.*

Cut two 7¼-inch rounds from the cake. (The trimmings make great snacks.) Using a small offset spatula, spread the pâte à glacer or melted chocolate over each cake round.

Line a sheet pan with a Silpat and position the cake ring toward one end of the pan. Center a cake round (pâte à glacer side down) in the ring. Place the second cake round next to the ring, and freeze for about 1 hour.

FOR THE CHOCOLATE CREAM: Whip the cream to soft peaks; refrigerate.

Melt the chocolate in the top of a double boiler. Transfer the chocolate to a large bowl and let cool to 100° to 120°F/37.7° to 48.8°C.

Meanwhile, whisk the eggs, egg yolks, and sugar in the (clean) top of the double boiler over simmering water. Initially the eggs will increase in volume and foam, but after 5 to 7 minutes, the foam will begin to subside and the eggs will thicken. Watch the temperature closely, as the eggs will begin to set if they get too hot; when the temperature reaches 183°F/83.8°C, immediately transfer them to the bowl of a stand mixer fitted with the whisk attachment and whip on medium-high speed for about 7 minutes, until the mixture thickens. When the whisk is lifted, the mixture should form a slowly dissolving ribbon.

Whisk one-third of the whipped cream into the chocolate to combine. Fold in the egg mixture, then fold in the remaining whipped cream. Transfer the chocolate cream to the pastry bag.

Continued on page 120

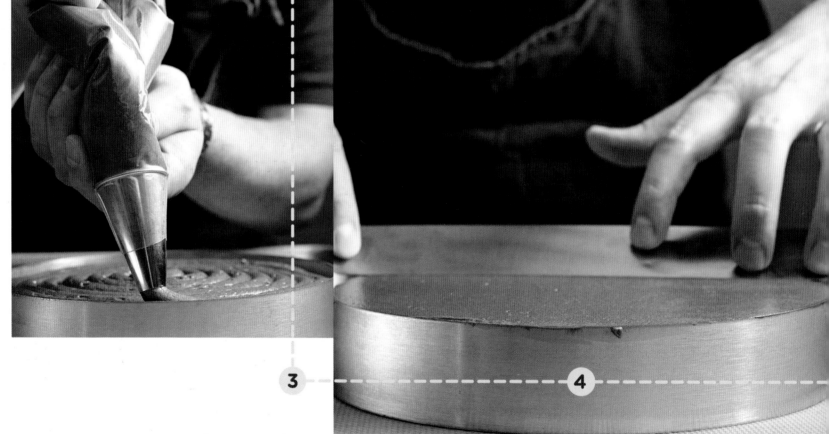

Remove the sheet pan from the freezer. Pipe a ring of cream to fill the gap between the edges of the cake and the ring. Then pipe a spiral, beginning in the center of the cake and extending to the edges of the pan. Center the second cake layer over the first layer. Repeat the piping, using enough cream to reach slightly above the rim of the ring. Sweep a long offset spatula over the cream from one side of the ring to the other for a perfectly smooth surface. Refrigerate the excess cream.

Place the sheet pan in the freezer. After several hours, check the cake. If the center has dipped, stir the reserved cream to soften it, then spread it over the top and smooth the surface again. Freeze overnight.

FOR THE CHOCOLATE GLAZE: Place the gelatin in a bowl of ice water to soften.

Place the cream, sugar, and water in a large saucepan and bring to a boil. Whisk in the cocoa powder, reduce the heat to keep the mixture at a gentle boil, and cook for about 15 minutes, until the mixture has reduced by about one-third. Test by spooning a small amount onto a plate: run your finger through it—if it runs together, continue to reduce it until your finger leaves a track. Once it has reached the desired consistency, remove the mixture from the heat. Wring the excess water from the gelatin and whisk it into the cocoa mixture.

TO ASSEMBLE THE CAKE: Line a sheet pan with parchment paper and set a cooling rack on top. Position the frozen cake, still in the ring, on the rack. Warm the sides of the ring with your hands or with warm towels, if necessary. (Do not use hot water—the cream must remain frozen.) Holding one side of the cake steady, lift up and remove the ring.

Reheat the glaze if necessary until hot, and strain through a fine-mesh strainer into a spouted measuring cup or directly over the cake. In one smooth, quick motion, pour the glaze over the top of the cake, beginning 1½ inches from the edges, allowing the glaze to flow down the sides and into the center to coat. Tap the sheet pan against the work surface to distribute the glaze evenly.

Let the glaze set for a few minutes and then, using a cake lifter or a wide spatula, lift the cake from the rack. If there are any drops of glaze clinging to the bottom of the cake, carefully scrape them against the rack to remove them, then place the cake on a serving platter.

Using the tip of a paring knife, lift a piece of gold leaf from the package (gold leaf is incredibly light and will want to fold onto itself, so keep it away from drafts) and lower it onto the cake. We like to leave part of the gold leaf standing up, rather than having it all lie flat. (The cake can be refrigerated, uncovered, for up to 1 day, and the glaze will remain shiny.)

TO SERVE: Run a slicing knife under hot water and dry it well. Slice the cake, heating the knife again as necessary to keep it clean. A palette knife is the best tool for transferring the slices to plates.

PHOTOGRAPHS ON PAGES 109, 118, AND 119   **SERVES 8**

NOTE ON PATE A GLACER: Pâte à glacer, sometimes referred to as compound chocolate, is used for coating. It can be used on fruits or on ice cream bars or cones, or to decorate cookies or desserts. Pâte à glacer is available in three different flavors—brune (dark), blonde (milk), and ivoire (white)—and it doesn't require tempering.

NOTE ON GELATIN: We use only silver-leaf gelatin sheets. Sheet gelatin comes in bronze, silver, or gold, which have increasing strengths; silver is medium strength. Sheet gelatin has a purer flavor than powdered gelatin and is easier to work with.

Chocolate Biscuit

BISCUIT AU CHOCOLAT

All-purpose flour	33 grams	3 tablespoons + 2 teaspoons
Almond flour/meal	25 grams	3 tablespoons + 2 teaspoons
Unsweetened alkalized cocoa powder	16 grams	3 tablespoons + ½ teaspoon
Eggs	123 grams	½ cup
Egg yolks	58 grams	3 tablespoons + 2 teaspoons
Granulated sugar	111 grams	½ cup + 1 tablespoon
	23 grams	1 tablespoon + 2½ teaspoons
Egg whites	74 grams	¼ cup + 1 tablespoon

A *biscuit,* like a génoise, is a French sponge cake, but unlike the génoise, where whole eggs are used, the yolks and whites are separated and the whites beaten before they are folded into the batter. This very thin cake, baked in a sheet pan, is flexible enough to be rolled up for our take on the Ho Ho (see Oh Ohs, page 122) and for other desserts. To make it especially pliable, we use less flour and more fat and chocolate than in a traditional chocolate *biscuit.* It's important not to overbake this, or it will dry out and then crack when you roll it. If you can, store the egg whites in the refrigerator for a few days before using them; the cake will have a better structure.

For this recipe, we use Guittard Cocoa Rouge.

Preheat the oven to 350°F (standard). Line a sheet pan with a Silpat or spray the pan lightly with nonstick spray, line with parchment paper, and spray the parchment.

Place the all-purpose flour in a large bowl. Sift in the almond flour; break up any lumps remaining in the sieve and add them to the bowl. Sift in the cocoa powder and whisk to combine.

Place the eggs, yolks, and the 111 grams/½ cup plus 1 tablespoon sugar in the bowl of a stand mixer fitted with the whisk attachment and mix on medium-low speed for about 1 minute to combine. Increase the speed to medium and whip for about 5 minutes, until the mixture is thick and pale yellow. Scrape down the sides and bottom of the bowl, then whip on medium-high speed for another 5 minutes, or until the mixture has thickened. When the whisk is lifted, the mixture should form a slowly dissolving ribbon. Remove the bowl from the mixer stand.

Whip the whites in a clean mixer bowl with the clean whisk attachment on medium speed for about 45 seconds, until foamy. Lower the speed and slowly add the remaining 23 grams/1 tablespoon plus 2½ teaspoons sugar, then increase the speed to medium-high and whip for 2 to 2½ minutes, until the whites are glossy with soft peaks.

Fold the dry ingredients into the yolk mixture in 2 additions, then do the same with the egg whites. Pour the batter into the prepared pan and, using an offset spatula, spread it in an even layer, making sure that it reaches into the corners. Bake for about 15 minutes, until a skewer inserted in the center comes out clean and the cake springs back when you touch it lightly. Set on a cooling rack and cool completely.

Lay a piece of parchment paper on the back of a sheet pan. Run a knife around the edges to loosen the cake and invert it onto the parchment. Remove the Silpat or parchment from the top of the cake.

Wrapped in a few layers of plastic wrap, the *biscuit* can be kept at room temperature for up to 4 hours, refrigerated for up to 3 days, or frozen for up to 2 weeks.

If you will be cutting the cake into shapes, the cake should be frozen before cutting. If frozen, and not being cut into shapes, the cake should be defrosted in the refrigerator still in the plastic wrap (this way, any condensation will form on the outside and not on the cake).

MAKES 1 SHEET CAKE

Oh Ohs

Chocolate Biscuit (page 121)

Sweetened Whipped Cream (page 378)	150 grams	1½ cups
Brune pâte à glacer (See Note, page 120)	400 grams	14 ounces
Crunchy dark chocolate pearls (optional)	18 grams	2 tablespoons
Crunchy white chocolate pearls (optional)	18 grams	2 tablespoons

I have to confess that I've loved Hostess Ho Hos since they were introduced in 1967, when I was twelve. People love our version of them. Adults get more excited than the kids—I suspect because these make them feel like kids again.

We coat ours in pâte à glacer, a chocolate coating that doesn't need to be tempered. The pearls add chocolaty crunch.

For this recipe, we use Cacao Barry pâte à glacer, Valrhona Les Perles 55%, and Cacao Barry white Crispearls.

Place a piece of parchment paper the size of the sheet pan on a cutting board and set the chocolate biscuit on the paper. Trim the edges to straighten them. Turn the biscuit so that a short end is facing you. Spread the whipped cream in a thin, even layer over the cake, leaving a ¼-inch border all around. Using the parchment paper to help you, lift the short end nearest you and fold about ½ inch of the cake over, just enough to begin rolling it, then continue to lift up the paper to roll the cake into as tight a roll as possible, stopping when you reach the center of the cake. Repeat, rolling from the opposite side, until the rolls meet in the center.

Cut the rolls apart. Cut two 12-by-8-inch pieces of parchment paper. Place a roll lengthwise along the edge of a paper and roll it up in the paper, pulling back on the roll from time to time to tighten it, using your hands, a paint shield, or a straightedge. Tape the paper in the center and at the ends, and repeat with the remaining roll. Freeze the rolls overnight.

TO ENROBE THE ROLLS: Trim the ends off the rolls, then cut each one into 4 pieces. You want to dip them while they are still frozen.

Lay a Silpat on the work surface. Heat the pâte à glacer until it is hot, then strain through a fine strainer into a small, deep bowl just large enough to hold an Oh Oh. Dip one piece at a time into the hot chocolate (preferably wearing latex gloves), making sure to cover the sides as well, then remove, letting the excess chocolate drip back into the bowl, and place on the Silpat. Let the glaze begin to set, then garnish each roll with several pearls, if using. Should any chocolate pool and harden around the base of the Oh Ohs, it can be trimmed away with a hot paring knife. Transfer to the refrigerator.

The Oh Ohs can be refrigerated for up to 3 days in a covered container.

MAKES 8 INDIVIDUAL CAKES

Note to Professionals: We add stabilizer to the whipped cream for this recipe.

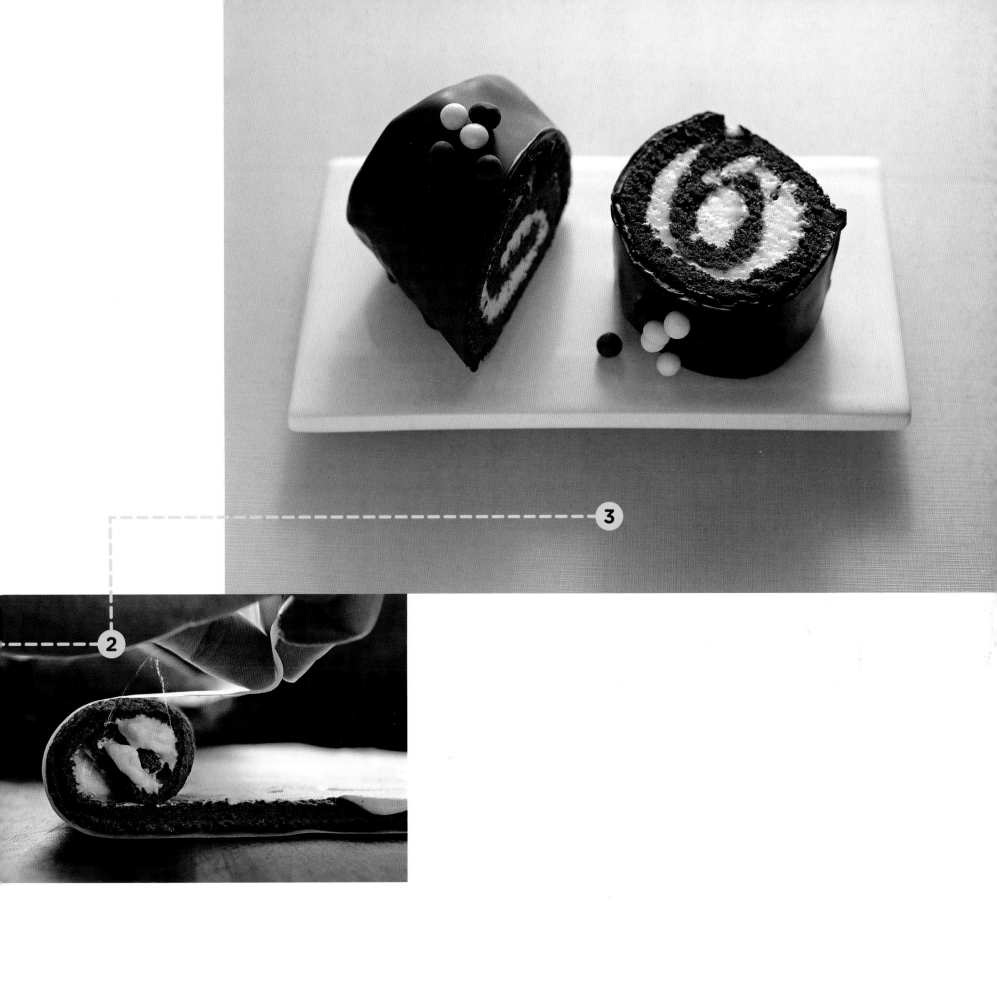

Crêpe Cake

GATEAU DE CREPES

Orange Diplomat Cream (page 375)	1 kilogram	4⅔ cups
13 Crêpes (recipe follows)		
Granulated sugar	60 grams	¼ cup + 2½ teaspoons

This fabulous dessert is also one of the easiest in the book—a stack of thirteen crêpes layered with orange diplomat cream (pastry cream lightened with whipped cream) and then sliced into serving portions. It's very light, and it can—and should—be made in advance, so it's an excellent dish for entertaining.

You'll need a 10-inch cardboard round (optional), a pastry bag with a ½-inch plain tip, and a propane torch.

Wrap a 10-inch cardboard round or a flat tray in plastic wrap.

Spoon the cream into the pastry bag. Choose the most attractive crêpe for the top of the cake. Place it with its better side down on the plastic wrap and pipe 80 grams/⅓ cup of the cream into the center. Using a small offset spatula, spread the cream over the crêpe, leaving a ¼-inch border. The crêpe is naturally thinner on the edges; to prevent a dome from forming as you fill and stack the crêpes, spread the filling at the edges a bit thicker. Top the cream with another crêpe, spread it with cream, and continue to layer the crêpes and cream, ending with a crêpe.

Wrap the cake in the plastic wrap and refrigerate for at least 4 hours, but preferably overnight.

TO SERVE: Unwrap the cake and invert it onto a serving platter. Sprinkle the top with an even layer of the sugar and, using the propane torch, caramelize the top of the cake, working from one side to the other. Cut the cake into 8 wedges and serve.

SERVES 8

Crêpes

Whole milk	500 grams	2 cups
Eggs	200 grams	¾ cup + ½ tablespoon
All-purpose flour	200 grams	1¼ cups + 3 tablespoons
Granulated sugar	20 grams	1 tablespoon + 2 teaspoons
Grand Marnier	60 grams	3½ tablespoons
Kosher salt	5 grams	1½ teaspoons
1 vanilla bean, split lengthwise		
Unsalted butter, melted and cooled	20 grams	0.7 ounce
Canola oil, for cooking		

Place the milk, eggs, flour, sugar, Grand Marnier, and salt in a Vitamix. Scrape the seeds from the vanilla bean and add them at medium-low speed for about 15 seconds. Scrape down the sides of the blender container. With the blender running on medium-low, drizzle in the melted butter. Strain through a fine-mesh strainer into a covered container; use a spatula to force through any batter remaining in the strainer. Refrigerate overnight.

Using a paper towel, rub a large crêpe pan or a 10-inch nonstick frying pan with a light coating of canola oil (if the crêpes begin to stick at any point, rub it again) and set it over medium to medium-high heat. Once the pan is hot, lift it from the heat and ladle 55 grams/¼ cup of the batter into the center of the pan. Immediately swirl and shake the pan so that the batter covers the bottom, then rotate the pan a couple of times so the batter comes ½ inch up the sides.

Return the pan to the heat and cook for 15 to 30 seconds, depending on the heat level, until the batter is set and the bottom is a light golden brown. Slip your fingers under the crêpe and flip it over (if you just grab the edge, it may tear as you flip). Cook on the second side until a light golden brown, then transfer the crêpe to a sheet pan. Repeat to make the remaining crêpes, stacking or overlapping them once they cool. Let them sit for at least 10 minutes before using.

MAKES 13 CREPES

A French tart and an American pie are essentially the same thing, but for me the refinement of the French tart is so satisfying, whether you're eating it or just looking at it in a pastry shop—even if it was made from leftovers, as tarts often are in France, using puff pastry dough, for instance. The French are so resourceful in using leftovers, and I really admire that. The other aspect of the tart that appeals to me deeply, beyond its elegance, is its versatility. A single technique offers you a range of desserts all year round—one simple crust gives you a cream and berry tart in spring, a stone-fruit tart in summer, an apple tart in fall, and a caramel or chocolate tart in winter. It allows you to feature what's best in each season. And, finally, I adore tarts because of Sebastien. His precision and ingenuity really shine in the tarts he's created for Bouchon Bakery: he's elevated the rhubarb tart, for example, by letting the shape of the vegetable determine the shape of the tart, and he's brought refinement and modernity to the peach tart. He's reimagined the apple tart as a band tart using both puff pastry and pâte sucrée doughs. His plum tart, a conventional round with traditionally layered fruit, looks both rustic and elegant at the same time and is a delicious example of how well sweet-tart elements work in tarts.

TARTS

FRAISER

Fraiser (or *fraisage*) is a French term and technique for smearing and blending the dough with the heel of your hand. Once combined, the dough is folded over and the method repeated until every ingredient is incorporated and the dough is uniform and smooth. As the dough bakes, the butter creates steam, and the resulting crust is light and flaky.

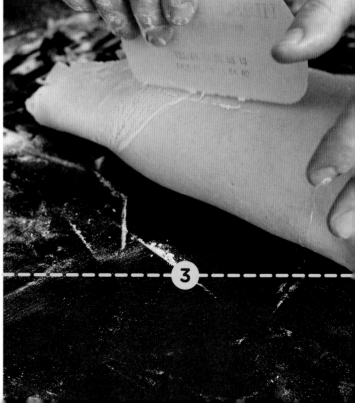

Pâte Sucrée

All-purpose flour	375 grams	2⅔ cups
Powdered sugar	46 grams	¼ cup + 2½ tablespoons
	94 grams	¾ cup + 1 tablespoon
Almond flour/meal (see Note)	47 grams	¼ cup + 3 tablespoons
Unsalted butter, at room temperature	225 grams	8 ounces
½ vanilla bean, split lengthwise		
Eggs	56 grams	3½ tablespoons

A traditional pâte sucrée is a basic sweet dough. But Sebastien is relentless in his pursuit of more flavor and a more refined technique, so he uses powdered sugar rather than granulated or superfine, because it blends into the butter better. He adds most of the sugar to the butter, which has been whipped to peaks, then adds the rest of the sugar with the flour; he uses not only wheat flour but also almond flour, for its rich flavor. For even more flavor, he adds the seeds of a vanilla bean and, for richness and its binding properties, some egg. The result is a wonderful sweet, delicate dough, which he likes to use with less-sweet fillings as in the Lemon Meringue Tarts (page 152). He uses pâte brisée (see page 130) with most very sweet fillings.

Place the all-purpose flour in a medium bowl. Sift the 46 grams/¼ cup plus 2½ tablespoons powdered sugar and the almond flour into the bowl; break up any lumps of almond flour remaining in the sieve, add them to the bowl, and whisk to combine.

Place the butter in the bowl of a stand mixer fitted with the paddle attachment and cream on medium-low speed, warming the bowl as needed (see Pommade, page 190), until the butter is the consistency of mayonnaise and holds a peak when the paddle is lifted. Sift in the remaining 94 grams/¾ cup plus 1 tablespoon powdered sugar and pulse to begin incorporating the sugar, then increase the speed to medium-low and mix for about 1 minute, until the mixture is fluffy. Scrape down the sides and bottom of the bowl. Scrape the seeds from the vanilla bean, add them to the butter mixture, and mix on low speed for about 30 seconds to distribute the seeds evenly.

Add the dry ingredients in 2 additions, mixing for 15 to 30 seconds after each, or until just combined. Scrape the bottom of the bowl to incorporate any dry ingredients that have settled there. Add the eggs and mix on low speed until just combined, 15 to 30 seconds.

Transfer the dough to the work surface. Use the heel of your hand to smear the dough and work it together (*fraiser*). Divide the dough in half and form each half into a 4-by-6-inch-rectangle, about ¾ inch thick.

Wrap each piece in a double layer of plastic wrap. Refrigerate until firm, about 2 hours, but preferably overnight. The dough can be refrigerated for up to 2 days or frozen for up to 1 month.

MAKES 800 GRAMS/1¾ POUNDS

NOTE ON NUT FLOURS: Almond and hazelnut flours, or meals, add texture and delicious flavor to pastries, but the nut oils can cause these flours to clump. So it's important to sift them before using, and then to break up any clumps remaining in the sieve and add them to the bowl.

Pâte Brisée

All-purpose flour	140 grams	1 cup
	165 grams	1 cup + 3 tablespoons
Kosher salt	3 grams	1 teaspoon
Cold unsalted butter, cut into ¼-inch cubes	227 grams	8 ounces
Ice water	58 grams	¼ cup

Our pâte brisée—butter, salt, and a little water to bring it all together—is as traditional as a crust gets. Sebastien likes to add a bit of milk and egg to many of his doughs, for richness and binding power, but this pâte brisée reflects my enduring respect for classical technique. It's something every cook should master—it's so easy and so versatile. Pâte brisée is used for savory tarts, such as quiches, and for very sweet tarts.

Place the 140 grams/1 cup flour and the salt in the bowl of a stand mixer fitted with the paddle attachment and mix to combine. With the mixer running on low speed, add the butter a small handful at a time. When all the butter has been added, increase the speed to medium-low and mix for about 1 minute, until the butter is thoroughly blended. Scrape down the sides and bottom of the bowl. Turn the speed to medium-low, add the remaining 165 grams/1 cup plus 3 tablespoons flour, and mix just to combine. Add the water and mix until incorporated. The dough will come up around the paddle and should feel smooth, not sticky, to the touch.

Remove the dough from the mixer and check to be certain that there are no visible pieces of butter remaining; if necessary, return the dough to the mixer and mix again briefly.

Pat the dough into a 7- to 8-inch disk and wrap in plastic wrap. Refrigerate for at least 1 hour, but preferably overnight. (The dough can be refrigerated for up to 1 day or frozen for up to 1 month.)

MAKES 585 GRAMS/1¼ POUNDS

Rolling Out Tart Dough

Line a sheet pan with parchment paper and place the ring(s) on the paper; or line a quarter sheet pan with parchment.

Unwrap the dough and place it between two large pieces of parchment or plastic wrap. With a rolling pin, pound the top of the dough, working from one side of the dough to the other, to begin to flatten the dough; turn the dough 90 degrees and repeat (this will help prevent the dough from cracking as it is rolled). Roll out the dough, in the parchment, from the center outward, rotating and flipping the dough over frequently, to the dimensions needed for the desired ring(s) or pan. If the dough feels stuck on the parchment, lift off the parchment and reposition it. Should the edges crack, tap the edge of the dough with the rolling pin to bring it back together. If the dough softens, refrigerate for a few minutes before placing it into the ring(s) or pan.

Remove the top piece of parchment (if you have not already done so). If using a ring or rings, invert the dough over the ring(s) along with the bottom piece of parchment and carefully lower it into the ring(s), pressing it gently against the sides and into the bottom edges. If using the sheet pan, make sure there are no thicker areas of dough in the corners of the pan. Run your hands over the parchment to smooth the dough and force out any air bubbles, then remove the parchment. Fold the excess dough outward over the rim of the ring(s) or pan. Repair any cracks in the dough.

If you are making the Apricot Flan Tart (page 141), fold the excess dough over against the outside of the ring (this will prevent it from shrinking down the sides as it bakes). For all other tarts, run your rolling pin over the ring(s) or pan to remove the excess dough. Reserve some of the excess dough in case your shell needs a repair after baking.

Freeze the dough for about 30 minutes, or refrigerate for an hour. If you are not blind-baking the shell(s), continue with the recipe.

Preheat the oven to 350°F (standard).

To Blind-Bake Tart Shells

Trim the dough evenly with the top of the ring(s), unless making the Apricot Flan Tart, or the sheet pan. Line the shell(s) with parchment paper or a large coffee filter, letting it extend over the top of the ring(s). Fill the shell(s) completely with raw rice (unlike dried beans or pie weights, rice won't leave an imprint in the dough), gently guiding it into the corners of the shell(s).

Bake according to the instructions in the individual recipe. Set the pan on a cooling rack and cool completely.

MEASURING THICKNESS

At the bakery, we often use guides or a sheeter (a large rolling machine) to roll out doughs to just the thickness we want. If you are gauging the thickness of a dough with a ruler, in general, don't check it at the edges, which are usually a bit thinner than the center. Instead, cut out a small piece from the center of the dough to measure the thickness, then push the dough back together. But don't cut into a laminated dough this way, or it will rise and bake unevenly.

DOUGH CHART

8-by-¾-inch tart ring	½ recipe Pâte Brisée, cold, or Pâte Sucrée, cold	Roll out a round about 11 inches in diameter and ⅛ inch thick
9-by-2-inch cake ring	1 recipe Pâte Brisée, cold, or Pâte Sucrée, cold	Roll out a round about 16 inches in diameter and just under ¼ inch thick
Six 3-by-¾-inch individual tart rings	1 recipe Pâte Brisée, cold, or Pâte Sucrée, cold	Roll out the dough to an 11-by-16-inch rectangle, about ⅛ inch thick, remove the top piece of plastic wrap, and cut six 5-inch circles (cutting right through the bottom piece of plastic wrap)
Quarter sheet pan	1 recipe Pâte Brisée, cold, or Pâte Sucrée, cold	Roll out a 12-by-16-inch rectangle, just under ⅛ inch thick

ROLLING OUT TART DOUGH

SKIMP ON FLOURING

Doughs are made with precise amounts of flour, and
for that reason, it's best not to use any additional flour
when rolling out cookie, scone, or tart doughs if at
all possible. Many of these doughs can be rolled out
between sheets of parchment paper or plastic wrap. If
you must add flour when rolling out a dough, use only
the minimum needed to keep the dough from sticking.

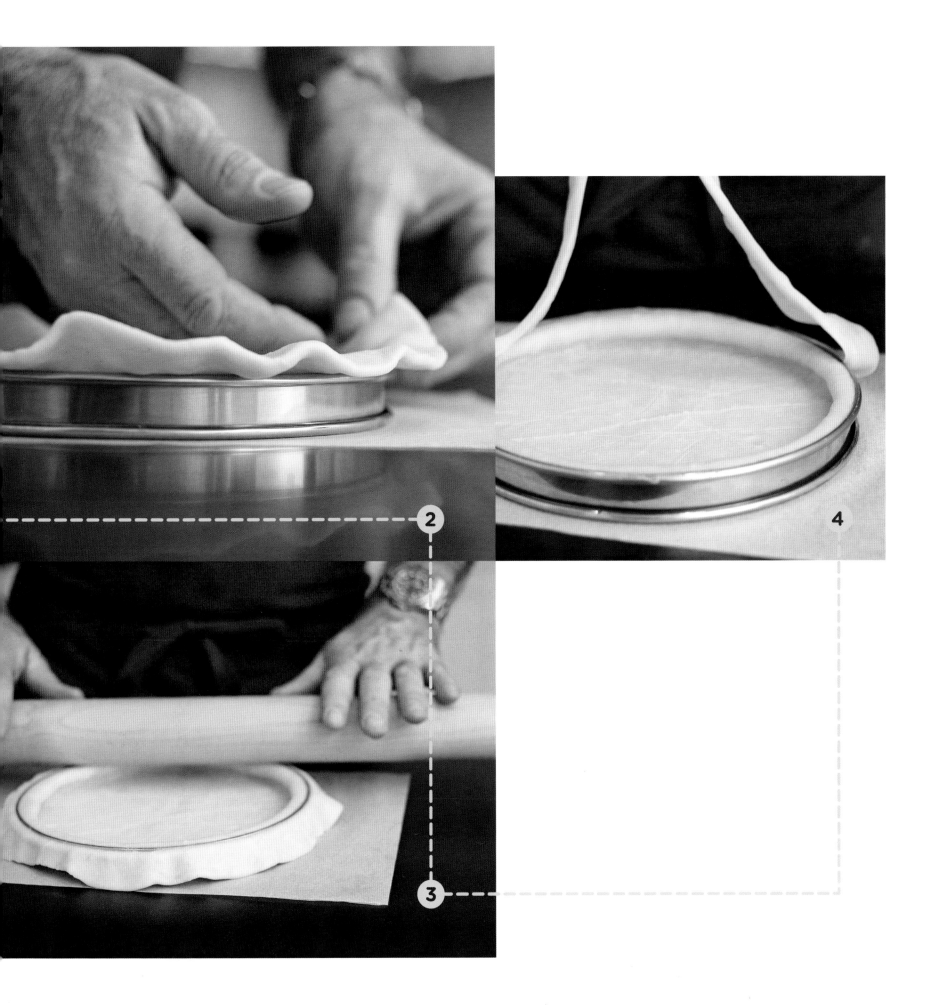

Chocolate, Praline, and Cocoa Nib Tart

TARTE AU CHOCOLAT NOIR AMER, AU PRALINE, ET AUX ECLATS DE FEVES DE CACAO

PRALINE

Hazelnut-almond praline paste	144 grams	5 ounces
40% milk chocolate	15 grams	0.5 ounce
Cocoa butter	12.5 grams	0.4 ounce
Feuilletine	60 grams	⅔ cup

½ recipe Pâte Sucrée (page 129)

CHOCOLATE DENTELLE

Skinned toasted hazelnuts	37 grams	¼ cup
Granulated sugar	75 grams	¼ cup + 2 tablespoons
Unsalted butter	62 grams	2.1 ounces
Light corn syrup	25 grams	1 tablespoon + 1 teaspoon
Whole milk	21 grams	1 tablespoon + 1 teaspoon
Cocoa nibs (see Note)	37 grams	¼ cup + 1 tablespoon
Cocoa powder, sifted	7 grams	1 tablespoon + 1 teaspoon

CHOCOLATE GANACHE

64% chocolate, coarsely chopped	200 grams	7 ounces
Heavy cream	170 grams	½ cup + 3½ tablespoons
Trimoline (invert sugar)	14 grams	1¾ teaspoons
Glucose	12 grams	½ tablespoon
Unsalted butter, at room temperature	14 grams	0.5 ounce

The beauty of the chocolate tart is that at heart it's so simple: a pâte sucrée crust and a ganache filling, with a couple of fun elements added for crunch and for visual appeal. There's a disk of chocolate praline and, on top of the tart, a chocolate dentelle ("lace" in French), a nougatine-like tuile made with hazelnuts and cocoa nibs.

You'll need an 8-by-¾-inch tart ring. ● *For this recipe, we use Cacao Barry hazelnut-almond praline paste, Valrhona Jivara 40% chocolate, Cacao Barry feuilletine, Valrhona cocoa powder, Valrhona Manjari 64% chocolate, and Erstein Trimoline.*

FOR THE PRALINE: Spoon the praline paste into a large bowl.

Melt the chocolate in a medium bowl (a microwave works best because of the small amount of chocolate). Melt the cocoa butter separately (chocolate and cocoa butter melt at different rates). Slowly, with a spatula, stir the cocoa butter into the chocolate until combined and smooth, then stir in the feuilletine. Add to the praline paste, stirring to combine well.

Place a large piece of parchment paper on the work surface. Spoon the mixture into the center and top with a second piece of parchment. Roll the praline to under ⅛ inch thick. Slide the praline, in the paper, onto a sheet pan. Freeze until solid, at least 4 hours, but preferably overnight. (The praline can be frozen, well wrapped, for up to 1 month.)

FOR THE TART SHELL: Preheat the oven to 325°F (standard). Line a sheet pan with a Silpat or parchment paper.

Following the instructions on page 130, roll out the dough, line the tart ring, and fill it with raw rice. Bake for 20 minutes, then rotate the pan and bake for another 20 minutes, or until the dough is set and no longer sticks to the parchment paper. Remove the parchment and rice (store the rice for future use), return the pan to the oven, and bake for another 20 minutes, or until the dough is cooked through and golden brown. Set the pan on a cooling rack and cool completely.

FOR THE DENTELLE: Preheat the oven to 350°F (standard).

Place the hazelnuts in a small heavy plastic bag and roll a rolling pin over them to crush them into pieces as small as the cocoa nibs. Set aside.

Combine the sugar, butter, corn syrup, and milk in a saucepan and stir over medium-high heat until the mixture reaches 230°F/110°C. Remove from the heat and stir in the hazelnuts, cocoa nibs, and cocoa powder.

Pour the mixture onto a piece of parchment paper and top with a second sheet. Roll out the dentelle as thin as possible.

Transfer it, still in the parchment paper, to a sheet pan. Remove the top piece of parchment and place the pan in the oven. After a few minutes, the mixture will begin to bubble. After about 12 minutes, the bubbles covering the surface will have become smaller and you will smell the aroma of the cocoa nibs and hazelnuts. Remove from the oven and set on a cooling rack.

After 2 to 3 minutes, the dentelle will have stiffened enough to be cut into a shape. Cut out a round to garnish the top of the tart. If you'd like, the remaining dentelle can be cut into pieces and used to garnish the individual slices. Set aside.

TO CUT THE PRALINE: Measure the bottom of the tart shell. Remove the praline from the freezer, remove the top sheet of parchment paper, and cut out a round of the same size. (It is best to work on the cold sheet pan, because the praline softens very quickly.) Return the praline to the freezer until it has hardened again.

Using a wide spatula, transfer the praline to the tart shell.

FOR THE GANACHE: Melt the chocolate in a medium bowl. Allow to cool to room temperature.

Place the cream, Trimoline, and glucose in a saucepan and bring to a simmer over medium heat, stirring to combine the ingredients. Remove from the heat, pour one-third of the mixture over the chocolate, and stir from the center, incorporating the chocolate from around the edges of the bowl. Repeat with the remaining cream. The ganache should be shiny and smooth. Stir in the butter (see Note on Repairing Broken Ganache).

Pour the ganache into the tart shell and let it set at room temperature for at least 4 hours. Run the tip of a paring knife between the top of the crust and the ring to loosen the crust, then lift off the ring.

The tart can be stored at cool room temperature for up to 2 days. (Do not refrigerate, or the ganache will lose its shine and become too firm.)

TO SERVE: Arrange the dentelle on top of the tart, placing it off center. Garnish the individual slices with the reserved dentelle, if desired.

PHOTOGRAPH ON PAGE 137   **SERVES 6 TO 8**

NOTE ON COCOA NIBS: Cocoa nibs are the particles of cacao beans left after the beans are roasted and shelled for making chocolate. They are not sweet, but they are the essence of cacao, the raw material that becomes chocolate. You might want to experiment with them in savory cooking as well as in dessert recipes.

NOTE ON REPAIRING BROKEN GANACHE: Ganache contains a high percentage of fat, and if it is heated too much, the fat may separate from the chocolate. Just as you can fix a broken mayonnaise by adding to it a fresh yolk and some mustard, you can whisk some fat-free milk into a broken ganache to restore the emulsion.

SEBASTIEN ON

TARTS

Tarts can be round or square, simple or complex, baked free-form or in a tart pan. Fluted pans are most common in the United States, but I prefer smooth French tart or cake rings, which rest directly on parchment or Silpat on a sheet pan, because that is how I was taught. The lack of fluting can cause the dough to shrink more, and the pans are more difficult to work with because they don't have a bottom for support, but I love the clean aesthetic of a straight-edged tart shell. If fluted pans are what you happen to have, though, of course use them.

At Bouchon Bakery, a tart typically has three components beyond the crust. For us, the more layers the better. A chocolate tart is traditional and fine, but it's a little sweet and one-dimensional. So I may make it more interesting by pouring in a layer of ganache, topping it with a thin round of génoise, and then pouring a mint custard over that. For the chocolate tart on page 134, we place a disk of praline in the tart shell for crunch, then pour ganache over it and add an off-center round of dentelle, a nougatine-like hazelnut tuile, for visual appeal, bite, and flavor.

This is not to say we don't make traditional tarts—and we keep them simple when simple is best. If you have amazing raspberries, you don't want to overembellish them: make the crust, add pastry cream or a mousseline cream or even sweetened whipped cream, and arrange fresh raspberries on top. Our Caramel Nut Tart (page 140) is nothing more than caramel jam and nuts, and it's fabulous.

Chocolate, Praline, and Cocoa Nib Tart (page 134)

The early bird gets the baguette.

Caramel Nut Tart

TARTE AUX FRUITS SECS ET AU CARAMEL

½ recipe Pâte Brisée (page 130)

Assorted unsalted nuts, toasted	185 grams	6.5 ounces
½ recipe Caramel Jam (page 380), hot	225 grams	¾ cup

This tart is at once simple and sophisticated. The filling is merely nuts bound with caramel, but when you use gorgeous nuts and a rich caramel "jam," something magical happens. As is always the case when you're working with just a few ingredients, you need to get it right. Here the critical factor is bringing the sugar to the proper temperature so that after the tart is assembled and cooled, it will slice cleanly and easily.

Be sure the nuts you choose are unsalted; if you're using hazelnuts, the skins should be removed. And in all our pastries we like to stress that nuts be completely toasted, toasted through to the center. Undercooking nuts is one of Sebastien's pet peeves.

You'll need an 8-by-¾-inch tart ring.

FOR THE TART SHELL: Preheat the oven to 325°F (standard). Line a sheet pan with a Silpat or parchment paper.

Following the instructions on page 130, roll out the dough, line the tart ring, and fill it with raw rice. Bake for 20 minutes, then rotate the pan and bake for another 20 minutes, or until the dough is set and no longer sticks to the parchment paper. Remove the parchment and rice (store the rice for future use), return the pan to the oven, and bake for another 15 to 20 minutes, or until the dough is cooked through and golden brown. Set the pan on a cooling rack and cool completely.

FOR THE FILLING: Toss the nuts together and spread them in the tart shell; the shell will be very full. Pour most of the hot caramel jam over the nuts, letting it run down between the gaps to fill the tart. The nuts will not be completely submerged in caramel, so drizzle some over the top to give them a beautiful sheen. Let cool. Run the tip of a paring knife between the top of the crust and the ring to loosen the crust, then lift off the ring.

The tart is best the day it is made, but it can be stored at room temperature for up to 2 days (do not refrigerate).

SERVES 6 TO 8

Apricot Flan Tart

FLAN PARISIEN

Pâte Brisée (page 130)

18 small ripe apricots, halved lengthwise and pitted

FLAN

Eggs	150 grams	½ cup + 1½ tablespoons
Egg yolks	100 grams	¼ cup + 3 tablespoons
Granulated sugar	300 grams	1½ cups
2 vanilla beans, split lengthwise		
Custard powder	75 grams	½ cup + 1 tablespoon
Cornstarch	75 grams	½ cup + 1 tablespoon
Whole milk	1.5 kilograms	6 cups

This is one of the simplest of all tarts—just a pâte brisée crust and a custard filling—and it's the best kind of comfort food there is. The custard is cooked twice, once on the stovetop and then in the tart shell. The tart takes a long time to bake because of the amount of filling, but to achieve the supple texture that makes a custard so exquisite, be careful not to overbake it. The filling should still have a very slight jiggle at the center; it will continue to cook when removed from the oven.

You'll need a 9-by-2-inch cake ring. ● *For this recipe, we use Bird's custard powder.*

FOR THE TART SHELL: Preheat the oven to 350°F (standard). Line a sheet pan with a Silpat or parchment paper. Brush the ring lightly with canola oil.

Following the instructions on page 130, roll out the dough, line the cake ring, and fill it with raw rice. Bake for 35 to 40 minutes, or until the edges of the dough are lightly browned and the bottom is set but still light in color. Remove the parchment and rice (store the rice for future use). Return the pan to the oven and bake for another 10 minutes, or until the bottom is golden brown. Set the pan on a cooling rack and cool completely.

Arrange the apricots cut side down in the bottom of the tart shell, overlapping them as necessary to fit in an even layer. (Depending on their size, you may not need all the apricots.)

FOR THE FLAN: Place the eggs, yolks, and sugar in the bowl of a stand mixer fitted with the whisk attachment and mix on low speed for about 30 seconds to combine. Scrape the seeds from the vanilla beans, add them to the egg mixture, and mix on low speed for about 30 seconds to distribute the seeds evenly. With the mixer running on the lowest setting, add the custard powder and the cornstarch and mix for 30 seconds to incorporate. Scrape down the sides and bottom of the bowl. With the mixer running on low speed, slowly pour in the milk. Pour the mixture through a fine-mesh strainer into a large saucepan.

Place the pan over medium-high heat and bring to a boil, whisking gently to prevent air bubbles. Boil for 1 minute, rotating the whisk around the edges of the pan to keep the mixture from scorching.

Pour the mixture through a fine-mesh strainer into the bowl of the mixer. Fit the mixer with the paddle attachment and mix on low speed for about 3 minutes to release steam and cool the mixture slightly.

Pour the mixture over the apricots, to the very top of the shell; the filling will shrink as it bakes. Place the pan in the oven and bake for 1 hour 20 minutes to 1 hour 40 minutes. (Some of the filling may spill over the edges of the tart, but that will be removed later when the tart is trimmed.) The tart should have a dark brown skin on top and the filling should be set but still jiggle slightly when the pan is moved.

Set the pan on a rack and let the tart cool to room temperature, then cover with plastic wrap and refrigerate overnight.

Using a bench scraper or a sharp knife, scrape away the excess crust from the top of the ring. Tilt the ring on its side, with the bottom facing you, and run a small paring knife between the crust and the ring to release the tart. Set the tart down and carefully lift off the ring.

Return the tart to the refrigerator until ready to serve. It will keep in the refrigerator for up to 2 days, but the apricots may release some moisture after a day.

Cut the cold tart into wedges, using a long slicing knife.

PHOTOGRAPHS ON PAGES 142 AND 143   **SERVES 8 TO 10**

Don't be chicken to try this eggscellent tart.

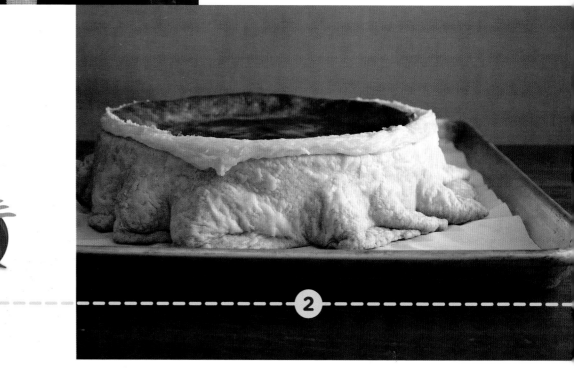

③

④

Apple Band Tart

TARTE AUX POMMES

½ recipe Pâte Sucrée (page 129)

Puff Pastry (page 214), cold, two 16½-by-1¼-by-¼-inch-thick strips	60 grams each	2 ounces each
Egg Wash (page 381)		
Pastry Cream (page 373)	200 grams	¾ cups + 2½ tablespoons
4 firm medium apples, such as Braeburn		
Unsalted butter	25 grams	0.8 ounce
Light brown sugar	25 grams	2 tablespoons

French apple tarts are typically made in a round pan with pâte sucrée, but this one is a band tart, rectangular in shape, and it uses two different doughs: pâte sucrée for the base and two strips of puff pastry for a border that holds the apples in (you won't need a full recipe of the puff pastry—freeze the rest for other desserts). The thin slices of apple are nestled into a pastry cream filling. When you fan the apple slices on the cream, they're higher than the puff pastry, but as the tart bakes, the dough rises and the apples deflate, evening out the surface, and you end up with a rustic-looking tart.

You'll need a dough docker (optional) and a pastry bag with a ⅜-inch plain tip.

Line a sheet pan with a Silpat or parchment paper. Roll the pâte sucrée out between two pieces of parchment paper or plastic wrap to a 5-by-16-inch rectangle, just under ¼ inch thick. Remove the top piece of parchment, flip the dough, and place it on the sheet pan. Remove the remaining piece of parchment. The ends of the pastry should touch the ends of the sheet pan; trim the dough or roll it slightly larger if necessary. Using a docker or a fork, prick the bottom of the dough to keep it from puffing as it bakes.

Set the puff pastry strips on the long edges of the pâte sucrée, lining up the edges exactly. Using the tip of a paring knife, cut ¼-inch-deep diagonal slits every ½ inch around the edges of the dough. This decorative edge will help to keep the two doughs from separating as the puff pastry rises.

Brush the tops of the puff pastry strips with egg wash. (If the egg wash drips down the sides onto the pan, the pastry will not rise evenly; transfer it to another lined pan.) Score the tops of the strips with 1/16-inch-deep diagonal lines ¼ inch apart. Refrigerate for at least 1 hour, or up to 1 day; or freeze for 20 minutes, or up to 3 days.

Place the pastry cream in the pastry bag and pipe strips of filling lengthwise over the pâte sucrée, covering it completely.

Peel the apples, cut them lengthwise in half, and remove the stems and cores. Set each half cut side down on the work surface, and slice across into ⅛-inch-thick slices, keeping the slices of each half together.

Fan out the apple slices, so that each slice overlaps the previous one by about one-third. Beginning at one corner of the tart and running down the length of that edge, stand the fanned apples in the filling. Repeat with more lines of apples until you have filled the entire tart.

The tart should be chilled before baking. Place it in the freezer for a few hours, or as long as overnight.

Preheat the oven to 350°F (standard).

Melt the butter in a small saucepan over medium heat. Whisk in the brown sugar until it has dissolved.

Carefully brush the top of the puff pastry with another coating of egg wash, then brush the apples with the warm brown sugar butter.

Bake for 30 minutes, or until the apples are beginning to lie flat against the crust; if necessary, rearrange any slices that have fallen in the wrong direction. Continue to bake for another 30 minutes, or until the apples are tender when pierced with the tip of a paring knife and the puff pastry is a rich golden brown. Set on a cooling rack and cool completely.

Serve warm or at room temperature, cut crosswise into pieces. The tart is best within a few hours of baking.

SERVES 8

The Vagaries of Dough

BY SEBASTIAN ROUXEL Making a good tart dough, a basic pâte brisée or pâte sucrée, is a fundamental pastry kitchen technique. It can be done in any number of ways. I make tart dough differently from the way my wife, Andrea, also a pastry chef, makes hers. She's American and likes a very flaky crust, so for her, it's good to see little flecks of fat in the dough. To me, that's wrong: the French way is to incorporate the fat uniformly into the flour before adding water or egg to bring the dough together. And even once

it's mixed and ready to chill, if my team sees even one speck of fat, I instruct them to get rid of it. To me it's an imperfection.

This is why for pâte sucrée, I prefer to paddle the butter until it's as soft as mayonnaise before adding the dry ingredients. This allows the flour to become uniformly coated with butter, which results in a perfectly uniform crust. For pâte brisée, I add the cold butter to the flour, which is the American tradition (and what my wife and Thomas both do), but still mix it until the butter is completely incorporated.

FAT: YOUR CHOICE

Different fats can be used for tart dough. I almost always use butter exclusively, for the richest, most flavorful crust, though I've made a pâte sablée with olive oil by thoroughly chilling the oil first and working quickly.

Sometimes Bouchon Bakery offers traditional pies. I'm not a pie guy, as Andrea will tell you. But I do love America, and so I make pies, using some lard to give the crust a savory depth you don't get using butter only. Lard also contributes to the flakiness. We use equal parts lard and butter for our pie doughs.

ROLLING DOUGH: BE GENTLE BUT FIRM

I think of all doughs as living things, even tart dough. It has an opinion. It will stretch only so far. You have to listen to the dough.

Once the dough has been chilled, it is ready to be rolled out. Rolling takes practice, care, and a gentle but firm hand. To start, I give the disk of dough a few fairly solid whacks with the rolling pin. This helps to loosen up the fat and get the dough ready to roll.

When you begin rolling, you may see the dough start to crack at the edges. I stop this when I see it by placing my left hand on top of the dough and firmly tapping the edge of the dough with the rolling pin to bring it back together. I roll in only one direction, back and forth. When I want to change directions, I turn the dough; I don't turn my rolling pin.

Anytime we can—with all tart doughs, for instance—we roll the dough between pieces of parchment paper or plastic wrap. This obviates the need to flour your work surface and thereby force more flour into your dough. It makes the dough easy to turn when you want to roll it in a different direction. The parchment also helps to prevent the dough from splitting at the edges as you roll it. And finally, it makes it easy to transfer the delicate dough to your tart pan without cracking or tearing it.

Have a look at the photograph of Thomas rolling out his tart dough, on page 132. It's perfect technique. He can work in my pastry kitchen anytime!

LIKE ANY OTHER DOUGH: THE NEED TO REST

As with any dough, tart dough needs to rest before changing environments. If you put a tart dough at room temperature into the tart pan and then into a hot oven, it will shrink and even crack. Wrap the dough and let it rest in the refrigerator before rolling it out, then chill the tart shell again before baking.

Rhubarb Tart

TARTE A LA RHUBARBE ET AU BEURRE NOISETTE

CURED RHUBARB

15 young rhubarb stalks (preferably at least 13 inches long and about ½ inch wide)	900 grams	about 2 pounds
Granulated sugar	100 grams	½ cup
Grenadine	120 grams	¼ cup + 2 tablespoons

Pâte Sucrée (page 129), cold

BROWN BUTTER FILLING

Almond flour/meal	75 grams	½ cup + 3 tablespoons
All-purpose flour	75 grams	½ cup + 1½ teaspoons
Eggs	150 grams	½ cup + 1½ tablespoons
Granulated sugar	210 grams	1 cup + 1 tablespoon
Whole milk	75 grams	¼ cup + 2 teaspoons
Heavy cream	75 grams	¼ cup + 1 tablespoon
Brown Butter (page 380), warm	165 grams	¾ cup + 1 tablespoon

Toasted Almond Streusel (recipe follows)

Powdered sugar for dusting

Without question, this is one of our favorite tarts: it's visually enticing, and it showcases the sweet-tart nature of rhubarb.

Cooks often err when making a fruit tart by not using enough fruit, given how much it will cook down; rhubarb in particular has a lot of water in it. Here we start by sprinkling the peeled rhubarb with sugar a day before cooking so it begins to release its moisture, then drain it before assembling the tart. Long, slender stalks of rhubarb are arranged in the tart shell and an almond-brown-butter filling is piped around them. It is important that the butter be warm, neither too hot nor too cool, so that it remains homogenized when added to the filling. We garnish the top with a toasted almond streusel.

We like to use small rhubarb from Holland when it comes into its short season, because it is very red, but it's fine to use whatever rhubarb is available to you. We "cure" the rhubarb with grenadine, a red syrup, which helps to color the rhubarb as well.

You'll need a 9-by-13-inch baking pan, a quarter sheet pan, and a pastry bag with a ½-inch plain tip.

FOR THE CURED RHUBARB: Trim the rhubarb so it fits lengthwise in a 9-by-13-inch baking dish. Using a paring knife (a vegetable peeler would remove too much), beginning at one end of each stalk, pull off the strings and any tough peel running the length of the rhubarb; if any of the stalks are very young and green and don't trim easily, they can be left unpeeled.

Arrange the rhubarb in the baking dish. Sprinkle with the sugar and drizzle the grenadine over the top. Cover with plastic wrap and refrigerate for 24 hours, turning and tossing the rhubarb every 8 hours to coat it evenly. (The sugar will pull out the moisture in the rhubarb as it sits.)

Drain the rhubarb on paper towels; discard the liquid in the pan.

FOR THE TART SHELL: Preheat the oven to 350°F (standard). Spray the quarter sheet pan with nonstick spray. Line the bottom with parchment paper.

Following the instructions on page 130, roll out the dough, line the sheet pan, and fill it with raw rice. Bake for 15 minutes, then rotate the pan and bake for another 15 to 20 minutes, until the dough is set and no longer sticks to the parchment paper. Remove the parchment and rice (store the rice for future use), return the pan to the oven, and bake for another 15 minutes, or until the dough is golden brown. Set the pan on a cooling rack and cool completely.

MEANWHILE, FOR THE FILLING: Whisk together the almond flour and all-purpose flour in a medium bowl, breaking up any lumps in the almond flour.

Combine the eggs and sugar in the bowl of a stand mixer fitted with the whisk attachment and mix on medium speed for about 2 minutes, until thickened. With the mixer running on medium-low, slowly add the milk and cream. Add the dry ingredients and mix on medium-low speed for a few seconds, until combined. With the mixer running, slowly add the brown butter and mix to combine. Transfer the filling to the pastry bag.

Pipe enough of the filling into the crust to cover the bottom with a ¼-inch-thick layer, and spread it evenly with a small offset spatula. Arrange the rhubarb rounded side up on top of the filling, running lengthwise in the pan (if any of the pieces are shorter than the pan, patch them with a piece cut from another stalk). Pipe the filling around the stalks, filling in any gaps, then spread any remaining filling over the top of the rhubarb (it may not be completely covered).

Bake for 40 minutes. Rotate the pan, reduce the oven temperature to 325°F, and bake for another 10 to 15 minutes, until the filling is set and golden. Set the pan on a cooling rack and cool completely.

TO SERVE: Lift the tart out of the pan with a large spatula and trim the edges of the crust. Cut into 12 pieces and garnish each piece with some streusel topping. Dust the tops lightly with powdered sugar.

PHOTOGRAPH ON PAGE 147   **SERVES 12**

Note to Professionals: In the bakery, we bake the tart in half sheet pans and trim the rhubarb to the width of the pan.

Toasted Almond Streusel

Almond Streusel Topping (page 77), cold	160 grams	1¼ cups

Preheat the oven to 325°F (standard).

Spread the streusel in an even layer on a sheet pan. Bake for about 12 minutes, turning the streusel with a metal spatula every 4 minutes, until it is golden brown and dry. Place the pan on a cooling rack and let cool completely.

Pour the streusel into a food processor and pulse to the consistency of brown sugar. The streusel can be stored in a covered container for up to 2 days.

MAKES 140 GRAMS/A GENEROUS 1 CUP

Plum Tart with Almond Cream

TARTE AUX PRUNES ET A LA CREME D'AMANDE

½ recipe Pâte Sucrée (page 129)

Almond Cream (page 376), at room temperature	250 grams	1¼ cups

8 to 10 small or 4 to 5 medium Santa Rosa plums or pluots (1½ to 2 inches in diameter)

A simple fruit tart becomes elegant when made with excellent ingredients and care. Here the filling is an almond cream topped with sliced fruit; you can use any fruit you like: peaches, apples, whatever is in season. We use plums because their color is so beautiful, and because they can be a little tart—that sweet-sour mix offsets the sweetness of the rich almond cream. (As always, we're careful about making desserts not overly sweet. To our tastes, many desserts in America are just too sweet. You shouldn't be overwhelmed by the sweetness. We use sugar judiciously, to keep all the flavors in balance.) Like most fruit, or any ingredient with a lot of water in it, the plums will shrink as they bake, so be sure to use enough fruit to fill the tart shell generously.

You'll need an 8-by-¾-inch tart ring and a pastry bag with a ½-inch plain tip.

Preheat the oven to 350°F (standard). Line a sheet pan with a Silpat or parchment paper.

Following the instructions on page 130, roll out the dough and place it in the tart ring; the shell will not be blind-baked.

Fill the pastry bag with the almond cream. Starting in the center, pipe a spiral out to the edges of the tart shell.

Cut the plums into ⅛-inch-thick wedges. Arrange a ring of plum slices, facing the same direction and each one overlapping the previous slice by about two-thirds, around the edge of the tart shell. Continue with a second ring that slightly overlaps the first. Arrange the remaining slices to fill the center of the tart.

Bake for about 45 minutes, until the crust is well browned, the filling has set, and the plums are softened and juicy. Set the pan on a cooling rack to cool completely. Although it is tempting to serve the tart right out of the oven, the juices would run and it would be difficult to cut; it is preferable to let it cool to room temperature. Or, if you want very precise slices, refrigerate the tart until cold, then cut into wedges and serve cold or at room temperature.

Run the tip of a paring knife between the top of the crust and the ring to loosen the crust, then lift off the ring.

SERVES 6 TO 8

Lemon Meringue Tarts

TARTES AU CITRON MERINGUEES

½ recipe Pâte Sucrée (page 129)

Egg whites (see Easier with the Freezer, page 108)	100 grams	¼ cup + 2½ tablespoons
Granulated sugar	200 grams	1 cup

Madeleine Cake for Lemon Meringue Tarts (page 115), frozen

Small batch of Lemon Curd (page 377)

I love individual desserts, whether they are cupcakes or cookies or these little lemon tarts, because I love having my very own. This dessert is all about contrasts in tastes and texture: the tartness of the creamy filling, the sweetness of the meringue, the crunch of the crust, and the surprise element of a layer of cake. Besides adding another textural element, the cake absorbs any moisture the meringue might release and prevents the meringue from sliding. You can use as much or as little meringue as you wish here, high or low.

You'll need a Thermapen or other candy thermometer, six 3-by-¾-inch tart rings, a pastry bag with a 1-inch plain tip, a 2¾-inch round cutter, a pastry bag with a ½-inch plain tip, and a propane torch.

FOR THE TART SHELL: Preheat the oven to 325°F (standard). Line a sheet pan with a Silpat or parchment paper.

Following the instructions on page 130, roll out the dough, line the tart rings, and fill with rice. Bake for 8 minutes, then rotate the pan and bake for another 8 minutes, or until the dough is set and no longer sticks to the parchment paper. Remove the parchment and rice (store the rice for future use), return the pan to the oven, and bake for another 12 minutes, or until the dough is cooked through and golden brown. Set the pan on a cooling rack and cool completely. Run the tip of a paring knife between the top of the crust and the ring to loosen the crust, then lift off the ring.

MEANWHILE, MAKE A SWISS MERINGUE: Place the egg whites and sugar in the bowl of a stand mixer and set over a saucepan of simmering water. Whisk until the mixture reaches 160°F/71.1°C, then immediately put the bowl on the mixer, attach the whisk attachment, and whip at medium-high speed for about 5 minutes, until the whites hold stiff peaks and are cool. Transfer to the pastry bag fitted with the 1-inch tip.

Use the round cutter to cut the frozen madeleine layer into 6 rounds.

Fill the pastry bag fitted with the ½-inch plain tip with the lemon curd.

Fill the tart shells with curd to ¼ inch from the rim of the shells (50 grams/¼ cup each). Place the cake rounds on top. Hold the pastry bag vertically over the center of each cake, about ½ inch from the surface, and pipe the meringue to cover about two-thirds of the surface (20 grams each), then pull the bag up to form a dome with as much additional meringue as you'd like. Hold a small offset spatula at the tip of the domed meringue and pull it to the edges of the crust, forming a smooth line from the tip to the outside of the shell. Wipe off the spatula and continue around the tart to form a cone shape, then use the spatula to form irregular peaks in the meringue. Using the propane torch, brown the top of the meringue.

The tarts are best the same day they are assembled. They can be refrigerated for 4 to 6 hours; remove them from the refrigerator 20 minutes before serving.

SERVES 6

Spiced Caramel Chiboust with Hazelnut Streusel and Peaches

CREME CHIBOUST AUX EPICES AVEC STREUSEL A LA NOISETTE ET PECHES SANGUINES

HAZELNUT STREUSEL

Cake flour	100 grams	¾ cup + 1 teaspoon
Almond flour/meal	100 grams	¾ cup + 2½ tablespoons
Hazelnut flour/meal	100 grams	¾ cup + 2½ tablespoons
Kosher salt	1 gram	⅜ teaspoon
Unsalted butter, cut into ½-inch pieces at room temperature	100 grams	3.5 ounces
Granulated sugar	100 grams	½ cup

CARAMEL CHIBOUST

¼ vanilla bean, split lengthwise		
A 1½-inch piece cinnamon stick		
Ground ginger	0.3 gram	⅛ teaspoon
Ground cinnamon	0.3 gram	⅛ teaspoon
Egg yolks	63 grams	¼ cup
Granulated sugar	15 grams	1 tablespoon + 1 teaspoon
	38 grams	3 tablespoons
	22 grams	2 tablespoons
Cornstarch, sifted	16 grams	2 tablespoons
Whole milk	150 grams	½ cup + 1½ tablespoons
Heavy cream	50 grams	3 tablespoons + 1 teaspoon
Egg whites	120 grams	½ cup
Silver leaf gelatin	4.8 grams	2 sheets

GARNISHES

Peach slices, cinnamon sticks, star anise, and/or a vanilla bean

---

The distinctive style of this more modern and more refined tart is characteristic of Sebastien's visual and architectural imagination as well as his taste-texture creativity. It looks very chic, and perhaps somewhat daunting to prepare at home, but most of the components can—and should—be made ahead. The crust is a pâte sucrée made with hazelnut and almond flours. The filling is a chiboust—pastry cream lightened with meringue—which is set with gelatin and frozen in a tart form. Then, shortly before serving, the chiboust is unmolded and placed on the crust, brûléed, and garnished with sliced peaches (and whole spices, if you wish). It's a wonderful tart to prepare in advance and an impressive showpiece.

A couple of touches make this even more special. A traditional crust can be flat, and a little boring, so we grate frozen hazelnut streusel over the top of the crust before baking it to add texture. And the chiboust is seasoned with bold spices, a very nontraditional touch. When you add the spices to the hot caramel, their aroma fills the room—our favorite part of making this dessert. Timing is important, so be sure to read through all the steps and have your *mise en place* organized before beginning. Note the clever way Sebastien slices the peaches, without cutting all the way down to the pits, so that the segments are very clean and uniform.

You'll need 6½- and 8-inch square tart forms, a pastry bag with a ½-inch plain tip, and a propane torch.

FOR THE HAZELNUT STREUSEL: Combine the three flours and the salt in a bowl and stir to break up any lumps.

Place the butter and sugar in the bowl of a stand mixer fitted with the paddle attachment and mix on medium-low speed until the mixture is smooth. Turn the speed to low, add the flour mixture, and mix until the dough begins to form a mass.

Transfer the dough to the work surface. Use the heel of your hand to smear the dough and work it together. Pat the dough into a square and wrap in a few layers of plastic wrap. Refrigerate until firm, about 2 hours, but preferably overnight. (The dough can be refrigerated for up to 2 days or frozen for up to 1 month.)

Roll the dough out on a piece of parchment paper into a square slightly larger than the 8-inch square tart form and just under ¼ inch thick. Place the tart form over the dough and press down to cut through the dough. Leave the form in place and remove the dough trimmings; pat the trimmings into a block and freeze overnight. Slide the parchment paper and dough (still in the form) onto a sheet pan and refrigerate overnight.

MEANWHILE, FOR THE CHIBOUST: It is important to be very organized before beginning to make the chiboust: Line a sheet pan with parchment paper and set the 6½-inch tart form in the center. Set a fine-mesh strainer over a medium saucepan. Set another strainer over a large bowl. Have a whisk and a heatproof spatula at hand.

Scrape the seeds of the vanilla bean into a small bowl and add the pod, the cinnamon stick, ginger, and ground cinnamon.

Place the egg yolks, the 15 grams/1 tablespoon plus 1 teaspoon sugar, and the sifted cornstarch in a large bowl and whisk to combine. Pour the egg whites into the bowl of a stand mixer fitted with the whisk attachment.

Place the 38 grams/3 tablespoons sugar in a large saucepan and set it on the stovetop. Pour the remaining 22 grams/2 tablespoons sugar into a small cup. Pour the milk and cream into separate small saucepans and set on the stovetop.

Place the gelatin in a small bowl of ice water to soften.

When you are ready to begin, turn the heat under both the milk and the cream to low and heat until hot. Turn the heat under the pan of sugar to medium. The sugar will begin to melt and caramelize around the edges first. As it does, use the heatproof spatula to drag any darker portions toward the center of the pan and then continue to move the sugar as needed to melt it evenly. Moving the sugar gently at this point will not adversely affect the caramel, but do not stir the sugar rapidly—it will make it harder to melt. If at any point the sugar seems to be darkening too quickly, lower the heat or remove the pan from the heat and swirl the pan to redistribute the sugar, then return it to the heat.

After about 3 minutes, the sugar should be melted and a deep caramel color. Remove the pan from the heat and carefully stir in the spices and vanilla bean. Return the pan to low heat for about 30 seconds to toast the spices, then add half of the cream to the caramel; it will bubble up and may seize. Continue stirring to remelt the caramel, then add the remaining cream. Whisk in about two-thirds of the milk. Remove from the heat and strain through the fine-mesh strainer into the saucepan. Discard the aromatics.

Whisk the remaining milk into the yolk mixture. Whisk the caramel mixture into the yolks, then strain through the fine-mesh strainer back into the saucepan.

At this point, you need to whip the egg whites and finish the caramel mixture. Turn the mixer to medium-low speed. When the whites are foamy, add half the sugar in the cup and whip to soft peaks, increasing the mixer speed as needed. The goal is for the meringue to reach stiff glossy peaks as close as possible to when the caramel mixture is ready

to be removed from the heat. If the whites are ready before the caramel, turn the mixer to the lowest setting.

Meanwhile, place the saucepan with the caramel mixture over medium-high heat and whisk until the mixture begins to thicken. This will happen very quickly; then reduce the heat to medium-low and whisk vigorously for 2 minutes to smooth the mixture. Squeeze the excess water from the gelatin and stir the gelatin into the caramel mixture to dissolve.

Immediately strain the mixture into the large bowl. Whisk one-third of the meringue into the caramel mixture to lighten it, then fold in the remaining meringue in 2 additions.

Transfer the chiboust to the pastry bag and, working from the center, pipe in a spiral to fill the 6½-inch tart form, then add more to fill the corners. Pipe in more of the mixture so it extends slightly above the top of the form. Use an offset spatula resting on the top of the form to sweep across the chiboust to create a level top. Reserve the remaining chiboust at room temperature.

Freeze the chiboust for 1 hour, during which time it may sink in the form. If so, whip the reserved chiboust slightly with a fork and spread it over the top. Freeze overnight. The chiboust can be frozen for up to 2 days.

TO BAKE THE CRUST: Preheat the oven to 325°F (standard).

Using the fine shredding holes of a box grater, grate the frozen dough onto the work surface. Pick it up with a metal spatula and gently arrange enough over the dough in the tart form to make a ¼-inch-thick layer. Bake for 18 to 20 minutes, until the color resembles that of peanut butter. Set the pan on a cooling rack and cool completely, then lift off the ring and transfer to a serving platter.

Just before serving, remove the chiboust from the freezer and warm the sides of the form with your hands. Remove the form and set the chiboust on the crust. Run the propane torch over the top of the chiboust to brûlée it. Garnish the tart with peach slices, cinnamon sticks, star anise, and/or the vanilla bean.

PHOTOGRAPH ON PAGE 157 SERVES 8

Note to Professionals: The chiboust can also be used for individual tarts or piped into fleximolds.

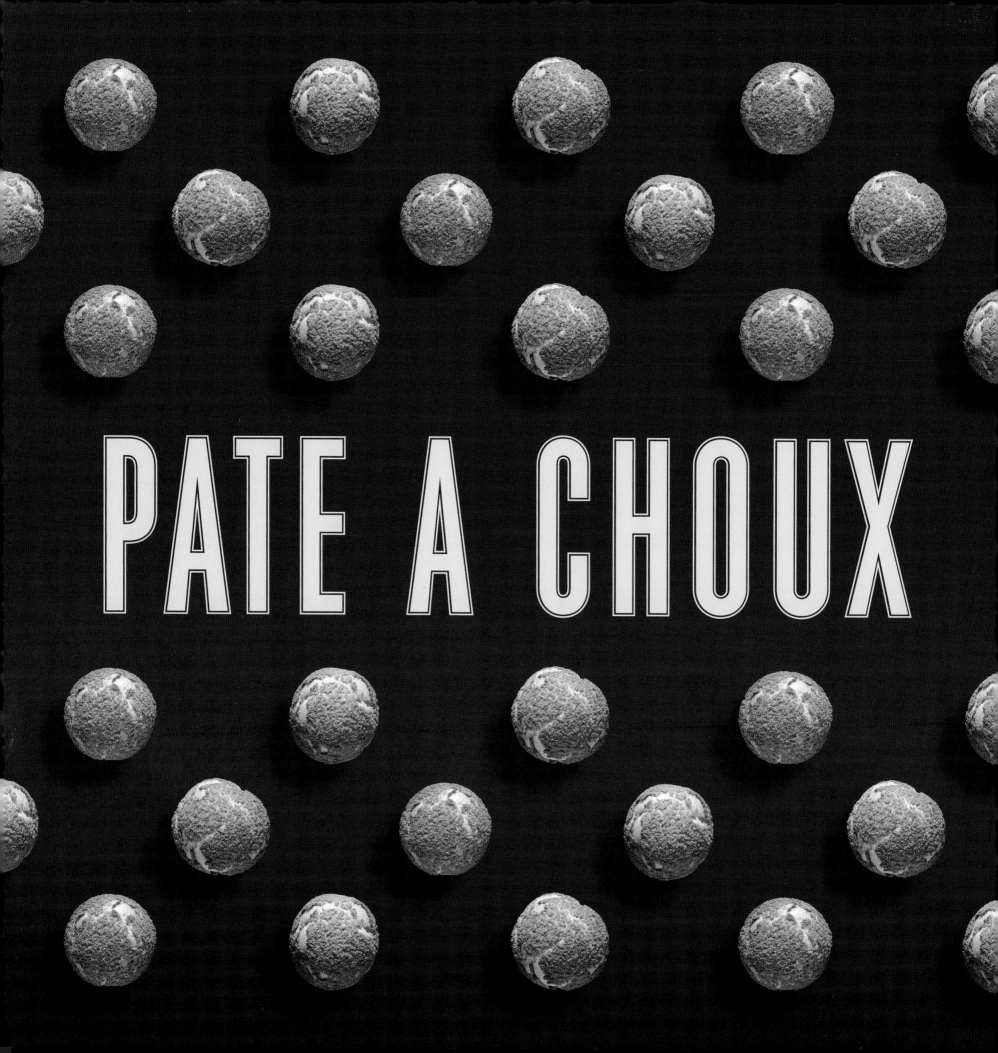

Pâte à choux is an amazing creation and, for me, a savory chef, a valuable preparation that can begin a meal (gougères), be the meal (gnocchi à la parisienne), or end the meal (profiteroles). ⊘ Sebastien loves pâte à choux in his pastry kitchen for traditional preparations such as cream puffs and éclairs. He likes to tell the story, perhaps apocryphal, of the young cook who was making pastry cream but forgot to add the sugar. To try to hide his mistake, he threw the pot into the oven. It resulted in something no one had seen before: a light, airy shell with a nearly hollow center, what we now call pâte à choux. (In the old days, pastry cream—milk, eggs, and sugar thickened with flour—was not as rich as it is now, and therefore was similar to pâte à choux in consistency.) True story or not, it underscores the mysterious nature of pastry itself and the way the most ordinary ingredients can result in the most extraordinary creations. ⊘ To make pâte à choux, you start by cooking flour in water and butter until it forms a paste, then you mix in the eggs. When you bake this mixture, the steam expands inside and the egg and flour coagulate into an airy shell that's ready to receive all sorts of fillings. The butter, of course, provides richness. ⊘ Pâte à choux is used to create some of my favorite things to eat. Cheese puffs, hot from the oven—just the smell of them is a pleasure, and to have a bite of one with a glass of Champagne is the height of refinement. A cream-filled éclair with a smooth, shiny coat of chocolate on top—heaven. All from this beguiling combination of flour, salt, water, butter, and egg.

Cream Puffs

DOUGH

Water	250 grams	1 cup + 1½ tablespoons
Unsalted butter, at room temperature	125 grams	4.4 ounces
Kosher salt	2.5 grams	¾ + ⅛ teaspoon
All-purpose flour	138 grams	1 cup
Eggs	250 to 275 grams	1 cup to 1 cup + 1½ tablespoons
Cookies for Cream Puffs (recipe follows)		
Pastry Cream (page 373)	340 grams	1½ cup
Powdered sugar for dusting		

These are traditional cream puffs, but Sebastien introduced two important innovations. The first is uniformity: unless you are extremely talented with a pastry bag, your cream puffs will be different sizes. He pipes the pâte à choux into silicone molds, so that they're completely uniform; he freezes the puffs in the molds until they are set and easy to unmold, then turns them out onto sheet pans and bakes them from frozen. Second, the crisp shell is one of the pleasures of eating a cream puff, but when the puffs sit, the shells can soften. To ensure that they stay crisp, Sebastien makes a thin cookie that rests on top of the dough. It bakes up very crisp, also giving the cream puff a visually appealing appearance. You can do this for profiteroles as well.

Because the cream puffs are frozen before they are baked, and can be kept frozen for up to 1 month, you can make the whole batch of dough and freeze the puffs, and then just bake as many as you want at a time.

You'll need medium silicone molds with spherical cavities that are 1½ inches wide and about ¾ inch deep, two pastry bags fitted with a ½-inch plain tip, a ¼-inch plain tip, a 1½-inch round cutter, and a spray bottle.

Put the molds on a sheet pan(s) and spray very lightly with nonstick spray. Set up a stand mixer with the paddle attachment.

Combine the water, butter, and salt in a medium saucepan, place over medium heat, and stir as the butter melts. (Starting at too high a temperature will evaporate some of the water before the butter has melted.) Once the butter has melted, increase the heat to medium-high and bring to a simmer, then remove the pan from the heat and, with a stiff heatproof or wooden spoon, stir in all of the flour. Continue to stir for about 2 minutes, or until the mixture has a paste-like consistency, then place over medium heat and stir rapidly for 1 to 2 minutes, until the dough pulls away from the sides of the pan and the bottom of the pan is clean; the dough should be glossy and smooth but not dry.

Immediately transfer the dough to the mixer bowl and mix on low for about 30 seconds to release some of the moisture. Slowly begin adding the eggs, about 50 grams/3 tablespoons at a time, beating until each addition is completely absorbed before adding the next one. Continue adding the eggs, reserving 25 grams/1½ tablespoons, until the dough comes away from the sides of the bowl when pulled with the paddle but then grabs back on again.

Increase the speed to medium and mix for 15 seconds to be sure all of the eggs are incorporated. Stop the mixer. When the paddle is lifted, the dough should form a bird's beak—it should hold its shape and turn down over itself but not break off. If the dough is too stiff, add the reserved egg.

Fill a spray bottle with water. Transfer the dough to a pastry bag and cool to room temperature. Pipe into the molds, filling each cavity. If the tops are uneven, dip your finger in water and smooth them.

Cover the molds with plastic wrap and freeze the puffs for about 4 hours, or until firm enough to be removed from the molds easily. The puffs can be frozen for up to 1 month.

Preheat the oven to 375°F (standard); if you will be baking more than one pan of puffs (see the headnote), position the racks in the upper and lower thirds of the oven. Line one or more sheet pans with Silpats, depending on the number of puffs you are baking.

Unmold the cream puffs and arrange on the sheet pan(s), leaving about 1½ inches between medium and 2 inches between large puffs. Spray them lightly with water.

Cut out 1½-inch cookies and set one on top of each puff. Place the pan(s) in the oven, immediately lower the oven temperature to 350°F, and bake for 25 to 30 minutes, until golden brown. If you are baking two sheets, rotate the pans after 20 minutes. Lower the oven temperature to 325°F and bake for about 10 minutes, until the puffs are light and feel hollow. Break one open if necessary: the center should appear completely cooked.

Set the pan(s) on a cooling rack and cool completely before filling or freezing (see Note).

MAKES ENOUGH FOR 48 MEDIUM PUFFS

TO FILL 12 CREAM PUFFS: Poke a hole in the bottom of each cream puff with the ¼-inch plain tip. Fill the second pastry bag with the pastry cream.

Insert the tip of the pastry bag into the hole in each puff and apply gentle pressure to fill the puff with 22 grams/about 1½ tablespoons pastry cream.

The cream puffs are best as soon as they are filled, but they can be refrigerated for up to 1 hour. Just before serving, dust the tops of the cream puffs with powdered sugar.

PHOTOGRAPH ON PAGE 163 · · · · · MAKES 12 FILLED CREAM PUFFS

NOTE ON FREEZING BAKED PATE A CHOUX PASTRIES: Once cooled, before filling, cream puffs, éclairs, and the Paris–New York can be wrapped individually, transferred to a covered container, and frozen for up to 2 weeks. To refresh, place the frozen item(s) on a sheet pan lined with a Silpat or parchment paper and bake in a 325°F (standard) oven for about 5 minutes, depending on size. Gougères can also be frozen and reheated as above, but it is not necessary to wrap individually. Store in a covered container.

FOR MISS DAISY (SEE PAGE 164): You will need 6 medium and 6 large cream puffs. For large, pipe the pâte à choux into a large silicone mold with spherical cavities that are 2 inches wide and 1¼ inches deep and freeze. When ready to bake, set on a Silpat-lined baking sheet. Cut out 1¾-inch cookies and set on the top of each puff. Place in a 375°F (standard) oven, immediately lower the oven temperature to 350°F, and bake for 30 to 35 minutes until golden brown. Lower the oven temperature to 325°F and bake for about 15 minutes, or until the puffs are light and feel hollow. Cool completely.

Cookies for Cream Puffs

Light brown sugar	180 grams	¾ cup + 3 tablespoons (lightly packed)
All-purpose flour	150 grams	1 cup + 1 tablespoon
Almond flour/meal	30 grams	¼ cup + 1 teaspoon
Cold unsalted butter, cut into ¼-inch pieces	85 grams	3 ounces

Place the brown sugar in the bowl of a stand mixer and use a fork to break up any lumps. Add the all-purpose flour, then sift the almond flour over the top; break up any lumps of almond flour remaining in the sieve, add them to the bowl, and whisk to combine.

Fit the mixer with the paddle attachment and mix on low to combine the dry ingredients. Add the butter and pulse the mixer on the lowest setting to begin incorporating and breaking up the butter. Increase the speed to low and mix for about 3 minutes, until the butter is broken up and completely incorporated into the dry mixture; the mixture will begin to come together in large crumbles but will not gather into one uniform mass.

Place two pieces of parchment paper on the work surface and divide the crumbles between the sheets. Using your hands, bring the crumbles together to begin to form a dough; it will still be crumbly. Then top each portion of dough with another piece of parchment paper and roll out to ¼ inch thick. Transfer to the back of a sheet pan, stacking one on top of the other, and freeze for 5 to 10 minutes.

Working with one sheet at a time, continue rolling, freezing the dough again as it softens, until it is ¹⁄₁₆ inch thick. During this process, the dough will crack and gaps will form; patch them as needed with bits of dough. Do not worry if the edges are a bit rough; the cookies will be cut with a cutter.

Freeze until cold before cutting out cookies. The dough can be frozen for up to 1 month. For more compact storage, once frozen the dough can be cut into rounds and refrozen between sheets of parchment paper.

Cut and bake the cookies on top of the cream puffs as directed in the recipe.

MAKES 50 MEDIUM COOKIES

A thin piece of the cookie dough is placed on top of each unbaked cream puff.

As it bakes, the cookie molds to the puff, browns, and crisps, ensuring a crunchy surface as you bite in.

MISS DAISY

Playful and fun, Miss Daisy is a special treat for kids or an impressive dessert centerpiece. To make 6, you will need 6 large cream puffs for the bodies and 6 medium cream puffs for the heads.

Color five 100-gram pieces of Carma rolling fondant five different colors, using 1 drop each of Rose Pink, Sky Blue, Leaf Green, Violet, and Lemon Yellow Chefmaster food coloring. Wrap them in plastic wrap and let rest overnight.

All the pieces of fondant should be rolled to just under $\frac{1}{8}$ inch thick, using a small fondant rolling pin. Keep any fondant you aren't working with wrapped in plastic wrap.

Roll out 800 grams of white fondant. Cut out six 4-inch rounds for the dresses, six $3\frac{1}{8}$-inch rounds for the hats, and six $2\frac{7}{8}$-inch rounds for the collars. Drape the rounds over ramekins, bowls, or other forms and crimp or shape the edges to make ruffled hems and collars and the brims of the hats. Use a Daisy Marguerite Plunger Set to cut a variety of daisies from the remaining white fondant. Let the fondant rest for 1 hour, or until it has stiffened.

Roll the pink, blue, green, and violet fondant into 8-inch rounds. Cut daisies from the pink round. Cut two 6-by- $\frac{3}{16}$-inch strips from each of the remaining colors. Shape each strip into a bow and trim the ends on an angle. Dab the back of each hat lightly with water and attach a bow to the hat, pressing lightly to secure it.

Roll the yellow fondant into an 8-inch round. Pinch off a piece the size of a pencil eraser and push it through a fine-mesh strainer to create the textured center of a flower. Using a small paintbrush, dab the center of a flower with water, then add a yellow center and press lightly to secure it. Continue with the remaining flowers; we like to leave some centers empty, turn up the petals, and use to garnish the platter. Attach a daisy to the center of each bow and arrange more flowers randomly on the dresses. (Any extra fondant can be wrapped in plastic wrap for future projects.)

If you'd like to fill the cream puffs, poke a hole in the bottom of each one using a $\frac{1}{4}$-inch plain tip. Fill a pastry bag fitted with a $\frac{1}{2}$-inch plain tip with Diplomat Cream (page 374) and pipe about 55 grams/1 generous tablespoon each into the large puffs and 25 grams/$\frac{1}{2}$ tablespoon each into the medium puffs.

Set the dresses over the large puffs. Dab the top of each dress with water, set a collar, ruffled side up, on top, and press lightly to secure. Position a medium cream puff on each collar and top with a hat.

PIPING WITH A PASTRY BAG

① Fold back the end of the pastry bag to form a cuff. Drop the pastry tip into the bag and cut off the point of the bag to form an opening, just large enough to expose about ½-inch of the tip. Fill the pastry bag with the piping mixture. ② Unfold the cuff and use a scraper to move the piping mixture down to the tip. ③ Twist the end of the bag until the piping mixture comes through the tip.

PLAIN

PASTRY BAGS AND TIPS

Canvas pastry bags used to be standard, but readily available disposable pastry bags are what we now prefer and recommend. They're cleaner, easier, and safer to work with.

There are all kinds of tips available; the three basic ones you need are a plain tip, a star tip, and a French star tip (which has many more teeth than the standard star tip—we use it to pipe éclairs; see page 168).

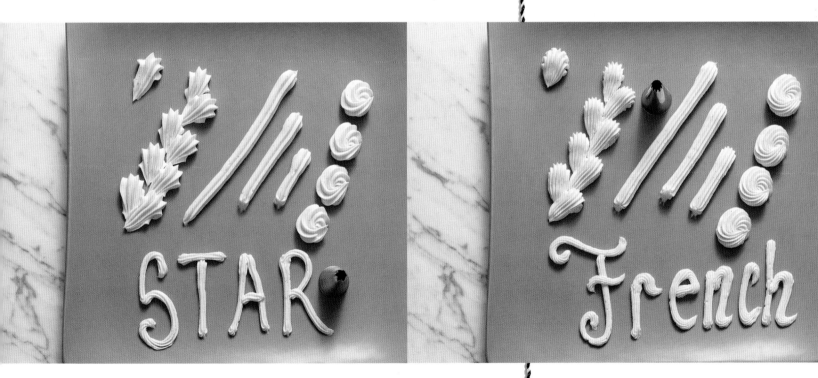

Eclairs

The éclair is a wonderful French tradition. For decades—centuries, probably—the only type made in France was the traditional pastry-cream-filled éclair with a chocolate, coffee, or plain white fondant glaze. As the craft of pâtisserie has evolved, éclairs with different fillings and different glazes have become common. (Some bakeshops now even sell savory éclairs, filled with vegetable purees.) Here we offer three versions.

I love that Sebastien has found a way to make uniform éclairs. He chills the pâte à choux before piping it, so that it pipes better. Then, rather than piping the dough using a plain tip and drawing a fork down the pastry to create the traditional grooves, he uses a French star tip, which results in uniform grooves over the entire surface; these give the éclair a better appearance and allow the pastry to expand evenly. Misting the éclairs with water right before baking also helps them to expand uniformly and without cracking.

Pâte à Choux for Eclairs

All-purpose flour	175 grams	1¼ cups
Granulated sugar	33 grams	2 tablespoons + 2 teaspoons
Water	240 grams	1 cup
Unsalted butter, at room temperature	120 grams	4.2 ounces
Kosher salt	2.5 grams	¾ + ⅛ teaspoon
Eggs	250 grams	1 cup

This pâte à choux dough is a little stiffer than the version we use for the cream puffs. Because the cream puffs are molded, the dough can be fairly loose. The éclair dough is piped onto sheet pans, so it needs extra body to hold up.

You'll need a pastry bag with an Ateco #867 French star tip.

Combine the flour and sugar in a small bowl. Using the proportions above, make the dough as directed in the cream puff recipe (page 160), adding the flour and sugar mixture in the same way and adding all the eggs.

Transfer the dough to the pastry bag and refrigerate until cold before using.

MAKES 785 GRAMS/28 OUNCES

NOTE ON FREEZING: Pâte à Choux for Eclairs (used for éclairs, Paris–New York, and Swans) is not ideal for freezing before baking because the lines created by using the French star tip can be compromised when you wrap or cover the dough in order to freeze it.

Chocolate Eclairs

Pâte à Choux for Eclairs (left), chilled in the pastry bag

Chocolate Pastry Cream (page 373)

Chocolate Glaze (page 377)

You'll need a spray bottle, a ¼-inch plain tip, and a pastry bag with a ½-inch plain tip.

Position the racks in the upper and lower thirds of the oven and preheat the oven to 375°F (standard).

TO MAKE A TEMPLATE: The guidelines for the éclairs should be visible through the lighter portion of a Silpat. Using a fine-tip marker, draw six 6-inch lines 2 inches apart on a large piece of parchment paper. Place the parchment on a sheet pan and position the Silpat over it.

Fill a small bowl and the spray bottle with water.

From left to right: Lime Coconut Eclair (page 174), Chocolate Eclair (page 168), Dulce de Leche Eclair (page 174)

TO PIPE AND BAKE THE ECLAIRS: (See photographs, pages 170–71.) Starting at the side of the Silpat farthest from you, hold the tip of the pastry bag ¾ inch above the Silpat and apply gentle, steady pressure as you pipe the first éclair. When the éclair is about 6 inches long, begin to lessen the pressure, and then stop it as you bring the dough back over itself, leaving a ½ inch curl at the end of the éclair. Pipe 5 more éclairs on the Silpat. Carefully slide out the template and repeat with a second sheet pan and Silpat. Wet your finger and press down the tip of each éclair, then spray them lightly with water. Place the sheet pans in the oven and immediately lower the oven temperature to 350°F. Bake for about 40 minutes, until the éclairs are beginning to brown; rotate the pans halfway through. Lower the temperature to 325°F and bake for an additional 20 minutes, or until golden brown. Lower the temperature to 300°F and bake for 10 minutes longer, or until the puffs are light and feel hollow. If you break one open, the center should be completely cooked. Set on a cooling rack and cool completely before filling or freezing (see Note on Freezing Baked Pâte à Choux Pastries, page 161).

TO FILL THE ECLAIRS: With the ¼-inch plain tip, poke 2 holes, 1½ inches in from each end, into the bottom of each éclair. Fill the pastry bag with the chocolate pastry cream. Place the tip of the pastry bag into one hole and apply gentle pressure to begin filling the éclair with pastry cream. (You may begin to see pastry cream through the second hole; this is okay.) Pipe cream as needed into the second hole until the éclair feels heavy; use 60 grams/about ¼ cup cream for each éclair. Repeat with the remaining éclairs and pastry cream.

TO GLAZE THE ECLAIRS: Pour the glaze into a deep bowl that is about 7 inches wide (just slightly larger than an éclair).

Hold an éclair parallel to the surface of the glaze and dip it into the glaze to coat the top; pull it out of the glaze, still parallel to it, and turn the éclair upward, letting the excess run off, then rotate slightly to one side to stop the glaze from dripping. Set on a serving platter and repeat with the remaining éclairs.

The éclairs are best eaten as soon as they are completed, but they can be refrigerated for up to 1 hour.

MAKES 12 ECLAIRS

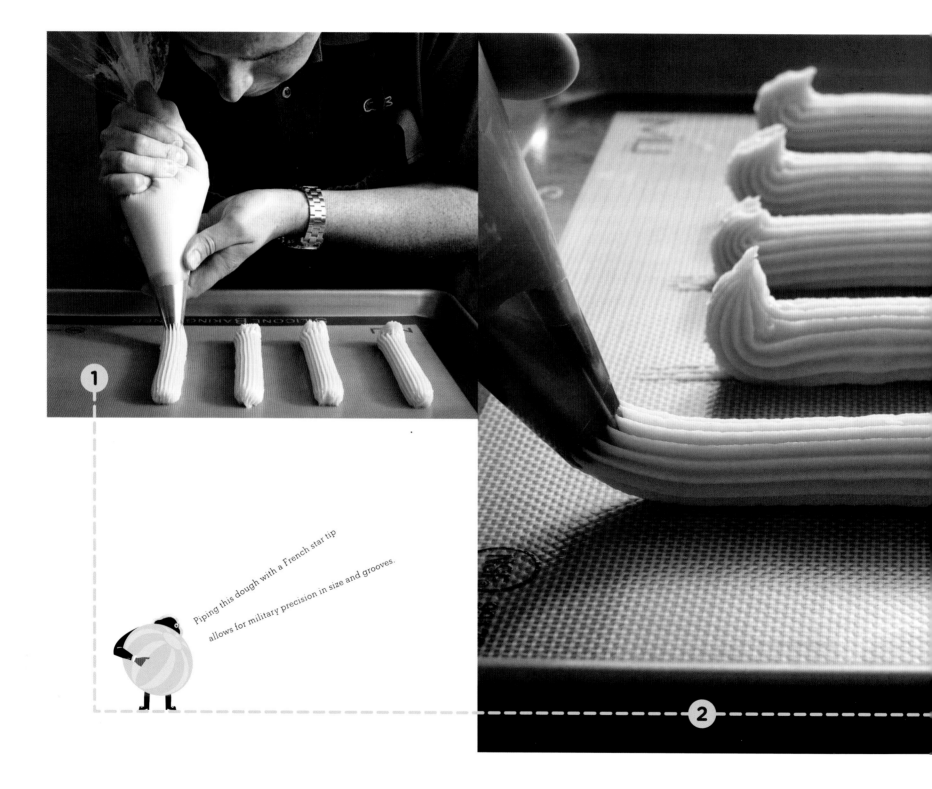

Piping this dough with a French star tip allows for military precision in size and grooves.

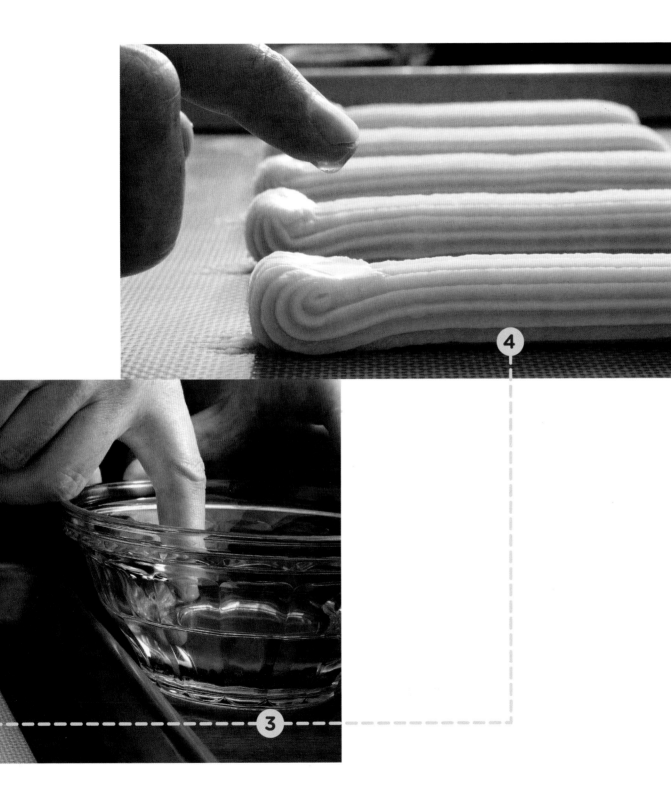

Lime Coconut Eclairs

Pâte à Choux for Eclairs (page 168), chilled in the pastry bag		
Unsweetened finely shredded dried coconut	200 grams	2¾ cups
Pouring/icing fondant	540 grams	1½ cups
Low-fat or nonfat milk	65 grams	¼ cup
Lime Curd (page 377)	800 grams	3½ cups

You'll need a spray bottle, a ¼-inch plain tip, and a pastry bag with a ½-inch plain tip. ● *For this recipe, we use Caullet pouring fondant.*

Create a template and pipe and bake the éclairs as directed on pages 168–69. Let cool completely.

Preheat the oven to 325°F (standard).

Spread the coconut on a sheet pan and bake for about 5 minutes, stirring as needed, until it turns an even golden brown. Let cool completely, then pour into a wide, shallow bowl. Place the fondant in a heatproof bowl that is about 7 inches wide (just slightly larger than an éclair) and set over a pot of simmering water, stirring to loosen the fondant. Add the milk 5 grams/1 teaspoon at a time as needed to help loosen it. Do not heat it beyond 95°F/35°C. Remove from the heat and let cool to room temperature. The fondant will be thick but fluid enough to glaze the éclairs.

TO FILL AND GLAZE THE ECLAIRS: Fill the éclairs with the lime curd, as directed in the recipe for chocolate éclairs (page 169). Then, one at a time, dip each one into the fondant to glaze, as directed in the recipe for chocolate éclairs, immediately dip the glazed top into the toasted coconut, and set on a serving platter.

The éclairs are best eaten as soon as they are completed, but they can be refrigerated for up to 1 hour.

PHOTOGRAPH ON PAGE 169   **MAKES 12 ECLAIRS**

Dulce de Leche Eclairs

Pâte à Choux for Eclairs (page 168), chilled in the pastry bag	
Dulce de Leche (recipe follows)	
Diplomat Cream (page 374)	
Candied Pecans (recipe follows)	
Caramélia Rectangles (recipe follows; optional)	

You'll need a spray bottle and a pastry bag with an Ateco #863 French star tip.

Create a template and pipe and bake the éclairs as directed on pages 168–69. Let cool completely.

Using a serrated knife, cut off the top third of each éclair (the tops will not be used).

TO FILL THE ECLAIRS: Spoon 30 grams/about 1½ tablespoons of the dulce de leche into each éclair bottom.

Fill the pastry bag with the diplomat cream. Pipe the cream in a spiral rosette pattern over the dulce de leche in each éclair, extending just past the top of the éclair. Arrange 6 or 7 pecans along the right edge of the spiral. Pipe a second spiral on top, leaving the right halves of the pecans exposed. Top with a Caramélia rectangle, if using, and set on a serving platter. Repeat with the remaining éclairs.

The éclairs are best eaten as soon as they are completed, but they can be refrigerated for up to 1 hour.

PHOTOGRAPHS ON PAGES 169, 172, AND 173   **MAKES 12 ECLAIRS**

Dulce de Leche

One 14-ounce (397-gram) can sweetened condensed milk

Remove the label from the can. Stand the can in a large saucepan that will hold the can upright with at least 1 inch of water to cover, and add water to cover the can generously (it is important to keep the can completely covered with water throughout the cooking process). Bring the water just to a boil for 4 hours. Cook at a low boil, adding more water as necessary to keep the can covered by at least 1 inch. Remove from the heat and let the can cool completely in the water.

The dulce de leche can be stored in the can at room temperature; once opened, it can be transferred to a covered container and refrigerated for up to 1 month.

MAKES 385 GRAMS / 1½ CUPS

Candied Pecans

Whole pecans	500 grams	4½ cups
Granulated sugar	114 grams	½ cup + 1 tablespoon
Water	30 grams	2 tablespoons

This is a simple recipe, but the timing is important. The nuts must be warm when they are added to the syrup, to speed the crystallization of the caramelized sugar on the pecans.

Preheat the oven to 325°F (standard).

Spread the nuts on a baking sheet and place in the oven to toast.

Meanwhile, when the nuts are becoming fragrant, after 5 to 6 minutes, combine the sugar and water in a large frying pan and bring to a boil over medium heat, stirring to dissolve the sugar.

Add the pecans to the syrup and stir constantly until they have a white crystallized appearance; the syrup should not take on any color. Transfer the nuts to a plate or platter and cool completely.

MAKES 570 GRAMS / 5½ CUPS

Caramélia Rectangles

Grapeseed or canola oil		
Valrhona Caramélia 34% chocolate, tempered (see page 370)	100 grams	3.5 ounces

You'll need a 6-by-12-inch piece of acetate and a bicycle cutter (see page 71; optional). ● *For this recipe, we use Valrhona Caramélia 34% chocolate.*

Lightly oil the work surface to anchor the acetate, lay the acetate on it, and press against it to be sure the acetate is perfectly smooth. Spoon about one-third of the chocolate onto the acetate and spread it in a thin, even layer extending past the edges of the acetate. Place the tip of a paring knife under a corner of the acetate, carefully lift it, and move it to a clean section of the work surface.

After about 2 minutes (the time will vary depending on the temperature in the room), the top of the chocolate will appear matte rather than shiny. The chocolate should be cut at this point, before it has hardened.

The size of the chocolate rectangles should match the length of the éclairs: we use 6-by-1-inch strips. A bicycle cutter works best, but you can also use a 1-inch-wide ruler. Hold the ruler above the chocolate and use it as a guide, running a knife down the length of the ruler to cut six 1-inch-wide lengthwise strips of chocolate. Then, make a cut across the center to make twelve 6-by-1-inch rectangles.

Line a sheet pan with parchment paper. Once the chocolate is no longer tacky to the touch, move the acetate to the sheet pan, cover with another piece of parchment, and set another sheet pan on top to keep the rectangles from curling.

Just before you are ready to use the chocolate, put the pan in the refrigerator for 5 minutes to harden it completely.

MAKES 12 RECTANGLES

PATE A CHOUX

Pâte à choux is wonderful but also unpredictable. It can puff out in all directions and often cracks, especially if you don't add enough egg. Perhaps people worry that the dough will become too loose if they add more egg, but not adding enough results in a stiff dough that's likely to develop big fissures while baking. And the dough needs the suppleness and flexibility the egg white provides.

Other tricks of the trade: If piping the dough free-form onto a Silpat or parchment paper, chill it before you pipe it, so it doesn't spread too much. Or pipe the dough into molds for perfect and uniform cream puffs every time. (They're also much easier to make this way.) Mist the pâte à choux with water before putting it into the oven to encourage a good even rise without cracking.

All pâte à choux is baked in the same way—it is put into a 375°F oven and then the temperature is immediately lowered. This helps to create steam quickly, facilitating the rise; lowering the temperature lets the interior cook without overcooking the shell. Baked pâte à choux pastries freeze very well; see the Note on page 161.

Swans

CYGNES A LA CHANTILLY

Pâte à Choux for Eclairs (page 168)

MOUSSELINE

Pastry Cream (page 373)	150 grams	½ cup + 2½ tablespoons
Basic Buttercream (page 375), at room temperature	150 grams	¾ cups + 2 tablespoons
Sweetened Whipped Cream (page 378)	1 small batch	
Powdered sugar for dusting		

These are very old-fashioned, and I love them for this reason—and also because they remind me of happy days cooking at La Rive, a restaurant in the Hudson Valley, when I was a young chef. They're a great thing to make with kids and are fun to present at the table. Work carefully when piping the batter so that you have nicely shaped bodies and elegantly curved necks—don't forget the cute little beaks.

If you have two ovens, use them, as the necks and the bodies bake for different times, and pâte à choux generally bakes best in the center of the oven. You will have extra batter, but it's a good idea to pipe extra bodies and heads/necks so you can use the best ones—or pipe and freeze the extras to bake another time.

You'll need a spray bottle and three pastry bags: one with a ¼-inch plain tip, one with an Ateco #829 star tip, and one with an Ateco #867 French star tip.

Position the racks in the upper and lower thirds of the oven and preheat the oven to 375°F (standard). Line two sheet pans with parchment paper and pipe a bit of pâte à choux under each corner to attach the paper to the pans. Fill the spray bottle with water.

Fill the pastry bag with the plain tip with about 80 grams/½ cup of the pâte à choux for the heads and necks. Fill the pastry bag with the #829 star tip with the remaining pâte à choux for the bodies.

FOR THE BODIES: Use about 50 grams of pâte à choux for each body: Begin by piping the rounded neck end of one body on one of the sheet pans, then continue piping, pulling the bag farther away each time, to narrow the body, and finally twisting the bag to create a tail. Repeat to form a total of 8 bodies.

FOR THE HEADS AND NECKS: Use about 5 grams of pâte à choux for each head and neck: Pipe a head ½ to ¾ inch in diameter on the second baking sheet, then continue piping an S shape, stopping short of completing the final curve of the S. Form a small beak by piping a dab of pâte à choux on the head and pulling the bag away from the head to narrow it and form a point. Repeat to form a total of 8 heads/necks.

Spray the bodies, heads, and necks lightly with water. Place the bodies in the upper third of the oven and the heads/necks in the lower third. Immediately reduce the oven temperature to 350°F. After 15 minutes, turn the heads/necks over and continue to bake for 5 minutes, or until they are golden brown and dry. Because the necks are so thin, it is important to keep a close eye on them. When they are done, remove from the oven and place on a cooling rack

Continue baking the bodies, for a total of 40 minutes, at 350°F. Then reduce the heat to 325°F and bake for 10 minutes. Reduce the heat to 300°F and bake for 20 minutes longer, or until the bodies are golden brown and thoroughly cooked; they should feel light. Remove from the oven and place on a cooling rack and cool completely before filling or freezing (see Note on Freezing Baked Pâte à Choux Pastries, page 161).

Using a serrated knife, cut off the top third of each body, being careful not to cut off the tails. Set the bottoms aside. Cut the tops lengthwise in half to create the wings; set aside.

FOR THE MOUSSELINE: Place the pastry cream in the bowl of a stand mixer fitted with the whisk attachment and whip on medium speed until smooth. Add the buttercream and whip until well combined and smooth.

Fill the pastry bag with the #867 tip with the whipped cream. Spoon the mousseline into the bodies. Beginning at the back end, pipe a spiral of the whipped cream over the mousseline in each body. Arrange the wings on the swans, gently pushing the cut sides of the wings into the whipped cream, just to anchor them, Do the same with the heads/necks.

Dust the swans with powdered sugar and serve immediately.

MAKES 8 SWANS

During my time at La Rive, in the Hudson Valley, I loved to make these pâte à choux swans, which I learned from my favorite book at the time, Jacques Pépin's *La Technique,* the book that taught a legion of chefs of my generation so much about classical French technique. (And I would miss a great opportunity if I failed to note an important connection: *La Technique* was published in 1976 by a young editor named Ann Bramson, the very person who has edited and published all my books, including this one.)

Ducky! Just ducky!

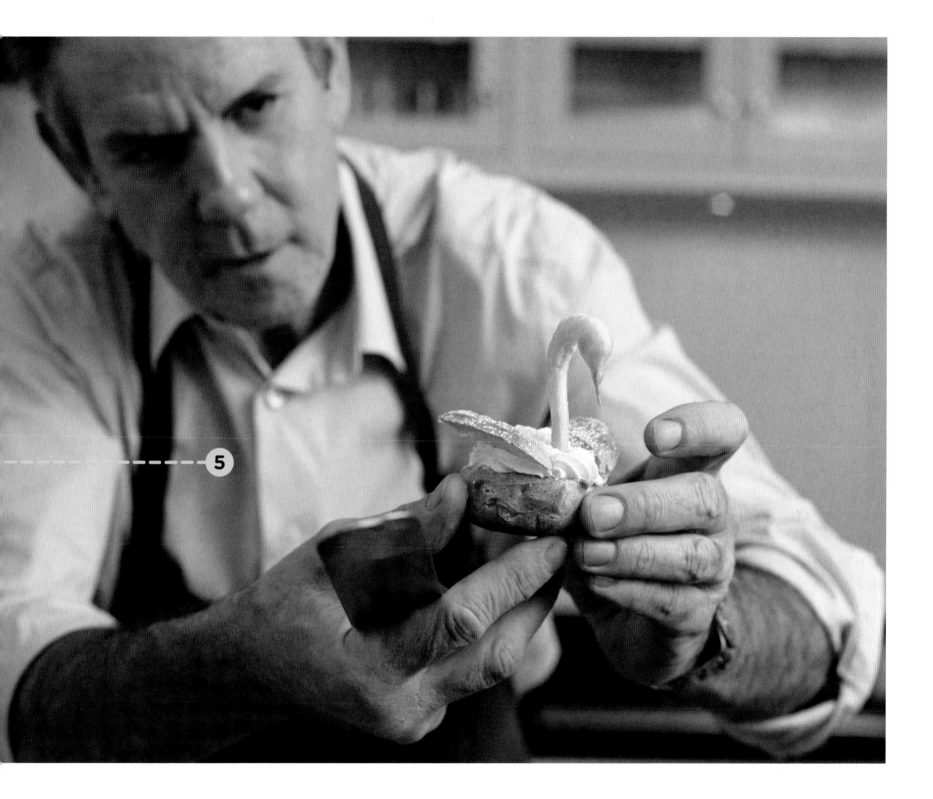

5

Paris-New York

Pâte à Choux for Eclairs (page 168)

Salted peanuts (without skin), coarsely chopped	120 grams	¾ cup

FILLING

Basic Buttercream (page 375)	125 grams	¾ cup + 1½ tablespoons
Creamy peanut butter	125 grams	½ cup
Kosher salt	0.4 gram	⅛ teaspoon
Diplomat Cream (page 374)	500 grams	2⅓ cups
Salted peanuts (without skin)	120 grams	¾ cup
Powdered sugar for dusting		

The Paris-Brest is more than a century old, invented to commemorate the famous bicycle race. The dessert is made with pâte à choux piped into a ring (the shape of a tire), baked, split, and filled with a praline pastry cream. I love classics, and Sebastien loves to put a twist on them. Here he combines a French creation with something very American—peanut butter (making this a reflection of his journey). We think of peanut butter as commonplace here, but it was new to Sebastien. He adds Skippy natural peanut butter to the pastry cream filling and garnishes the dessert with whole and chopped salted peanuts rather than using the traditional praline buttercream and almonds.

These are impressive individual desserts to serve at a dinner party.

You'll need a 3½-inch oval cutter, a spray bottle, a pastry bag with an Ateco #867 French star tip, and a pastry bag with an Ateco #864 French star tip. ● For this recipe, we use Skippy natural creamy peanut butter.

Position the racks in the upper and lower thirds of the oven and preheat the oven to 375°F (standard).

TO MAKE A TEMPLATE: The templates for the pâte à choux should be visible through the lighter part of a Silpat. Using a fine-tip marker and the oval cutter as a guide, draw 6 ovals about 2 inches apart on a large piece of parchment paper. Place the parchment on a sheet pan and position the Silpat over it.

TO PIPE AND BAKE THE PATE A CHOUX: Fill a small bowl and the spray bottle with water. Fill the pastry bag with the #867 star tip with the pâte à choux. Pipe the pâte à choux around the oval templates, overlapping the ends of each one to make a solid oval. Carefully slide out the template and repeat with a second sheet pan and Silpat.

Wet your finger and press down the overlap to smooth it. Sprinkle 10 grams/1 tablespoon chopped peanuts on top of each oval, pressing them lightly into the batter. Spray the ovals lightly with water.

Place the sheet pans in the oven, immediately lower the oven temperature to 350°F, and bake for 40 minutes, or until the pastry is beginning to brown. Lower the temperature to 325°F and bake for 5 minutes more, or until golden brown. Lower the temperature to 300°F and bake for about 10 minutes longer, until the puffs are light and hollow. If you break one open, the center should be completely cooked. Set on a cooling rack and cool completely before filling or freezing (see Note on Freezing Baked Pâte à Choux Pastries, page 161).

TO MAKE THE FILLING: Combine the buttercream, peanut butter, and salt in the bowl of a stand mixer fitted with the paddle attachment and mix until smooth. Remove the bowl from the mixer and fold in the diplomat cream.

TO FILL THE PASTRIES: Using a serrated knife, cut off the top third of each oval. Set the tops aside.

Fill the pastry bag with the #864 star tip with the peanut butter cream. Pipe the cream in a spiral rosette pattern toward the outer edge of each oval, then make a second spiral around the inside edge. Arrange 10 grams/1 tablespoon of the whole peanuts between the spirals in each oval. Dust the tops with powdered sugar and place over the filling. Set the assembled pastries on a serving platter.

The pastries are best eaten as soon as they are completed, but they can be refrigerated for up to 1 hour.

MAKES 12 PASTRIES

Gougères

Water	144 grams	½ cup + 1½ tablespoons
Unsalted butter	63 grams	2.2 ounces
Kosher salt	1.8 grams	½ + ⅛ teaspoon
Freshly ground black pepper	0.3 gram	⅛ + 1/16 teaspoon
All-purpose flour	90 grams	½ cup + 2½ tablespoons
Eggs	150 grams	½ cup + 1½ tablespoons
Shredded aged Gruyère	63 grams	scant 1 cup

These gougères go back to the earliest days of The French Laundry. It was always one of my favorite moments of the day when, just before service, they came out of the oven and filled the kitchen with their comforting aroma. They are basic and delicious.

As with the cream puffs, we pipe these into silicone molds to ensure that they are uniform, freeze them, and then bake them. It's a great trick. Like the cream puffs, the unbaked gougères can be frozen for up to 1 month, allowing you to bake as many or as few as you like at a time.

We often pipe Mornay, a rich cheese sauce, into the centers of the baked gougères for an over-the-top canapé.

You'll need small silicone molds with spherical cavities that are 1.2 inches wide and 0.6 inches deep, a spray bottle, and a pastry bag with a ⅜-inch plain tip.

Put the molds on a sheet pan and spray very lightly with nonstick spray. Set up a stand mixer with the paddle attachment.

Combine the water, butter, salt, and pepper in a medium saucepan, place over medium heat, and stir to combine as the butter melts. (Starting at too high a temperature will evaporate some of the water before the butter has melted.) Once the butter has melted, increase the heat to medium-high and bring to a simmer, then remove the pan from the heat and, with a stiff heatproof or wooden spoon, stir in all of the flour. Continue to stir for about 1½ minutes, until the mixture has a paste-like consistency, then place over medium heat and stir rapidly for about 1 minute, until the dough pulls away from the sides of the pan and the bottom of the pan is clean; the dough should be glossy and smooth but not dry.

Immediately transfer the dough to the mixer bowl and mix on low for about 30 seconds to release some of the moisture. Slowly begin adding the eggs, 50 grams/3 tablespoons at a time, beating until each addition is completely absorbed before adding the next one. Continue adding the eggs, mixing until the dough pulls away from the sides of the bowl when pulled with the paddle but then grabs back on again.

Increase the speed to medium and mix for 15 seconds to be sure all of the eggs are incorporated. Stop the mixer. When the paddle is lifted, the dough should form a bird's beak—it should hold its shape and turn down over itself but not break off. Add the cheese and pulse to incorporate.

Fill a spray bottle with water. Transfer the dough to the pastry bag and pipe it into the molds, filling each cavity. If the tops are uneven, dip your finger in water and smooth them.

Freeze the gougères for about 4 hours, or until firm enough to be removed from the molds easily. (The gougères can be frozen for up to 1 month.)

Preheat the oven to 375°F (standard); if you will be baking more than one sheet of gougères, position the racks in the upper and lower thirds of the oven. Line one or more sheet pans with Silpats, depending on the number of gougères you are baking.

Unmold the gougères and arrange on the sheet pan(s), leaving about 1 inch between them. Spray the gougères lightly with water. Place in the oven, immediately lower the oven temperature to 350°F, and bake for 25 to 30 minutes, until golden brown. If you are baking two sheets, rotate the pans after 20 minutes. Lower the temperature to 325°F and bake for about 10 minutes, until the gougères are light and feel hollow. If you break one open, the center should be completely cooked. Set the pan(s) on a cooling rack and cool completely before filling or freezing (see Note on Freezing Baked Pâte à Choux Pastries, page 161).

To serve warm, put back in the oven for about 5 minutes.

MAKES 4 DOZEN BITE-SIZE GOUGERES

NOTE ON MAKING OTHER SIZES: We like to make these in bite-size portions, but they can also be piped into the medium or large molds used for the Cream Puffs (page 160). This recipe will make about 2½ dozen medium gougères or 1 dozen large. The baking time will need to be increased.

Of the vast array of breads we enjoy, brioche is among the aristocracy, loaded as it is with eggs and butter. We call doughs to which butter and/or eggs are added "enriched," and of the enriched breads, brioche is the easiest to make. It's also one of the most fun, because you can make so many different things using brioche dough, from *brioche à tête,* with its traditional topknot, to doughnuts to sticky buns. ⊘ I have a powerful emotional association with brioche that's bound up with the memory of my friend Jean-Louis Palladin, who died in 2001 at age fifty-five. It was at his restaurant Jean-Louis at the Watergate, in Washington, D.C., that I first had foie gras paired with brioche. It seems somewhat counterintuitive, combining a very rich dough with the richest of all kitchen preparations, *foie gras au torchon,* but it is a case where rich elevates rich. It was a revelation to me. For years, we've used Jean-Louis's brioche recipe and served it with our *torchon.* That excellent all-purpose brioche recipe appears on page 313. Most of the following recipes call for the brioche to be mixed the night before baking.

Sticky Buns

SCHMEAR

Light brown sugar	255 grams	1⅓ cups (lightly packed)
Unsalted butter, at room temperature	168 grams	6 ounces
Clover honey	30 grams	1½ tablespoons
Myers's dark rum	5 grams	1 teaspoon
Vanilla paste	2.6 grams	½ teaspoon
Whole pecans	215 grams	2 cups
Brioche Dough for Sticky Buns (page 313)		
Pastry Cream (page 373)	140 grams	½ cup + 2 tablespoons
Ground cinnamon	1.3 grams	½ teaspoon

Sticky buns are the American version of *pain aux raisins,* a favorite French breakfast bread. Here brioche dough is rolled into a square, spread with pastry cream and a layer of our "schmear"—a mixture of brown sugar, butter, honey, rum, and vanilla—and sprinkled with pecans. The dough is rolled up and sliced into disks, which are put in muffin pans that have been filled with more schmear and pecans. This can bake up fantastically messy, with caramelizing sugar bubbling up and over the buns. The result is a very moist and delicious sticky bun.

You'll need a 6-cup jumbo muffin pan.

FOR THE SCHMEAR: Place the brown sugar in a bowl and break up any lumps with a fork.

Place the butter in the bowl of a stand mixer fitted with the paddle attachment. Turn to medium-low speed and cream the butter, warming the bowl as needed (see Pommade, page 190), until the butter is the consistency of mayonnaise and holds a peak when the paddle is lifted. Add the sugar and mix for 3 to 4 minutes, until fluffy. Scrape the bowl again. Add the honey, rum, and vanilla paste and mix on low for 1 minute to combine.

Place 35 grams/2 tablespoons of the schmear in each muffin cup. Set the pan in the oven for about 1 minute to melt the schmear.

Sprinkle 15 grams/2 tablespoons of the pecans into each cup. Place on a baking sheet and set aside.

TO SHAPE AND BAKE THE BUNS: Run a bowl scraper around the sides and bottom of the bowl of brioche to release the dough and turn it onto a lightly floured work surface. Using a rolling pin, roll out the dough, flipping and fluffing it (see Note, page 215), into a 16-inch square.

Spread the pastry cream in an even layer over the dough, then spread 140 grams/½ cup plus 1 tablespoon of the schmear in an even layer over the pastry cream. Dust with the cinnamon and sprinkle with the remaining 125 grams/1¼ cups pecans.

Lift the end nearest you and roll the dough up as tightly as possible. Turn the roll seam side down, trim the ends, and cut into 6 equal portions. Tuck the end of each roll underneath itself to keep it from unraveling as it bakes and set in a muffin cup. Put your index finger in the center of each roll and push the center layers outward, making a small opening in the center. (The opening will close up as the buns proof.) Then gently press the top of each bun so the edges reach the sides of the cup. (See Note on Freezing Unbaked Brioche Pastries, page 193.)

Cover with a plastic tub or a cardboard box and let proof for 1 to 1½ hours, or until the buns have expanded to fill the cups and risen about ½ inch above the top of the pan.

Preheat the oven to 350°F (standard).

Bake for 35 to 40 minutes, or until the sticky buns are a rich golden brown and, when tested with a toothpick, there are no undercooked areas in the center. Set a Silpat on the work surface and immediately invert the muffin pan onto the Silpat, letting the melted schmear run down the sides of the sticky buns. Any schmear that pools on the Silpat can quickly be spooned back over the sticky buns. Let cool completely.

The sticky buns are best the day they are baked, but they can be stored wrapped in a few layers of plastic wrap or in a single layer in a covered container at room temperature for up to 3 days or frozen for up to 1 week. (See Note on Defrosting Frozen Baked Brioche Pastries, page 193.)

MAKES 6 BUNS

THE BUTTER CONTINUUM

CHILLED

We chill shaped butter so that we can lock it into a dough (that has also been chilled) of the same consistency, as for puff pastry or croissants. For pâte brisée we dice the butter and chill until it is very cold so that the flour will coat the butter as it's mixed, before it has a chance to soften.

ROOM TEMPERATURE

We use room-temperature butter in a number of cookies, such as TKOs, shortbread, and speculoos, when we want the butter to combine easily with the other ingredients. We also use it in pâte sucrée.

POMMADE

Before we cream butter for some cookie doughs or some tart doughs, we want the butter to be so soft and creamy that it forms soft peaks and has a consistency like mayonnaise. Typically we warm the mixer bowl with the butter in it, by holding the bowl over a burner, or using a blowtorch against the outside of the bowl, to encourage the softening.

MELTED

We add melted butter to the lemon–poppy seed muffins, blueberry muffins, savarins, and crêpes. When we want a richer flavor, we melt butter and cook it to the point that it browns and has a nutty aroma and flavor; we then add it to the financiers and rhubarb tart.

BETTER BUTTER

The quality of the butter really matters in pâtisserie. Most butter in the United States is 80% butterfat and 15% water; in France, the butterfat is typically 83%. For certain recipes, we use butter containing up to 84% butterfat. The higher the ratio of fat to water, the brighter the color, the better the flavor, and the better the structure of the dough. Butter with a higher butterfat ratio is especially good for laminated doughs, such as those for puff pastry and croissants. However, occasionally we use a butter with a lower butterfat ratio and a paler color (in our buttercreams, for example). Plugra is an excellent higher-fat (82%) European-style butter that's widely available here. For more about butter, see page 195.

Hot Cross Buns

FOR THE BUNS

Dried currants	122 grams	¾ cup
Dried cranberries	61 grams	½ cup
Vanilla paste	3 grams	½ teaspoon
Brioche Dough for Hot Cross Buns (page 313)		
Egg Wash (page 381)		

ICING

Powdered sugar	258 grams	2¼ cups
Ground cinnamon	1 gram	⅜ teaspoon
Ground cardamom	1 gram	⅜ teaspoon
Whole milk	40 grams	2½ tablespoons

This recipe was developed by Bouchon Bakery's head baker, Matthew McDonald. The buns are loaded with currants and cranberries and piped with an icing spiced with cinnamon and cardamom. It's the beguiling addition of cardamom to just the right amount of cinnamon in the icing, and the way the spices play off the fruit, that gives these buns their zing. Hot cross buns are an English tradition on Good Friday, but they're so good we hope you'll make them all year round.

You'll need a quarter sheet pan and a disposable pastry bag. ● *Buns baked in a convection oven will have a slightly higher rise and a more even color.*

FOR THE BUNS: Combine the currants and cranberries in a medium bowl and pour 2 cups boiling water over them. Let sit for 5 minutes to plump the fruit, then drain and pat dry with paper towels. Dry the bowl, return the fruit to it, and toss with the vanilla paste. Set aside.

Spray a large bowl with nonstick spray. Run a bowl scraper around the sides and down to the bottom of the bowl of brioche dough to release the dough and turn it out onto a lightly floured work surface, adding flour only as needed to keep it from sticking.

With your hands, gently pat the dough into a rectangular shape. Pour the currant-cranberry mixture onto the dough and knead it into the dough (which will be sticky) to distribute it evenly. Pat the dough into a rectangle again.

Stretch the left side of the dough out and fold it over two-thirds of the dough, then stretch and fold it from the right side to the opposite side, as if you were folding a letter. Repeat the process, working from the bottom and then the top. Turn the dough over, lift it up with a bench scraper, and place it seam side down in the prepared bowl. Cover the bowl with plastic wrap or a clean dish towel and let the dough sit at room temperature for 45 minutes.

Repeat the stretching and folding process, then return the dough to the bowl, seam side down, cover, and let sit for another 45 minutes.

Spray the quarter sheet pan with nonstick spray. Line the bottom with parchment paper and spray the paper.

Use the bowl scraper to release the dough and turn it out onto a lightly floured work surface. Using a bench scraper, divide the dough into 12 equal portions (78 grams each). Cup your fingers around a portion of dough and, using the palm of your hand, roll it against the work surface to form a ball. Continue to roll until the dough is completely smooth. Repeat with the remaining dough. (When you become proficient at rolling with one hand, you can use both hands and roll 2 portions at a time.) Set the balls on the prepared pan in 3 rows of 4. (See Note on Freezing Unbaked Brioche Pastries, page 193.) Brush the tops with egg wash.

Cover the pan with a plastic tub or a cardboard box and let proof for 1 to 1½ hours, until the balls have risen and are touching.

Preheat the oven to 325°F (convection) or 350°F (standard).

Brush the tops of the buns with egg wash again. Bake for 17 to 22 minutes in a convection oven, 25 to 30 minutes in a standard oven, until the tops are a rich golden brown and, when tested with a toothpick, the centers are baked through. Set the pan on a cooling rack and let cool completely. (If freezing, do not ice the buns at this point.)

FOR THE ICING: Sift the sugar, cinnamon, and cardamom into the bowl of a stand mixer. Fit the mixer with the paddle attachment and mix on the lowest setting for about 15 seconds to distribute the spices evenly. With the mixer running, slowly add the milk. Scrape down the sides and bottom of the bowl, increase the speed to low, and mix for 30 seconds to 1 minute, until smooth.

Transfer the icing to the pastry bag. Cut off ¼ inch of the tip. Starting at the left side of the top corner bun, pipe a continuous strip of icing across the center of the first row of 3 buns. Repeat with the remaining 3 rows. Then repeat in the opposite direction, across the 3 rows of 4 buns, working in the opposite direction, to create a cross of frosting on each bun. Serve the whole pan, or cut into individual buns.

The buns are best the day they are baked, but they can be stored, before icing, wrapped tightly in a few layers of plastic wrap or in a single layer in a covered container at room temperature for up to 3 days or frozen for up to 1 week (see Note on Defrosting Frozen Baked Brioche Pastries).

MAKES 12 BUNS

NOTE ON FREEZING UNBAKED BRIOCHE PASTRIES: Unbaked brioche pastries can be frozen after they are formed, but before they are proofed, wrapped in a few layers of plastic wrap, for up to 1 week. When ready to use, remove from the freezer and proof the dough as directed, keeping in mind that the proofing may take up to 5 hours.

NOTE ON DEFROSTING FROZEN BAKED BRIOCHE PASTRIES: Defrost, still in the plastic wrap or in the container, in the refrigerator. Leaving the pastries wrapped or in the container means any condensation will form on the outside, not on the pastries. Place on a sheet pan and refresh in a 325°F oven (standard) for about 5 minutes.

WASHING UP

We use egg washes often. If you want a nice shine on a dough, give the dough two brushings of it: the first brushing acts as a sealer, and the second is more like a glaze. At the bakery, because we egg-wash great volumes of products, we put the egg wash, strained, into a spray gun, paint gun, or airbrush. This not only gives us a uniform coating, it's also very gentle on the dough, which is important if it's a proofed and delicate croissant, for example. If you're only egg-washing a small quantity, use a pastry brush.

DIANE ST. CLAIR ON

KELLER THE COW

"Keller is a six-year-old Jersey, the breed with the highest butterfat in its milk (of course!). Her mom was one of my foundation cows and one of two cows I had when I started selling butter to The French Laundry. For five years, Dyedee, her mom, only had bulls and then, voilà, a heifer. Due to the celebratory nature of this event, we called the heifer Keller. She's always gotten a lot of attention and is pretty spoiled.

"I was a little nervous about the photo shoot. When you have a photographer with no large animal experience, it can turn ugly (animals walking away, not cooperating). But when Thomas arrived, he walked right into the field with Keller and started scratching her neck and whispering sweet nothings in her ear, and from then on she followed him around everywhere, kind of like a dog. (She does like to eat; maybe she sensed he was a chef?) There was great chemistry between the Kellers."

{ Artisanal Butter Makers }

Butter is a cornerstone ingredient in baking. Our preference is to buy from small-scale farmers like Diane St. Clair. Her production is too small for her butter to be widely available, but I think it's important to recognize farmers such as Diane who commit their lives to making natural products. I was amazed when I saw how small her strainer was. A little handheld kitchen strainer is what she uses for washing her entire butter production. I said, "Diane, I know what to get you for Christmas! A bigger strainer."

She truly does devote her life to her cows, their offspring, their milk, and the resulting butter, seven days a week. Because her butter is directly influenced by what the cows eat, it changes color throughout the year—from deep yellow, almost orange, when the cows are grazing on summer grass, to pale in the winter, when they feed on hay. And there are about six weeks in the spring, after the cows calve, when no butter at all is available.

Diane and farmers like her are a different breed, and the world is better and richer for such people. Look at the color of the butter, at how healthy those cows are. The quality of the grass dairy cows eat, and how we treat those cows, gets expressed in the mille-feuilles Sebastien makes, the Nanterre that Matthew bakes.

These photographs from one of my favorite farms are, in effect, an ode to small artisanal farmers throughout America. I'm grateful to them all.

Doughnuts

Brioche dough makes outstanding doughnuts. You don't need as much richness for something that will be deep-fried and, in some cases, filled with rich cream as well, so this dough has less butter than some of our other brioche recipes.

Here we offer a traditional American-style ring-shaped doughnut that's simply tossed in vanilla sugar, along with two more decadent versions that remind Sebastien of his childhood summers on the Atlantic coast, where food trucks at carnivals sold beignets filled with all kinds of creams and fruits. One of these is filled with diplomat cream (pastry cream lightened with whipped cream) and glazed with chocolate, and the other is filled with cherry jam and topped with whipped cream.

Sugared Doughnuts

DOUGH

All-purpose flour	518 grams	3½ cups + 3 tablespoons
Instant yeast	10 grams	1 tablespoon
Granulated sugar	74 grams	¼ cup + 2 tablespoons
Kosher salt	9 grams	1 tablespoon
Whole milk at 75°F/23.8°C	212 grams	¾ cup + 1½ tablespoons
Eggs	111 grams	¼ cup + 3 tablespoons
Vanilla paste	9 grams	1½ teaspoons
Unsalted butter, cut into ½-inch pieces, at room temperature	5 grams	2 ounces
Canola oil for deep-frying		
Vanilla sugar (see Note)	300 grams	1½ cups

You'll need 3¼-inch and 1½-inch round cutters and a deep-fat thermometer.

FOR THE DOUGH: Dust the surface with flour and spray a large bowl with nonstick spray.

Place the flour and yeast in the bowl of a stand mixer fitted with the dough hook and mix for about 15 seconds to distribute the yeast evenly. Add all of the remaining dough ingredients, except the butter, and mix on low speed for 4 minutes to incorporate. Continue to mix on low speed for 30 minutes. (At this point there will be some dough sticking to the sides of the bowl.) Add the butter a few pieces at a time, incorporating each addition before adding the next. Stop and scrape down the sides and bottom of the bowl and push the dough off the hook. Continue to mix for 5 minutes.

Run a bowl scraper around the sides and bottom of the bowl to release the dough and turn it out onto the work surface, adding flour only as needed to keep it from sticking. With your hands, gently pat the dough into a rectangular shape; the dough will be sticky.

Continued on page 198

Stretch the left side of the dough out and fold it over two-thirds of the dough, then stretch and fold it from the right side to the opposite side, as if you were folding a letter. Repeat the process, working from the bottom and then the top. Turn the dough over, lift it up with a bench scraper, and place it seam side down in the prepared bowl. Cover the bowl with plastic wrap or a clean dish towel and let sit at room temperature for 1 hour.

Use the bowl scraper to release the dough and turn it out onto a lightly floured work surface. Gently but firmly pat the dough into a rectangle, pressing any large bubbles to the edges and then out of the dough. Repeat the stretching and folding process, then return the dough to the bowl, seam side down, cover, and refrigerate overnight. Dough for filled doughnuts (see right and page 199) will be made through this point.

TO ROLL OUT THE DOUGH AND SHAPE THE DOUGHNUTS: On a lightly floured work surface, roll out the dough, flipping and fluffing it (see Note, page 215), into an 11-inch round. Transfer to a parchment-lined sheet pan and refrigerate for about 30 minutes or freeze for about 10 minutes, until the dough is firm enough to cut.

Line a sheet pan with parchment paper and lightly spray the parchment with nonstick spray.

Using the 3¼-inch cutter, cut 8 rounds from the dough, then cut holes in the centers with the 1½-inch cutter. Brush off any excess flour and place on the prepared pan. The holes can be proofed and fried, or discarded (see Note on Freezing Unbaked Brioche Pastries, page 193).

TO PROOF THE DOUGHNUTS: Cover the baking sheet with a plastic tub or a cardboard box and proof for 1 to 1½ hours, until the doughnuts have about doubled in size; when the dough is delicately pressed with a finger, the impression should remain.

TO FRY THE DOUGHNUTS: Pour 3 inches of oil into a Dutch oven or a heavy stockpot; ideally, the oil should come no more than one-third of the way up the sides of the pot, but it should be deep enough to allow the doughnuts to float freely. Heat the oil to 350°F/177°C.

Set a cooling rack over a baking sheet. Pour the vanilla sugar into a large shallow bowl. Gently lower 4 doughnuts into the oil and fry for 30 seconds, without moving the doughnuts, to allow the dough to set; adjust the heat as needed to maintain the temperature. Flip the doughnuts over and fry on the second side for 45 seconds. Flip them over again and fry for 45 seconds, or until they are a rich golden brown. Transfer the doughnuts to the rack and cool while you cook the second batch. Just before you transfer the second batch to the rack, toss the first batch in the sugar, coating them on all sides, then transfer to a serving plate or platter. Let the second batch cool and then coat them with the sugar.

The doughnuts are best the day they are fried, but they can be stored in a covered container for up to 1 day.

MAKES 8 DOUGHNUTS

NOTE: When you use vanilla beans, you are often left with the pods. Place the pods in a jar and fill the jar with granulated sugar: the sugar will take on the flavor of the vanilla. Use the sugar whenever you'd like to add a vanilla flavor. Alternatively, you can mix 100 grams/½ cup sugar with the seeds of 1 vanilla bean.

Chocolate-Glazed Diplomats

Dough for Sugared Doughnuts (page 196), refrigerated overnight		
Canola oil for deep-frying		
Chocolate Glaze (page 377)		
Crunchy dark chocolate pearls	112 grams	¾ cup
Diplomat Cream (page 374)	375 grams	1¾ cups

You'll need a 3-inch round cutter, a deep-fat thermometer, and a pastry bag with a ¼-inch plain tip. ● *For this recipe, we use Valrhona Les Perles 55%.*

Roll out the dough and chill it as directed on page 198.

TO SHAPE AND PROOF THE DOUGHNUTS: Line a sheet pan with parchment paper and lightly spray the parchment with nonstick spray. Using the 3-inch cutter, cut 10 rounds from the dough. Brush off any excess flour and place on the prepared pan (see Note on Freezing Unbaked Brioche Pastries, page 193). Proof the dough as directed.

TO FRY THE DOUGHNUTS: Pour 3 inches of canola oil into a Dutch oven or heavy stockpot; ideally, the oil should come no more than one-third of the way up the sides of the pot, but it should be deep enough to allow the doughnuts to float freely. Heat the oil to 335°F/168°C. Set a cooling rack over a baking sheet.

Gently lower 4 doughnuts into the oil and fry for 30 seconds, without moving the doughnuts, to allow the dough to set; adjust the heat as needed to maintain a temperature of 335° to 345°F/168° to 174°C. Flip the doughnuts over and fry for 5 to 5½ minutes, flipping them every 30 to 45 seconds, until they are a rich golden brown. Transfer to the rack and cook the remaining doughnuts in 2 batches of 3 each. Let the doughnuts cool completely before glazing and filling.

TO FILL AND GLAZE THE DOUGHNUTS: Pour the glaze into a bowl just large enough to hold one doughnut. Spread the pearls on a small plate.

Spoon the diplomat cream into the pastry bag. Push the tip into the side of a doughnut and, applying gentle pressure, pipe in 30 to 35 grams/2 to 2½ tablespoons of cream; the doughnut will feel heavy. Continue with the remaining doughnuts.

One at a time, dip the top of each doughnut into the glaze, then turn the doughnut over, letting the excess glaze run off, and dip the glazed side into the pearls. Set on a serving plate or platter.

The doughnuts are best as soon as they are made, but they can be refrigerated for up to 1 hour.

PHOTOGRAPH ON PAGE 201 **MAKES 10 DOUGHNUTS**

Cherry–Whipped Cream Doughnuts

Dough for Sugared Doughnuts (page 196), refrigerated overnight		
Canola oil for deep-frying		
Cherry Jam (page 379)	400 grams	1 cup
Sweetened Whipped Cream (page 378)	240 grams	2¼ cups + 2 tablespoons
5 cherries, pitted and cut in half		
10 stemmed cherries for garnish (optional)		

You'll need a 3-inch cutter, a deep-fat thermometer, a pastry bag with a ¼-inch plain tip, and a pastry bag with an Ateco #865 star tip.

Roll out the dough and chill it as directed on page 198, then cut out 10 rounds as for Chocolate-Glazed Diplomats (page 198), and proof the dough.

Fry the doughnuts as for Chocolate-Glazed Diplomats, and let cool completely before filling.

TO FILL THE DOUGHNUTS: Spoon the jam into the pastry bag with the plain tip. Spoon the whipped cream into the pastry bag with the star tip.

Push the tip of the jam-filled bag into the side of a doughnut and, applying gentle pressure, pipe in 35 to 40 grams/1 tablespoon plus 1 teaspoon to 1 tablespoon plus 2 teaspoons of jam; the doughnut will feel heavy. Continue with the remaining doughnuts.

Pipe whipped cream in a tall spiral rosette on top of each doughnut and garnish with half a cherry.

The doughnuts are best eaten as soon as they are completed, but they can be refrigerated for up to 1 hour before serving. If desired, garnish each plate with a stemmed cherry.

PHOTOGRAPH ON PAGE 200 **MAKES 10 DOUGHNUTS**

Craquelins

STARTER

Whole milk at 75°F/23.8°C	60 grams	3½ tablespoons
Instant yeast	8 grams	2⅜ teaspoons
All-purpose flour	90 grams	½ cup + 2 tablespoons + ¾ teaspoon

DOUGH

Candied Orange Peel (page 379), cut into ⅛-inch pieces	150 grams	½ cup + 2½ tablespoons
Grated orange zest	15 grams	2½ tablespoons
Cointreau or Grand Marnier	8 grams	1½ teaspoons
All-purpose flour	390 grams	2¾ cups + 2 teaspoons
Granulated sugar	52 grams	¼ cup + ½ teaspoon
Kosher salt	12 grams	1 tablespoon + 1 teaspoon
Eggs	225 grams	¾ cup + 2 tablespoons
Unsalted butter, cut into ½-inch pieces, at room temperature	300 grams	10.5 ounces

12 sugar cubes

Egg Wash (page 381)

Pearl sugar	36 grams	3 tablespoons

Craquelins are made with an enriched dough and baked in individual paper molds. Just before baking, they are sprinkled with pearl sugar, a large-crystal sugar that doesn't dissolve in the oven and gives them a crunchy topping. Our version includes grated orange zest, candied orange peel, and orange liqueur, and in the tradition of this Belgian preparation, we add a sugar cube to the center of each craquelin, for additional sweetness and moisture. But even so, these are not overly sweet.

You'll need twelve 2¾-inch paper panettone baking molds. • Craquelins baked in a convection oven will have a slightly higher rise and more even color.

FOR THE STARTER: Place the milk in a small bowl and stir in the yeast, followed by the flour. Mix with your hands to combine. The mixture will be dense and dry.

Cover with plastic wrap and let sit at room temperature for 1 hour. The starter will be softer to the touch.

FOR THE DOUGH: Combine the candied orange peel, zest, and Cointreau in a small bowl.

Place the flour, sugar, and salt in the bowl of a stand mixer fitted with the dough hook and mix on the lowest setting to distribute the sugar and salt evenly. Add the starter and mix for 30 seconds to incorporate. With the mixer running, add the eggs in 3 additions. The dough will be very dry. Increase the speed to low and mix for 15 minutes, stopping once to scrape down the sides and bottom of the bowl.

Push the dough off the hook and continue to mix on low speed. Add the butter a few pieces at a time, incorporating each addition before adding the next. Once all the butter has been added, mix for 2 minutes. The dough will be very sticky.

Dust the work surface with flour and spray a large bowl with nonstick spray. Run a bowl scraper around the sides and bottom of the mixer bowl to release the dough and turn it out onto the work surface, adding flour only as needed to keep it from sticking. With your hands, gently pat the dough into a rectangular shape. Pour the orange mixture onto the dough and knead it into the dough, which will be sticky, to distribute it evenly. Pat the dough into a rectangle again.

Stretch the left side of the dough out and fold it over two-thirds of the dough, then stretch and fold the dough from the right side to the opposite side, as if you were folding a letter. Repeat the process, working from the bottom and then the top. Turn the dough over, lift it up with a bench scraper, and place it seam side down in the prepared bowl. Cover the bowl with plastic wrap or a clean dish towel and let sit at room temperature for 1 hour.

Use the bowl scraper to release the dough and turn it out onto a lightly floured work surface. Gently but firmly pat the dough into a rectangle, pressing any large gas bubbles to the edges and then out of the dough. Repeat the stretching and folding process, then return the dough to the bowl, seam side down, cover, and refrigerate overnight.

Spray the paper baking molds with nonstick spray and arrange on a sheet pan. Release the dough and turn it out onto a lightly floured work

surface. Using a bench scraper, divide the dough into 12 equal portions (100 to 105 grams each). Cup your fingers around a portion of dough and, using the palm of your hand, roll it against the work surface to form a ball. Continue to roll until the dough is completely smooth. Repeat with the remaining dough. (When you become proficient at rolling with one hand, you can use both hands and roll 2 portions at a time.)

Turn the balls over and push a sugar cube one-third of the way into each one. Turn over again and reroll each one to encapsulate the sugar cube and move it into the center of the roll. Place the balls in the prepared molds (see Note on Freezing Unbaked Brioche Pastries, page 193). Brush with egg wash.

Cover the sheet pan with a plastic tub or a cardboard box and let proof for 1½ to 2 hours, until the balls have risen to ⅜ inch below the tops of the papers.

Preheat the oven to 325°F (convection) or 350°F (standard).

Brush the tops of the craquelins with egg wash again and sprinkle with 3 grams/¾ teaspoon pearl sugar each. Bake for 18 to 22 minutes in a convection oven, 26 to 30 minutes in a standard oven, until the tops are a rich golden brown and the centers are baked through when tested with a toothpick. Cool completely on a cooling rack.

The craquelins are best the day they are baked, but they can be stored wrapped tightly in a few layers of plastic wrap or in a single layer in a covered container at room temperature for up to 3 days or frozen for up to 1 week (see Note on Defrosting Frozen Baked Brioche Pastries, page 193).

MAKES 12 CRAQUELINS

Tropézienne

Brioche Dough for Tropézienne
 (page 313)

Egg Wash (page 381)

Pearl sugar	12 grams	1 tablespoon
Nutella (see Note to Professionals)	240 grams	¾ cup + 1 tablespoon
Pastry Cream (page 373)	360 grams	1½ cups + 2 tablespoons

I n 1955, the movie . . . *And God Created Woman* was filming in Saint-Tropez, the chic beach town of southern France. A Polish pastry chef who had a shop there began selling his pastries to the crew and cast, including the young Brigitte Bardot. One of his preparations was a round of brioche dough, baked into what resembles a large hamburger bun, split, and spread with mousseline cream. He named it *tarte tropézienne*. Traditionally the pastry cream is flavored with orange blossom water. We flavor the cream with Nutella.

You'll need a 9-by-2-inch cake ring and a pastry bag with an Ateco #863 French star tip. ● A tropézienne baked in a convection oven will have a slightly higher rise and more even color.

Line a sheet pan with parchment paper. Run a bowl scraper around the sides and bottom of the bowl of brioche to release the dough and turn it out onto a lightly floured work surface. Using a rolling pin, roll it out, flipping and fluffing it (see Note, page 215), into a ¼- to ⅜-inch-thick round that is just slightly larger than the cake ring. Transfer the dough to the prepared sheet pan.

Dip the bottom of the cake ring in flour and tap off any excess. Center the ring over the dough and press it down into the round of dough in one clean motion; remove the trimmings around the ring and discard. (See Note on Freezing Unbaked Brioche Pastries, page 193.) Brush the top of the brioche with egg wash. Cover the sheet pan with a plastic tub or a cardboard box, and let proof for about 1½ hours, until the dough has risen halfway up the sides of the ring.

Preheat the oven to 325°F (convection or standard).

Brush the top of the dough with egg wash again and sprinkle with the pearl sugar. Bake for 18 to 22 minutes in a convection oven, 28 to 32 minutes in a standard oven, until the top is a rich golden brown and the center is baked through when tested with a toothpick. Set the pan on a cooling rack and cool completely. The uncut, unfilled tropézienne can be stored wrapped tightly in a few layers of plastic wrap at room temperature for up to 3 days or frozen for up to 1 week (see Note on Defrosting Frozen Baked Brioche Pastries, page 193).

Carefully run a paring knife around the edges of the brioche to loosen it and lift off the ring. Using a serrated knife, cut the tropézienne horizontally in half. Lift off the top and set aside.

Place the Nutella in a medium bowl, add one-third of the pastry cream, and stir to loosen the consistency. Fold in the remaining pastry cream. Transfer to the pastry bag and, beginning in the center of the bottom layer of brioche, pipe a spiral to within ¼ inch of the edges. Pipe a second spiral of filling on top to within ½ inch of the edges. Replace the top half of the brioche and press down gently.

The tropézienne is best the day it is made, but the dough can be baked up to 1 day ahead, wrapped in plastic wrap, and stored at room temperature. The tropézienne can be filled up to 2 hours before serving and refrigerated.

Note to Professionals: Gianduja can be used instead of Nutella. Or Diplomat Cream (page 374) rather than the Nutella and pastry cream mixture.

SERVES 6 TO 8

Savarins

SAVARINS AUX FRUITS

DOUGH

All-purpose flour	250 grams	1¾ cups + 1½ teaspoons
Granulated sugar	25 grams	2 tablespoons + ¼ teaspoon
Kosher salt	5 grams	1½ + ⅛ teaspoons
Instant yeast	5 grams	1½ teaspoons
Eggs	125 grams	½ cup
Water, at 75°F/23.8°C	88 grams	¼ cup + 2 tablespoons
Unsalted butter, melted and still warm	94 grams	3.3 ounces

SYRUP

Water	750 grams	3 cups + 2 tablespoons
Granulated sugar	338 grams	1½ cups + 3 tablespoons
Passion fruit puree	188 grams	6.6 ounces
1½ vanilla beans, split lengthwise		
Sweetened Whipped Cream (page 378)	420 grams	4¼ cups
1 banana		
1 small pineapple, peeled, cored, and cut into ½-by-¼-inch pieces; small leaves reserved for garnish		
1 mango, peeled, pitted, and cut into ¼-inch dice		
1 papaya, peeled, halved lengthwise, and seeded, and cut into ⅛-inch slices		
1 orange, rind removed and segmented (see Note)		
4 lychees, cut in half lengthwise		
Granulated sugar (optional)		

These brioche creations, baked in ring-shaped molds, are named for the French lawyer and politician Jean Anthelme Brillat-Savarin, one of the earliest, and best known, writers on gastronomy. (His *Physiology of Taste*, first published in 1825, has never been out of print.) Traditionally the baker grabs a handful of dough, squeezes it so that a ball of dough rises out of his fist, and scrapes that into the mold; the dough can also be piped into the molds. Usually savarins are soaked with rum, but preferring to avoid using alcohol here, we soak them in a passion fruit syrup; the tart fruit balances the sweetness of the sugar syrup.

You'll need four 5-inch savarin molds, preferably nonstick, a pastry bag with ½-inch plain tip (optional), a Thermapen or other candy thermometer, a pastry bag with an Ateco #865 French star tip, and a propane torch. ● For this recipe, we use Boiron or Perfect Puree passion fruit puree. ● Savarins baked in a convection oven will have a slightly higher rise and a more even color.

FOR THE DOUGH: Place the flour, sugar, salt, and yeast in the bowl of a stand mixer fitted with the paddle attachment and mix on the lowest setting for 30 seconds. With the mixer running, add the eggs and mix for 1 minute. Continue to mix on low speed for 2 minutes. Reduce the speed to the lowest setting, slowly add the water, and mix for 1 minute. Increase the speed to low and mix for 2 minutes. Scrape down the sides and bottom of the bowl and the paddle. Mix for 8 to 10 minutes, or until the dough, which will be very sticky, begins to pull away from the sides of the bowl.

Scrape down the bowl and the paddle again and turn the mixer to the lowest setting. Gradually add the butter, then mix for 3 minutes. Continue to mix on low speed for 7 to 9 minutes, until the dough is completely smooth and very soft, like a batter. Refrigerate for 30 minutes.

Spray the savarin molds (even if nonstick) with nonstick spray.

Traditionally the dough is portioned by hand, but it can also be piped through a pastry bag. If portioning by hand (it is best to use gloves for this), grab a handful of dough and make a fist, squeezing a ball of dough above your fingers, and place it in a mold. Continue making balls and adding them until you have filled the mold, then repeat with the remaining dough and molds. Or, using a pastry bag fitted with a ½-inch plain tip, pipe equal amounts of dough into the molds (use 130 grams of dough for each one). This dessert is meant to be shared; it makes 4 savarins to serve 8.

Dip your finger in water and spread the dough evenly in the molds. Arrange the molds on a sheet pan and proof, uncovered, for about 30 minutes, until the dough fills the bottoms of the molds and has risen slightly.

Preheat the oven to 325°F (convection) or 350°F (standard).

Bake the savarins for 25 to 30 minutes in a convection oven, 35 to 40 minutes in a standard oven, rotating the sheet pan halfway through, until golden brown. Unmold the savarins onto a cooling rack, set over a sheet pan, and cool.

FOR THE SYRUP: Meanwhile, combine all of the ingredients in a large saucepan, scraping the vanilla bean seeds and adding them and the pods. Bring to a simmer over medium heat, stirring to dissolve the sugar. Strain into a 6- to 8-inch-wide bowl.

The savarins should be soaked when the syrup is 130°F/54°C: if it is too hot, the savarins could fall apart; too cold, and they won't absorb the syrup. One at a time, submerge the savarins in the syrup, turning to soak all sides. Return to the rack. Let stand for 2 to 4 hours before serving. (Reserve the syrup.)

Just before serving, brush the savarins with syrup again. Place a savarin on each serving plate. Spoon the whipped cream into the piping bag with the star tip and fill the centers with whipped cream, then pipe rosettes over half of each ring. Cut the banana into ⅛-inch-thick slices. Arrange the fruit over and around the savarins and serve.

PHOTOGRAPH ON PAGE 209   **MAKES 4 SAVARINS TO SERVE 8**

NOTE ON SECTIONING CITRUS FRUIT: To remove the suprêmes (sections) from an orange or other citrus fruit, cut off the top and bottom of the fruit to expose the flesh. Stand the fruit on a cutting board and use a paring knife to cut away the peel and white pith in wide strips from top to bottom. Cut between the membranes to release the suprêmes.

Note to Professionals: If you'd like a more refined appearance, cut the banana slices into uniform circles, using a round cutter, and caramelize them: set the slices on a sheet pan, sprinkle with granulated sugar, and caramelize the tops with a propane torch.

PUFF PASTRY & CROISSANTS

I remember my first attempts at making puff pastry at Rakel in 1986. I didn't have a sheeter, which we use now for rolling dough, and if I didn't roll the dough evenly, it wouldn't rise evenly. The process was very difficult and time-consuming—and it took two days. So I found a company that sold five-pound blocks of very good puff pastry, and that's what we used. It's what everyone used. But by the time I got to Checkers in Los Angeles in the early 1990s, I realized we were in danger of losing the craft altogether, and I decided we'd go back to making our own. There are countless ways to put this special dough to use, including my favorite dessert, the mille-feuille (see page 230). I love its butteriness, its textural contrasts, and the flavor of the burnt sugar on top, like a crème brûlée. It makes me really happy to eat. Croissant dough, another layered (or laminated) dough, is closely related to puff pastry, but it includes yeast. Croissants are one of my favorite things. I love the delicate crisp shell and the open, elastic, airy crumb. We need to consider what we may be losing in our perpetual quest for convenience. Once we lose the knowledge of something learned and refined over centuries, it's gone for good.

Puff Pastry

European-style unsalted butter (in one piece)	400 grams	14 ounces

DOUGH

Water	225 grams	¾ cup + 3 tablespoons
White wine vinegar	25 grams	1 tablespoon + 2½ teaspoons
All-purpose flour, plus more for dusting	500 grams	3½ cups + 1 tablespoon
Kosher salt	10 grams	1 tablespoon + ⅜ teaspoon
Unsalted butter, melted but not hot	50 grams	1.7 ounces

Puff pastry is an ingenious dough composed of alternating layers of pastry and butter, hundreds and hundreds of ultrathin layers—it's what's referred to in the profession as a laminated dough. When it's baked, the water in the butter turns to steam, forcing the dough to puff, and the pastry layers become shatteringly delicate and light, with a delicious buttery crunch.

The concept is simple: a dough is wrapped around a block of butter to encase it, then the dough is rolled out into a long, thin sheet, with a thin layer of butter sandwiched between the two layers of dough. When this sheet is folded over on itself and rolled out, the layers of butter and dough multiply exponentially.

FOR THE BUTTER BLOCK: Place a piece of parchment paper on the work surface. Center the butter on the parchment paper. Top with a second piece of parchment paper and pound the top of the butter from left to right with a rolling pin to begin to flatten it. The parchment paper will be stuck to the butter: lift off the top piece and place it butter side up on the work surface. Flip the butter onto the parchment, turning it 90 degrees. Top with the second piece of parchment paper. Continue to flatten the butter as before until you have a rectangle approximately 6½ by 8 by ½ inch thick.

Remove the top piece of parchment paper. Cut the sides to straighten them and place the trimmings on top of the block. Return the parchment and roll the butter to a 6½-by-8-by-½-inch-thick rectangle. Wrap tightly in plastic wrap and refrigerate for at least 8 hours, but preferably overnight.

MEANWHILE, FOR THE DOUGH: Combine the water and vinegar in a liquid measuring cup.

Place the flour and salt in the bowl of a stand mixer fitted with the dough hook and mix on the lowest setting for about 15 seconds to combine. Increase the speed to low, slowly add about half the water mixture, and mix for 30 seconds to combine. Add more of the water-vinegar mixture, reserving about 30 grams/2 tablespoons, until the flour is thoroughly moistened. Scrape down the sides and bottom of the bowl. With the mixer running on low speed, mix in any dry ingredients that have settled in the bottom, then slowly pour in the butter. After about 30 seconds, the dough should begin to gather together in the center of the bowl. Stop the mixer before it comes together around the hook and feel the dough: it should feel tacky but shouldn't stick to your fingers. If it feels at all dry, turn the mixer to low and add the reserved water in very small amounts as needed.

Spray a medium bowl with nonstick spray, and lightly dust the work surface with flour. Turn the dough out onto the work surface and knead it for several minutes. The dough will not be completely smooth but will have some variance in texture, much like a bread dough. Lift the dough and tuck under the edges to form a ball, then place it seam side down in the prepared bowl.

With a sharp paring knife, score a large ½-inch-deep X in the top of the dough to help it relax. Cover the bowl tightly with plastic wrap, pressing it against the surface of the dough, and refrigerate for at least 8 hours, but preferably overnight.

TO ENCASE (LOCK IN) THE BUTTER BLOCK IN THE DOUGH: Lightly flour the work surface and a heavy rolling pin. Turn the dough out onto the work surface and lightly dust the top with flour. Roll the dough outward from the center, rotating it frequently and adding just enough flour to the work surface, dough, and/or pin to prevent sticking, flipping and fluffing the dough from time to time (see Note on Flipping and Fluffing), until you have a 12- to 13-inch circle about ⅜ inch thick. The dough should still be cold; if not, transfer it to a parchment-lined sheet pan and refrigerate until chilled.

Lay the block of butter in the center of the dough. Stretch and fold the two opposite sides of the dough over the longer sides of the butter block to touch in the center, without overlapping. Fold over the other two sides to meet in the center, without overlapping. Pinch the edges together to seal. There should be no exposed butter.

FOR TURN 1: Using the rolling pin, press down firmly on the dough, working from one side to the other, to expand the dough. Turn the dough so a short end faces you. Roll to expand the length of the dough, flipping, fluffing, and turning the dough over and adding flour only as needed, until you have a rectangle approximately 24 by 9 inches and ⅜ inch thick.

Fold the bottom third of the dough up as if you were folding a letter, then fold the top third down to cover the bottom third. Turn the block 90 degrees so the dough resembles a book, with the opening on the right. You will continue this pattern with each roll, and keeping the opening on the right will help you remember how to position the dough. You have completed your first turn; gently press a finger into a corner to mark it. Wrap in plastic wrap and refrigerate for 2 hours.

FOR TURN 2: Lightly dust the work surface with flour. Place the dough on the work surface with the opening on the right. Expand the dough by pressing down firmly with the rolling pin, working up the length of the dough. Then pound the dough, also working up the length of the dough. Hitting the dough will warm the butter—if it is too cold, it will shatter rather than spread as you roll the dough. Then roll out the dough as you did before to a 24-by-9-by-⅜-inch-thick rectangle. At this point, the short ends may have become rounded. If they are, trim the more rounded end to create a straight edge. Fold in the untrimmed third of dough and use the trimmings to patch and square off the rounded edges, cutting the trimmings as necessary to fit. As you patch, be certain that all the layers of dough are running in the same direction. Fold over the top third of the dough. Turn the block 90 degrees, so the opening is on the right. You have completed the second turn; gently press two fingers into a corner to mark the dough. Wrap in plastic wrap and refrigerate for 2 hours.

FOR TURNS 3 AND 4: Repeat all of the steps for turn 2, marking the dough with the corresponding number of fingerprints and refrigerating it for 2 hours after each turn.

FOR TURN 5, THE FINAL TURN: Repeat the steps and mark the dough with five fingerprints. Refrigerate for at least 8 hours, but preferably overnight (see Note on Storing Puff Pastry).

TO FINISH THE DOUGH: Line the back of a sheet pan with parchment paper and lightly dust the work surface with flour. Place the dough on the work surface with the opening on the right. It is especially critical at this stage that the dough remain cold; refrigerate as needed. Lightly dust the top of the dough and roll it outward from the center, flipping, fluffing, and rotating it and turning it over, adding only enough flour to the work surface, dough, and/or pin as necessary to prevent sticking. Roll the dough to the size of the sheet pan, about ⅜ inch thick. If the dough becomes too difficult to roll, place it on the pan and refrigerate until cold, then return to the work surface and continue to roll it.

Return the dough to the sheet pan and refrigerate for at least 1 hour, or freeze for 15 minutes, to chill and relax the dough before using it.

PHOTOGRAPHS ON PAGES 216 AND 217   **MAKES 1.2 KILOGRAMS/2⅔ POUNDS**

NOTE ON FLIPPING AND FLUFFING: "Flipping and fluffing" (see photograph, page 231) refers to gently lifting and aerating the dough to keep it moving during the rolling process. This helps keep the dough from contracting during the rolling as well as from sticking to the work surface.

While rolling, rotate the dough from top to bottom to ensure that the butter remains in the center of the dough layers.

NOTE ON STORING PUFF PASTRY: After the last turn, or after it has been rolled out, the puff pastry can be refrigerated for up to 3 days (or frozen for up to 1 month). The time the dough has been refrigerated must be taken into account when you are refrigerating a formed pastry. For example, if you make apple turnovers on the same day you made the puff pastry, the turnovers can be refrigerated for up to 3 days before baking. But if the dough was refrigerated for 2 days before you shaped the turnovers, the turnovers can be held for only 1 day before baking.

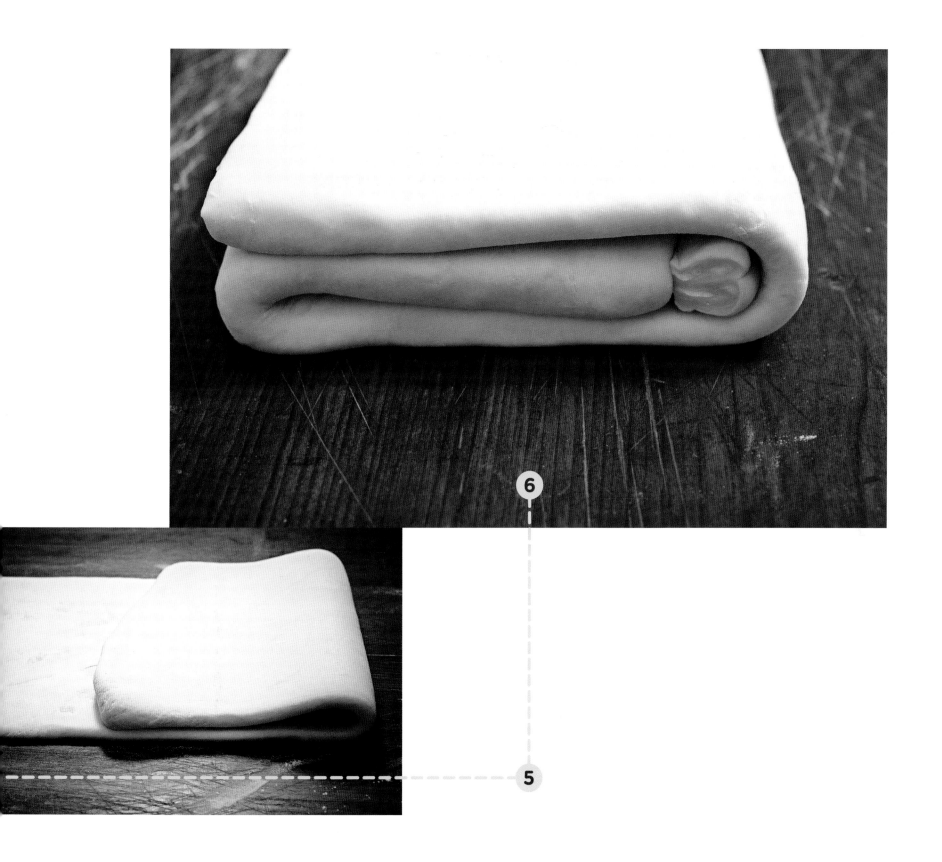

6

5

Palmiers à la Framboise

Granulated sugar	about 200 grams	¾ cup
Puff Pastry (page 214), prepared through the third turn and chilled for 2 hours		
Raspberry Jam (page 379)	375 grams	¾ cup + 3 tablespoons
Powdered sugar for dusting (see Note to Professionals)		

Classic palmiers, also called elephant ears, are made by folding two opposite sides of the rolled-out dough over onto itself to meet in the center before slicing, resulting in a heart shape when baked. We skip that folding step to make neat rectangular palmiers, both large and, for petits fours, small. Traditionally the puff pastry is sliced and the pieces are rolled in sugar before baking, but we think the pastries are more elegant if you incorporate the sugar into the dough itself, which we do by making the sugar part of the turns. Here the dough gets five turns; for the final two turns, we dust the work surface and the dough with sugar so that the sugar gets incorporated inside as we complete the turns.

Sugar attracts moisture, both from the dough and from ambient humidity. So don't dawdle, and don't let the dough rest in the refrigerator for longer than 1 day, or the sugar will melt, making the dough soft and sticky.

Because of the sugar, these bake to a lovely golden brown. Once cooled, the pastry strips are sandwiched with the jam and dusted with powdered sugar. A savory version, substituting a grated hard cheese such as Parmigiano-Reggiano for the sugar, is also delicious.

FOR TURN 4: Sprinkle the work surface with a generous, even layer of sugar. There should be enough to keep the dough from sticking as you flip, fluff, and turn it. Roll out the dough and trim and patch as necessary. Sprinkle the surface of the rectangle with 24 grams/2 tablespoons sugar, finish the turn, and refrigerate for 2 hours.

FOR TURN 5: Sprinkle the work surface with sugar again and roll out the dough. Sprinkle with sugar as before, and finish the turn. The dough is best used at this point, but it can be refrigerated for up to 1 day. (After that, the sugar will begin melting.)

TO SHAPE THE PALMIERS: Position the racks in the upper and lower thirds of the oven and preheat the oven to 350°F (standard). Line two sheet pans with Silpats or parchment paper.

Sprinkle the work surface with granulated sugar. Place the block of dough on the sugar and trim all sides so they are perfectly straight; this will expose the layers. Cut four ⅜-inch-thick slices from the dough; wrap and refrigerate the remaining dough.

FOR LARGER SANDWICHES: Lay 2 slices flat on each sheet pan, with the layers running parallel to the long sides of the sheet, positioning them 2 to 3 inches from the sides of the pan and leaving 2 to 3 inches between them.

FOR SMALLER SANDWICHES: Cut each slice in half crosswise. Lay 4 slices flat on each sheet pan, with the layers running parallel to the short ends of the sheet, positioning them 2 to 3 inches from the sides of the pan and leaving about 6 inches between them.

TO BAKE THE PALMIERS: Bake for 10 minutes. If the pieces are touching, carefully separate them with a spatula. Rotate the pans from top to bottom and front to back, and bake for about 8 minutes, until the tops are golden brown. Flip the pieces over and bake until the tops are golden brown. Using an offset spatula, transfer the pieces to a flat surface to cool completely.

Slice and bake the remaining dough. Cool completely.

TO ASSEMBLE THE PALMIERS: Sandwich the pastries with jam, using 24 to 48 grams/1 to 2 tablespoons for large palmiers, 12 to 24 grams/½ to 1 tablespoon for small palmiers.

Just before serving, dust the tops of the palmiers with powdered sugar. (For a decorative element, lay a palette knife or an offset spatula diagonally across the top of each palmier before dusting.)

The palmiers are best the day they are made; they will begin to soften after a few hours.

MAKES 7 LARGE OR 14 SMALL PALMIERS

Note to Professionals: Deco White (non-melt sugar) will not dissolve on the surface of the palmiers, as powdered sugar will.

LAMINATED DOUGHS

Puff pastry and croissant doughs are called laminated doughs, because of the intricate layering of sheets of butter and dough. Puff pastry is a dough wrapped around half its weight in butter, then rolled and folded and rolled and folded to create hundreds of layers of butter between hundreds of layers of dough. When the moisture in the butter vaporizes, it separates all those layers of dough, and the dough puffs. Croissant dough is similar in its layering, but it's a sweet dough to which yeast is added.

Don't be afraid to make laminated doughs. While it does take some care, practice, and planning, it's not as difficult as you might think. And it results in a very elegant, satisfying product that you can use in many, many ways. You should judge puff pastry by three main criteria:

- Brittleness—it should shatter pleasantly when you eat it.
- Lightness—it should feel light on the palate.
- Butteriness—you should detect a melting sensation from the large quantity of butter.

Cutting a laminated dough is something that must be done carefully. The dough should be very cold when you cut it. The knife must be sharp, and it must go down straight, perpendicular to your board. Cuts that are rough or not perpendicular to the cutting board can disturb the layers, and the dough will bake unevenly. You've got literally hundreds and hundreds of layers—you don't want to smash them.

I always add a little vinegar to puff pastry dough to prevent the butter from oxidizing and turning gray.

Puff pastry cut for Palmiers à la Framboise (page 218)

Because puff pastry freezes well, you can make a big batch so that you always have it on hand. Puff pastry and sugar—whether decorative or in the form of royal icing, for example—is really all you need for an elegant and easy dessert; see the Allumettes Glacées (page 235).

Croissant dough is the pinnacle of what we do. The enriched dough continuum begins with brioche, an easy yeasted dough with lots of butter and eggs, mixed with a dough hook, shaped, and baked. One step up is the Danish, which is a laminated brioche. The dough is rolled with a butter inlay, but there are fewer turns with this dough than with puff pastry, and they aren't as critical to the finished product. The next dough up is puff pastry—a pure laminated dough that must be handled and cut precisely and thoughtfully. And then there is croissant dough, which relies on two elemental processes, lamination and fermentation.

When you bake puff pastry, it rises in one direction. When you bake a croissant, though, because it's laminated, yeasted, and also rolled, it bakes up and out in all directions. Notice its golden-brown crust, composed of layers of dough so fine that they shatter when you bite into them. Cut a croissant horizontally in half. Examine the crumb, the intricate webbing of the dough, the waxy-looking interior of the gas pockets. It's a beautiful creation.

Croissant dough is the most difficult of the enriched doughs to get right because of this double action, and it's also the most satisfying dough at which a baker can succeed. You can never master it completely. Every time you attempt it, it's new. The temperature of your kitchen, the humidity in the air, the absorbency of the flour, the activity of the yeast—all these factors affect the dough.

TRICKS OF THE TRADE

WATER	Don't add all of the water the recipe calls for. Always hold back a bit, because flours are variable and may absorb water differently depending on the brand and the conditions of your kitchen. So you need to go by feel.
MIXING	Don't mix the dough too much, or it will contract when it's rolled and baked. Overmixing can also make the dough tough. What you're after is a weak dough, one with little gluten formation and little elasticity.
ELASTICITY	The idea is to achieve a dough that's as pliable as the butter when it's chilled. If one is softer than the other, this can cause problems. If you have a very soft dough or a very stiff dough, you can break through the layers, which will result in a puff pastry that bakes unevenly.

Apple Turnovers

CHAUSSONS AUX POMMES

Puff Pastry (page 214)	800 grams	28 ounces
Apple Filling (recipe follows)	180 grams	½ cup + 2 tablespoons
Egg Wash (page 381)		

These are classic apple turnovers, *chaussons aux pommes,* a sweetened cooked apple filling enclosed in puff pastry. We shape them on the baking sheet, then flip them over so we have a flat surface on top to score for decoration. We give these a double egg wash, brushing them before they go into the refrigerator and then before they go into the oven, which results in a beautiful color and shine.

You'll need a Matfer #95 4-inch fluted cutter and a pastry bag with a ½-inch plain tip.

Line a sheet pan with parchment paper. Lightly flour the work surface and a rolling pin. Lightly dust the top of the puff pastry and roll it outward from the center, flipping, fluffing, and rotating it and turning it over (see Note on Flipping and Fluffing, page 215), adding only enough flour to the work surface, dough, and/or pin as necessary to prevent sticking. Roll the dough out to a ¼-inch-thick rectangle. Cut out 6 rounds with the fluted cutter. (Reserve the trimmings for another use.)

Roll each round of puff pastry outward from the center to form an oval about 6½ inches long. Place the pastry on the prepared sheet pan and refrigerate until cold.

Spoon the filling into the pastry bag.

Brush a 1-inch border of egg wash around the edges of each oval. Turn an oval so a short end is toward you. Pipe 30 grams/about 1½ tablespoons of the apple filling just below the center line, leaving a ¾-inch border all around. Fold the top of the dough over the filling, leaving a 1/16-inch edge of dough exposed, and press the edges to seal the dough around the filling. Repeat with the remaining ovals and filling. Turn the turnovers over, brush with egg wash, and refrigerate until cold.

Preheat the oven to 350°F (standard). Line a sheet pan with a Silpat.

Brush the tops a second time with egg wash. Using the tip of a paring knife, score the top of each turnover in a leaf pattern. (The turnovers can be refrigerated for up to 1 day or frozen for up to 3 days. If frozen, bake them directly from the freezer; the baking time will be slightly longer.)

Transfer the turnovers to the sheet pan and bake for 40 to 45 minutes, rotating the pan halfway through baking, until they are a rich golden brown. Let cool completely on a cooling rack.

The turnovers are best the day they are made, but they can be stored in a covered container for up to 1 day.

MAKES 6 TURNOVERS

Apple Filling

Granulated sugar	80 grams	¼ cup + 2½ tablespoons
Water	15 grams	1 tablespoon
Fresh lemon juice (optional)	4 drops	
About 8 medium apples, peeled, cored, and cut into ½-inch-thick wedges	1.25 kilograms	2¾ pounds

We like sweet-tart Braeburn apples for this filling; if they are not available, Golden Delicious or Fuji also work well.

Place the sugar in a large saucepan and stir in the water until the sugar is evenly moistened. Cook over medium-high heat, stirring often as the sugar melts. If the sugar begins to crystallize, add the lemon juice. Once the sugar has melted, but not taken on any color, stir in the apple. The sugar mixture may seize, but it will melt again as the apples cook. When the mixture begins to bubble, reduce the heat to medium and simmer, breaking the apples apart as they cook and stirring often, until the apples are broken down and thickened, about 40 minutes. Remove from the heat and let cool. The filling can be refrigerated in a covered container for up to 1 week.

MAKES 500 GRAMS/1¾ CUPS

Pithiviers

Puff Pastry (page 214)

Egg Wash (page 381)

Frangipane (page 376)

Simple Syrup (page 378)   65 grams | ¼ cup

This is another example of the versatility of puff pastry dough. Once you have the dough, you can simply use it to enclose a sweet creamy filling, here frangipane, almond cream lightened with pastry cream. With some scoring work for garnish, it becomes an elegant dessert. Simple shape, classic flavors. If you want to vary it, add dried fruit or chocolate chips to the frangipane. Or enclose a bean or trinket in the filling to make it a proper *galette des rois,* or "kings' cake."

You'll need 7- and 9-inch vol-au-vent cutters (optional) and a pastry bag with a ½-inch plain tip.

Line a sheet pan with parchment paper.

Lightly flour the work surface and a rolling pin. Lightly dust the top of the puff pastry and roll it outward from the center, flipping, fluffing, and rotating it and turning it over (see Note on Flipping and Fluffing, page 215), adding only enough flour to the work surface, dough, and/or pin as necessary to prevent sticking. Roll the dough out to an 18-by-16-inch rectangle, ¼ inch thick. Using a 9-inch vol-au-vent cutter or plate as a guide, cut the dough into two 9-inch rounds. Transfer the rounds to the sheet pan and chill in the refrigerator or freezer until cold. (Reserve the large trimmings for Allumettes Glacées, page 235, or for another use.)

Gently press a 7-inch vol-au-vent cutter or plate into the center of one round to give it a 1-inch border. Brush the border with egg wash. Place the frangipane in the pastry bag and, beginning in the center of the dough, pipe a spiral of frangipane out to the border. Pipe a second spiral of frangipane on top, beginning in the center and stopping ½ inch short of the edges of the bottom spiral. Line up an edge of the second pastry round with one edge of the bottom layer and carefully lay the round over the filling, letting the sides gently drape over the frangipane. Rub your palm in a circular motion over the top of the dough to soften it enough so it covers the filling and to work any air bubbles toward the outside.

With your fingertips, press the edges of the dough, moving around the filling, to seal the top and bottom, leaving a small section of the dough unsealed, then gently press your fingertips over the top of the dough to move any air bubbles toward the opening. Finally, press your thumb around the bottom of the mound of filling to give it definition. Seal the final section of the rim.

Using the tip of a paring knife, cut ¼-inch-deep diagonal slits every ½ inch around the edges of the dough. Brush the surface of the cake with egg wash. Freeze for 5 to 10 minutes, or refrigerate for about 20 minutes, until cold.

Brush the Pithiviers again with egg wash. We like to score the top with a flower: score an elongated S, working from a far edge of the dough through the center, finishing on the opposite edge. Then, beginning at the same point, repeat in the opposite direction to form a figure 8. Repeat from the two opposite sides to form an X shape. Score the sections between each with a petal shape, for a total of 8 petals. Add additional scorings to the petals if desired. Using the tip of the knife, poke a hole in the center of the cake. Freeze for 5 to 10 minutes, or refrigerate for 20 minutes, or until cold and firm.

Meanwhile, preheat the oven to 350°F (standard). Line a sheet pan with parchment paper.

Using a cake lifter or a large spatula, transfer the cake to the lined sheet. Bake for 30 minutes. Rotate the pan from front to back: as it bakes there may be one area that rises more than another; if this happens, gently press down on that area.

Bake for 30 more minutes, then lower the oven temperature to 325°F and bake for 50 minutes, or until the surface is a rich golden brown.

Set the sheet pan on a cooling rack and brush the top of the Pithiviers once with the simple syrup. Return to the oven for about 2 minutes to set the syrup. Cool completely on the rack.

The Pithiviers is best the day it is baked.

PHOTOGRAPH ON PAGE 224   **SERVES 6 TO 8**

PATIENCE & PRACTICE

One of the things I advise home cooks to do is to make the same recipe over and over. If you just jump from one recipe to the next to the next, you don't really learn. But when you do the same recipe again and again, you become attuned to the nuances of the way ingredients behave.

So much of working with doughs has to do with feel—with the way a dough feels in your hands, how moist it is or how dry, how elastic it is, how cold or warm it is. Paying attention to these indicators when following a recipe not only helps you make it better and better each time you prepare it, but it makes you more skillful when you work with other doughs. It helps you to become a better cook. And this is especially true in the pastry kitchen, where variables such as ambient temperature and humidity can really affect the final outcome of a pastry or a bread.

In the pastry kitchen, we work with ingredients that seem simple at first—granulated sugar, chocolate—but that are actually very complex. They undergo dramatic changes depending on the temperature you bring them to. Sugar that you heat to 250°F/120°C looks, tastes, and behaves differently from sugar you heated to 320°F/160°C. You only begin to understand the nuances of these simple-seeming but extraordinary ingredients by working with them over and over.

Handling dough, whether a pastry dough, a bread dough, or a croissant dough, is a lesson in understanding the effects of time and the need for patience. You can't rush dough. When water is added to flour, gluten forms, giving dough its elasticity. It's what allows us to roll out a tart dough; it's what allows bread doughs to trap gas bubbles without breaking and thereby leaven bread. You can't speed gluten development, or force gluten to relax. A dough needs to be mixed for a specific amount of time to develop this gluten. The more you develop the gluten, the more it needs to relax, which means leaving it alone. When you're rolling out a dough, it may want to pull back or contract; sometimes you've got to let it sit, and allow the gluten to relax to avoid stressing the dough. It's a matter of time.

Often a dough must be chilled before being rolled, especially if it contains butter. You need to chill the dough for an adequate time, which means learning patience. Patience, practice, time, care, and touch are never more important than in baking.

Pear Feuilletés

Puff Pastry (page 214)

Almond Cream (page 376),　　　100 grams | ½ cup
　at room temperature

Poached Pears (recipe follows),
　drained well on paper towels

Egg Wash (page 381)

We like to cut puff pastry into a variety of appealing shapes; here we use a pear-shaped cutter. We fill the pastries with almond cream and slices of pear (try to find pears close to the size of your cutter), and then cover them with a lattice topping made with a lattice bicycle cutter. It's a fun tool and it makes it very easy to create the lattice. The open topping is visually appealing and also allows some of the fruit juices to reduce, concentrating the flavor.

You'll need a pear-shaped cutter (about 5 by 3½ inches), a pastry bag with a ½-inch plain tip, and a lattice bicycle cutter.

Lightly flour the work surface and a rolling pin. Lightly dust the top of the puff pastry and roll it outward from the center, flipping, fluffing, and rotating it and turning it over (see Note on Flipping and Fluffing, page 215), adding only enough flour to the work surface, dough, and/or pin as necessary to prevent sticking. Cut the puff pastry in half. Roll each piece into an 11-by-16-inch rectangle, about ⅛ inch thick. Line the backs of two sheet pans with parchment paper. Top each with a piece of puff pastry. Trim the edges so that they are straight.

Using the pear-shaped cutter, and working 1 inch from the edges, press 6 impressions into one piece of pastry: Make the first impression and then rotate the cutter 180 degrees so that the top of the next impression is beside the bottom of the first one, then rotate the cutter again, and repeat.

Place the almond cream in the pastry bag. Pipe filling, about 16 grams/1 generous tablespoon, into each impression, leaving a ½-inch border all around.

Trim the pears as necessary so they will just cover the almond cream. Cut each pear half crosswise into slices about ⅛ inch thick. Keeping them together, fan the slices of each half slightly as you lay them over the filling; they should be ½ inch from the sides. If any of the almond cream spreads when the pears are added, wipe the border of dough clean. Brush the borders with egg wash.

Cut the remaining piece of dough crosswise into 6 rectangles. The pastry must be very cold before it is cut with the lattice cutter, so place it in the freezer or refrigerator if necessary.

Using the lattice cutter, cut 1 piece of dough from one short end to the other. Lift it and pull the long sides apart to form the lattice. Lay the dough over one of the pears and let it drape down and over the scoring from the pear cutter. Line up the pear cutter with the scoring and cut through both layers of pastry. Remove the trimmings, and continue with the remaining pastry and tarts.

Brush egg wash over the pastry and refrigerate for 1 hour, or until cold.

Brush the feuilletés with egg wash a second time and refrigerate for another hour. (The feuilletés can be refrigerated for up to 1 day or frozen for up to 3 days. If frozen, bake them directly from the freezer; the baking time will be slightly longer.)

Preheat the oven to 350°F (standard). Line a sheet pan with a Silpat or parchment.

Carefully transfer the feuilletés to the sheet pan. Bake for about 35 minutes, rotating the pan once halfway through, until the feuilletés are a rich golden brown. Set the pan on a cooling rack and cool completely.

The feuilletés are best the day they are baked.

PHOTOGRAPH ON PAGE 228　　　　　　　　　　　　　　　　SERVES 6

Note to Professionals: At the bakery, we make puff pastry in large batches and it almost always needs to be trimmed, so we have lots of leftover pieces. Trim pieces work well for feuilletés because they tend to puff less.

Poached Pears

Sauvignon blanc	150 grams	½ cup + 3 tablespoons
Water	300 grams	1¼ cups
Granulated sugar	110 grams	½ cup + 1 tablespoon
1 vanilla bean, split lengthwise		
Fresh lemon juice	2 grams	⅜ teaspoon
3 small Bartlett or Comice pears, peeled		

You'll need a melon baller.

Combine the wine, water, and sugar in a medium saucepan. Scrape the seeds from the vanilla bean and add the seeds and pod to the pan. Bring to a simmer over medium heat, stirring to dissolve the sugar. Remove from the heat, stir in the lemon juice, and let cool, then refrigerate until cold.

Peel the pears. Halve them, core them with the melon baller, and remove the stems. Add the pears to the poaching liquid and refrigerate overnight, or for up to 3 days.

MAKES 6 PEAR HALVES

FLEURER!

In France, there's a name for the act of throwing down flour on your work surface, that sideways snap of the wrist that sends a flurry of flour across the surface on which you're rolling out your dough: *fleurer*. Remember, though, you want only as much as is needed to keep the dough from sticking. You want the dough to be gliding over the granules of flour, not picking up excess flour.

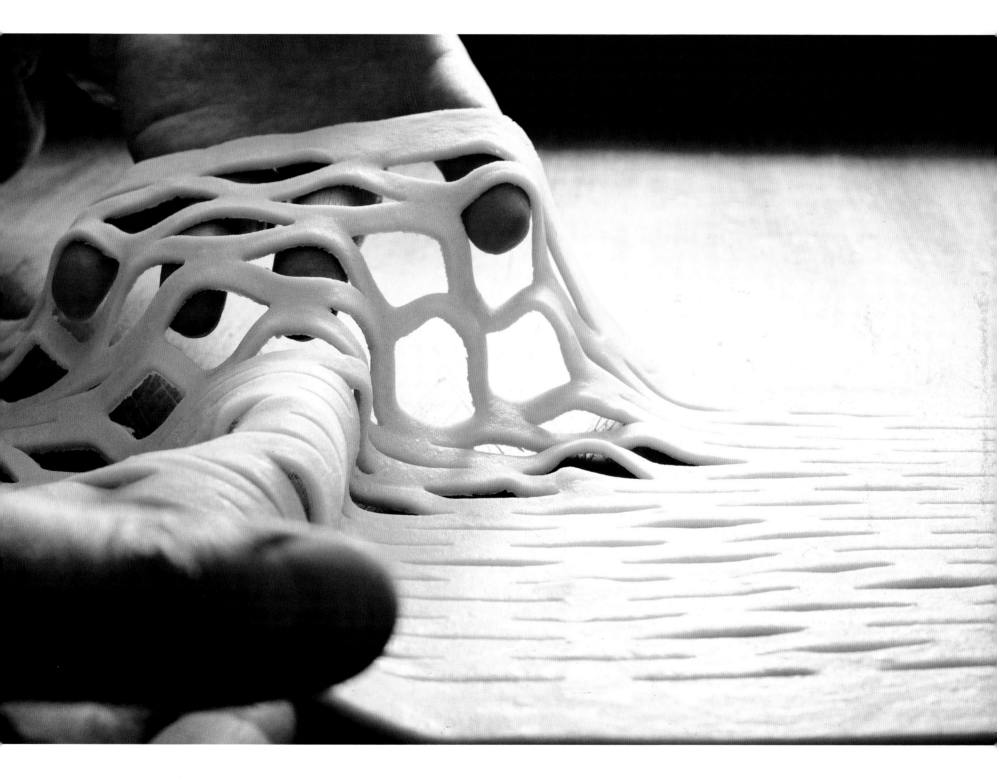

Mille-feuille

MOUSSELINE

Pastry Cream (page 373)	375 grams	1½ cups + 2½ tablespoons
Basic Buttercream (page 375)	375 grams	2½ cups
Puff Pastry (page 214)	600 grams	21 ounces
Sweetened Whipped Cream (page 378)	300 grams	3 cups
1 vanilla bean, split lengthwise (optional)		

This traditional French dessert, called a napoleon in America, is quite simple once you've made the dough: it's essentially puff pastry and a mousseline cream. Sebastien never liked how difficult it was to cut the mille-feuille into slices: you inevitably press out some of the cream as you cut down through the layers of pastry. So, he thought, why not serve it on its side, as it were, so that you cut through the layers of pastry at the same time without compressing the cream filling? It's an ingenious solution. Served this way, it slices beautifully. We decorate it with whipped cream piped through a St.-Honoré tip, a flat fluted tip, to make teardrop shapes. Garnish it with a whole vanilla bean, if you like.

You'll need a 9-by-13-inch baking pan and a pastry bag with a #20 St.-Honoré tip.

FOR THE MOUSSELINE: Place the pastry cream in the bowl of a stand mixer fitted with the whisk attachment and whip on medium speed until smooth. Add the buttercream and whip until well combined.

Line the baking pan with plastic wrap so that it extends slightly over all four sides (use two sheets if necessary, overlapping them slightly). Pour the mousseline into the pan and smooth the top with an offset spatula. Freeze overnight.

TO ROLL OUT THE PASTRY: Lightly flour the work surface and a rolling pin. Lightly dust the top of the puff pastry and roll it outward from the center, flipping, fluffing, and rotating it and turning it over (see Note on Flipping and Fluffing, page 215), adding only enough flour to the work surface, dough, and/or pin as necessary to prevent sticking. Roll the dough to a 12½-by-16-inch rectangle. If the dough becomes too difficult to roll, place it on a sheet pan and refrigerate until cold, then return it to the work surface and continue to roll it.

Set the dough on a sheet pan and refrigerate it for at least 1 hour, or freeze for 30 minutes, to chill and relax.

TO BAKE THE DOUGH: Preheat the oven to 350°F (standard).

Cut a piece of parchment paper the size of the sheet pan. Lay the parchment paper on top of the dough and, using a pizza wheel or a large chef's knife, trim the dough to the size of the sheet.

Spray the sheet pan lightly with nonstick spray and line it with parchment paper. Roll the puff pastry up on the rolling pin and unroll it on the lined sheet pan. Place the sheet pan in the freezer for 5 to 10 minutes, or refrigerate it for about 20 minutes, until the puff pastry is cold.

Top the puff pastry with a piece of parchment paper and another sheet pan. If you have them, add up to three more sheet pans to weight the dough and keep it very flat. If you don't, set other weights, such as baking pans, on top; be sure that the weight is evenly distributed. Bake for 1 hour and 10 minutes, or until the bottom of the pastry is a rich golden brown.

Remove the sheet and/or baking pans from the top of the pastry, but leave the parchment paper in place. Invert the pastry onto the back of a sheet pan. Cover the pastry with a piece of parchment and another sheet pan. Bake for another 15 minutes, or until the bottom is light golden brown.

Remove the top sheet pan and parchment paper and bake for 8 to 10 minutes more, until the pastry is cooked through and a very rich golden brown. Remove from the oven and let the pastry cool on the pan on a cooling rack.

TO ASSEMBLE THE MILLE-FEUILLE: Carefully transfer the pastry to a cutting board. Using a serrated knife, trim the edges to make a 10-by-12-inch rectangle. To cut 4 lengthwise strips of pastry, first cut marks every 2½ inches on both ends of the pastry. Carefully use a sawing motion to cut the pastry in a straight line from one end to the other. (If you aren't assembling the mille-feuille immediately, place the pieces on a parchment-lined sheet pan, wrap completely in plastic wrap, and set aside for up to 1 day.)

Turn the frozen mousseline out onto a cutting board. Trim the edges to even them. Measure the finished puff pastry strips and cut the mousseline into 3 matching strips; you may have extra mousseline.

Place one strip of puff pastry on a serving platter or board. Top with a strip of mousseline, and repeat the layering with the remaining puff pastry and mousseline. Turn the mille-feuille on its side. (It is much easier to slice the mille-feuille with this presentation.)

Place the whipped cream in the pastry bag and, starting in one corner, holding the tip with the opening facing up, pipe a line of teardrops (moving the bag slightly forward, then raising it slightly and pulling back to form the bottom of each teardrop) onto the mille-feuille. Work vertically in one line, piping one from the right, then one from the left to form a V. Repeat to cover the entire surface. If you will be garnishing the top with the vanilla bean, pipe a few more teardrops to anchor the bean. Arrange the vanilla bean atop them on an angle. Refrigerate until ready to serve.

The mille-feuille should be served the day it is assembled, and it is at its best if refrigerated for no more than 2 hours. Use a serrated knife to cut it into 2-inch slices.

PHOTOGRAPHS ON PAGES 232 AND 233   SERVES 6

FLUFF YOUR DOUGH

For doughs that we don't roll between parchment—the laminated doughs for puff pastry and croissants, for instance—we like to "fluff" them, just as you would a cotton sheet. The gentle fluffing helps the gluten relax and so makes the dough easier to roll out. It will be less likely to tense up on you.

Allumettes Glacées

Puff Pastry (page 214)	250 grams	8.8 ounces
Royal Icing for Allumettes (page 378)	38 grams	2 tablespoons

I n France, these small, elegant, sweet crunchy bites are served after dessert with champagne. They are nothing more than rectangles of puff pastry painted with royal icing. As they bake, the top layer of dough with the icing on it lifts away from the rest of the dough, resulting in two different textures and a lovely duotone appearance. The effect is magical. Freeze the dough before spreading a thin, even layer of icing over it, then freeze again until the icing is very cold, so you can make precise, clean cuts when you slice the dough into rectangles. I love the way Sebastien bakes these beneath a wire cooling rack so that when they puff, they all puff to exactly the same height.

You'll need four ¾-inch-high molds or small ramekins and a cooling rack that fits inside the rim of the baking sheet.

Lightly flour the work surface and a rolling pin. Lightly dust the top of the puff pastry with flour and roll it outward from the center, flipping, fluffing, and rotating the dough and turning it over (see Note on Flipping and Fluffing, page 215), adding only enough flour to the work surface, dough, and/or pin as necessary to prevent sticking, until you have an 11-by-8-by-⅛-inch-thick rectangle. If the dough becomes too difficult to roll, place it on a sheet pan and refrigerate until cold, then return it to the work surface and continue to roll it.

Set the dough on a sheet pan and refrigerate for at least 1 hour, or freeze for 20 to 30 minutes, to chill and relax it.

TO BAKE THE DOUGH: Preheat the oven to 350°F (standard). Lay a piece of parchment paper on the back of a small baking pan.

Trim the dough to a 7½-by-8-inch rectangle and put on the parchment. Freeze until frozen, 10 to 15 minutes. (It is much easier to spread the icing on frozen dough.)

Remove the dough from the freezer and, using an offset spatula, spread the icing in a very thin, even layer over the surface, reaching the edges. The spatula can be lightly moistened to help create a smooth edge. Freeze for 5 to 10 minutes (the puff pastry and icing must be cold and firm to cut).

Trim the rectangle of dough to 6 by 7½ inches. Freeze again.

It is crucial that the allumettes have very clean edges, so have a pitcher of water and a towel nearby to clean the knife between cuts. Cut the iced dough crosswise in half and then cut each half across into twelve 3-by-⅝-inch rectangles, returning the dough to the freezer as necessary if the icing or dough softens. If any of the edges are ragged, they can be smoothed with a small offset spatula, though the results will not be as good. Chill again, until firm, about 10 minutes.

Line a sheet pan with a Silpat or parchment paper. Position a mold or ramekin in each corner to support a cooling rack. Arrange 12 of the allumettes evenly on the sheet pan, leaving about 1½ inches between them. Put the cooling rack upside down on top of the molds. Bake for 15 minutes, or until the icing is a pale golden brown and the puff pastry is golden brown. Reduce the oven temperature to 325°F and bake for 5 more minutes to ensure the puff pastry is cooked through. Let cool completely on a cooling rack and turn the oven to preheat to 350°F.

Repeat with the remaining allumettes.

Serve the allumettes within 1 hour (if allowed to stand for longer, the tops will soften).

MAKES 24 ALLUMETTES

Croissant Dough

POOLISH

All-purpose flour	100 grams	½ cup + 3 tablespoons + 1 teaspoon
Instant yeast	0.1 gram	¹⁄₃₂ teaspoon or a pinch
Water at 75°F/23.8°C	100 grams	¼ cup + 2 tablespoons + 2½ teaspoons
European-style unsalted butter (in one piece)	330 grams	11.6 ounces

DOUGH

All-purpose flour	500 grams	3½ cups + 1 tablespoon + ¼ teaspoon
Granulated sugar	75 grams	¼ cup + 2 tablespoons + ¼ teaspoon
Instant yeast	10 grams	1 tablespoon
Diastatic malt powder	3 grams	1 teaspoon
Water at 75°F/23.8°C	200 grams	¾ cup + 1 tablespoon + 1¾ teaspoons
Unsalted butter, at room temperature	100 grams	3.5 ounces
Kosher salt	15 grams	1 tablespoon + 2 teaspoons

When making croissant dough, you want to make sure that the butter and the dough are chilled and are the same consistency so that the layers of dough and butter will remain distinct. That's why we freeze this dough between turns, to make sure it is thoroughly chilled.

Because croissant dough is yeasted, however, it's handled a little differently from puff pastry. With puff dough, the only leavening comes from the layering, and so we give it five turns to get those many hundreds of layers (some people give it six turns). Since croissant dough is also leavened by the yeast, we don't need as many layers and so only give it three turns. After the first turn, the butter will no longer be visible. And keep in mind that as soon as the dough is warm enough to be rolled, the yeast will begin to release gas, so it's important to work quickly.

You'll need a quarter sheet pan.

FOR THE POOLISH: Combine the flour and yeast in a medium bowl and mix with your fingers. Pour in the water and mix until thoroughly combined; the mixture should have the consistency of pancake batter.

Cover the bowl loosely with plastic wrap and let it sit at room temperature for 12 to 15 hours. The mixture will be bubbly, but the best indication that it is ready are lines on the surface that look like cracks that are beginning to fall in at the center, as the yeast exhausts its food supply (see photograph on page 270).

FOR THE BUTTER BLOCK: Place a piece of parchment paper on the work surface. Center the butter on the paper. Top with a second piece of parchment paper and pound the top of the butter from left to right with a rolling pin to begin to flatten it. The parchment paper will be stuck to the butter; lift off the top piece and place it butter side up on the work surface. Flip the butter over onto the parchment, turning it 90 degrees. Top with the second piece of parchment paper. Continue to flatten the butter as before until you have a 6¾-by-7½-inch rectangle. Wrap tightly in the parchment paper and refrigerate.

FOR THE DOUGH: Spray a large bowl with nonstick spray.

Combine the flour, sugar, yeast, and malt powder in the bowl of a stand mixer fitted with the dough hook and give it a quick mix on the lowest setting to distribute all of the ingredients evenly.

Pour about half the water around the edges of the bowl of poolish to help release the poolish, then add the contents of the bowl, along with the water (reserving 50 grams/3½ tablespoons), to the mixer. Add the butter and mix on low speed for 2 minutes to moisten the dry ingredients. Scrape down the sides and bottom of the bowl to make sure all the flour has been incorporated.

Sprinkle the salt over the top and mix on low speed for 2 minutes to dissolve the salt. If the mixture feels at all dry, add the reserved water in very small amounts as needed. Continue to mix on low speed for 20 minutes.

Run a bowl scraper around the sides and bottom of the bowl to release the dough and turn it out onto the work surface. Stretch the left side of the dough outward and fold it over the center of the dough, then stretch and fold the right side over to the opposite side, as if you were folding a letter. Repeat the process, working from the bottom and then the top. Turn the dough over, lift it up with a bench scraper, and place it seam side down in the prepared bowl. Cover the bowl with plastic wrap or a dish towel and let sit at room temperature for 1 hour.

Line the quarter sheet pan with parchment paper. Uncover the dough, run the bowl scraper around the sides and bottom of the bowl to release the dough, and turn it out onto a lightly floured work surface, disturbing the structure as little as possible. Gently but firmly pat the dough into a rectangle about 10 by 7½ inches, pressing any large gas bubbles to the edges and then out of the dough. Transfer to the sheet pan, cover with plastic wrap, and freeze for 20 minutes.

TO ENCASE (LOCK IN) THE BUTTER BLOCK AND ROLL THE DOUGH: Lightly flour the work surface and a heavy rolling pin. Turn the dough out onto the work surface and lightly dust the top with flour. Roll the dough outward from the center, rotating it frequently and flipping and fluffing it from time to time (see Note on Flipping and Fluffing, page 215), adding just enough flour to the work surface, dough, and/or pin to prevent sticking, until you have a 16-by-7½-by-½-inch-thick rectangle.

Lay the block of butter across the center of the dough. Stretch and fold over the two longer sides so they meet in the center and pinch together to seal. There should be no exposed butter at the top of the block, but you will see the butter on the sides.

FOR TURN 1: Using the rolling pin, press down firmly on the dough across the seam from one side to the other to expand the dough. Turn the dough so a short end faces you. Roll to expand the length of the dough, flipping, fluffing, and turning the dough over and adding flour only as

needed, until you have a rectangle approximately 22 by 9 inches and ³/₈ inch thick.

Fold the bottom third of the dough up as if you were folding a letter. Fold the top third down to cover the bottom third. Turn the block 90 degrees so the dough resembles a book, with the opening on the right. You will continue this pattern with each roll, and keeping the opening on the right will help you remember how to position the dough. You have completed your first turn; gently press a finger into a corner to mark it. Return to the sheet pan, cover with plastic wrap, and freeze for 20 minutes or until the dough has stiffened but is not hard.

FOR TURN 2: Lightly dust the work surface with flour. Place the dough on the work surface with the opening on the right. It is important to work with the dough as quickly as possible, but not at the risk of exposing

the butter. Pressing on the dough will warm the butter; if it is too cold, it will shatter rather than spread as you roll it. Expand the dough by pressing down firmly with the rolling pin, working up the length of the dough. If the dough cracks at all along the edges, stop and let it warm slightly at room temperature. Then roll out the dough as you did before to a 22-by-9-by-⅜-inch-thick rectangle and repeat the folding. Turn the block 90 degrees, so the opening is on the right. You have completed the second turn; gently press two fingers into a corner to mark the dough. Return to the sheet pan, cover with plastic wrap, and freeze for 20 minutes, or until the dough has stiffened but is not hard.

FOR TURN 3: Repeat all of the steps for turn 2 and mark the dough with three fingerprints.

TO FINISH THE DOUGH: Line a sheet pan with parchment paper and lightly dust the work surface with flour. Place the dough on the work surface with the opening on the right.

It is especially critical at this stage that the dough remain cold; freeze as needed. Lightly dust the top of the dough and roll it outward from the center, flipping, fluffing, and rotating the dough and turning it over, adding only enough flour to the work surface, dough, and/or pin as necessary to prevent sticking. Roll the dough out to 24 by 9 inches.

Cut the dough crosswise in half, making two 12-by-9-inch rectangles. Stack on the sheet pan with a piece of parchment paper between them, cover with plastic wrap, and freeze for 20 minutes, or until the dough has stiffened but is not hard. The dough is now ready to be used.

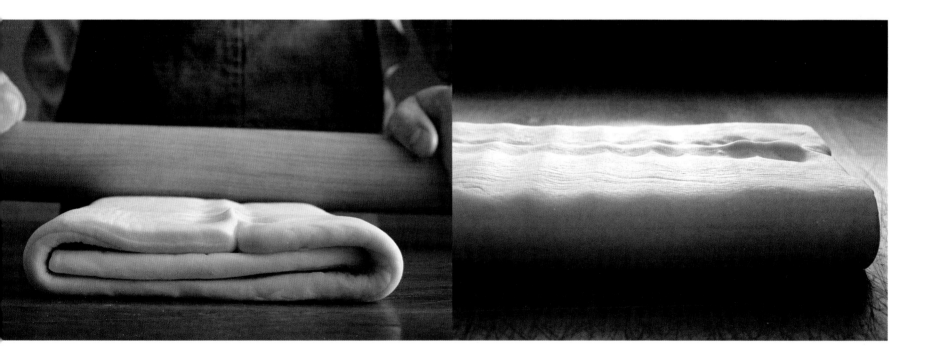

Traditional Croissants and Pains au Chocolat

There's only one word for it: *shatter*. It's what a good croissant does when you bite into it—and an indication that you've succeeded in making one of the most special doughs in the baker's repertoire. You've created layers of dough so exquisitely thin, brittle, and browned that they shatter into sweet, delicate shards that all but melt in your mouth.

Traditional Croissants

Croissant Dough (page 237)
Egg Wash (page 381)

Croissants baked in a convection oven will have a better rise and more even color.

Spray two sheet pans with nonstick spray and line with parchment paper.

Lightly flour the work surface. Remove one piece of dough from the freezer and position it on the work surface with a short end toward you; transfer the second piece of dough to the refrigerator. Roll the dough out to a rectangle about 19 by 9 inches.

Turn the dough so a long side is facing you and trim it to 18 inches long. Trim the remaining sides only as needed for straight edges.

Starting at the left side, measure 3¾ inches along the bottom edge of the dough and cut from this point to the top left-hand corner of the dough, making a triangle. For the second triangle, measure 3¾ inches along the top of the dough and cut from this point straight down. Continue cutting, alternating between the top and bottom of the dough, to make 8 triangles.

Hold one triangle up by the base with one hand and, using your fingertips, gently pull the dough until it is stretched to about 12 inches.

Put the dough on the work surface, with the base of the triangle close to you. Fold over the corners to the center of the base and roll the dough up from the wide end to the tip. Put on a prepared sheet pan with the tail down. (If the tail is not tucked under, the croissant could unroll when proofed and/or baked.) Press down slightly, flattening the croissant just enough so that it will not roll on the pan. Repeat with the remaining 7 triangles of dough, spacing them evenly on the sheet pan.

Remove the second piece of dough from the refrigerator, and, if necessary, let sit at room temperature until warmed enough to roll, then repeat to make 8 more croissants.

Brush the croissants with egg wash. Cover the pans with plastic tubs or cardboard boxes and let proof for about 2 hours. When the dough is delicately pressed with a finger, the impression should remain.

Position the racks in the upper and lower thirds of the oven and preheat the oven to 350°F (convection or standard).

Brush the croissants again with egg wash. If using a convection oven, reduce the heat to 325°F. Bake for 25 to 30 minutes in a convection oven, 35 to 40 minutes in a standard oven, rotating the pans once halfway through baking and separating the croissants if they are touching, until the tops are a rich golden brown and no portions, particularly between the layers, look undercooked. Set the pans on a rack and cool completely.

The croissants are best the day they are baked, but they can be wrapped individually in a few layers of plastic wrap and frozen for up to 1 month (see Note).

PHOTOGRAPHS ON PAGES 236 AND 243   **MAKES 16 CROISSANTS**

NOTE ON DEFROSTING FROZEN BAKED CROISSANTS: Defrost the croissants, still in the plastic wrap, in the refrigerator. (Leaving them wrapped means any condensation will form on the outside of the wrap, not on the croissants.) Place on a sheet pan and refresh in a 325°F oven (standard) for about 5 minutes.

I grew up eating Pillsbury Crescent Rolls for dinner. They made the house smell good as they baked, and they were delicious, from a kid's perspective, but they're not real croissants, which I would first taste when I went to France as a young cook. Those croissants were such a revelation to me that I've never had a croissant as good as the ones in my memory, and I don't think I ever will. I can't go back to the person I was then.

Croissant dough is used for pains au chocolat and pains aux raisins. Almond croissants, one of my favorite items the bakery makes, are essentially a leftover. They were created to make use of croissants that didn't sell the day before, and yet they are so rich and satisfying.

Pains au Chocolat

Croissant Dough (page 237)

40 chocolate baking sticks,
    (3 inches by ½ inch thick)

Egg Wash (page 381)

For this recipe, we use Cacao Barry 44% chocolate baking sticks.

Spray three sheet pans with nonstick spray and line with parchment paper.

Lightly flour the work surface. Remove one piece of dough from the freezer and position it on the work surface with a short end toward you; transfer the second piece of dough to the refrigerator. Roll the dough out to a rectangle about 19 by 9 inches.

Turn the dough so a long side is facing you and trim it to a rectangle 17½ by 8 inches.

Cut the dough lengthwise in half, then cut each half into five 4-by-3½-inch rectangles.

Set a chocolate baking stick ½ inch up from the bottom of each rectangle. Turn the bottom edge up and over to cover the baking stick. Set a second baking stick next to the folded dough. Brush the top of the dough with egg wash, roll the dough over the second stick, and continue to roll, finishing with the seam on the bottom. Set on one of the sheet pans. Repeat with the remaining 9 dough rectangles, spacing them evenly on the sheet pans.

Remove the second piece of dough from the refrigerator and, if necessary, let sit at room temperature until warmed enough to roll, then repeat to make 10 more pains au chocolat.

Brush the pains au chocolat with egg wash. Cover the pans with plastic tubs and or cardboard boxes and let proof for about 2 hours. When the dough is delicately pressed with a finger, the impression should remain.

Position the racks in the upper and lower thirds of the oven and preheat the oven to 350°F (convection or standard; see Note).

Brush the pains au chocolat again with egg wash. If using a convection oven, reduce the heat to 325°F. Bake for 25 to 30 minutes in a convection oven, 35 to 40 minutes in a standard oven, rotating the pans once halfway through baking and separating the pains if they are touching, until the tops are a rich golden brown and no portions, particularly between the layers, look undercooked. Set the pans on a rack and cool completely.

The pains au chocolat are best the day they are baked, but they can be wrapped individually in a few layers of plastic wrap and frozen for up to 1 month (see Note on Defrosting Frozen Baked Croissants, page 242).

MAKES 20 PAINS AU CHOCOLAT

NOTE ON BAKING THE PAINS AU CHOCOLAT: If you have two ovens, now is the time to use both. If not, move the third sheet pan, still covered, to a cooler spot in the kitchen while the others bake. Then, if baking in a convection oven, return the oven to 350°F before baking.

Pains aux Raisins

½ recipe Croissant Dough
(page 237; see Note)

Pastry Cream (page 373) | 140 grams | ½ cup + 2 tablespoons

Rum-Soaked Raisins
(recipe follows), drained

Egg Wash (page 381)

This is a great traditional breakfast pastry akin to the American cinnamon roll in its pinwheel construction. A sheet of croissant dough is spread with sweet pastry cream and sprinkled with rum-soaked raisins, then rolled, sliced, and baked. Feel free to vary the components—exchanging dried cranberries for the raisins, for instance, or almond cream for the pastry cream—or to add nuts.

Pastries baked in a convection oven will have a better rise and more even color.

Spray two sheet pans with nonstick spray and line with parchment paper.

Lightly flour the work surface. Roll the dough out to a 19-by-9-inch rectangle. Turn the dough so a short end is toward you. Spread the pastry cream evenly over the dough. Sprinkle the raisins on top. The surface will be dense with raisins, but they should not overlap.

Lift the side of the dough nearest you and roll up the dough as compactly as possible, pressing gently on the roll as it spreads, ending with the seam side down. Trim the ends if needed. Cut the roll into 10 pieces, ¾ to 1 inch wide each.

Transfer to the prepared sheet pans, spacing the rolls about 2 inches apart and tucking the end of each one under to keep it from unraveling as it proofs and bakes. Brush with egg wash. Cover the sheet pans with plastic tubs or cardboard boxes and let proof for 1 to 1½ hours. When the dough is delicately pressed with a finger, the impression should remain.

Position the oven racks in the upper and lower thirds of the oven and preheat the oven to 350°F (convection) or 375°F (standard).

Brush the pastries again with egg wash. Bake for 15 to 20 minutes in a convection oven, 17 to 22 minutes in a standard oven, rotating the pans once halfway through baking, until the tops are a rich golden brown and no portions, particularly between the layers, look undercooked. Set on a cooling rack and cool completely.

Pains aux raisins are best the day they are baked, but they can be wrapped individually in plastic wrap and frozen for up to 1 month.

PHOTOGRAPHS ON PAGES 246 AND 247   **MAKES 10 PASTRIES**

NOTE: The full recipe of croissant dough needs to be used once it is made. Since only half is used here, the remaining half can be used for 8 traditional croissants, 10 pains au chocolat, or 10 more pains aux raisins. (You will need 280 grams/1¼ cups pastry cream and a double batch of rum-soaked raisins.)

Rum-Soaked Raisins

SYRUP

Water	200 grams	¾ cup + 1½ tablespoons
Granulated sugar	200 grams	1 cup
Myers's dark rum	30 grams	2 tablespoons
Raisins	300 grams	2 cups

Combine the syrup ingredients in a medium saucepan and bring to a boil over medium heat, stirring to dissolve the sugar.

Place the raisins in a medium bowl and pour the hot syrup over them. Let cool completely, then refrigerate overnight before using. (The raisins can be refrigerated for up to 1 week.)

MAKES 700 GRAMS/2⅔ CUPS

Almond Croissants

CROISSANTS AUX AMANDES

6 Traditional Croissants
(page 242)

Almond Cream (page 376), cold	300 grams	1¼ cups + 2 tablespoons
Sliced blanched almonds	190 grams	2¼ cups
Almond Syrup (recipe follows)		

The almond croissant is an example of the pâtissier's ingenuity. A bakery invariably has croissants left over. (If it doesn't, it didn't make enough.) So, how to sell those the next day? Turn them into something almost better than a fresh croissant. Split the croissants, fill them with almond cream, and top with more almond cream and sliced almonds, then bake them. So good.

Sebastien is very attentive to sweetness levels, and he always likes to give things his own twist. To that end, he sometimes includes tart raspberry jam, which brings flavor and balance to the croissants.

You'll need a pastry bag with a ½-inch plain tip.

Preheat the oven to 350°F (standard). Line a sheet pan with a Silpat or parchment paper.

Spoon the almond cream into the pastry bag, and spread the almonds in a shallow bowl.

Cut the croissants horizontally in half, as if slicing them open to make sandwiches. Brush the cut side of each one with 10 grams/1½ teaspoons of the almond syrup. Pipe 25 to 30 grams/2 to 2½ tablespoons almond cream onto the bottom half of each croissant, and spread it evenly with a small offset spatula. Place the top halves back on and gently press together. Pipe 20 grams/1½ tablespoons almond cream on top of each croissant, and spread it evenly.

Dip the tops of the croissants into the almonds, coating the almond cream generously, and press down to compact. Arrange the croissants on the prepared sheet pan.

Bake for 18 to 20 minutes, until the nuts are golden brown. (Don't worry if some of the almond cream drips onto the Silpat.) Set the pan on a rack and cool completely.

The croissants are best the day they are baked, but they can be stored in a covered container for up to 1 day.

MAKES 6 CROISSANTS

Almond Raspberry Croissants

Pipe 25 grams/1 tablespoon Raspberry Jam (page 379; 150 grams/¼ cup plus 2 tablespoons total) into each croissant with the almond cream.

Almond Syrup

Sugar	75 grams	¼ cup + 2 tablespoons
Water	75 grams	¼ cup + 1 tablespoon
Almond flour/meal	15 grams	2 tablespoons

Combine the sugar, water, and almond flour in a small saucepan and bring to a simmer over medium heat, stirring to dissolve the sugar. Remove from the heat and let steep for 1 hour.

Strain the syrup into a small bowl or covered container. It can be refrigerated for up to 1 month.

PHOTOGRAPHS ON PAGES 250 AND 251   MAKES 128 GRAMS/SCANT ½ CUP

I remain nostalgic for Wonder Bread because it was a part of my childhood, inseparable from a time when my life was easy and without responsibilities. Back then great bread as we know it today didn't really exist for most people in the United States. We had known great bread, but as with much of the food that came with the immigrant tides, we lost it. We had the tradition and the knowledge to make great bread, and beer, and salami, and wine, and cheese, but we gave them up and allowed them to become homogenized, inexpensive, ersatz versions of truly great food. Fortunately, we realized what we'd lost and have rediscovered these elemental crafts. The speed with which we've resuscitated them is breathtaking and wonderful. How lucky we are to be making such quality foods in this country, bread chief among them. Now it's the exception rather than the rule when a town doesn't have an independent baker. And artisanal bakeries flourish in the bigger cities. Bouchon Bakery now makes all the things an ambitious *boulangerie* should, but we built it first and foremost to make bread.

BREADS

Bread is the reason Bouchon Bakery exists. I conceived the bakery to make bread for my restaurants. And while the bakery has become so much more than a producer of specialty breads, it's the simplicity and universality of the plainer breads—a baguette, a country loaf—that is the source of much of my pride in the bakery. I love bread. Bread is both the simplest of foods—flour, water, yeast, and salt—and infinitely complex. It's one of the easiest foods to make (if it were difficult, it wouldn't have

been around for millennia), but it's also fantastically nuanced. Truly great bread does indeed take great care.

Enter Matthew McDonald, our head baker and bread guru. Matthew came to us, like Sebastien, due to a benevolently conniving spouse. Matthew met his wife, Kristina, at the Culinary Institute of America in St. Helena, and from there they moved all over the United States. But before that, Kristina had been my pastry sous-chef at Rakel in Manhattan in the late 1980s and then opening pastry chef at The French Laundry. It was she who kept insisting that I hire her husband. When, unbeknownst to Matthew, she called me from Phoenix in 2007, a head baker was exactly what I needed. The timing was perfect.

Matthew was one of the key forces in making Bouchon Bakery successful. First

off, his baguette was amazing. He also impressed me with his great respect for and knowledge about bread. His intelligence and ability to articulate it was truly astounding. And, finally, he showed me he could really nail down production schedules and baking times. Bread baking is tricky. Bread has a shorter shelf life than virtually any other food. Oven space is limited. It takes serious experience and knowledge to get it right, to make an excellent product while not losing money. Matthew took charge.

Bakers are a unique breed. A restaurant chef works with countless ingredients. We have new menus every night at The French Laundry and per se. The chefs are working with meat, fish, poultry, offal, produce, dairy, and spices and aromatics, making a range

of soups, salads, appetizers, and entrées. A baker plies his skills with just four basic ingredients—flour, water, yeast, and salt— night after night.

Matthew's unique nature combines a bulldog's tenacity to get things right and a Zen-like patience that spiritually parallels the bread he bakes.

There are very few people who understand bread baking, who can execute it and who can teach it at the level that Matthew can. It's an honor to give voice to his knowledge and convictions about the art and craft of great bread. I'll let him explain his highly individualistic methods in the pages that follow. Like most bakers, he's quite opinionated on the subject of bread, just one of the reasons I wanted him on our team.

Above, from left to right: Multigrain Bâtard (see page 296), Demi-Baguette (page 286), Pain Palladin (page 306), Pain-au-Lait Pullman Loaf (page 317), and Nanterre (page 314). Opposite: Demi-Baguette (page 286).

MATTHEW ON

THE BAGUETTE

For me, it's all about the baguette, perfecting the baguette, the baker's touchstone. I've never made a perfect baguette, nor have I eaten a perfect baguette. We bake between 800 and 1,000 baguettes a day. I try to find the best balance of flavor, texture, crumb, crust, and aroma, and I do feel we're baking one of the best baguettes around. We are also baking hundreds of brioches and croissants and pains au chocolat, épis for the bistro, pain Palladin for Ad Hoc, and specialty breads for The French Laundry, as well as bread for about thirty local establishments.

It's a balancing act: we are limited by time and space, and each product must receive its proper attention and care. Every single piece of dough has to go into one of the eight narrow decks we have for baking (about 24 inches wide, 7 inches high, and 8 feet deep), and each one must go in and come out at the right time in order not to jeopardize the piece that's ready to take its place once the deck has had time to recover its heat. All made even more difficult when you work for a chef famed for his perfectionism, and with the general ethos of a company determined never to compromise.

It's the baguette that pushes me forward. And that's what most bread bakers measure themselves against. I've done some high-level competitive baking, and the one product common to all of them has been the baguette. It's a dough of extraordinary simplicity—just flour, water, yeast, and salt—and yet the interactions of these four basic ingredients are complex.

You can't hide anything about the bread (or about yourself) when you're making a baguette. Every aspect of bread baking is represented in the baguette. For a baguette to be excellent, it requires extraordinary balance at every stage of the dough's creation. And if there's any flaw in the process, or in the baker, it will be revealed really clearly in the finished baguette.

I love that. The baguette speaks clearly and it never lies.

Bread Fundamentals BY MATTHEW MCDONALD

This section outlines our fundamental techniques and convictions, and they apply to both "lean" doughs and "enriched" doughs, doughs that contain fat, eggs, and/or dairy, for instance. But keep in mind that after you've read what we have to say, the most important voice to listen

to is that of the dough. The dough will tell you what to do. You just need to pay attention to it.

BEFORE YOU BEGIN

Good bread is a commitment—you have to tend to it frequently throughout its creation—but it's a rewarding and fun commitment if you're organized.

Most of these doughs require some sort of pre-ferment stage, in the form of either a poolish, made 12 to 15 hours before you mix the dough, or a levain, which takes several days to develop. (We discuss these pre-ferments in detail on pages 270–71.) And then making the bread, from mixing to cooling once it's out of the oven, spans about 6 hours. So if you want something such as fresh bâtards for a six o'clock dinner, you'll need to mix the poolish at nine the night before. Making a poolish is not difficult or time-consuming—it takes about 3 minutes—but it makes a *huge* contribution to the flavor of the bread. You just have to plan. It's a good idea to write down the timing for all the steps. For many of these recipes, we've created a timeline for you to follow and use as a guide (see page 275).

Part of our process requires generating steam in the oven using a hotel pan or sheet pan filled with rocks and chain (see page 267). Get this set up ahead of time too so that you don't have to think about it while making the dough.

Before setting up your *mise en place*, consider what we think of as the X factor: the environment in which the dough will be created, and all the things that make it what it is and may become while it ferments and proofs. The environment will affect the dough. Warm temperatures speed the yeast activity. Dough that hits 82°F/27.7°C will ferment too fast, and the yeast can release hexanol, a gas that will mask the flavor of the finished bread. If it's very hot in your kitchen, take the temperature of your flour. If it's already warm, consider using ice water rather than tap water in the recipe to cool the dough down to the mid- to low-70-degree range. On the other hand, if it's very cold in your kitchen, the yeast activity is going to be slow, so the fermenting and proofing times will be different. If we had our way, everything would happen at 75°F/23.8°C: that's the optimal temperature for dough development.

COMMON MISTAKES IN BREAD BAKING

You've tried to hurry, reducing the mixing, fermenting, and/or proofing times. That's almost always the biggest problem. You can't rush dough. You have to be patient; you have to listen to the dough.

When the bread is less than what you had hoped, it's usually because you fudged at least one of the steps, perhaps failing to preheat the oven sufficiently.

To do bread really well requires a commitment, and therefore planning and organization. That's not to say there's anything criminal about rushing things, or not giving the dough enough time to ferment, or chilling it so that you can do something else—it's just something to be aware of and recognize: everything you do is going to affect that dough.

Also keep in mind the outdoor temperature. People coming in and out of your kitchen can let that weather inside.

If it's very dry in your kitchen, you'll need to keep the dough well covered so that it doesn't develop a skin, which could restrict its development. High humidity is good for proofing dough, but not for baking; it can turn a crisp crust soggy.

THE PRIMARY STEPS FOR GREAT BREAD

Most baking instructors talk about the five basic steps of making bread—mixing, fermenting, shaping, proofing, and baking—but there are actually more than that, in our opinion. We cover them all here.

CHOOSING THE BEST INGREDIENTS

The first step in making bread is no different from the first step in making any good food: find the best possible ingredients.

FLOUR We recommend all-purpose flour milled from hard red winter wheat (which is grown in the Plains states). The hardness of the kernel and the quality of the protein result in superior gluten development; overall, it has the best combination of characteristics for making bread. At the bakery, we use Harvest King brand. Contact the companies of the flours available to you to find out which ones are most likely to be milled from low-protein, hard red winter wheat. For whole wheat and rye flour, I recommend Keith Giusto Bakery Supply (Central Milling).

YEAST We recommend SAF instant yeast. Bakers once used only cakes of compressed fresh yeast, but fresh yeast doesn't keep for long. Given that and the improvements made in manufacturing dried yeast, we use only instant dry. Active dry yeast has a coating of dead yeast cells surrounding the live ones and in our experience behaves less consistently than instant yeast. If you prefer fresh yeast, you can calculate the amount needed by multiplying the amount of instant dry yeast by 2.25.

There are other brands that are fine too. Red Star yeast is actually owned by SAF, and the yeast is the same. Store yeast in the refrigerator once the package has been opened.

SALT Salt is critical in bread both for flavor and for specific chemical reactions (it regulates the yeast, slows oxidation, and is, to a small degree, a preservative). We salt all our doughs with 2 percent of the weight of the flour. Unlike in other forms of cooking, the kind of salt you use in bread dough doesn't matter; any type will do. We prefer fine sea salt because it's easily available and dissolves more quickly than coarse kosher salt, but that works fine as well provided you measure by weight. You could even use iodized table salt if you wanted—there's not enough iodide to make a difference in the flavor of the bread.

WATER As to water, tap water is fine. Its temperature is more important than its source.

SCALING YOUR INGREDIENTS

The quality of a bread dough is determined by the proportion of the ingredients relative to each other. While we give volume measurements here, precision in measuring can only be achieved by using a scale. And all these recipes can be easily doubled, tripled, or quintupled if you use a scale—but not if you measure by volume. (For more about scales, see page 24.)

SETTING UP THE WORKSTATION

You should have your workstation set up and ready for each stage of production.

Before mixing, all ingredients should be weighed or measured and ready to go. Spray the bowl you'll transfer the mixed dough to, or rub it with oil. Lightly dust a clean board or the work surface with flour. Have a small bowl of flour at the ready.

For dividing, preshaping, and shaping, be sure to have plenty of clear working space, areas where the dough will be placed during these stages.

Have the linen, or whatever you'll use for proofing the dough, nearby. Also have the tub or box for covering the dough during proofing handy.

MIXING

Mixing involves two stages.

FIRST STAGE, INCORPORATION This stage involves combining the flour, yeast, and water uniformly, thereby hydrating the flour and yeast. Add the flour to the mixing bowl, sprinkle the yeast over it, and stir with a whisk or the dough hook to distribute the yeast evenly throughout it. Then add the wet ingredients, the pre-ferment and the water. Turn the mixer to low just to mix all the ingredients until they are uniformly combined, 2 to 3 minutes. The purpose of hydrating the dough first is

Slice of Pain-au-Lait Pullman Loaf (page 317)

to activate the yeast and to form the gluten before adding the salt. Then add the salt and continue mixing for 1 minute to dissolve the salt.

SECOND STAGE, MIXING Now the second stage begins. Continue to mix on low (see Stand Mixer, page 26). We give exact times for every step, but it's important to know that bakers think of mixing not in terms of time, but in terms of revolutions of the dough hook. The mixing of dough is a succession of stretches and folds. Our times are based on a KitchenAid Artisan mixer, and we refer to three basic levels of mixing: short, improved, and intensive. Short is about 600 revolutions of the dough hook, improved is about 1,000 revolutions, and intensive is about 1,600. The more a dough is mixed, the more uniform its structure and the smaller the gas bubbles—and, therefore, the more gas it can contain, giving it greater volume. Most of our doughs get an improved mix, which results in a slightly irregular crumb but not one as wide open and holey as a short mix would create.

The only way to know if you are mixing the dough right is through practice, and by keeping track of your results. We don't believe that being able to stretch a piece of dough until it becomes translucent, as is often taught, is adequate to determine if dough is mixed enough. Also, our doughs are fairly slack—that is, loose—so you couldn't use this "windowpane" test anyway; when you scrape them out of the bowl and onto your work surface, they will spread out into fairly flat blobs. Slack, or wet, doughs can ferment longer and develop more flavor.

Once you turn off your mixer, the next step, fermentation, begins. Timing is important here—and it begins the moment you turn the mixer off, not when you get the dough into the bowl it will ferment in and cover it.

FERMENTATION

During the fermentation period, typically more than 3 hours, the dough develops flavor, and during this time, you usually give the slack dough some structure by folding it at three different points.

FIRST FOLD When you've finished mixing, using a plastic bowl scraper, scrape the dough out of the bowl onto a lightly floured surface and give it its first fold. Pat it down into a rectangle, give it a fold from left to right and then a fold from right to left, just as you would fold a letter, then repeat the process, working from the bottom and then the top, and set it seam side down in an oiled bowl (see Stretching and Folding the Dough, page 278). You can either spray the bowl or rub it with canola oil; the amount of fat the dough will pick up is negligible, but oiling the bowl will allow you to remove the dough for further folding without destroying the structure that you've been working to develop. As a rule, always be as gentle as possible with the dough. This is why we use a bowl scraper to remove it from the bowl, so that we don't have to tear it away from the bowl. Always perform each step with an eye to making the next step as close to perfect as you can.

SUBSEQUENT FOLDS After every hour of fermentation, turn the dough gently out onto a floured surface, using the bowl scraper; give it another fold left then right, bottom then top; and return it to the bowl, seam side down. By the end of the fermenting period, the dough will clearly have more structure and strength than when it came out of the mixer bowl.

DIVIDING, PRESHAPING, AND SHAPING

The dough is now fermented and structured, ready to be divided, preshaped, and shaped (some recipes do not involve a dividing and preshaping step).

DIVIDING Turn the dough out again onto a floured surface, using the bowl scraper, and pat it gently into a round, if you are making a boule, or into a rectangle. Cut it into the desired number of pieces, weighing each one: it's important that all the pieces weigh exactly the same. Don't worry about cutting off small pieces to make the right weight. It's best for the structure of the bread to make as few cuts as possible, but it's more important that the weights be even.

PRESHAPING When the pieces have been divided, preshape them by pressing them gently but firmly into either a round shape for bâtards or a rectangular shape for demi-baguettes and longer breads. Everything we do along the way is meant to prepare the dough for its next step, all the way up until we bake it. In the bakery, we keep the dough on speed racks and have special slipcovers to keep drafts out and the humidity in. At home, rest the dough under a plastic tub or a cardboard box to protect it from drafts. Let it rest for 15 minutes, or as otherwise directed in the recipe you are using.

SHAPING Shaping takes a lot of patience and the most practice. Your hands should be firm but gentle. You need to shape the dough but you don't want to smash all the gas that you've been developing out of it. For more on the specific steps, see pages 284–85 and page 292.

Place the shaped dough in its proofing place, whether a linen cloth (see page 269) or a sprayed baking sheet. Most doughs need structural support as they proof to help them maintain the shape you've given them. And they need to be covered, with a plastic tub or a cardboard box (they need room to rise), to protect them from any circulating air that might create a skin.

If you want to practice shaping, make a "dead dough," a dough without yeast; see page 322.

PROOFING

Proofing begins as soon as you have finished shaping the dough. Most doughs proof for one and a half to two hours. To tell when it's ready to bake, touch the dough gently with a finger: if the dough springs back, it needs a little longer; if the impression remains, it's ready. If it collapses, you'd better get it in the oven fast (and shame on you for neglecting your dough after having taken such good care of it all this time; overproofing will result in a flatter and denser loaf).

BAKING

TRANSFER AND SCORING As gently as possible, to avoid damaging the dough's structure, transfer it to the transfer peel and then to the oven peel. Score the dough if specified in the recipe.

BAKING Slip it onto the baking stone and quickly shut the oven door. (See pages 266–67 for creating steam in your oven and general baking issues.)

The bread is done when the color is an appealing dark gold-brown and it feels light, as though it's filled with air, not heavy

with moisture (a dough tends to lose about 20 percent of its weight as it bakes). Pay attention—you don't want underbaked bread. We like a dark crust, because that gives the best flavor. If you are new at this, you can stick a thermometer in the dough—we give temperatures in most of the recipes.

COOLING Set the bread on a rack and (this is one of the hardest parts of bread baking) keep your hands off that beautiful crusty bread for at least an hour, or until it is completely cool. You will be dying to cut into that gorgeous warm bread, the crust crackling as it cools, but remember that it's still cooking inside; the crumb is still jelling, and the crust still developing. The crust will soften partway through the cooling time, but it will crisp again as it cools completely.

AFTER BAKING

Keep cut bread cut side down on a cutting board. You can wrap it if you will be toasting or reheating it, but wrapping bread will soften the crust.

Once it's completely cool, bread can also be wrapped in a few layers of plastic wrap and then in aluminum foil and frozen. Allow the bread to thaw, still wrapped in the foil, for an hour or so at room temperature before reheating it. To reheat frozen breads, preheat the oven to 450°F, preferably with the stone in the oven. Remove the foil and plastic wrap and put the bread on the stone or directly on an oven rack (not a baking sheet; the stone or hot rack conducts heat better than a thin pan) and reheat until it is warm and the exterior is crusty, usually 3 to 5 minutes.

Great Crust at Home

Bread baked in a professional deck oven with steam injection will have an excellent crust if the baker knows how to use his or her steam (at the bakery, we give our deck oven a blast before opening the door, then a second blast as soon as the dough has been loaded). When the steam rolls over the cool dough, it condenses on the dough so that it becomes uniformly coated with a fine layer of water. The water prevents the crust from setting and keeps the exterior supple and cool longer, allowing for easier expansion of the dough. The crust of a dough that doesn't get steam will set quickly and become thick and hard as it bakes. It will also become dull and chalky. The shiny, caramelized crust of bread treated with steam is thinner than on breads that haven't been steam-treated, and has the crispy, chewy texture of great bread.

You can create a similar effect in a home oven with a little effort. What you need is sufficient thermal mass over adequate surface area in your oven. By thermal mass, I mean heat stored in stone and metal, here in the form of rocks and metal (we use chain) in a hotel pan or sheet pan that's allowed to heat thoroughly in the oven. In order to transform 350 grams/1½ cups of water entirely to steam, you need to build up enough heat. You also need that heat spread over enough surface area to do that work fast. Plenty of mass plus plenty of surface area, heated to the temperature of your oven, will give you voluminous, instantaneous steam. With your hotel pan or baking sheet, you create thermal mass by hitting it with a blast of water to begin the baking process. You also need plenty of water to create plenty of steam, and you need the rocks and metal to be hot enough so that the injection of water won't cool down the oven as the water converts to steam. That's what this abundant use of rock and metal is for.

ASSEMBLY AND OVERVIEW OF THE PROCESS

Place all the stones and the chain in your pan and set the pan on the bottom of your oven, if the oven doesn't have a heating element there, or on the lowest oven rack. Position a rack above the pan, making sure there's enough room that you'll be able to hit the rocks and chain with the water, and put the baking stone on this rack. Remove all the other racks.

Preheat the oven for at least 1 hour, preferably 2 hours, before baking. Oven temperatures cycle as the oven preheats, rising above the set temperature, turning off, and then turning back on when the temperature goes below the set temperature. Typically a light indicates when the oven is heating back up again. When the oven hits the desired temperature, the light will go off, then come on again; this is one cycle. It's best to let your oven cycle three times before baking. Your goal when adding the dough is to open the oven, put the bread on the stone, and spray in the water when the oven is at the set temperature or even slightly higher, since the temperature will drop when the door is opened. Stop and take a minute to think about the steps involved and where your tools should be to make this a quick process. The faster it happens, the less heat the oven loses.

Open the oven door, slide the dough off the oven peel onto the stone, hit the rocks and metal with the water (be careful of the steam that will billow out), and close the oven door. If for any reason you must open the oven during baking, wait for at least 10 minutes after you put the bread in before doing so.

Can you bake bread without going to all this trouble? Of course. But we guarantee you will get an excellent crust if you follow the method described here. It may seem hyper rigid, but in fact it's simply highly organized, and because it's organized, it's actually very easy.

Mini Pretzel Bâtards (see page 331)

STEAM-GENERATING KIT

Hotel pan	13 x 21 x 3 inches	Hotel pans can be purchased from restaurant supply stores. They're best because their higher sides will hold a lot of rocks and metal, but you can use rimmed sheet pans.
River rocks	9–10 pounds	Rocks can be purchased at stone yards, landscape or garden supply stores, and even Home Depot. Get golf-ball-sized or smaller for maximum surface area relative to the weight. Do not use sedimentary rocks, which can break apart or even explode with the rapid change of temperature.
Metal chain link	10 feet	The metal chain is arranged in the pan between the rocks.
Super Soaker water gun		Whatever water gun you use, you'll need to be able to deliver about 350 grams/1½ cups of water to the thermal mass quickly and from far enough away that the steam doesn't burn you (see photograph opposite). If you're concerned about getting burned by the steam, you may want to wear protective gloves long enough to cover your forearms as well as your hands.

Tools for Making Bread at Home

SCALE Some scales measure in tenths of grams up to kilos. If yours does not measure tenths of a gram, consider buying an inexpensive palm scale (see page 24).

MIXER The mixer we used for testing all the recipes is the KitchenAid Artisan model (see page 26).

THERMOMETERS The first time you make bread, set an oven thermometer next to the baking stone. During the preheat time, monitor the temperature to get a sense of how long it takes your oven to preheat and to come to temperature. Then remove it and allow the oven to reheat, compensating for the temperature loss when you opened the door.

You should also have a good instant-read thermometer. If you cook a lot, it's worth investing in a good probe thermometer, like the Thermapen (see page 345).

BOWL AND BENCH SCRAPERS An inexpensive plastic bowl scraper helps to maintain the structure of the dough as it is removed from the bowl.

A bench scraper has a metal blade and a handle and is useful for scraping your board clean and for portioning the dough.

TRANSFER PEEL A transfer peel is used to move proofed dough from the linen to the oven peel. It can be a piece of heavy cardboard or a thin piece of wood cut to size; it should be a little larger than the size of the loaf you are moving.

OVEN PEEL An oven peel is the best way to transfer the dough onto the baking stone. Use a piece of heavy cardboard, a thin piece of wood, or Masonite, cut to the size of your baking stone.

PIZZA/BREAD STONE A large, flat rectangular heating stone, about 14 by 16 inches, is best.

BUS TUB, CARDBOARD BOX, OR LARGE PLASTIC STORAGE CONTAINER At the bakery, breads are proofed in a proofing box or in a large rolling rack that is covered with a plastic cover. At home, we suggest proofing the dough under a plastic bus tub or a cardboard box. You can also use a deep plastic storage container from a housewares store, and restaurant supply stores sell plastic storage containers with lids. A 20-by-15-by-8-inch container is ideal.

LINEN CLOTH, OR BAKER'S COUCHE A large linen cloth is the best surface for proofing many doughs once they are shaped. It helps in creating a chewier, crunchier crust and a better crumb, because it supports the sides but then releases the proofed dough so easily. For a boule that will proof in a bowl, use a soft linen cloth or a clean kitchen towel.

DOUGH SCORING TOOL You'll need something with a very thin, very sharp blade for scoring dough. An old-fashioned razor blade works well. Bakers use what's referred to as a *lame* (French for "blade," pronounced *lahm*), a double-edged razor blade affixed to the end of a thin handle.

HANDLING THE LINEN

When you first purchase a linen, it will be stiff. Roll and unroll it a few times to start to soften it and make it pliable. Starting from a short end, roll it up as tightly as possible. Repeat two more times. If time allows, let it sit rolled up for a few days.

After using the linen, shake it over a trash can to remove excess flour and any pieces of dough. The linen will have absorbed moisture from the dough, so hang it on a clothesline or drape it over something overnight to let it dry completely. Then put it on the work surface with the side that wasn't used facing up and roll it up as tightly as possible. (This way the next time the linen is used you will work on the other side.)

Pre-ferments *(the secret to great-tasting bread)*

We add pre-ferments to our doughs because they result in stellar flavor. A pre-ferment is nothing more than a mixture of flour, water, and yeast that's left to stand for many hours, then added to the remaining flour and water when making the dough. It goes by many names—*biga, pâte fermentée,* mother, sponge, and sourdough starter, among others—but the principle is the same: yeast is left alone to gorge on flour for the better part of a day, sometimes

Top: A poolish, ready to use (after 12 to 15 hours)

Above: A levain, ready to use (after 4 days)

longer, to release gases and alcohol, and when it is added to the bread dough, it results in the complex fermented flavors we want in our bread.

At the bakery, we use two types of pre-ferments: poolish (flour, water, and instant yeast) and levain (flour and water).

POOLISH

A poolish is a mixture of flour and water cultured with a small amount of instant yeast. Our poolish is hydrated at 100 percent, meaning it is equal parts (by weight) flour and water, and so has the consistency of a batter. The amount of yeast we use varies, depending on how long we want it to ferment. The less yeast, the more time needed to let it ferment; the longer the fermentation, the more complex the flavor of the bread. Typically we use only a fraction of poolish relative to the flour, about two-thirds, in any given dough, and it has a fairly fast fermentation.

When adding the poolish to the mixer bowl, in order to get as much of it into the bowl as possible, pour some of the water called for in the recipe around the edges of the poolish to loosen it, and allow it all to slip into the mixer bowl.

LEVAIN

Levain is a pre-ferment cultured only with wild yeast. This type of pre-ferment, sometimes called a sourdough starter, is developed by taking advantage of the flora naturally present in the flour and in the air in your kitchen. It's customary to hydrate a levain at 100 percent, like a poolish, to a batter-like consistency—that is, equal parts flour and water by weight. A loose levain encourages the growth of more lactic acid bacteria relative to acetic acid bacteria, and results in a less sour flavor. If all things are equal, the stiffer your levain, the more sour it will become.

When using a levain to make bread dough, we often add nearly equal weights of flour and levain. A dough leavened with a levain is slower to rise than a dough that uses a poolish. The dough will have a little more tensile strength, the ability to stretch, and the flavor will be more acidic.

MAKING YOUR OWN LEVAIN

Make the levain by combining equal parts (by weight) flour and water: let it sit for 24 hours. Then you must feed it. The natural yeast and bacteria in the mixture are living organisms that need food to multiply. If you don't feed a levain, the bacteria will die.

So feed your levain twice a day with flour and water. In practice, you add a small amount of the growing levain to a larger amount of flour and water. We like to use starter in the amount of 60 percent of the weight of the flour (bakers measure everything relative to the weight of the flour) in the recipe. So if you are using 250 grams each of flour and water, add 150 grams of the levain.

All you need for a vigorous levain is the flour you'll be using to make your bread and some water. The flour already has plenty of flora in it, and there's plenty in the air in your kitchen and on your hands to develop a healthy starter. We've found that 4 days is the minimum for developing a levain, and it will keep growing in strength with regular feedings. For strength and flavor, I think a 2-week-old starter is best.

As far as the age of starter goes, or its place of origin, after a few feedings it's going to be fresh again, containing the flora of its environment, so thinking of a starter as you might an old grapevine is silly.

A levain will ferment most efficiently at 78°F/25.5°C. If your kitchen is cold, it may take a day or two longer. If your kitchen is very warm, you may need to watch it so that it doesn't become too sour; feeding it more frequently can help you control yeast and bacteria activity in a hot environment. If this is your first time, it's best to ferment it at 75°F/23.8°C.

Feeding the starter frequently also means that you'll be throwing a lot of starter away. There's really no avoiding it when you're growing a culture. You need enough to get it going and to ensure the right environment for your yeast. Once your levain is solidly established, you can reduce the amount of flour and water you use to feed it by 100 grams if you have a good environment for the yeast and bacteria.

An important note: Don't throw extra starter down your drain. Gluten is not water-soluble (as your sponge will show you, if you've ever used it to clean dough out of a mixing bowl), and it can clog your pipes over time. It's better to dispose of the starter in the garbage can or compost heap. A tip for cleaning dough off your hands: Rub some flour between your hands over the garbage can.

Feeding your starter more or less frequently has varying effects. If you feed it, say, three times a day, it will be very active and less sour. If you feed it once a day, it will be a little more sluggish, and a little more sour.

BAKING BREAD ON A SATURDAY

If you want to make your own yeast culture and have bread that same week, for any of the recipes that call for a levain, here's what you can do:

CREATE THE STARTER	9:00 A.M. TUESDAY
FIRST FEEDING	9:00 A.M. WEDNESDAY
SECOND FEEDING	9:00 P.M. WEDNESDAY
THIRD FEEDING	9:00 A.M. THURSDAY
FOURTH FEEDING	9:00 P.M. THURSDAY
FIFTH FEEDING	9:00 A.M. FRIDAY
SIXTH FEEDING	9:00 P.M. FRIDAY
LEVAIN READY	9:00 A.M. SATURDAY

Any remaining levain can continue to be fed or refrigerated or frozen; see page 272.

Liquid Levain

TO STOP AND START FEEDING: If you need to stop feeding your starter, you can refrigerate it or freeze it indefinitely. Then you can get it back up and running in a day or two. To restart the levain, remove it from the refrigerator or freezer; if it's frozen, allow it to thaw in the refrigerator. Pour off any liquid that's risen to the top. Weigh it out into a clean container and feed it with flour and water as follows: 100 percent each flour and water, 60 percent starter. (You'll be weighing the starter first to see how much you have; to calculate the weight of the flour and water needed using your starter weight, multiply the weight of the starter by 1.67, which will give you an approximately 100 percent flour-and-water ratio.) You can bake with your restored levain after one feeding, but giving it a couple more feedings will ensure that it's fully awake. Judge by sight—it should look as bubbly as it did when you last used it.

Here are guidelines for starting and feeding a levain, with amounts given for the first six feedings.

STARTING YOUR LEVAIN

All-purpose flour	250 grams
Water, ideally at 75°F/23.8°C	250 grams

Combine the flour and water in a plastic or glass container large enough to contain the ingredients comfortably and stir with your hand until uniformly combined. Cover the container. If it has a lid, leave it loose to let out the gas the yeast will produce; if you're using plastic wrap, leave it loose or poke some holes in it.

Put the container in a place that's most likely to maintain a steady 72° to 78°F/23.8° to 25.5°C temperature (i.e., not in a cold basement or a sunny window); the top of the refrigerator is often an excellent place to keep your levain. After 24 hours, you will start to see bubbles—not a lot, but enough to let you know some yeast is active in there.

FEEDING YOUR LEVAIN

All-purpose flour	1500 grams
Water, ideally at 75°F/23.8°C	1500 grams

Combine 250 grams each water and flour in a plastic or glass container. Add 150 grams of the 24-hour-old starter; discard the rest. Stir to combine well, then cover and return to the same place.

Repeat the feeding every 12 hours, using 250 grams each flour and water and 150 grams starter (discard the excess starter). You should notice an increasing amount of bubbles at each feeding, indicating increased yeast activity. After six feedings, your starter should be sufficiently developed to use in any of the doughs calling for levain here, but it will grow stronger with continued feedings and will be at optimal strength after 2 weeks of twice-daily feedings.

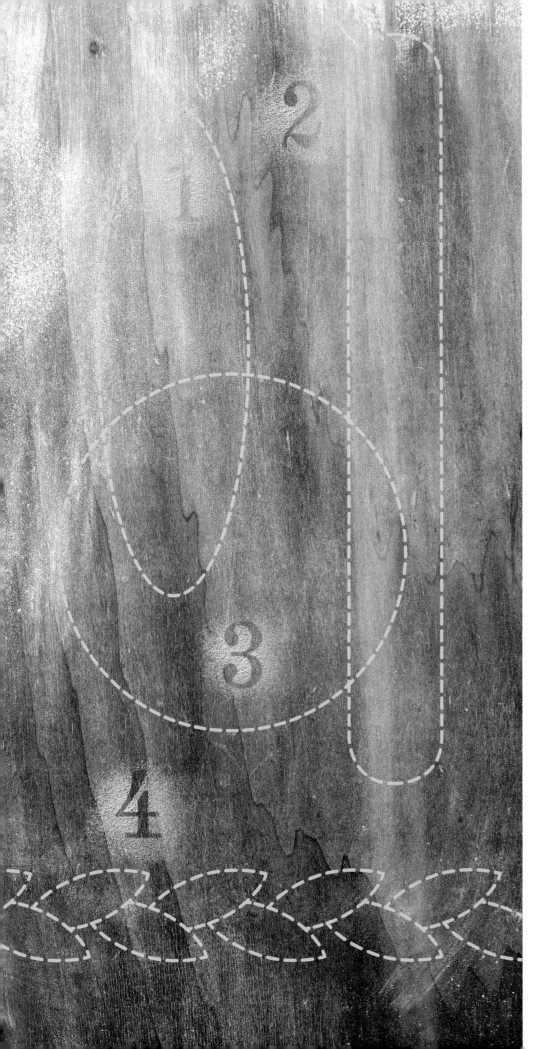

BREAD DOUGH SHAPES

1. BATARD Choose the bâtard shape when you want a large cross section, say for a sandwich. *Bâtard* means "bastard"; it's kind of an illegitimate baguette. It's a much easier shape to manage.

2. BAGUETTE Choose the baguette shape when you want to showcase both the crust and the crumb, to eat the bread with a meal or some wine and cheese. Here we give a recipe for demi-baguettes because a true baguette is longer than the stones most people will have available to bake on. But since a baguette is defined by its circumference rather than its length, the baguette and the demi-baguette are essentially the same shape.

If you like to work with dough, the baguette is one of the great tests for a baker. It's easy to shape a baguette, but it's impossible to shape a perfect one—so the baguette is an exciting challenge. You can always get better. You can spend a lifetime perfecting your baguette skills.

3. BOULE The boule, a large round loaf, is the natural and easy shape for bread (indeed, the French word for "bakery," *boulangerie,* comes from *boule*); dough wants to be round. We use it for pain de campagne and a sourdough loaf as well.

4. EPI The word *épi* refers to the kernels at the tops of cereal plants, such as the tip of a blade of wheat, which this shape resembles. That the bread is shaped to resemble the plant of which it is composed makes it especially elegant. It's also just too cool. At the bakery, guests press up against the glass when we are cutting épis and when they come out of the oven. It looks like magic, but all it really requires is a shaped baguette and a pair of scissors. Here again, we give a recipe for demi-épis rather than full épis.

TIMELINES

Bread baking takes time, and although not all of the time is active, a timeline is a great tool for planning. It will show where there are gaps in the day that will provide you time for other activities. Timelines are essential when you want to make multiple batches at home in one day. And, in a professional setting, timelines are invaluable for creating a production schedule, especially when it comes to baking a large amount and variety of product in a limited amount of oven space(s).

To create a timeline, begin by writing down the time each step takes. Decide on the time you want the bread to come out of the oven and, working backward, lay out each step to determine the time the recipe needs to be started.

All of the loaves of bread (except for brioche) are illustrated in timelines here. Each step is illustrated in a different color. The black slashes indicate when to make a fold. The timelines assume that the poolish or the levain is made and ready to go at the start time; they assume a finish time of 4:00 p.m. to allow ample cooling time before dinner.

If you go the next step and create timelines for making multiple batches at home, just be sure to leave as much time between baking as possible for the stone and the steam-generating system to reheat, at least one, but preferably two hours between batches.

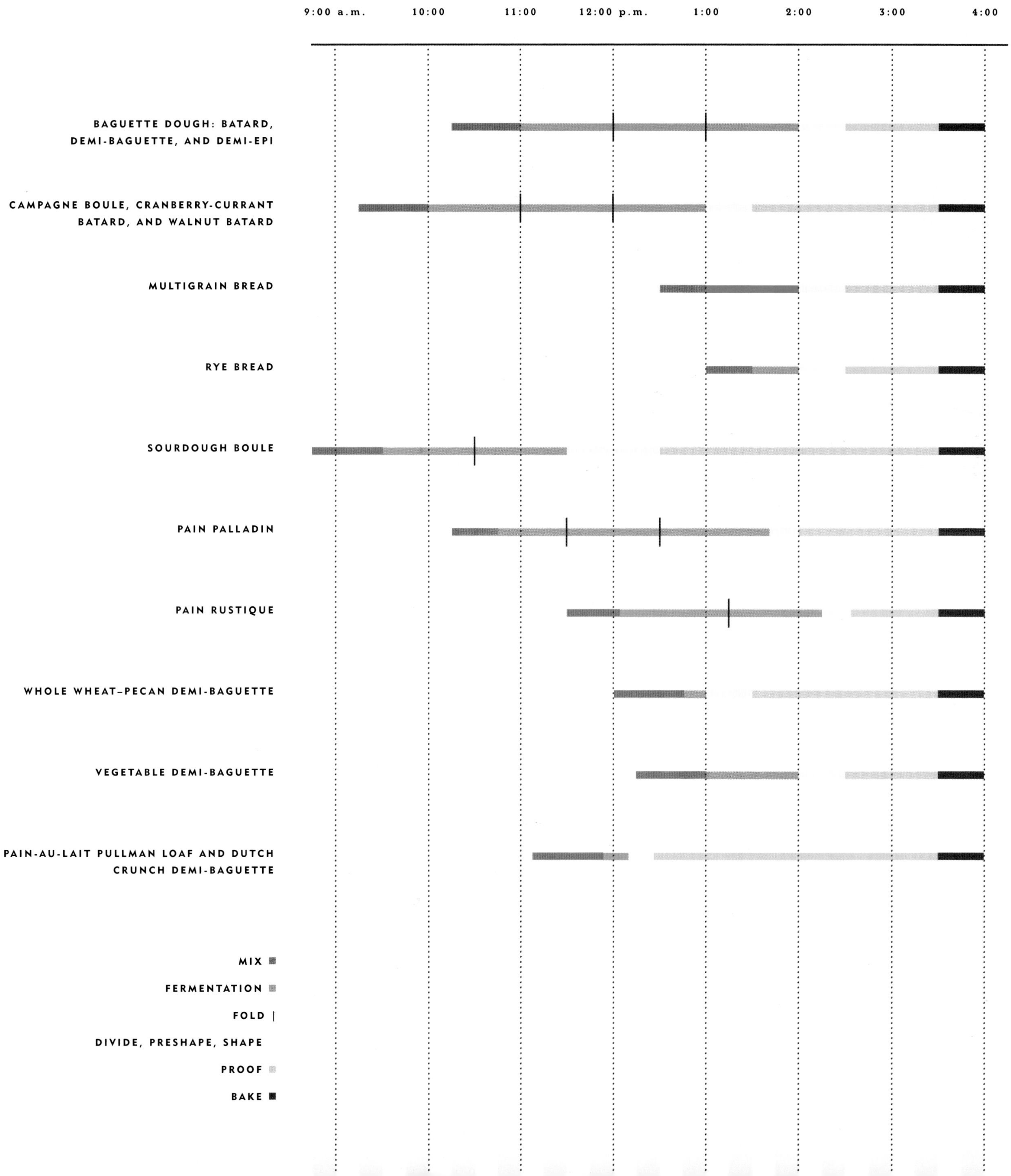

	9:00 a.m.	10:00	11:00	12:00 p.m.	1:00	2:00	3:00	4:00

BAGUETTE DOUGH: BATARD,
DEMI-BAGUETTE, AND DEMI-EPI

CAMPAGNE BOULE, CRANBERRY-CURRANT
BATARD, AND WALNUT BATARD

MULTIGRAIN BREAD

RYE BREAD

SOURDOUGH BOULE

PAIN PALLADIN

PAIN RUSTIQUE

WHOLE WHEAT–PECAN DEMI-BAGUETTE

VEGETABLE DEMI-BAGUETTE

PAIN-AU-LAIT PULLMAN LOAF AND DUTCH
CRUNCH DEMI-BAGUETTE

MIX ▪

FERMENTATION ▪

FOLD |

DIVIDE, PRESHAPE, SHAPE

PROOF ▪

BAKE ▪

Master Recipe: Baguette Dough for Bâtards

POOLISH

All-purpose flour	146 grams	1 cup + 1¾ teaspoons
Instant yeast	0.1 gram	⅟₃₂ teaspoon or a pinch
Water, at 75°F/23.8°C	146 grams	½ cup + 1 tablespoon + 2½ teaspoons

DOUGH

All-purpose flour	437 grams	3 cups + 2 tablespoons
Instant yeast	0.9 gram	¼ teaspoon
Water, at 75°F/23.8°C	279 grams	1 cup + 3½ tablespoons
Fine sea salt	12 grams	2 teaspoons

True baguettes are around 2 feet/60 centimeters long, longer than most baking stones for home ovens, and a length that's difficult to achieve without a proper oven loader. So, for this, our master bread recipe, we give quantities and shaping directions for bâtards. We've taken great care in these instructions to convey the nuances of each step, and we recommend that you read through and then refer to this recipe before making any of the breads—and whenever you want further elucidation when making the other recipes in this chapter.

FOR THE POOLISH: Combine the flour and yeast in a medium bowl and mix with your fingers. Pour in the water and continue to mix until thoroughly combined; the mixture should have the consistency of pancake batter. Cover the bowl loosely with plastic wrap and let sit at room temperature for 12 to 15 hours.

The poolish will be bubbly, but the best indication that it is ready are lines on the surface that look like cracks that are beginning to fall in at the center, as the yeast exhausts its food supply. At this point, the yeast is ready to begin its leavening work in the dough.

TO MIX THE DOUGH: Spray a large bowl with nonstick spray.

Place the flour and yeast in the bowl of a stand mixer fitted with the dough hook and give it a quick mix on the lowest setting to distribute the yeast evenly.

Pour about half the water around the edges of the poolish to help release it, and add the contents of the bowl, along with the remaining water, to the mixer bowl. Mix on low speed for 3 minutes to moisten the dry ingredients and hydrate the flour and yeast.

Using a bowl scraper, scrape down the sides and bottom of the bowl to make sure all the flour has been incorporated. Sprinkle the salt over the top and mix on low speed for 1 minute to dissolve the salt. Continue to mix on low speed for 20 minutes. This is a fairly slack dough, so it will not form a ball or pull away from the sides of the bowl.

FERMENTATION: The dough is now in the 3-hour fermentation stage. Write down the time and set a timer for 1 hour. Referring to the photographs for Stretching and Folding the Dough, pages 278–79, ❶ use a bowl scraper to release the dough and turn it out onto a lightly floured board. The dough will be very sticky. ❷ Gently pat it into a rectangular shape, removing any large bubbles and adding flour only as needed to keep the dough from sticking to the board. Don't dust the top of the dough; it should stick to your fingers.

❸ Stretch the left side of the dough upward and outward and ❹ fold it over two-thirds of the dough, then ❺ stretch and fold the dough from the right side to the opposite side, as if you were folding a letter. ❻ Repeat the process, working from the bottom and then ❼ the top. ❽ Turn the dough over, lift it up with a bench scraper, and place seam side down in the prepared bowl. Cover the bowl with plastic wrap or a clean dish towel and set aside.

When the timer goes off, 1 hour after you stopped the mixer, set it for 1 hour again. Use the bowl scraper to release the dough and pat, stretch, and fold it as before, from side to side, then bottom to top. The dough will have gained structure. Gently return it to the bowl, seam side down, cover, and set aside.

When the timer goes off once again, set it for 1 more hour. Use the bowl scraper to release the dough and pat, stretch, and fold it as before. The dough will have become pillowy. Gently return it to the bowl, seam side down, cover, and set aside.

Meanwhile, set up your baking stone and steam-generating kit (see Assembly and Overview of the Process, page 267) and preheat the oven to 460°F (standard; see Note on Baking Temperatures, page 280).

TO DIVIDE THE DOUGH: Spread a linen cloth on a large cutting board or the back of a sheet pan. Flour the linen.

Use the bowl scraper to release the dough and turn it out onto a lightly floured board. Gently pat the dough into a rectangular shape, removing any large bubbles and adding flour only as needed to keep the dough from sticking to the board. Divide the dough into 2 equal (500-gram/17.6-ounce) portions (see Note on Portioning, page 280).

TO PRESHAPE THE BATARDS: ❶ Gently fold the edges of each piece of dough into the center to form a ball and ❷ turn seam side down on the board (see the photographs for Short Preshape on page 281). Let rest for 15 minutes.

TO SHAPE THE BATARDS: Referring to the photographs for Shaping, pages 284–85, working with one piece of dough at a time, turn the dough seam side up and pat to remove any air bubbles. Position your hands with your fingertips touching at the bottom of the dough. ❶ ❷ Using the sides of your hands, lift up the bottom of the dough and fold it over two-thirds of the dough, then ❸ fold the top over and bring it down so it covers two-thirds of the dough.

Continued on page 280

The bâtard has a great crust-to-crumb ratio. The Master Baguette Dough recipe uses a poolish (yeast, flour, and water) for flavor and follows our standard procedure for mixing, fermenting, and proofing.

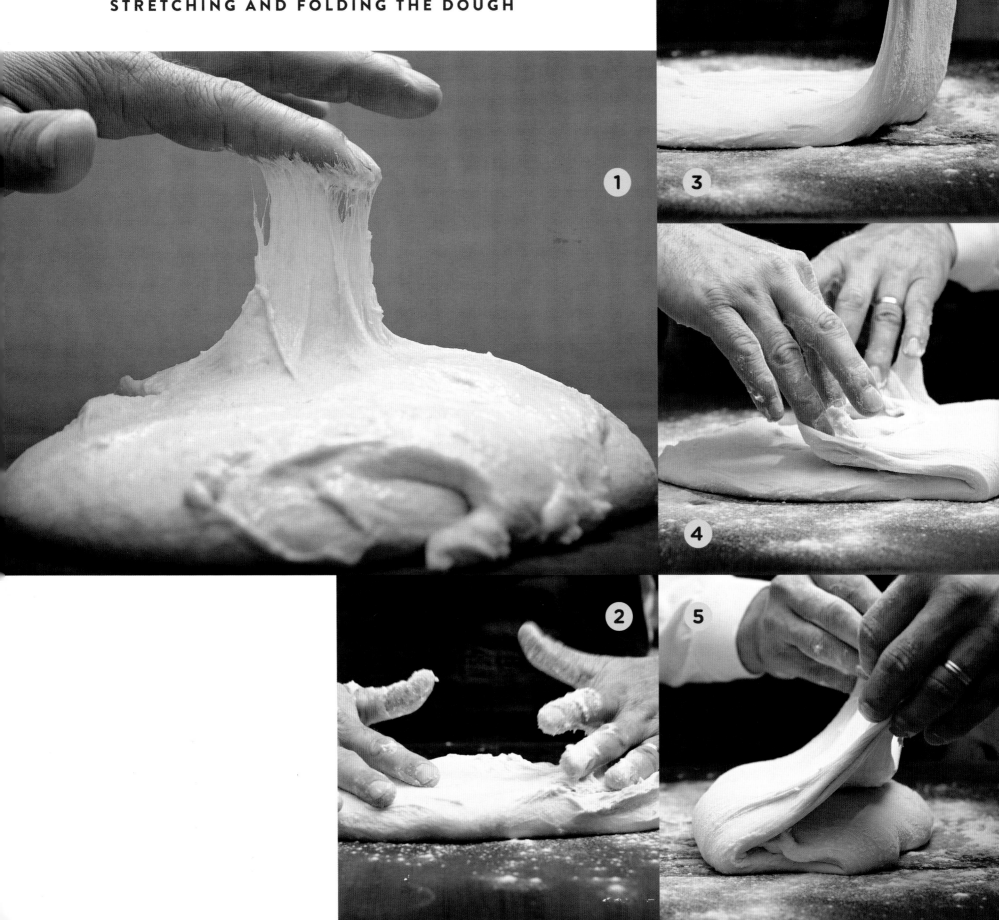

STRETCHING AND FOLDING THE DOUGH

1. Using a bowl scraper, turn the dough out onto a lightly floured work surface; the dough will be very sticky.

2. Gently pat the dough into a rectangular shape, removing any large bubbles and adding flour only as needed to keep the dough from sticking to the surface. Don't dust the top of the dough; it should stick to your fingers.

3. Stretch the left side of the dough upward and outward and 4. fold it over two-thirds of the dough, then 5. stretch and fold the dough from the right side to the opposite side, as if you were folding a letter. 6. Repeat the process, working from the bottom 7. and then the top. 8. Turn the dough over, lift it up with a bench scraper, and place seam side down in the prepared bowl; cover the bowl with plastic wrap or a clean dish towel

④ ⑤ Use the heel of one hand to form an indentation in the dough. ⑥ Fold the dough so that the top and bottom edges meet and use the heel of your hand to seal the seam. Turn the dough seam side down. ⑦ With your hands one on top of the other on the center of the dough, rock the dough back and forth, applying gentle pressure while slowly moving your hands apart, until you reach the ends; keep the diameter consistent. ⑧ Once your hands are no longer touching each other, the heels of your hands and your fingertips should be resting on the board. As you roll the dough, it will increase in length and the structure will tighten. It's best to keep an eye on the center diameter, as this will dictate the length. The finished diameter of the center of the bâtard should be 2¾ inches. Lay the loaves on a linen. Fold or bunch the linen to create small walls on both sides of each loaf to help maintain the shape as the dough proofs.

TO PROOF THE DOUGH: Cover with a plastic tub or a cardboard box and let proof for about 1 hour, or until when the dough is delicately pressed with a finger, the impression remains.

TO BAKE THE BREAD: Using the linen, move the dough, one piece at a time, to the transfer peel, seam side up, and then to the oven peel, seam side down, spacing them evenly. Score the bâtards by making one single cut down the center (see Six Types of Scoring, page 324).

Transfer the dough to the baking stone. Immediately spray water from the Super Soaker onto the steam generator (rocks and chain). Quickly shut the oven door and bake for 25 to 30 minutes, until the bread feels lighter than you'd expect for its size and the internal temperature is 200° to 210°F/93.3° to 98.8°C (see Note on Venting the Oven).

Let cool completely on a cooling rack. As tempting as it is to eat warm, the bread will continue to cook when removed from the oven. Eat the bread at room temperature or rewarm in a hot oven.

PHOTOGRAPH ON PAGE 289   **MAKES 2 BATARDS**

NOTE ON PORTIONING: At the bakery, we always make a little bit more dough than we need to ensure that all portions are exactly the same weight. Although this is less crucial at home, we still encourage you to portion to the gram weights given. As you progress, it will help you recognize and achieve consistency of product.

NOTE ON BAKING TEMPERATURE: The ideal temperature for baking this bread (as well as others noted) at home is 460°F/238°C (standard). If your oven has a digital setting, it is easily set to 460°F; for an oven with a dial setting, position the dial between 450°F/232°C and 475°F/246°C.

NOTE ON VENTING THE OVEN: If the exterior of the loaf reaches the desired golden brown color or begins to darken too qickly before the internal temperature reaches 200° to 210°F/93.3° to 98.8°C, open the oven door slightly (if your oven door will not stay open, fold a towel or a pot holder and use it to prop the door slightly open) and continue to bake until done.

Note to Professionals: If you are a more experienced baker, you may want to hold back some of the water during the hydration phase so that you can better control the dough and achieve the consistency that works best for you. For instance, if your dough is difficult to shape, try using less water.

At the bakery, we often use an autolyse, created by the godfather of modern bread baking, Raymond Calvel. The process is simply combining the flour and water and letting it stand for 20 to 30 minutes, which releases an enzyme in the flour that breaks down the protein, thereby weakening the dough, so that it will require less mixing. With less mixing, there's less oxidation of the dough, and you have more control over its temperature, as the friction from mixing can heat the dough up past where you might want it.

SHORT PRESHAPE

For bâtards, ① gently fold the edges of the dough into the center to form a ball. ② Turn seam side down to rest.

LONG PRESHAPE

For demi-baguettes, demi-épis, pain-au-lait Pullmans, or pretzels, ① gently fold the edge that is closest to you over to the far side and roll the seam side under. ② Turn seam side down to rest.

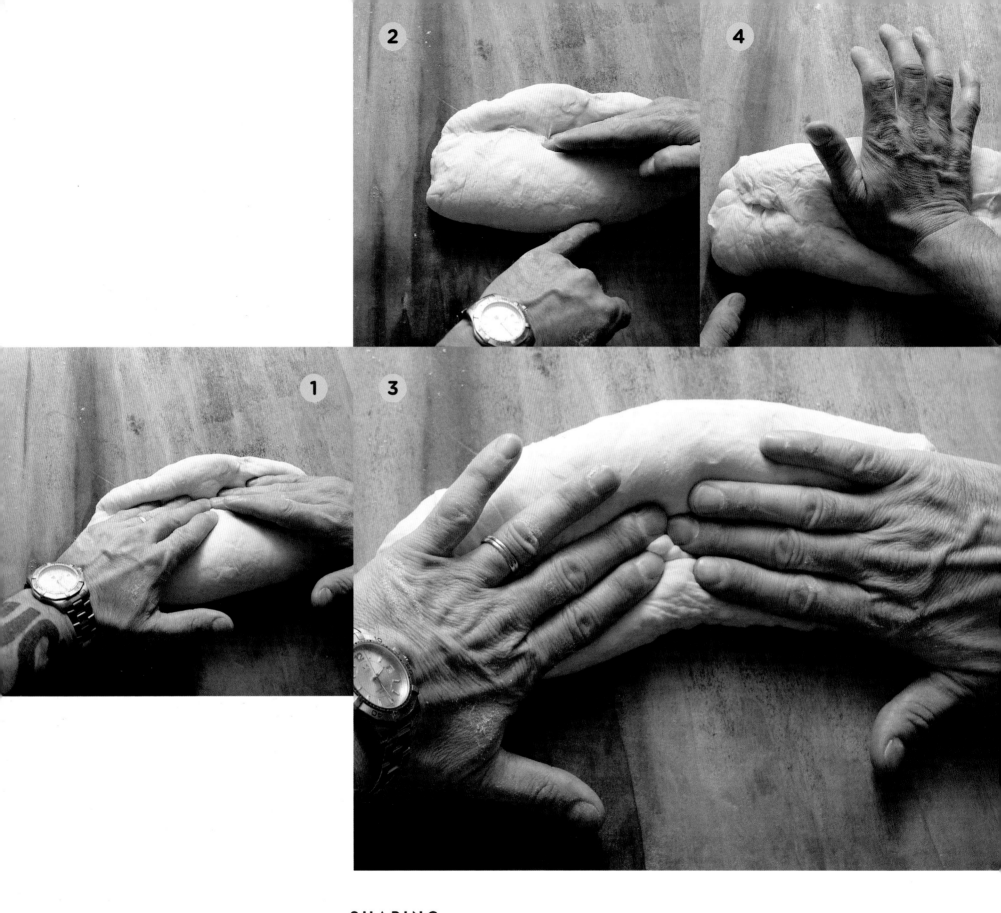

SHAPING FOR BATARDS, DEMI-BAGUETTES, EPIS, PAIN-AU-LAIT PULLMANS, OR PRETZELS

• PRETZELS: ¾ INCH

• DEMI-BAGUETTES, DEMI-EPIS, AND
  DUTCH CRUNCH DEMI-BAGUETTES: 1½ INCHES

• PAIN-AU-LAIT PULLMANS: 2½ INCHES

• BATARDS: 2¾ INCHES

5

6

7

8

Turn the dough seam side up and pat to remove any air bubbles. Position your hands with your fingertips touching at the bottom of the dough. ❶ ❷ Using the sides of your hands, lift up the bottom of the dough and fold it over two-thirds of the dough, then ❸ fold the top over and bring it down so it covers two-thirds of the dough. ❹ ❺ Use the heel of one hand to form an indentation in the dough. ❻ Fold the dough so that the top and bottom edges meet and use the heel of your hand to seal the seam. Turn the dough seam side down. ❼ With your hands one on top of the other on the center of the dough, rock the dough back and forth, applying gentle pressure while slowly moving your hands apart, until you reach the ends; keep the diameter consistent. ❽ Once your hands are no longer touching each other, the heels of your hands and your fingertips should be resting on the board. As you roll the dough, it will increase in length and the structure will tighten. It's best to keep an eye on the center diameter, as this will dictate the length.

Demi-Baguettes and Demi-Epis

POOLISH FOR DEMI-BAGUETTES

All-purpose flour	83 grams	½ cup + 1 tablespoon + 1¼ teaspoons
Instant yeast	0.1 gram	⅟₃₂ teaspoon or a pinch
Water, at 75°F/23.8°C	83 grams	¼ cup + 1½ tablespoons

POOLISH FOR DEMI-EPIS

All-purpose flour	55 grams	¼ cup + 2 tablespoons + ½ teaspoon
Instant yeast	0.2 gram	⅟₃₂ teaspoon or a pinch
Water, at 75°F/23.8°C	55 grams	3 tablespoons + 2½ teaspoons

DOUGH FOR DEMI-BAGUETTES

All-purpose flour	249 grams	1¾ cups + 1½ teaspoons
Instant yeast	0.7 gram	¼ teaspoon
Water, at 75°F/23.8°C	159 grams	⅔ cup
Fine sea salt	5 grams	¾ teaspoon

DOUGH FOR DEMI-EPIS

All-purpose flour	166 grams	1 cup + 3 tablespoons
Instant yeast	0.3 gram	⅟₁₆ teaspoon
Water, at 75°F/23.8°C	106 grams	¼ cup + 3 tablespoons
Fine sea salt	5 grams	¾ teaspoon

This is our basic baguette dough, 100 percent flour and 73 percent water, a fairly wet dough. These amounts are the same proportions we use for the bâtard in the preceding recipe. It's a truly versatile dough, and here we give proportions and instructions for both demi-baguettes and demi-épis. Do read Bread Fundamentals and the master recipe for baguette dough before you begin.

FOR THE POOLISH: Place the flour and yeast in a medium bowl and mix with your fingers. Pour in the water and continue to mix until thoroughly combined; the mixture should have the consistency of pancake batter. Cover the top of the bowl loosely with plastic wrap and let sit at room temperature for 12 to 15 hours.

TO MIX THE DOUGH: Spray a large bowl with nonstick spray. Place the flour and yeast in the bowl of a stand mixer fitted with the dough hook and give it a quick mix on the lowest setting to distribute the yeast evenly.

Pour about half of the water around the edges of the poolish to help release it, and add the poolish, along with the remaining water, to the mixer bowl. Mix on low speed for 3 minutes. Scrape down the sides and bottom of the bowl. Sprinkle the salt over the top and mix on low speed for 1 minute to dissolve the salt. Continue to mix on low speed for 20 minutes.

FERMENTATION: The dough is now in the 3-hour fermentation stage. Set a timer for 1 hour. Using a bowl scraper, release the dough and turn it out onto a lightly floured board. Pat, stretch, and fold the dough (see Stretching and Folding the Dough, page 278), and place in the prepared bowl. Cover and set aside.

Set the timer for 1 hour again. Repeat the pat, stretch, and fold, place the dough back in the bowl, cover, and set aside.

Set the timer for 1 hour again. Repeat the pat, stretch, and fold, place the dough back in the bowl, cover, and set aside.

Meanwhile, set up your baking stone and kit (see Assembly and Overview of the Process, page 267) and preheat the oven to 460°F (standard; see Note on Baking Temperature, page 280).

TO DIVIDE, PRESHAPE, AND SHAPE THE DOUGH: Spread a linen cloth on a large cutting board or on the back of a sheet pan. Flour the linen.

Use the bowl scraper to release the dough and turn it out onto a lightly floured board. Gently pat the dough into a rectangular shape, removing any large bubbles and adding flour only as needed to keep the dough from sticking to the board. Divide the dough into 190-gram/6.7-ounce portions: 3 for demi-baguettes, 2 for demi-épis.

Preshape the dough long. ❶ Gently fold the edge that is closest to you over to the far side and roll the seam side under. ❷ Turn seam side down on the board (see the photographs for Long Preshape on page 282). Let rest for 15 minutes.

Shape for demi-baguettes (see Shaping, page 284; cutting for demi-épis happens after proofing) and lay the loaves on the linen. Fold or bunch the linen to create small walls on both sides of each loaf to help maintain the shape as the dough proofs.

TO PROOF THE DOUGH: Cover with a plastic tub or a cardboard box and let proof for 1 hour, or until when the dough is delicately pressed with a finger, the impression remains.

TO BAKE THE BREAD: Using the linen, move the dough, one piece at a time, to the transfer peel, seam side up, and then to the oven peel, seam side down, spacing them evenly. Score the demi-baguettes by making 3 cuts down the center (see Six Types of Scoring, page 324) or cut the loaves for demi-épis (see instructions at right).

Transfer the bread to the baking stone. Immediately spray water onto the steam generator (rocks and chain). Quickly shut the oven door and bake demi-épis for 15 minutes, demi-baguettes for 20 minutes, or until the bread feels lighter than you'd expect for its size and the internal temperature is 200° to 210°F/93.3° to 98.8°C (see Note on Venting the Oven, page 280).

Let cool completely on a cooling rack.

MAKES 3 DEMI-BAGUETTES OR 2 DEMI-EPIS

CUTTING A BAGUETTE INTO AN EPI

Set the demi-baguette on a floured peel. Beginning 2½ to 3 inches from one end of the baguette, holding a pair of sharp scissors at a 60-degree angle, make the first cut, leaving a little of the dough attached to anchor the leaf. Move the leaf to one side of the épi. Continue to the end of the épi, alternating the cuts from one side to the other.

From left to right: Baguette Dough Bâtard (page 276), Walnut Bâtard (page 294), Multigrain Demi-Baguette (page 296),

Sourdough Boule (page 302), Rye Bâtard (page 301), and Cranberry-Currant Bâtard (page 294)

Pain de Campagne

Campagne Boule

All-purpose flour	459 grams	3¼ cups + 1 teaspoon
Rye flour	32 grams	¼ cups
Whole wheat flour	25 grams	3 tablespoons + 1 teaspoon
Instant yeast	0.5 gram	⅛ teaspoon
Liquid Levain (page 272)	169 grams	6 ounces
Water, at 75°F/23.8°C	322 grams	1¼ cups + 2 tablespoons
Fine sea salt	12 grams	2 teaspoons

Historically, the classic country loaf (*campagne* means "country") was made with a variety of whole-grain flours and rye flours, rather than the more refined and more expensive white flour. We use more rye in this bread than whole wheat, and that gives it a deeper, earthier flavor; a richer color; a denser crumb; and a heavier crust. It can be served by itself or to accompany a meal. It's also a great sandwich bread, especially for a juicy sandwich. It satisfies something primal, something deep down in a place that maybe you didn't know you had in you.

The campagne is great plain, but it also accommodates dried fruits and nuts well, so we often incorporate walnuts and cranberries (see page 294).

TO MIX THE DOUGH: Spray a large bowl with nonstick spray. Place the flours and yeast in the bowl of a stand mixer fitted with the dough hook and give it a quick mix on the lowest setting to combine the flours and distribute the yeast evenly. Make a well in the center, add the levain and water, and mix on low speed for 3 minutes. Sprinkle the salt over the top and mix on low speed for 1 minute to dissolve the salt. Continue to mix on low for 20 minutes.

FERMENTATION: The dough is now in the 3-hour fermentation stage. Set a timer for 1 hour. Using a bowl scraper, release the dough and turn it out onto a lightly floured board. Pat, stretch, and fold the dough (see Stretching and Folding the Dough, page 278) and place in the prepared bowl. Cover and set aside.

Set the timer for 1 hour again. Repeat the pat, stretch, and fold, place the dough back in the bowl, cover, and set aside.

Set the timer for 1 hour again. Repeat the pat, stretch, and fold, place the dough back in the bowl, cover, and set aside.

Meanwhile, set up your baking stone and kit (see Assembly and Overview of the Process, page 267) and preheat the oven to 460°F (standard; see Note on Baking Temperature, page 280).

TO SHAPE THE DOUGH: (See Note on the Strength of a Boule.) Line a large bowl, about 11 inches across at the top, with a linen cloth, trying to keep the folds as flat against the surface as possible (see Note on Docking the Dough). Flour the linen.

Referring to the photographs for Shaping a Boule, page 292, ❶ use the bowl scraper to release the dough and turn it out onto a lightly floured board; it will feel tacky to the touch. Gently pat the dough into a round, removing any large bubbles and adding flour only as needed to keep the dough from sticking to the board. Trim the dough to a weight of 1 kilogram/2 pounds, 3.2 ounces. Let rest for 20 minutes.

❷ Fold the edges of the dough into the center to form a ball. ❸ Hold the dough on its side, with the seam away from you. Place your other hand slightly above the edge of the dough and pull the side of your hand along the seam, rolling the dough toward you, to close the seam. As you close the seam, a small tail will form. ④ Fold the tail down to hold the seam closed.

TO DOCK THE DOUGH: Following the sequence of photographs on page 293, ① use a bench scraper to mark the dough in a deep crosshatch pattern, almost all the way through the dough. ② Invert and place in the lined bowl.

TO PROOF THE DOUGH: Set a sheet pan on top of the bowl or cover with a plastic tub or a cardboard box and let proof for 2 hours, or until when the dough is delicately pressed with a finger, the impression remains.

TO BAKE THE BREAD: Using the linen, move the dough to the oven peel, docked side up. Transfer the bread to the baking stone. Immediately spray water onto the steam generator (rocks and chain). Quickly shut the oven door and bake for 30 minutes, or until the bread feels lighter than you'd expect for its size and the internal temperature is 200° to 210°F/93.3° to 98.8°C (see Note on Venting the Oven, page 280).

Let cool completely on a cooling rack.

MAKES 1 ROUND LOAF

NOTE ON THE STRENGTH OF A BOULE: A boule is the strongest structure for a loaf of bread, and the shaping should be sufficient for giving it the structure it needs, so generally it does not need to be preshaped. However, until you are proficient at shaping a boule, adding the step of preshaping short (see Short Preshape, page 281) will only increase the structure. After dividing, preshape the dough short, as for bâtards, and let rest for 15 minutes, then shape the dough.

NOTE ON DOCKING THE DOUGH: Because of the cuts in the surface area of the dough, there is a greater likelihood that the dough will stick to the linen. Use a linen that is very supple and dust it well with flour. Alternatively, the boule can be scored with a square cut, as for the Sourdough Boule (page 302).

SHAPING A BOULE

① Release the dough from the bowl, seam side up, onto a lightly floured board. Gently pat the dough into a mound, removing any large air bubbles. Trim the dough as needed (according to the recipe). ② Fold the edges of the dough into the center to form a ball. ③ Hold the dough on its side, with the seam away from you. Place your other hand slightly above the edge of the dough and pull the side of your hand along the seam, rolling the dough toward you, to close the seam. As you close the seam, a small tail will form.

④ Fold the tail down to hold the seam closed.

DOCKING A CAMPAGNE BOULE

① Use a bench scraper to mark the dough in a deep crosshatch pattern almost all the way through the dough. ② Invert and place in a linen-lined bowl.

Cranberry-Currant Bâtards and Walnut Bâtards

DOUGH FOR CRANBERRY-CURRANT BATARDS

All-purpose flour	395 grams	2¾ cups + 1 tablespoon
Rye flour	27 grams	3 tablespoons + 2 teaspoons
Whole wheat flour	22 grams	3 tablespoons
Instant yeast	0.4 gram	⅛ teaspoon
Liquid Levain (page 272)	146 grams	5.1 ounces
Water, at 75°F/23.8°C	277 grams	1 cup + 3 tablespoons
Fine sea salt	11 grams	2 teaspoons
Dried cranberries (see Note)	70 grams	½ cup + 1½ tablespoons
Dried currants (see Note)	70 grams	¼ cup + 3 tablespoons

DOUGH FOR WALNUT BATARDS

All-purpose flour	404 grams	2¾ cups + 2 tablespoons
Rye flour	28 grams	3 tablespoons + 2¼ teaspoons
Whole wheat flour	22 grams	3 tablespoons
Instant yeast	0.4 gram	⅛ teaspoon
Liquid Levain (page 272)	149 grams	5.2 ounces
Water, at 75°F/23.8°C	284 grams	1 cup + 3½ tablespoons
Fine sea salt	11 grams	2 teaspoons
Coarsely chopped walnuts	120 grams	1 cup + 1 tablespoon

Nuts and tart fruits are good in breads. Hazelnuts and currants is a common pairing in breakfast breads in southern France. Here the astringent cranberry and sweet currant pair nicely with the flavors of wheat and rye. Walnuts also complement rye well. They're a great nut and they grow out here in Napa. When we add nuts to bread, we always add them raw, skin on—no blanching, no roasting—because we like the clean nut flavor to come through in the bread. Adding this kind of garnish is all about proportion, so pay attention to the amounts here, and feel free to improvise with other garnish in these proportions. It should be noted that this is the same campagne dough used for the boule.

TO MIX THE DOUGH: Spray a large bowl with nonstick spray. Place the flours and yeast in the bowl of a stand mixer fitted with the dough hook and give it a quick mix on the lowest setting to combine the flours and to distribute the yeast evenly. Make a well in the center, add the levain and water, and mix on low speed for 3 minutes. Sprinkle the salt over the top and mix on low speed for 1 minute to dissolve the salt. Continue to mix on low for 20 minutes.

Meanwhile, if making the walnut bâtards, toss the nuts in a fine-mesh strainer to remove any small particles and pieces.

Add the cranberries and currants or walnuts to the dough and mix on low just to incorporate.

FERMENTATION: The dough is now in the 3-hour fermentation stage. Set a timer for 1 hour. Using a bowl scraper, release the dough and turn it out onto a lightly floured board. Pat, stretch, and fold the dough (see Stretching and Folding the Dough, page 278) and place it in the prepared bowl. Cover and set aside.

Set the timer for 1 hour again. Repeat the pat, stretch, and fold, place the dough back in the bowl, cover, and set aside.

Set the timer for 1 hour again. Repeat the pat, stretch, and fold, place the dough back in the bowl, cover, and set aside.

Meanwhile, set up your baking stone and kit (see Assembly and Overview of the Process, page 267) and preheat the oven to 460°F (standard; see Note on Baking Temperature, page 280).

TO DIVIDE, PRESHAPE, AND SHAPE THE DOUGH: Spread a linen cloth on a large cutting board or on the back of a sheet pan. Flour the linen.

Use the bowl scraper to release the dough and turn it out onto a lightly floured board. Gently pat the dough into a rectangular shape, removing any large bubbles and adding flour only as needed to keep the dough from sticking to the board. Divide the dough into two 500-gram/17.6-ounce portions.

Preshape short (see Short Preshape, page 281). Let rest for 15 minutes.

Shape for bâtards (see Shaping, page 284) and lay the loaves on the linen. Fold or bunch the linen to create small walls on both sides of each loaf to help maintain the shape as the dough proofs.

TO PROOF THE DOUGH: Cover with a plastic tub or a cardboard box and let proof for 2 hours, or until when the dough is delicately pressed with a finger, the impression remains.

TO BAKE THE BREAD: Using the linen, move the dough, one piece at a time, to the transfer peel, seam side up, and then to the oven peel, seam side down, spacing them evenly. Score the cranberry-currant bread with the Vs of the chevron cut (see Six Types of Scoring, page 324) or the walnut bread with the 10 to 12 parallel cuts of the sausage cut (see Six Types of Scoring, page 324).

Transfer the bread to the baking stone. Immediately spray water onto the steam generator (rocks and chain). Quickly shut the oven door and bake for 20 to 25 minutes, until the bread feels lighter than you'd expect for its size and the internal temperature is 200° to 210°F/93.3° to 98.8°C (see Note on Venting the Oven, page 280).

Let cool completely on a cooling rack.

PHOTOGRAPH ON PAGE 289   **MAKES 2 BATARDS**

NOTE: If your dried fruit is not plump, rehydrate it by pouring hot water over it and letting it sit for 20 minutes. Drain, let cool, and pat dry before beginning.

Multigrain Bread

SOAKER FOR BATARDS

Rolled oats	33 grams	¼ cup + 2½ tablespoons
Sesame seeds	33 grams	3 tablespoons + 2 teaspoons
Hulled sunflower seeds	33 grams	¼ cup
Flaxseeds	33 grams	¼ cup + 1 teaspoon
Quinoa	33 grams	2 tablespoons + 2½ teaspoons
Cold water	100 grams	¼ cup + 3 tablespoons

SOAKER FOR DEMI-BAGUETTES

Rolled oats	18 grams	3½ tablespoons
Sesame seeds	18 grams	2 tablespoons
Hulled sunflower seeds	18 grams	2 tablespoons + 1 teaspoon
Flaxseeds	18 grams	2 tablespoons + 1 teaspoon
Quinoa	18 grams	1½ tablespoons
Cold water	54 grams	3 tablespoons + 2 teaspoons

DOUGH FOR BATARDS

All-purpose flour	311 grams	2 cups + 3½ tablespoons
Whole wheat flour	89 grams	¾ cup
Rye flour	44 grams	¼ cup + 2 tablespoons
Instant yeast	3 grams	¾ + ⅛ teaspoon
Liquid Levain (page 272)	89 grams	3.1 ounces
Water, at 75°F/23.8°C	311 grams	1 cup + 5 tablespoons
Fine sea salt	10 grams	1¾ teaspoons

DOUGH FOR DEMI-BAGUETTES

All-purpose flour	169 grams	1 cup + 3 tablespoons
Whole wheat flour	48 grams	¼ cup + 2½ tablespoons
Rye flour	24 grams	3 tablespoons + 1 teaspoon
Instant yeast	2 grams	½ + ⅛ teaspoon
Liquid Levain (page 272)	48 grams	1.6 ounces
Water, at 75°F/23.8°C	169 grams	½ cup + 3 tablespoons + 1 teaspoon
Fine sea salt	5 grams	¾ teaspoon

A soaker is baker-speak for whole grains and seeds that are soaked in water before being added to the dough. Here we use rolled oats, sesame seeds, sunflower seeds, flaxseeds, and quinoa. The most important step in making this multigrain bread is adding the soaker at the very end of mixing; adding it too early will interfere with the dough's gluten development, resulting in a flatter, denser bread.

FOR THE SOAKER: Combine the oats and all the seeds in a medium bowl. Pour in the water and mix well. Let sit at room temperature for 1 hour.

TO MIX THE DOUGH: Spray a large bowl with nonstick spray. Place all the flours and the yeast in the bowl of a stand mixer fitted with the dough hook and give it a quick mix on the lowest setting to combine the flours and to distribute the yeast evenly. Make a well in the center, add the levain and water, and mix on low speed for 3 minutes. Sprinkle the salt over the top and mix on low speed for 1 minute to dissolve the salt. Continue to mix on low for 20 minutes.

Add the seeds and any water remaining in the bowl and mix on low just to incorporate.

FERMENTATION: The dough is now in the fermentation stage. Set a timer for 1 hour. Using a bowl scraper, release the dough and turn it out onto a lightly floured board. Pat, stretch, and fold the dough (see Stretching and Folding the Dough, page 278) and place in the prepared bowl. Cover and set aside.

Meanwhile, set up your baking stone and kit (see Assembly and Overview of the Process, page 267) and preheat the oven to 460°F (standard; see Note on Baking Temperature, page 280).

TO DIVIDE, PRESHAPE, AND SHAPE THE DOUGH: Spread a linen cloth on a large cutting board or on the back of a sheet pan. Flour the linen.

Use the bowl scraper to release the dough and turn it out onto a lightly floured board. Gently pat the dough into a rectangular shape, removing any large bubbles and adding flour only as needed to keep the dough from sticking to the board. Divide the dough into two 550-gram/19.4-ounce portions for bâtards or three 200-gram/7-ounce portions for demi-baguettes.

Preshape short for bâtards (see Short Preshape, page 281) or long for demi-baguettes (see Long Preshape, page 282). Let rest for 15 minutes.

Shape for bâtards or demi-baguettes (see Shaping, page 284) and lay the loaves on the linen. Fold or bunch the linen to create small walls on both sides of each loaf to help maintain the shape as the dough proofs.

TO PROOF THE DOUGH: Cover with a plastic tub or a cardboard box and let proof for 1 hour, or until when the dough is delicately pressed with a finger, the impression remains.

TO BAKE THE BREAD: Using the linen, move the dough, one piece at a time, to the transfer peel, seam side up, and then to the oven peel, seam side down, spacing them evenly. Score the bâtards by making a single cut down the center (see Six Types of Scoring, page 324) or the demi-baguettes by making 3 cuts down the center (see Six Types of Scoring, page 324).

Transfer the bread to the baking stone. Immediately spray water onto the steam generator (rocks and chain). Quickly shut the oven door and bake demi-baguettes for 15 minutes, bâtards for 20 minutes, or until the bread feels lighter than you'd expect for its size and the internal temperature is 200° to 210°F/93.3° to 98.8°C (see Note on Venting the Oven, page 280).

Let cool completely on a cooling rack.

PHOTOGRAPHS ON PAGES 255 AND 289   **MAKES 2 BATARDS OR 3 DEMI-BAGUETTES**

FRIED EGG ON TOASTED MULTIGRAIN This bread is ideal for toasting on a griddle next to some fried eggs. Top each slice of toast with an egg and sprinkle with salt and black pepper, and you have a great breakfast, or even lunch with a side salad.

For Matthew, the most important aspect of a multigrain bread is its taste. "If it's got some extra nutritional value, that's great," he says, "but if it doesn't taste good, why eat it?" This recipe has been taught for decades by his mentor Didier Rosada. "My goal was to keep our version in balance with what he created. I've changed the seeds a little, but it's right in line with the bread he made when I studied with him in the mid-nineties. It's all about proportions (mainly white flour, about 85 percent, with whole wheat and rye making up the rest), levain (sourdough starter), and a soaker."

Opposite: Multigrain Soaker. Above: Multigrain Demi-Baguette (page 296).

HAM AND CHEESE ON RYE Nothing fancy here, but I urge you to try a ham and cheese made with the best possible ingredients. Spread slices of our rye bread with Edmund Fallot Dijon mustard and add slices of Comté or Gruyère and some beautiful French ham. For a little crunch, serve cornichons on the side.

Rye Bread

Rye flour	295 grams	2¼ cups + 3 tablespoons
All-purpose flour	236 grams	1½ cups + 3 tablespoons
Instant yeast	4 grams	1¼ teaspoons
Liquid Levain (page 272)	131 grams	4.6 ounces
Water, at 75°F/23.8°C	341 grams	1¼ cups + 3 tablespoons
Fine sea salt	12 grams	2 teaspoons

Rye flour gives breads a powerful flavor, but the dough is actually a little more fragile than other doughs; you can't mix it as hard to develop it, and you must score it *before* proofing. We make a traditional rye, which by definition has at least 50 percent rye flour. We don't use caraway seeds in rye bread, because we enjoy the pure rye flavor, but add 10 grams/ 1 tablespoon caraway if you want (or better, add caraway to sourdough— that's a combination we love).

Set up your baking stone and kit (see Assembly and Overview of the Process, page 267) and preheat the oven to 460°F (standard; see Note on Baking Temperature, page 280).

TO MIX THE DOUGH: Spray a large bowl with nonstick spray. Place the flours and yeast in the bowl of a stand mixer fitted with the dough hook and give it a quick mix on the lowest setting to combine the flours and to distribute the yeast evenly. Make a well in the center, add the levain and water, and mix on low speed for 3 minutes. Sprinkle the salt over the top and mix on low speed for 1 minute to dissolve the salt. Continue to mix on low for 16 minutes.

FERMENTATION: The dough is now in the fermentation stage. Set a timer for 30 minutes. Using a bowl scraper, release the dough and turn it out onto a lightly floured board. Pat, stretch, and fold the dough (see Stretching and Folding the Dough, page 278) and place in the prepared bowl. Cover and set aside. (This dough is not folded again during fermentation.)

TO DIVIDE, PRESHAPE, SHAPE, AND SCORE THE DOUGH: Spread a linen cloth on a large cutting board or on the back of a sheet pan. Flour the linen.

Use the bowl scraper to release the dough and turn it out onto a lightly floured board. Gently pat the dough into a rectangular shape, removing any large bubbles and adding flour only as needed to keep the dough from sticking to the board. Divide the dough into two 500-gram/17.6-ounce portions.

Preshape short (see Short Preshape, page 281). Let rest for 15 minutes.

Shape for bâtards (see Shaping, page 284) and lay the loaves on the linen. Fold or bunch the linen to create small walls on both sides of each loaf to help maintain the shape as the dough proofs. Score the bâtards with freestyle cuts or with the 10 to 12 parallel cuts of the sausage cut (see Six Types of Scoring, page 324).

TO PROOF THE DOUGH: Cover with a plastic tub or a cardboard box and let proof for 1 hour, or until when the dough is delicately pressed with a finger, the impression remains.

TO BAKE THE BREAD: Using the linen, move the dough, one piece at a time, to the transfer peel, seam side up, and then to the oven peel, seam side down, spacing them evenly.

Transfer the bread to the baking stone. Immediately spray water onto the steam generator (rocks and chain). Quickly shut the oven door and bake for 25 minutes, or until the bread feels lighter than you'd expect for its size and the internal temperature is 200°F to 210°F/93.3° to 98.8°C (see Note on Venting the Oven, page 280).

Let cool completely on a cooling rack. The rye bread will be good the day it is made, but even better if it sits and is eaten the next day.

PHOTOGRAPH ON PAGE 289   **MAKES 2 BATARDS**

Sourdough Boule

All-purpose flour	424 grams	3 cups + 1½ teaspoons
Instant yeast	0.5 gram	⅛ teaspoon
Liquid Levain (page 272)	403 grams	14.2 ounces
Water, at 75°F/23.8°C	181 grams	¾ cup
Fine sea salt	12 grams	2 teaspoons

There are all kinds of myths and theories about starting a yeast culture: Put organic grapes into the flour and water, or purple cabbage. You can only develop a true sourdough in the Bay Area. So-and-so's grandmother's 400-year-old starter has amazing complexity and distinction. Nonsense. Sourdough is the world's oldest leavened bread and it's all more or less the same, with the variations depending on climate, amount of hydration, how often you feed the starter, and so on. The distinction of sourdough is the level of sour you bring to it. The French tend to make milder sourdoughs. Generally, the looser the starter, the less sour it will be. This boule is tangy but not super sour.

TO MIX THE DOUGH: Spray a large bowl with nonstick spray. Place the flour and yeast in the bowl of a stand mixer fitted with the dough hook and give it a quick mix on the lowest setting to distribute the yeast evenly. Make a well in the center, add the levain and water, and pulse the mixer (to prevent the flour from flying out of the bowl) to begin incorporating the levain and water, then mix on low speed for 3 minutes. Sprinkle the salt over the top and mix on low speed for 1 minute to dissolve the salt. Continue to mix on low for 20 minutes.

FERMENTATION: The dough is now in the fermentation stage. Set a timer for 2 hours. Using a bowl scraper, release the dough and turn it out onto a lightly floured board. Pat, stretch, and fold the dough (see Stretching and Folding the Dough, page 278) and place in the prepared bowl. Cover and set aside. (This dough is not folded again during fermentation.)

TO SHAPE THE DOUGH: (See Note on the Strength of a Boule, page 291.) Line a large bowl, about 11 inches across at the top, with a linen cloth, trying to keep the folds as flat against the surface as possible. Flour the linen.

Use the bowl scraper to release the dough and turn it out onto a lightly floured board. Gently pat the dough into a round, removing any large bubbles and adding flour only as needed to keep the dough from sticking to the board. Trim the dough to a weight of 1 kilogram/ 2 pounds, 3.2 ounces. Let rest for 40 minutes.

Shape the dough for a boule (see Shaping a Boule, page 292). Invert and place in the lined bowl.

TO PROOF THE DOUGH: Set a sheet pan on the top of the bowl or cover with a plastic tub or a cardboard box and let proof for 3 hours, or until when the dough is delicately pressed with a finger, the impression remains.

Meanwhile, set up your baking stone and kit (see Assembly and Overview of the Process, page 267) and preheat the oven to 425°F (standard).

TO BAKE THE BREAD: Using the linen, move the dough to the oven peel, tail side down. Score with a square cut (see Six Types of Scoring, page 324).

Transfer the bread to the baking stone. Immediately spray water onto the steam generator (rocks and chain). Quickly shut the oven door and bake for 30 minutes, or until the bread feels lighter than you'd expect for its size and the internal temperature is 200° to 210°F/93.3° to 98.8°C (see Note on Venting the Oven, page 280).

Let cool completely on a cooling rack.

PHOTOGRAPH ON PAGE 289   **MAKES 1 ROUND LOAF**

SOURDOUGH CROUTONS

There isn't much that can beat the aroma of fresh-baked sourdough coming out of the oven. But as good as it is the day it is baked, the day-old bread can be made into excellent croutons. Rather than toasting them in the oven, brown them in a skillet with some butter, turning them for even color on all sides, until they are crisp on the outside without being dried throughout. Your Caesar salad will never be the same.

Pain Palladin

All-purpose flour	481 grams	3¼ cups + 2 tablespoons + 2 teaspoons
Instant yeast	1 gram	¼ teaspoon
Liquid Levain (page 272)	96 grams	3.3 ounces
Water, at 75°F/23.8°C	323 grams	1¼ cups + 2 tablespoons
Extra virgin olive oil	14 grams	1 tablespoon
Fine sea salt	11 grams	2 teaspoons

This bread is similar in technique and shape to the pain rustique—if you saw them side by side, you might not know they were different breads—but this recipe uses less commercial yeast and has a shorter mixing time and longer fermentation. The result is a little more tanginess and a thicker crust. It is named for the late chef Jean-Louis Palladin.

TO MIX THE DOUGH: Spray a large bowl with nonstick spray. Place the flour and yeast in the bowl of a stand mixer fitted with the dough hook and give it a quick mix on the lowest setting to distribute the yeast evenly. Make a well in the center, add the levain, water, and olive oil, and mix on low speed for 3 minutes. Sprinkle the salt over the top and mix on low speed for 1 minute to dissolve the salt. Continue to mix on low for 20 minutes.

FERMENTATION: The dough is now in the 3-hour fermentation stage. Set a timer for 1 hour. Using a bowl scraper, release the dough and turn it out onto a lightly floured board. Pat, stretch, and fold the dough (see Stretching and Folding the Dough, page 278) and place in the prepared bowl. Cover and set aside.

Set the timer for 1 hour again. Repeat the pat, stretch, and fold, place the dough back in the bowl, cover, and set aside.

Set the timer for 1 hour again. Repeat the pat, stretch, and fold, place the dough back in the bowl, cover, and set aside.

TO DIVIDE THE DOUGH: Spread a linen cloth on a large cutting board or on the back of a sheet pan. Flour the linen.

Use the bowl scraper to release the dough and turn it out onto a lightly floured board. Gently pat the dough into a rectangular shape, removing any large bubbles and adding flour only as needed to keep the dough from sticking to the board. Let rest for 10 minutes.

Meanwhile, set up your baking stone and kit (see Assembly and Overview of the Process, page 267) and preheat the oven to 460°F (standard; see Note on Baking Temperature, page 280).

Divide the dough into two 450-gram/15.8-ounce portions. There is no preshaping or shaping, as the pieces will naturally fall into a rectangular to diamond shape.

Lay the loaves on the linen and fold or bunch the linen to create small walls on all four sides of each loaf to help maintain the shape as the dough proofs.

TO PROOF THE DOUGH: Cover with a plastic tub or a cardboard box and let proof for 2 hours, or until when the dough is delicately pressed with a finger, the impression remains.

TO BAKE THE BREAD: Using the linen, move the dough, one piece at a time, to the transfer peel, top side down, and then to the oven peel, top side up, spacing them evenly. Transfer the loaves to the baking stone. Immediately spray water onto the steam generator (rocks and chain). Quickly shut the oven door and bake for 20 minutes, or until the bread feels lighter than you'd expect for its size and the internal temperature is 200° to 210°F/93.3° to 98.8°C (see Note on Venting the Oven, page 280).

Let cool completely on a cooling rack.

PHOTOGRAPHS ON PAGES 255, 304, AND 305 (RIGHT)   **MAKES 2 LOAVES**

Pain Rustique

All-purpose flour	593 grams	4 cups + 3 tablespoons
Instant yeast	3 grams	¾ + ⅛ teaspoon
Liquid Levain (page 272)	98 grams	3.5 ounces
Water, at 75°F/23.8°C	393 grams	1½ cups + 2½ tablespoons
Fine sea salt	13 grams	2¼ teaspoons

Pain rustique is plain, simple, and easily shaped, with a soft, airy crumb and a thin, crisp crust. The dough and the shaping were created by Professor Raymond Calvel. Bakers in the industry asked him to create a dough that was faster and easier to make than standard doughs. What he decided to use for flavor was *pâte fermentée,* or fermented dough (such as leftover baguette dough, which any bakery would have on hand). Adding fresh flour, water, yeast, and salt resulted in a great flavor and performance in less time. He also used a simple, quick folding technique to develop the strength of the dough without shaping it. It's so easy and yet it's elegant as well. This is the slicing bread we serve at The French Laundry.

TO MIX THE DOUGH: Spray a large bowl with nonstick spray. Place the flour and yeast in the bowl of a stand mixer fitted with the dough hook and give it a quick mix on the lowest setting to distribute the yeast evenly. Make a well in the center, add the levain and water, and mix on low speed for 3 minutes. Sprinkle the salt over the top and mix on low speed for 1 minute to dissolve the salt. Continue to mix on low speed for 20 minutes.

FERMENTATION: The dough is now in the 2¼-hour fermentation stage. Set a timer for 1 hour. Using a bowl scraper, release the dough and turn it out onto a lightly floured board. Pat, stretch, and fold the dough (see Stretching and Folding the Dough, page 278) and place in the prepared bowl. Cover and set aside.

Set the timer for 1¼ hours. Repeat the pat, stretch, and fold, place the dough back in the bowl, cover, and set aside.

Meanwhile, set up your baking stone and kit (see Assembly and Overview of the Process, page 267) and preheat the oven to 460°F (standard; see Note on Baking Temperature, page 280).

TO DIVIDE THE DOUGH: Spread a linen cloth on a large cutting board or on the back of a sheet pan. Flour the linen.

Use the bowl scraper to release the dough and turn it out onto a lightly floured board. Gently pat the dough into a rectangular shape, removing any large bubbles and adding flour only as needed to keep the dough from sticking to the board. Let rest for 10 minutes.

Divide the dough into two 500-gram/17.6-ounce portions. There is no preshaping or shaping, as the pieces will naturally fall into rectangular to diamond shapes.

Lay the loaves on the linen, and fold or bunch the linen to create small walls on all four sides of each loaf to help maintain the shape as the dough proofs.

TO PROOF THE DOUGH: Cover with a plastic tub or a cardboard box and let proof for 1 hour, or until when the dough is delicately pressed with a finger, the impression remains.

TO BAKE THE BREAD: Using the linen, move the dough, one piece at a time, to the transfer peel, top side down, and then to the oven peel, top side up, spacing them evenly.

Transfer the bread to the baking stone. Immediately spray water onto the steam generator (rocks and chain). Quickly shut the oven door and bake for 20 minutes, or until the bread feels lighter than you'd expect for its size and the internal temperature is 200° to 210°F/93.3° to 98.8°C (see Note on Venting the Oven, page 280).

Let cool completely on a cooling rack.

PHOTOGRAPH ON PAGE 305 (LEFT)   **MAKES 2 LOAVES**

Whole Wheat–Pecan Demi-Baguettes

All-purpose flour	331 grams	2¼ cups + 1 tablespoon + 2 teaspoons
Whole wheat flour	37 grams	¼ cup + 1 tablespoon
Light brown sugar	18 grams	1½ tablespoons, lightly packed
Instant yeast	2 grams	½ + ⅛ teaspoon
Brown Butter (page 380), warm	18 grams	1½ tablespoons
Ice-cold water	221 grams	¾ cup + 2 tablespoons + 2½ teaspoons
Fine sea salt	7 grams	1⅛ teaspoons
Coarsely chopped pecans	74 grams	½ cup + 2½ tablespoons

We love the flavor and sweetness of brown sugar with smoked turkey, so when we wanted a bread specifically for a smoked turkey sandwich, it was a natural to use brown sugar. The negatives about whole wheat bread—the bitterness of the bran, the texture—are actually positives with brown sugar and nuts. We add nuts to the dough raw rather than pretoasted, for a sweeter, cleaner flavor.

Set up your baking stone and kit (see Assembly and Overview of the Process, page 267) and preheat the oven to 375°F (standard). Spray a large bowl with nonstick spray. Spray a sheet pan with nonstick spray, line with parchment paper, and lightly spray the parchment.

TO MIX THE DOUGH: Place the flours, sugar, and yeast in the bowl of a stand mixer fitted with the dough hook and give it a quick mix on the lowest setting to combine the flours and sugar and to distribute the yeast evenly. Add the butter and then the water and mix on low speed for 4 minutes. Sprinkle the salt over the top and mix on low speed for 1 minute to dissolve the salt. Continue to mix on low for 30 minutes.

Meanwhile, toss the pecans in a fine-mesh strainer to remove any small particles and pieces.

Add the pecans to the dough and mix on low just to incorporate them.

FERMENTATION: The dough is now in the fermentation stage. Set a timer for 15 minutes. Using a bowl scraper, release the dough and turn it out onto a lightly floured board. Pat, stretch, and fold the dough (see Stretching and Folding the Dough, page 278) and place in the prepared bowl. Cover and set aside.

TO DIVIDE, PRESHAPE, AND SHAPE THE DOUGH: Use the bowl scraper to release the dough and turn it out onto a lightly floured board. Gently pat the dough into a rectangular shape, removing any large bubbles and adding flour only as needed to keep the dough from sticking to the board. Divide the dough into three 225-gram/7.9-ounce portions.

Preshape long (see Long Preshape, page 282). Let rest for 15 minutes.

Shape for demi-baguettes (see Shaping, page 284). Transfer the loaves to the sheet pan, spacing them evenly.

TO PROOF THE DOUGH: Cover the sheet pan with a plastic tub or a cardboard box and let proof for 2 hours, or until when the dough is delicately pressed with a finger, the impression remains.

TO BAKE THE BREAD: Score each loaf with the 10 to 12 parallel cuts of the sausage cut (see Six Types of Scoring, page 324).

Transfer the bread to the baking stone. Immediately spray water onto the steam generator (rocks and chain). Quickly shut the oven door and bake for 35 minutes, or until the bread feels lighter than you'd expect for its size and the internal temperature is 200° to 210°F/93.3° to 98.8°C (see Note on Venting the Oven, page 280).

Let cool completely on a cooling rack.

MAKES 3 DEMI-BAGUETTES

WHOLE WHEAT–PECAN TOAST We use our whole wheat–pecan bread for sandwiches, but its rich, nutty flavor is also the perfect match to a ripe blue cheese. Toast the long slices of bread in a toaster or under a broiler, or brush them lightly with olive oil and brown them on a griddle.

Vegetable Demi-Baguettes

All-purpose flour	339 grams	2¼ cups + 1½ tablespoons
Instant yeast	1 gram	¼ teaspoon
Vegetable Stock (recipe follows), at room temperature	235 grams	1 cup
Fine sea salt	7 grams	1⅛ teaspoons

When you get amazing, abundant tomatoes in summer, you want a bread that will do them justice. We developed this as a sandwich bread for tomato season, to give our tomato sandwiches as much flavor as possible. Instead of water, we use a vegetable stock for the hydration. The bread is a great framework for a tomato, Brie, and basil sandwich; brush the slices of bread with olive oil.

Set up your baking stone and kit (see Assembly and Overview of the Process, page 267) and preheat the oven to 460°F (standard; see Note on Baking Temperature, page 280). Spray a large bowl with nonstick spray.

TO MIX THE DOUGH: Place the flour and yeast in the bowl of a stand mixer fitted with the dough hook and give it a quick mix on the lowest setting to distribute the yeast evenly. Add the vegetable stock and mix on low speed for 3 minutes. Sprinkle the salt over the top and mix on low speed for 1 minute to dissolve the salt. Continue to mix on low for 20 minutes.

FERMENTATION: The dough is now in the fermentation stage. Set a timer for 1 hour. Using a bowl scraper, release the dough and turn it out onto a lightly floured board. Pat, stretch, and fold the dough (see Stretching and Folding the Dough, page 278) and place in the prepared bowl. Cover and set aside.

TO DIVIDE, PRESHAPE, AND SHAPE THE DOUGH: Spread a linen cloth on a large cutting board or on the back of a sheet pan. Flour the linen.

Use the bowl scraper to release the dough and turn it out onto a lightly floured board. Gently pat the dough into a rectangular shape, removing any large bubbles and adding flour only as needed to keep the dough from sticking to the board. Divide the dough into three 200-gram/7-ounce portions.

Preshape long (see Long Preshape, page 282). Let rest for 15 minutes.

Shape for demi-baguettes (see Shaping, page 284). Lay the loaves on the linen and fold or bunch the linen to create small walls on both sides of each loaf to help maintain the shape as the dough proofs.

TO PROOF THE DOUGH: Cover with a plastic tub or a cardboard box and let proof for 1 hour and 15 minutes, or until when the dough is delicately pressed with a finger, the impression remains.

TO BAKE THE BREAD: Using the linen, move the dough, one piece at a time, to the transfer peel, seam side up, and then to the oven peel, seam side down, spacing them evenly. Score the demi-baguettes by making 3 cuts down the center (see Six Types of Scoring, page 324). Transfer the demi-baguettes to the baking stone. Immediately spray water onto the steam generator (rocks and chain). Quickly shut the oven door and bake for 15 to 20 minutes, until the bread feels lighter than you'd expect for its size and the internal temperature is 200° to 210°F/93.3° to 98.8°C (see Note on Venting the Oven, page 280).

Let cool completely on a cooling rack.

MAKES 3 DEMI-BAGUETTES

Vegetable Stock

Leeks, trimmed, washed well, and coarsely chopped	680 grams	1½ pounds
Carrots, peeled and coarsely chopped	453 grams	1 pound
Spanish onions (2 large), coarsely chopped	680 grams	1½ pounds
Fennel bulb (1 small)	340 grams	12 ounces
Canola oil	56 grams	¼ cup
2 bay leaves		
2 thyme sprigs		
Italian parsley sprigs	56 grams	2 ounces

Combine all the vegetables in a food processor and finely chop.

Cook the vegetables in the canola oil in a medium stockpot over low heat for 5 to 8 minutes, or until softened. Add the bay leaves, thyme, parsley, and enough water to cover, bring to a gentle simmer, skimming frequently, and cook for 45 minutes.

Prepare an ice bath. Strain the stock through a chinois or fine-mesh strainer into a container and submerge the container in the ice bath. Stir the stock occasionally until completely cool, then refrigerate for 1 to 2 days or freeze (in several containers) for up to 1 month.

MAKES 3.3 KILOGRAMS/3½ QUARTS

Brioche

BRIOCHE DOUGH FOR STICKY BUNS

All-purpose flour	263 grams	1¾ cups + 2 tablespoons
Instant yeast	6 grams	1¾ teaspoons
Granulated sugar	31 grams	2 tablespoons + 1¾ teaspoons
Fine sea salt	6 grams	1 teaspoon
Eggs	132 grams	½ cup + 1½ teaspoons
Whole milk	44 grams	2 tablespoons + 2¼ teaspoons
Unsalted butter, cut into ½-inch cubes	118 grams	4.1 ounces

BRIOCHE DOUGH FOR HOT CROSS BUNS

All-purpose flour	372 grams	2½ cups + 2½ tablespoons
Instant yeast	8 grams	2⅜ teaspoons
Granulated sugar	44 grams	3 tablespoons + 2 teaspoons
Fine sea salt	9 grams	1½ teaspoons
Eggs	186 grams	½ cup + 3½ tablespoons
Whole milk	63 grams	¼ cup
Unsalted butter, cut into ½-inch cubes	167 grams	5.8 ounces

BRIOCHE DOUGH FOR TROPEZIENNE

All-purpose flour	175 grams	1¼ cups
Instant yeast	4 grams	1¼ teaspoons
Granulated sugar	21 grams	1 tablespoon + 2¼ teaspoons
Fine sea salt	4 grams	½ + ⅛ teaspoon
Eggs	88 grams	¼ cup + 1½ tablespoons
Whole milk	29 grams	1½ tablespoons
Unsalted butter, cut into ½-inch cubes	79 grams	2.7 ounces

BRIOCHE DOUGH FOR NANTERRE

All-purpose flour	271 grams	1¾ cups + 3 tablespoons
Instant yeast	6 grams	1¾ teaspoons
Granulated sugar	32 grams	2 tablespoons + 2 teaspoons
Fine sea salt	7 grams	1⅛ teaspoons
Eggs	136 grams	½ cup + 2¼ teaspoons
Whole milk	46 grams	2 tablespoons + 2½ teaspoons
Unsalted butter, cut into ½-inch cubes	122 grams	4.3 ounces

Brioche is a bread that's enriched with butter and eggs. There are different ways of making it, with different proportions of butter. Everything should be at room temperature so the dough comes together beautifully. The dough then gets folded and is fermented in the refrigerator overnight.

This recipe is for our all-purpose brioche dough, with different proportions depending on which of the brioche preparations you will be using it for.

Spray a large bowl with nonstick spray (unless making hot cross buns).

TO MIX THE DOUGH: Place the flour and yeast in the bowl of a stand mixer fitted with the dough hook and mix for about 15 seconds to distribute the yeast evenly. Add all of the remaining dough ingredients, except the butter, and mix on low speed for 4 minutes. Continue to mix on low speed for 30 minutes. (At this point there will be some dough sticking to the sides of the bowl.) Add the butter a few pieces at a time, incorporating each addition before adding the next. Stop and scrape down the sides and bottom of the bowl and push the dough off the hook. Continue to mix for 10 minutes.

For hot cross buns, the dough is used at this point.

FERMENTATION: For all other doughs, the dough is now in the fermentation stage. Set a timer for 1 hour. Using a bowl scraper, release the dough and turn it out onto a lightly floured board; the dough will be sticky. Pat, stretch, and fold the dough (see Stretching and Folding the Dough, page 278) and place it in the prepared bowl. Cover and set aside.

Repeat the pat, stretch, and fold, place the dough back in the bowl, cover, and refrigerate overnight. The dough is now ready to be used.

Nanterre

Brioche Dough for Nanterre
(page 313)

Egg Wash (page 381)

Nanterre is a classic brioche shape, baked in a loaf pan. We originally made ours to serve with foie gras at The French Laundry. It has a fairly uniform shape end to end, so the whole loaf can all be used, and the slices provide a contrast in texture with the smooth foie gras as well as a decorative presentation.

You'll need two 8½-by-4½-by-2¾-inch loaf pans.

Spray the loaf pans with nonstick spray. Line the bottoms with parchment paper and spray the parchment.

TO DIVIDE, PRESHAPE, AND SHAPE THE DOUGH: Use a bowl scraper to release the dough from the bowl and turn it out onto a lightly floured board. Gently pat into a rectangular shape, removing any large air bubbles and adding flour only as needed to keep the dough from sticking to the board. Divide the dough into twelve 50-gram/1.7-ounce portions.

Cup your fingers around a portion of dough and, using the palm of your hand, roll it against the board to form a ball. Continue to roll until the top is completely smooth. Repeat with the remaining dough. (When you become proficient at rolling with one hand, you can use both hands to roll 2 portions at a time.)

TO PROOF THE DOUGH: Set 6 balls in each pan. Brush the tops with egg wash. Cover the pans with a plastic tub or a cardboard box and let proof for 2½ to 3 hours, until the balls have risen and are touching.

Meanwhile, position a rack in the lower third of the oven and place a baking stone on it. Preheat the oven to 350°F (standard).

TO BAKE THE BREAD: Brush the tops again with egg wash. Slide the pans onto the stone and bake for 20 to 25 minutes, until the tops are a rich golden brown and the loaves are baked through (a wooden skewer inserted in the center should come out clean).

Turn out immediately and let cool completely on a cooling rack.

PHOTOGRAPH ON PAGE 312   MAKES 2 LOAVES

MY BLT This is the perfect summer sandwich, a classic, but one you never tire of. Spread two slices of brioche toast with a generous layer of mayonnaise (you don't have to make it—Best Foods/Hellmann's is perfect). Put some butter lettuce over one of the slices and top with slices of fresh, ripe, juicy heirloom tomatoes. Cover with a layer of warm, crisp applewood-smoked bacon, top with the second slice of toast, and enjoy!

Pain-au-Lait Pullman Loaf

All-purpose flour	547 grams	3¾ cups + 2 tablespoons + 1 teaspoon
Instant yeast	6 grams	1¾ teaspoons
Granulated sugar	32 grams	2 tablespoons + 2 teaspoons
Fine sea salt	11 grams	2 teaspoons
Water	285 grams	1 cup + 3½ tablespoons
Eggs	35 grams	2 tablespoons + ½ teaspoon
Unsalted butter	25 grams	0.8 ounce
Cream cheese	79 grams	2.7 ounces
Egg Wash (page 381)		

This dough is traditionally made with milk, as the name indicates, but milk results in a slightly drier crumb than we like. So we use cream cheese—a richer dairy product—and water and add some egg for the softening effect it has in the finished bread. And, as with the Brioche (page 313), we start with all the ingredients at room temperature.

Pullman loaves, named after the train cars they were designed for (to save space), are baked in special rectangular lidded pans, resulting in a fine, uniform crumb and a soft crust. They are fun because you can cut nice square slices or cut the slices into elegant crustless disks to use for canapés.

You'll need a 2-pound Pullman loaf pan.

Spray a large bowl and the Pullman loaf pan with nonstick spray.

TO MIX THE DOUGH: Place the flour and yeast in the bowl of a stand mixer fitted with the dough hook and give it a quick mix on the lowest setting to distribute the yeast evenly. Add all of the remaining ingredients except the egg wash and mix on low speed for 4 minutes. Continue to mix on low for 30 minutes.

FERMENTATION: The dough is now in the fermentation stage. Set a timer for 15 minutes. Using a bowl scraper, release the dough and turn it out onto a lightly floured board. Pat, stretch, and fold the dough (see Stretching and Folding the Dough, page 278) and place in the prepared bowl. Cover and set aside.

TO PRESHAPE AND SHAPE THE DOUGH: Use the bowl scraper to release the dough and turn it out onto a lightly floured board. Gently pat the dough into a rectangular shape, removing any large bubbles and adding flour only as needed to keep the dough from sticking to the board. Trim the dough to a weight of 1 kilogram/2 pounds, 3.2 ounces.

Preshape long (see Long Preshape, page 282) and let rest for 5 minutes.

Shape for a Pullman as close to the length of the pan as possible (see Shaping, page 284) and lay it in the prepared pan. Brush the top with egg wash.

TO PROOF THE DOUGH: Slide the lid onto the pan, leaving it open about ½ inch so you can see inside, and let proof for 2½ to 3 hours, until the dough has nearly reached the top of the pan.

Meanwhile, position a rack in the lower third of the oven and place a baking stone on it. Preheat the oven to 375°F (standard).

TO BAKE THE BREAD: Close the top of the pan, slide it onto the stone, and bake for 25 minutes. Carefully remove the top of the pan and bake for 10 minutes, or until the top is a rich golden brown and the loaf is baked through (a wooden skewer inserted in the center should come out clean).

Turn the bread out onto a cooling rack and let cool completely.

PHOTOGRAPHS ON PAGES 255 AND 263　　　　　　　　　　**MAKES 1 LOAF**

Dutch Crunch Demi-Baguettes

DOUGH

All-purpose flour	328 grams	2¼ cups + 1 tablespoon + 1 teaspoon
Instant yeast	4 grams	1¼ teaspoons
Granulated sugar	19 grams	1 tablespoon + 1¾ teaspoons
Fine sea salt	7 grams	1⅛ teaspoons
Water	171 grams	½ cup + 3 tablespoons + 2 teaspoons
Eggs	21 grams	1 tablespoon + 1 teaspoon
Unsalted butter	15 grams	0.5 ounce
Cream cheese	48 grams	1.6 ounces

TOPPING

Rice flour	177 grams	¼ cup + 3 tablespoons + 2 teaspoons
Granulated sugar	27 grams	2 tablespoons + ¾ teaspoon
Instant yeast	10.5 grams	1 tablespoon + ⅛ teaspoon
Fine sea salt	7.5 grams	1¼ teaspoons
Water	162 grams	½ cup + 2 tablespoons + 2½ teaspoons
Canola oil	66 grams	¼ cup + 2 teaspoons

To add visual and textural appeal to this sandwich bread, we pipe on a topping that adds flavor and a quasi-exotic appearance (it's sometimes called tiger bread). It is the contrast of the crunch and grittiness of the topping to the soft bread that makes it appealing. And the salty-sweet flavor of the topping is what makes it a great complement to a sandwich made with something like roast beef.

You'll need a pastry bag with a Wilton 789 tip. ● *All the ingredients should be at room temperature.*

Spray a large bowl with nonstick spray. Spray a sheet pan with nonstick spray, line with parchment paper, and lightly spray the parchment.

TO MIX THE DOUGH: Place the flour and yeast in the bowl of a stand mixer fitted with the dough hook and give it a quick mix on the lowest setting to distribute the yeast evenly. Add all of the remaining ingredients and mix on low speed for 4 minutes. Continue to mix on low for 30 minutes.

FERMENTATION: The dough is now in the fermentation stage. Set a timer for 15 minutes. Using a bowl scraper, release the dough and turn it out onto a lightly floured board. Pat, stretch, and fold the dough (see Stretching and Folding the Dough, page 278) and place in the prepared bowl. Cover and set aside.

TO DIVIDE, PRESHAPE, AND SHAPE THE DOUGH: Use the bowl scraper to release the dough and turn it out onto a lightly floured board. Gently pat the dough into a rectangular shape, removing any large bubbles and adding flour only as needed to keep the dough from sticking to the board. Divide the dough into three 200-gram/7-ounce portions.

Preshape long for demi-baguettes (see Long Preshape, page 282). Let rest for 5 minutes.

Shape for demi-baguettes (see Shaping, page 284). Lay the loaves on the prepared sheet pan.

TO PROOF THE DOUGH: Cover with a plastic tub or a cardboard box and let proof for 2 to 2½ hours, or until when the dough is delicately pressed with a finger, the impression remains.

Meanwhile, position a rack in the lower third of the oven and place a baking stone on it. Preheat the oven to 375°F (standard) and make the topping.

FOR THE TOPPING: Combine the rice flour, sugar, yeast, and salt in a medium bowl. Whisk in the water and oil. Transfer to the pastry bag.

With the flat side of the tip down, pipe a strip of the topping down the center of each demi-baguette and then, using a small offset spatula, spread the topping over the top of the loaves. Some of the topping may run over the ends and down the sides, which is fine. (There may be leftover topping.)

TO BAKE THE BREAD: Slide the sheet pan onto the stone and bake for 35 minutes, or until the tops are a rich golden brown and the baguettes are baked through (a wooden skewer inserted into the center should come out clean).

Let cool completely on a cooling rack.

MAKES 3 DEMI-BAGUETTES

ROAST BEEF ON DUTCH CRUNCH A Dutch Crunch demi-baguette turns a roast beef sandwich into something extraordinary. Split the loaf lengthwise and add mayonnaise, thinly sliced rare roast beef sprinkled with salt, ripe tomatoes, red onions, and watercress or arugula.

Dead Dough

All-purpose flour	500 grams	3½ cups + 1 tablespoon
Instant yeast	1 gram	¼ teaspoon
Fine sea salt	25 grams	1 tablespoon + 1 teaspoon
Water, at 75°F/23.8°C	325 grams	1¼ cups + 2 tablespoons

Shaping and scoring dough takes practice, practice, and more practice. Making a batch of dead dough is a great way to get a feel for preshaping, shaping, and scoring.

Combine the flour, yeast, and salt in the bowl of a stand mixer fitted with the dough hook and mix on the lowest setting. With the mixer running on low, add the water and mix for 3 to 4 minutes, or until the dough comes together around the hook. Continue to mix on low speed for about 10 minutes, until the dough is smooth. Let the dough rest for 15 minutes.

The dough can be used now or put in a bowl sprayed with nonstick spray, covered with plastic wrap, and refrigerated.

Lightly flour a board. Cut the dough into the desired portions and then practice preshaping, shaping, and scoring. Once you are done, push the pieces together and knead for a few minutes, until uniform. Refrigerate to be reused. When the dough becomes less pliable or begins to discolor, discard it.

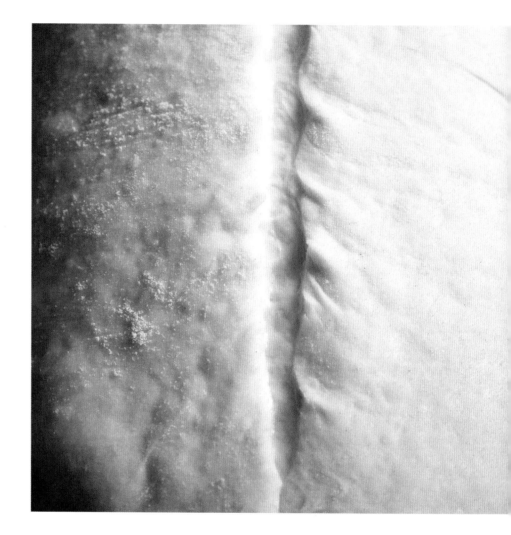

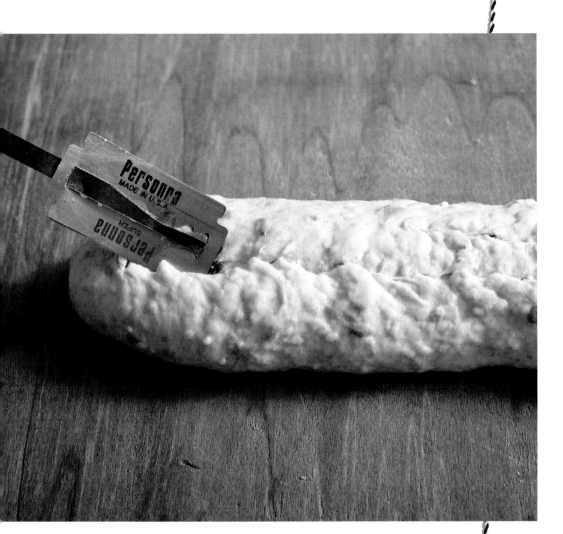

Scoring a Multigrain Demi-Baguette (page 296)

SCORING

Loaves are scored for both functional and aesthetic reasons. Scoring weakens the dough at the point where it is scored, allowing controlled expansion.

The key to successful scoring is a very sharp blade. We like to use a *lame,* a double-edged blade with a removable handle. When you are starting out, the speed at which you cut is less important than the accuracy of the cuts.

For most loaves, the cuts should stay within the center third of the loaf, the exceptions being the square cut (4), freestyle (5), and chevron (6). Visualize where the cuts will go before you start. Or practice them on Dead Dough (opposite) or on dough trimmings. Draw lines on the dead dough or trimmings with a Sharpie or other dark marker to indicate the lines you want to stay between when making the cuts.

For all cuts, insert the tip of the blade at the upper end of the cut and, in one straight motion, cut down to the end of the cut (for a square cut, the cuts can be from left to right rather than from top to bottom). For single and triple cuts (1 and 3), the blade should be almost horizontal. For sausage, square, freestyle, and chevron cuts, the blade should be at a 90-degree angle to the dough. The cuts should be about ⅛ inch deep. If there are any areas in the cut that are uneven, go back over them a second time.

Err on the side of a lighter touch. You will know it is too light if the cuts have some tearing. And, conversely, you will know the cuts were too deep if the loaf bakes up a little flat.

SIX TYPES OF SCORING

1. Single Cut | One straight line. Starting at the top of the scoring area, make one straight cut down the center of the loaf to the other end. Shown here on a baguette-dough Bâtard (page 276); we also use this on the Multigrain Bâtards (page 296).

2. Sausage Cut | A series of ten to twelve shorter parallel diagonal cuts. Starting at the top of the left side of the scoring area, make a cut on a 45-degree angle across to the right side of the scoring area. Repeat to make parallel cuts down the loaf, finishing at the other end. Shown here on a Walnut Bâtard (page 294); we also use this on the Rye Bâtards (page 301) and Whole Wheat–Pecan Demi-Baguettes (page 308).

3. Triple Cut | A series of three longer parallel diagonal cuts. Starting at the top right of the scoring area, make a long cut on a 30-degree angle across to the left side of the scoring area, running about one-third of the length of the loaf. For the second cut, start about two-thirds down the length of the first cut and make a long cut running to about two-thirds down the length of the dough. For the final cut, start two-thirds down the length of the second cut and make a cut down to the end of the loaf. Shown here on a Multigrain Demi-Baguette (page 296); we also use this on the baguette-dough Demi-Baguettes (page 276) and on Vegetable Demi-Baguettes (page 310).

4. Square Cut | Four separate cuts making a square. Starting about a quarter of the way in from the edge of the dough, cut four straight lines in the dough to form a square. Shown here on a Sourdough Boule (page 302)

5. Freestyle | A series of cuts done in a more random, decorative way. As the name indicates, this series of cuts allows for creative license; however, it is still important to be sure the cut surface area is fairly uniform. Shown here on a Rye Bâtard (page 301).

6. Chevron | A series of ten parallel diagonal cuts on each side of the top of the loaf, forming a series of Vs. Visualize a line running down the center of the loaf, and start each series of cuts just slightly to the left or right of that center line. Starting at the top of the scoring area, make a cut on a 45-degree angle from just right of the center down the right side of the loaf. Repeat to make 9 more parallel cuts down the end of the loaf. Then, starting from the top again, repeat the series of cuts down the left side of the loaf. Shown here on a Cranberry-Currant Bâtard (page 294).

English Muffins

All-purpose flour	274 grams	1¾ cups + 3 tablespoons + ¾ teaspoon
Granulated sugar	25 grams	2 tablespoons
Instant yeast	11 grams	1 tablespoon + ⅛ teaspoon
Fine sea salt	3 grams	½ teaspoon
Liquid Levain (page 272)	247 grams	8.7 ounces
Whole milk, at 75°F/23.8°C	274 grams	1 cup + 1 tablespoon + 1¾ teaspoons
Canola oil	22 grams	1 tablespoon + 1¾ teaspoons
Coarse cornmeal for sprinkling	22 grams	2 tablespoons

The recipe calls for a huge amount of levain, some yeast, some milk, a little oil, and a touch of sugar. The dough is almost batter-like, and while English muffins are typically cooked in rings on a griddle, we wanted to give these time to rise, so we use a mold where they proof for about half an hour before going into a hot oven. Of course, cornmeal goes into the molds first, for the classic English muffin bottom.

You'll need one Flexipan cylinder mold. ● *We use Flexipan Cylinders from JB Prince. These are only available in a full sheet pan size (with 24 molds), so you will have to cut one in half—and share with a friend.*

Set up your baking stone and kit (see Assembly and Overview of the Process, page 267) and preheat the oven to 425°F (standard).

TO MIX THE DOUGH: Combine the flour, sugar, yeast, and salt in the bowl of a stand mixer fitted with the paddle attachment and give it a quick mix on the lowest setting to distribute the yeast evenly. Make a well in the center, add the levain, and mix on low for about 2 minutes to begin to moisten the dry ingredients. With the mixer running on low, slowly add the milk, followed by the oil, and mix for 2 minutes, or until smooth. Scrape down the sides and bottom of the bowl and pulse to incorporate. Increase the speed to medium and mix for 2 minutes.

Let the dough rest at room temperature, uncovered, for 1 hour.

TO SHAPE AND PROOF THE DOUGH: Spray the mold with nonstick spray and set on a sheet pan. Sprinkle 1.8 grams/½ teaspoon of cornmeal in each cup.

Scoop 60 grams/about ¼ cup of the dough into each cup. Cover with a plastic tub or a cardboard box and proof for 30 to 45 minutes, or until the dough has risen about ¼ inch over the tops of the molds. When the top of a muffin is touched, it will begin to collapse on itself.

TO BAKE THE MUFFINS: Wet your finger and gently smooth any uneven spots on the surface of the muffins. Place the pan on the baking stone. Immediately spray water onto the steam generator (rocks and chain). Quickly shut the oven door and bake for 20 to 25 minutes, until the muffins are a rich golden brown.

Let cool completely on a cooling rack.

MAKES 12 MUFFINS

Garlic Comté Breadsticks

Garlic Oil (page 381)	28 grams	2 tablespoons
Comté cheese, grated	136 grams	1¾ cups + 2 tablespoons
All-purpose flour	234 grams	1½ cups + 2 tablespoons + 2 teaspoons
Fine sea salt	5.5 grams	1 teaspoon
Instant yeast	4.5 grams	1¼ teaspoons
Water, at 75°F/23.8°C	117 grams	½ cup

C heez-Its are one of Matthew's favorite crackers. He took it as a challenge to make a version that was even better (and better for you). Matthew tweaked the cracker dough he'd made for Ad Hoc and added cheese melted in garlic oil, and the result was this breadstick. They're really easy to make, and fun to do with kids. Shape them into dinosaurs, or twist them around something metal to make a coil. There's only one problem— you can't stop eating them.

You'll need a pizza wheel.

Spray a large bowl with nonstick spray.

TO MIX THE DOUGH: Heat the garlic oil in the top of a double boiler over barely simmering water. Add the cheese and stir as it melts. The mixture will not emulsify; the melted cheese will be separated from the oil. Remove from the heat, leaving the mixture over the hot water to keep warm.

Combine the flour, salt, and yeast in the bowl of a stand mixer fitted with the paddle attachment and give it a quick mix on the lowest setting to distribute the yeast evenly. With the mixer running, add the water. With the mixer still running on the lowest speed, add the warm oil and cheese. The oil will pour out of the pan and be incorporated first; the cheese should still be hot when it is added, or it will not be evenly distributed in the dough. If any of the cheese clumps on the sides of the small bowl, stop adding it; it is better to leave some out than to try to incorporate it. Continue to mix until the oil and cheese have been incorporated; if necessary, increase the speed to low for 15 seconds.

Stop the mixer and switch to the dough hook. Mix on low for 30 minutes. Using a bowl scraper, release the dough and turn it out onto a lightly floured board. Pat, stretch, and fold the dough (see Stretching and Folding the Dough, page 278) and place in the prepared bowl. Cover and let stand for 15 minutes.

Line a sheet pan with parchment paper. Using as little flour as possible, roll the dough out to a 5-by-4-by-1-inch-thick rectangle. Transfer to the sheet pan, cover with plastic wrap, and refrigerate for 3 to 4 hours, or until cold enough to roll.

TO SHAPE THE BREADSTICKS: Roll the dough out on a lightly floured board to a 15-by-9-by-¼-inch rectangle. Set on the lined sheet pan, top with another piece of parchment paper, and cover with plastic wrap. Refrigerate for 1 hour or freeze for 20 minutes, or until firm enough to trim.

Trim the dough to a 14-by-7¾-inch rectangle; the trimmings can be baked for a chef's snack. Refrigerate the dough for 1 hour or freeze for 20 minutes, or until cold enough to cut.

Set up your baking stone and kit (see Assembly and Overview of the Process, page 267) and preheat the oven to 325°F (standard). Line two sheet pans with Silpats or parchment paper.

Using a pizza wheel or a chef's knife, cut the dough into ⅜-inch-wide strips. It is important that the strips be uniform in size, or they will bake unevenly. Carefully lift up the sticks and arrange on the sheet pans, leaving about ¼ inch between them; use the side of a chef's knife or a ruler to make sure the sides are straight. At this point the sheet pans can be wrapped in a few layers of plastic wrap and frozen for up to 2 weeks.

TO PROOF THE DOUGH: Cover with plastic tubs or cardboard boxes and let proof for 1 to 1½ hours, until when the dough is delicately pressed with a finger, the impression remains.

TO BAKE THE BREADSTICKS: Place one pan onto the baking stone. Immediately spray water onto the steam generator (rocks and chain). Quickly shut the oven door and bake for 22 minutes, or until golden brown. Repeat with the second pan.

Let cool completely on cooling racks.

MAKES 3 DOZEN BREADSTICKS

Pretzels

STIFF LEVAIN

All-purpose flour	113 grams	¾ cup + 1 tablespoon
Water, at 75°F/23.8°C	57 grams	¼ cup
Liquid Levain (page 272)	11 grams	0.4 ounce

DOUGH

All-purpose flour	483 grams	3¼ cups + 3 tablespoons
Instant yeast	5 grams	1½ teaspoons
Diastatic malt powder	6 grams	2 teaspoons
Fine sea salt	12 grams	2 teaspoons
Water, at 75°F/23.8°C	242 grams	1 cup + 1¾ teaspoons
Unsalted butter, at room temperature	60 grams	2.1 ounces

DIPPING LIQUID

Water, at 75°F/23.8°C	500 grams	2 cups + 3 tablespoons
Food-grade lye	21 grams	1 tablespoon + ½ teaspoon
Fleur de sel	10 grams	2½ teaspoons

French Laundry chef de cuisine Tim Hollingsworth asked Matthew to make pretzels. For The Laundry they had to be really nice: elegantly shaped into mini-bâtards, buttery, and flavorful (see photograph on page 267).

Now we do a lot of other pretzels at the bakery too—regular pretzels, croissant pretzels, and brioche pretzels. Pretzels are a lot of fun.

What gives pretzels their distinctive flavor is sodium hydroxide, also known as lye, a powerful alkaline corrosive. But don't be afraid of it; just be sure to buy food-grade lye, and be careful when using it. The lye is neutralized by the carbon dioxide in the oven during baking, leaving a dark brown, shiny, delicious crust. The manufacturer we recommend suggests a 4 percent lye solution; we use a 4.2 percent solution, so we leave the dough in the bath for a shorter time. This is the same dough as the French Laundry pretzels, but these are shaped traditionally. They need to be started the night before you intend to bake them.

You'll need two perforated baking sheets; heavy-duty plastic, such as a large garbage bag; and latex gloves.

FOR THE STIFF LEVAIN: Combine the flour and water in a medium bowl and mix together with your fingers. Mix in the levain. Cover the bowl loosely with plastic wrap and let sit at room temperature for 12 hours.

TO MIX THE DOUGH: Spray a large bowl with nonstick spray. Combine the flour, yeast, malt powder, and salt in the bowl of a stand mixer fitted with the dough hook and give it a quick mix on the lowest setting. Make a well in the center, add the levain, water, and butter, and mix on low speed for 4 minutes. Continue to mix on low for 30 minutes.

Using a bowl scraper, release the dough and turn it out onto a lightly floured board. Pat, stretch, and fold the dough (see Stretching and Folding the Dough, page 278) and place in the prepared bowl. Cover and let sit at room temperature for 15 minutes.

TO DIVIDE AND PRESHAPE THE DOUGH: Use the bowl scraper to release the dough and turn it out onto a lightly floured board. Gently pat the dough into a rectangular shape, removing any large bubbles and adding flour only as needed to keep the dough from sticking to the board. Divide the dough into ten 90-gram/3.2-ounce portions.

Preshape (see Long Preshape, page 282). Let rest for 5 minutes.

TO SHAPE THE PRETZELS: (See Shaping Pretzels, pages 332–33.) Line two sheet pans with parchment paper and lightly spray with nonstick spray. Form the pretzels and arrange 5 pretzels on each sheet pan. Refrigerate, uncovered so a skin forms, for 2 to 3 hours, until thoroughly chilled.

Meanwhile, position a rack in the lower third of the oven and place a baking stone on it. Preheat the oven to 350°F (standard). Spray the perforated baking sheets generously with nonstick spray, and set them on top of two sheet pans to catch any dipping liquid.

TO DIP AND BAKE THE PRETZELS: Line your work surface with the heavy-duty plastic. Put on the latex gloves.

FOR THE DIPPING LIQUID: Pour the water into a large bowl and whisk in the lye; some of the particles may not dissolve. Let sit for 5 to 10 minutes, and whisk again.

Place 3 of the pretzels in the dipping liquid, and one at a time, turn them over to thoroughly moisten, moving them around in the liquid for about 20 seconds (they should not touch each other). Lift from the bowl, letting the excess run off into the bowl, and arrange on a perforated sheet pan, leaving 2 to 3 inches between them. Repeat with the remaining pretzels, placing 5 on each pan.

Lift the perforated sheets off of the sheet pans. Sprinkle each pretzel with 1 gram/1¼ teaspoons of the fleur de sel. Slide one perforated sheet pan at a time onto the baking stone and bake for 25 minutes, or until a rich golden brown.

Let cool completely on a rack.

MAKES 10 PRETZELS

NOTE ON MAKING MINI PRETZEL BATARDS: To make mini-bâtards, divide the dough into 30-gram/1-ounce portions. Preshape (see Long Preshape, page 282), let rest for 5 minutes, and then shape (see Shaping, page 284). Dip and arrange on the perforated sheets, sprinkle with salt, and bake for 12 to 15 minutes.

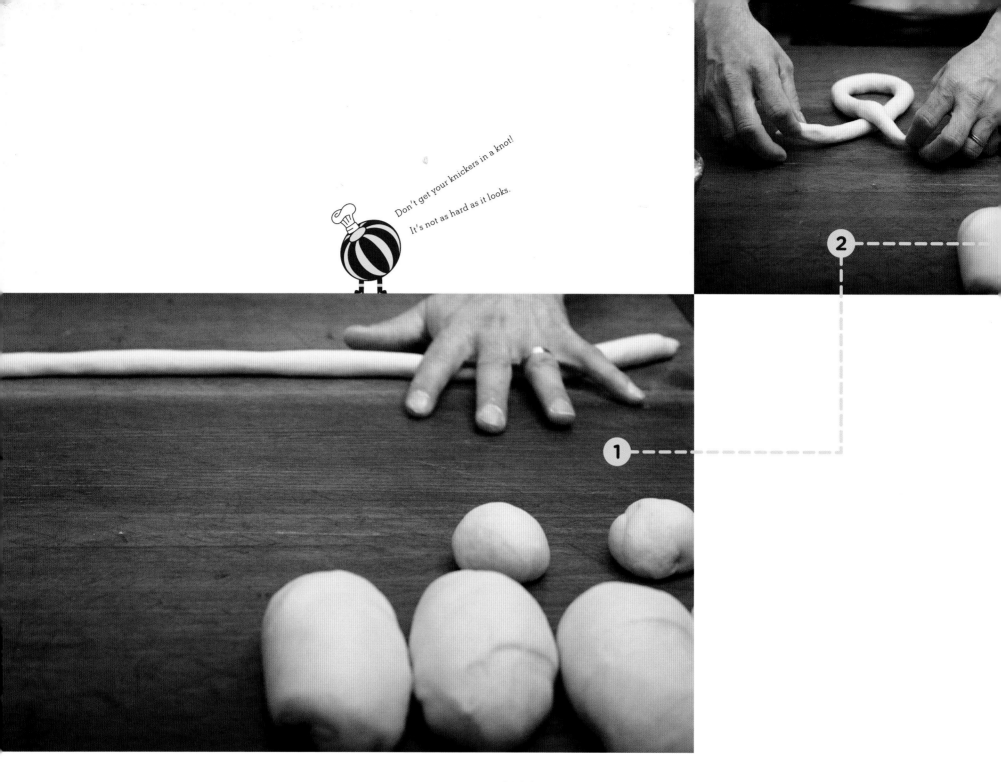

Don't get your knickers in a knot!

It's not as hard as it looks.

SHAPING PRETZELS

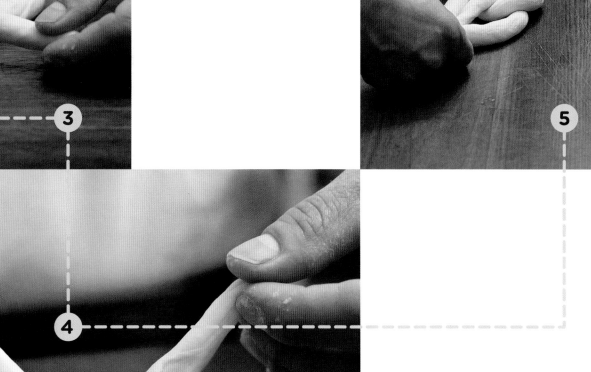

① Use your palms and fingertips to stretch the dough. ② Lift up one end of the dough and overlap it over the other end to create a loop. ③ Lift the bottom end over the top so it rests on the opposite end. ④ Lift the two ends and ⑤ push the ends down against the sides of the rounded bottom of the pretzel to form the pretzel shape (press down until you feel the work surface, to make sure the shape is secure).

Gluten-Free Brioche Rolls

Instant yeast	7 grams	2 teaspoons
Granulated sugar	20 grams	1 tablespoon + 2 teaspoons
Warm water, at 75°F/23.8°C	230 grams	¾ cup + 2 tablespoons + 1¾ teaspoons
Cup4Cup	535 grams	3¾ cups + 1 tablespoon
Kosher salt	20 grams	2 tablespoons + ¾ teaspoon
Eggs	158 grams	½ cup + 2 tablespoons
Egg yolks	22 grams	1½ tablespoons
Honey	80 grams	¼ cup
Unsalted butter, melted and cooled	100 grams	3.5 ounces
Egg Wash (page 381)		
Maldon salt for sprinkling	6 grams	1 teaspoon

In 2007, a young chef, Lena Kwak, did an internship at The French Laundry, and we asked her to stay. She was interested in nutrition, and as we found ourselves increasingly responding to diners who had specific dietary requests and restrictions, we often looked to Lena (pronounced "Lenna") to test new recipes.

One of the most common requests we get is for gluten-free breads, cakes, cookies, pasta, and other preparations. And gluten intolerance is a condition we take seriously.

Every meal at The French Laundry begins with a cornet, a savory cone-shaped tuile filled with crème fraîche and salmon tartare. So Corey Lee, chef de cuisine at the time, asked Lena to develop a gluten-free tuile. And she moved on to other gluten-free products. Lena didn't realize how important her work was until a diner came back to the kitchen, not to thank the chef, but to see her.

"She wanted to thank me for the brioche," Lena recalls. "She started crying. She hadn't been able to eat bread in seven years. People don't realize how special the simplest pleasures are until they can't have them."

Lena had worked hard to create an all-purpose mixture, based on different rice flours, potato flours, and cornstarch, that she could use in any gluten-free baked good, one that could be substituted cup for cup, gram for gram, for wheat flour.

It was so good that Corey suggested she talk to me about developing a product we could market. It was 2010, and I was already making a number of products for Williams-Sonoma, but this one was potentially the most special of all. And that's how Cup4Cup was born. It's something we're very proud of, as we are of these gluten-free brioche rolls. These are not just "pretty good for gluten-free," they are fantastic brioche rolls, period.

You'll need a 12-cup muffin pan.

Combine the yeast and sugar in a small bowl. Stir in the warm water, and set in a warm spot to proof for 10 minutes or until the yeast mixture is foaming and bubbly.

Meanwhile, combine the Cup4Cup and salt in the bowl of a stand mixer fitted with the paddle attachment. Whisk together the eggs, yolks, honey, butter, and proofed yeast mixture in a medium bowl.

Turn the mixer to low speed and slowly add the egg mixture. Increase the speed to medium and mix the dough for 10 minutes. It will be very silky and not as stiff as regular bread dough.

Scrape down the sides of the bowl, cover with plastic wrap, and set the bowl in a warm spot until the dough has about doubled in size, about 1 hour.

Using a rubber spatula, deflate the dough, turning it over a few times in the bowl. Scrape down the sides of the bowl, cover the bowl tightly with plastic wrap, and refrigerate for 2 hours.

Spray the muffin pan with nonstick spray. Spoon 75 grams/⅓ cup of the dough into each cup. Brush the tops of the rolls with egg wash, sprinkle with the Maldon salt, and set in a warm spot to proof uncovered for about 40 minutes until they rise (but are not doubled) and spread slightly.

Preheat the oven to 350°F (standard). Bake the rolls for 15 to 17 minutes, until the tops are a golden brown and a wooden skewer inserted in the center of a roll comes out clean.

Transfer to a cooling rack to cool completely.

MAKES 12 ROLLS

CONFECTIONS

What exactly are confections? You don't go to the grocery store for a quart of milk, a dozen eggs, and some confections. But it is a meaningful term in that it allows us to assemble a miscellany of sweets that don't fit neatly into any other group: caramel popcorn, for example, caramel apples, and Fuhgeddaboudits, our version of Rice Krispies Treats, coated with caramel and enrobed in chocolate. ◎ At Bouchon Bakery, we love classics, and we love to elevate them, to explore them and see how refined we can make them. The *pâtes de fruits* (fruit jellies), for instance, are a favorite of mine. Nougat and marshmallows are other time-honored preparations that are dear to me. And so are those preparations born of nostalgia: our peppermint patties and caramels. Making our own versions of foods we grew up with has become almost second nature to us. ◎ No matter what the category, much of my pleasure comes from Sebastien's skill and craftsmanship in making these treats the very best they can be. I also love that the items in this section make great gifts. There's no better gift you can give than something that comes from the work of your own hands and your heart.

Caramel Popcorn

POPCORN AU CARAMEL ET AUX CACAHUETES

Canola oil		
Salted Spanish peanuts	225 grams	1½ cups
Water	112 grams	½ cup
Granulated sugar	225 grams	1 cup + 2 tablespoons
Light brown sugar	112 grams	½ cup + 1½ tablespoons (lightly packed)
Light corn syrup	100 grams	¼ cup + 1 tablespoon
Unsalted butter, at room temperature	70 grams	2.5 ounces
Popped popcorn	about 135 grams	10 cups
Baking soda	9 grams	2 teaspoons
Kosher salt	13 grams	1 tablespoon + 1¼ teaspoons

Among the many culinary surprises that awaited Sebastien in America was the butter and salt on the popcorn at the movies. In France popcorn is only served with caramel, which maintains the freshness of the popcorn and adds crunch. At the bakery, we add nuts as well. Caramel popcorn is a simple, special treat when you make it yourself.

Use a popcorn that produces really large kernels; we prefer Newman's Own (jarred, not the microwave kind). The best way to get evenly coated popcorn is to toss the popcorn and the caramel in a hot bowl so the caramel doesn't seize up when it hits the bowl.

You'll need a 14-inch-wide metal bowl, a Thermapen or other candy thermometer, and heatproof gloves or two pairs of latex gloves.

Preheat the oven to 350°F (standard). Lightly oil two sheet pans with canola oil. Lay a kitchen towel on your work surface. Spray two heatproof or wooden spoons with nonstick spray.

Put the metal bowl in the oven to heat while you make the caramel. Spread the peanuts on a small sheet pan.

Combine the water, sugars, corn syrup, and butter in a large saucepan and cook over medium-high heat, stirring to dissolve the sugar, until the mixture (which will bubble up considerably) reaches 270°F/132°C, about 7 minutes.

Letting the syrup continue to cook, remove the bowl from the oven, and place the peanuts in the oven. Spray the bowl with nonstick spray and place it on the towel. Pour 108 grams/8 cups of the popcorn into the bowl and form a well in the middle. Put on the heatproof or latex gloves.

When the caramel reaches 300°F/149°C, remove it from the heat and immediately stir in the baking soda and salt (be careful, as it will foam up). Remove the peanuts from the oven and add them to the caramel. Immediately pour the caramel mixture into the well and over the popcorn in the bowl, avoiding the sides of the bowl, then cover with the remaining 27 grams/2 cups of popcorn. Using the two spoons, quickly toss the ingredients together, drawing the popcorn from the edges into the center. Continue to stir and toss to coat as much of the popcorn as possible. (Any uncoated kernels will become stale more quickly.)

Pour the hot mixture onto one of the prepared sheet pans. Using your hands—taking care, as the caramel will still be quite hot—break up any larger clumps of popcorn. As you work, transfer half the popcorn to the second sheet. Let the caramel popcorn set until cooled and hardened.

Store in a covered container at room temperature; if the kernels are well coated, the popcorn will remain fresh for 2 to 3 days.

MAKES 800 GRAMS/4 QUARTS

1

2

3

Caramel Apples
POMMES FONDANTES AU CARAMEL

Skin-on whole almonds	177 grams	1 cup + 3 tablespoons
4 medium Granny Smith or other firm, crisp apples		
Caramel Jam (page 380)	450 grams	1½ cups
70% chocolate, tempered (see page 370)	144 grams	5 ounces

How fluid the caramel is will dictate how thick the layer of caramel on the apples is. If you like a thinner layer, heat the caramel more to make it more fluid; if you like a thicker layer of caramel, don't heat it as much. The caramel for the apples we make is very thick. Sometimes kids have a hard time getting through to the apple—but we look at this as a good thing, since it's all about the caramel. We also like to add nuts for their texture and flavor. Be sure to buy unwaxed apples so that the caramel adheres to them.

Because the apples must be dipped in enough caramel to coat them, there will be leftover caramel. Heat it up, thin it out with a little cream, and you'll have a delicious caramel sauce for ice cream.

Popsicle or wooden craft sticks can be found at craft stores and some kitchen supply or cake decorating stores. Clear or colored cellophane for wrapping the apples is available at craft and party stores and some florists.

You'll need 4 Popsicle sticks or wooden craft sticks and clear cellophane (optional). ● *For this recipe, we use Valrhona Guanaja 70% chocolate.*

Preheat the oven to 350°F (standard). Line a sheet pan with a Silpat.

Spread the nuts on a small baking sheet and toast in the oven for 10 minutes, or until golden brown: break one open to check the color. Let cool.

Coarsely chop the nuts. Toss the nuts in a strainer to remove any dusty particles, which would detract from the look of the finished apples. Spread the nuts on a plate or in a shallow bowl.

Remove the apple stems and push a stick through the stem end into the center of each apple.

Put the caramel jam in a microwave-safe bowl, preferably one with slightly sloped sides, that is deep enough for dipping the apples. Heat the caramel in the microwave, checking it every 10 seconds or so and giving it a stir, until you reach the consistency you want: the more you liquefy the caramel, the thinner the coating will be on the apples. If the caramel becomes too thick as you work with the apples, simply heat it again.

Holding it by the stick, dip an apple into the caramel, angling the apple and rotating it as necessary to coat the entire apple, leaving a ½-inch ring exposed around the stick. Lift up the apple, letting the excess caramel run back into the bowl, and, working quickly, use a small spatula or a palette knife to remove any extra caramel that has settled on the bottom of the apple, then dip the bottom of the apple into the nuts and turn it to coat the sides. There won't be a solid layer of nuts, but if the nuts don't adhere to the caramel easily, press them in lightly with your fingertips. Place the apple on the Silpat and repeat with the remaining apples. Let stand until the caramel sets.

The caramel (and nuts) may pool at the bottom of the apples. If you'd like a more refined look, trim the edges of the bottom with a pair of scissors (see Note).

Place a piece of parchment paper on the work surface. Hold an apple over the parchment paper and drizzle it with some of the chocolate. Return it to the Silpat and continue with the remaining apples. Let the apples sit at room temperature for at least 30 minutes until the chocolate is firm.

If you are not serving the apples within a few hours, wrap them individually in clear cellophane. Gather the paper at the top and tie with kitchen twine or decorative ribbons. Caramel apples are best the day they are made, but they can be kept at room temperature for up to 3 days.

MAKES 4 CARAMEL APPLES

NOTE: If you'd like, the caramel trimmings can be rolled into caramel nut chews and served as is, or dipped into melted chocolate and sprinkled with fleur de sel.

Toffee

Skin-on whole almonds	412 grams	2¾ cups
Unsalted butter	150 grams	5.25 ounces
Granulated sugar	375 grams	1¾ cups + 2 tablespoons
Water	100 grams	¼ cup + 3 tablespoons
Light corn syrup	75 grams	3 tablespoons + 2 teaspoons
Baking soda	4.8 grams	1 teaspoon
Kosher salt	4.5 grams	1½ teaspoons
Vanilla paste	5.6 grams	1 teaspoon
70% chocolate, tempered (see page 370)	180 grams	6.3 ounces

Toffee is another form of cooked sugar and butter, taken to a higher temperature than for chewy caramels. We add a little baking soda, which gives the toffee a lighter, crisper texture. Be sure to use a deep pot when cooking the toffee, as the sugar will really bubble up when you add the baking soda. We coat the toffee with chocolate and chopped toasted almonds.

You'll need two 24-by-¼-inch-square confectionery rulers and a Thermapen or other candy thermometer. ● *For this recipe, we use Valrhona Guanaja 70% chocolate.*

Preheat the oven to 350°F (standard).

Spread the nuts on a small baking sheet and toast in the oven for 10 minutes, or until golden brown: break one open to check the color. Let cool.

Coarsely chop 330 grams/2¼ cups of the nuts. Finely chop the remaining 82 grams/½ cup nuts. Toss the coarsely chopped and finely chopped nuts separately in a fine-mesh strainer to remove any dusty particles, which would detract from the look of the toffee.

Place a Silpat on the work surface. Position the confectionery rulers lengthwise along the edges of the Silpat and tape the ends to the work surface to prevent them from shifting.

Melt the butter in a large, deep saucepan over medium heat. Stir in the sugar, water, and corn syrup, increase the heat to high, and bring to 310°F/154°C. Stir in the baking soda and salt (the mixture will bubble up), then continue to cook to 320°F/160°C.

Remove the pan from the heat and stir in the vanilla paste and coarsely chopped almonds. Carefully pour the mixture onto the Silpat and cover with a second Silpat.

Using a rolling pin, roll over the Silpat to spread the toffee evenly between the bars and smooth the top. Let cool completely, about 4 hours.

Line the work surface with a piece of parchment paper slightly larger than the toffee. Spread half the chocolate in a very thin layer over the parchment and sprinkle it evenly with half of the finely chopped nuts. Remove the top Silpat, invert the toffee onto the chocolate, and remove the remaining Silpat. Spread the remaining chocolate in a thin layer over the toffee and sprinkle evenly with the remaining nuts. It is best to let the toffee set up in a cool room (60° to 65°F/15.5° to 18°C); let stand for at least an hour so the chocolate sets. (The toffee would set up in the refrigerator, but there would be condensation.)

Place a piece of parchment paper over the toffee and hit it with a rolling pin to break it into irregular pieces.

The toffee can be stored in a covered container at room temperature for up to 1 month.

MAKES 954 GRAMS/ABOUT 2 POUNDS

Toffee (left; page 342) and Fuhgeddaboudits (right; page 365)

Caramels

Crème fraîche	500 grams	2¼ cups
2 vanilla beans, split lengthwise		
Glucose	352 grams	1 cup
Granulated sugar	380 grams	1¾ cups + 2½ tablespoons
Salted butter	30 grams	1 ounce

The key to good caramels, aside from cooking the mixture to the proper temperature, is the ingredients. We use crème fraîche, rather than the typical cream, and the best butter. We prefer salted butter for caramels, to balance the sweetness; if you don't use salted butter, you will need to add a little salt. If you want perfectly smooth, uniform caramels, use confectionery rulers.

You can make the caramels very special by enrobing them in chocolate; see page 371.

You'll need four 24-by-½-inch-square confectionery rulers or an 8-inch-square baking pan, a Thermapen or other candy thermometer, and cellophane.

If using confectionery rulers, place a Silpat on the work surface. Arrange the rulers on the Silpat to form an 8-inch square and tape the ends of the rulers to the work surface to prevent them from shifting. If using the baking pan, line it with a double layer of plastic wrap; make sure there are no gaps in the plastic wrap.

Place the crème fraîche in a small saucepan. Scrape the seeds from the vanilla beans, add them to the crème fraîche, and stir to distribute them. Heat the crème fraîche over medium-low heat, stirring, until warm.

Meanwhile, put the glucose in a large saucepan and bring to a boil over high heat. Reduce the heat to medium-high and stir in the sugar one-third at a time, stirring just to incorporate before adding the next batch. (Adding all the sugar at once could cause it to caramelize too quickly and unevenly.) After about 3 minutes, when the sugar has dissolved, the bubbles are a rich amber color, and the temperature is about 350°F/176°C, reduce the heat to medium. Working quickly, stir in the butter. Reduce the heat to medium-low and slowly, because the mixture will bubble up, add the crème fraîche. Cook, stirring and scraping to keep the mixture from scorching, until the temperature reaches 242° to 244°F/116° to 118°C. To test the consistency, drop a small amount of the caramel onto a cold plate. It should firm up quickly, not spread; lift easily from the plate; and not feel sticky to the touch.

Strain the caramel through a fine-mesh strainer onto the Silpat or into the prepared pan. Let sit at room temperature until cool and set, at least 2 hours.

Cut about 5 dozen 3-by-2½-inch pieces of cellophane.

Transfer the slab of caramel to a cutting board; discard the plastic wrap, if you used it. Using scissors, trim any uneven edges. Cut the caramel into 1-inch-wide strips, then cut them crosswise into ¾-inch pieces. Wrap each caramel in a piece of cellophane, twisting the ends in opposite directions to seal them tightly.

The caramels can be stored in a covered container at room temperature for up to 1 week. After a week, the flavor begins to fade.

MAKES ABOUT 5 DOZEN CARAMELS

CANDY THERMOMETERS

The Thermapen is an excellent instant-read thermometer that registers high temperatures. It's our thermometer of choice and what we recommend. The Taylor candy thermometer is very good, and we use it as well, but it's fragile. We don't recommend using it for both deep-frying and candy making, because the high temperatures of deep-frying reduce its accuracy at the lower temperatures of cooked sugar. If you deep-fry a lot, buy a second one exclusively for that (they're inexpensive). We go through ours quickly: when you see a gap in the mercury, it's time to get a new thermometer.

When working with small quantities of sugar, you may need to tilt the pot to submerge the bulb in the sugar syrup; if you do this, make sure gas flames aren't licking up the side of the pot and making the thermometer too hot. Never take the thermometer out of the cooking sugar and put it immediately under cold water. To clean the thermometer, just soak it in hot water—the cooked sugar will dissolve.

Lemon Caramels

CARAMELS ACIDULES

35% white chocolate, coarsely chopped	125 grams	4.5 ounces
Valrhona Caramélia 34% milk chocolate, coarsely chopped	200 grams	7 ounces
Cocoa butter	15 grams	0.5 ounce
Kosher salt		pinch
Granulated sugar	250 grams	1¼ cups
Salted butter	62 grams	2 ounces
Fresh lemon juice	90 grams	¼ cup + 2 tablespoons
Grated lemon zest	4 grams	2 teaspoons

We call these caramels because they're chewy like caramels and have a caramel flavor, but they're actually made from a mixture of white chocolate and Valrhona Caramélia 34%, a milk chocolate that has caramel in it. There's really no substitute for the Caramélia, because it's what makes these unique "caramels" what they are.

We flavor these with lemon, but you could use tangerine, orange, or blood orange in the same proportions. To make plain caramels, simply eliminate the juice and zest.

You'll need four 24-by-¼-inch-square confectionery rulers or a 6-inch-square baking pan, a Thermapen or other candy thermometer, and cellophane. • *For this recipe, we use Valrhona Ivoire 35% white chocolate and Valrhona Caramélia 34% milk chocolate.*

If using confectionery rulers, place a Silpat on the work surface. Arrange the rulers on the Silpat to form a 6-inch square and tape the ends of the rulers to the work surface to prevent them from shifting. If using the baking pan, line it with a double layer of plastic wrap; make sure there are no gaps in the plastic wrap.

Combine the chocolates and melt them. Melt the cocoa butter and stir it into the chocolate; add the pinch of salt. Pour into a food processor.

Meanwhile, combine the sugar, butter, and lemon juice in a medium saucepan and cook over medium-high heat, stirring from time to time, until the temperature reaches 248°F/120°C. Remove the pan from the heat and let cool to 212°F/100°C.

With the food processor running, pour the butter mixture through the feed tube and process until well combined and smooth. Scrape down the sides of the bowl, add the zest, and pulse to combine.

Pour the mixture onto the Silpat or into the prepared pan. Smooth the top with an offset spatula. Let sit at room temperature until set, at least 6 hours.

Cut about 4 dozen 3-by-2-inch pieces of cellophane.

Transfer the slab of caramel to a cutting board; discard the plastic wrap, if you used it. Using scissors, trim any uneven edges. Cut the caramel into ¾-inch-wide strips, then cut them crosswise into 1-inch rectangles. Wrap each caramel in a piece of cellophane, twisting the ends in opposite directions to seal them tightly.

The caramels can be stored in a covered container at room temperature for up to 1 week. After a week, the flavor begins to fade.

MAKES ABOUT 4 DOZEN CARAMELS

WORKING WITH SUGAR

Cooking sugar allows us to achieve many different outcomes. But cooked sugar gets very, very hot, so pay attention when working with it; if you turn your head at the wrong moment, it can quickly rise above the temperature you want.

Use a refined granulated sugar made from beets or sugarcane. If the sugar is not refined, impurities can cause it to crystallize and clump up when it's melting. For the same reason, it's important that your pan be very clean. Any particles in the pan can cause the liquefied sugar to crystallize.

Choose the right pan. A copper pan is best because it distributes heat so well, but a heavy-bottomed stainless steel pan is also fine. Choose a pan that's big enough, especially if you'll be adding cream or liquid, which can bubble up violently.

Although you can make what is called a "dry caramel," starting with just sugar in a dry pan, we combine the sugar with a little bit of water, which makes it easier to melt the sugar uniformly (as a rule, add 30 percent of the weight of the sugar). Begin the cooking over medium heat to dissolve the sugar. When the sugar has become a syrup, turn up the heat, but make sure that the flame stays under the pan—you don't want flames climbing up the sides, which could burn any sugar splattered on the inside of the pan—if you wish, you can use a wet pastry brush to dissolve any sugar crystals clinging to the side of the pan.

The best way to monitor the temperature is to use a thermometer. When I first started in the industry, all apprentices were taught to dip three fingers first in ice water, then in the boiling syrup, then back in the ice water to feel the consistency of the cooled sugar. I don't recommend you do this at home. (Sugar burns are painful!)

KEY SUGAR TEMPERATURES

212°F/100°C	Sugar dissolves into a transparent and fluid syrup.
230°F/110°C	Most of the water has evaporated and it is time to start whipping egg whites if you're making a meringue with hot syrup.
235–240°F/113–116°C	Soft ball: the temperature needed to make fudge, fondant, and some caramels.
250–266°F/121–130°C	Hard ball: the temperature needed to cook honey for nougat and syrup for marshmallows and Italian meringue.
300–310°F/150–160°C	Hard crack: the temperature needed to cook sugar for hard candy, toffee, brittle, and our glaze for pâte à choux.
320°F/160°C	Sugar begins to caramelize.
338–356°F/170–180°C	The hotter the caramel gets, the darker it becomes. Past this temperature, the sugar will turn black and can ruin your pan.

The consistency of the sugar syrup changes depending on how hot you get it. When your sugar reaches the desired temperature, you can stop the syrup from cooking further by immediately submerging the pan in an ice bath. You can also remove the syrup from the heat when it is a few degrees below the desired temperature so that the temperature will be reached by carryover cooking. The smaller the amount of sugar, the faster the temperature goes up: stay alert.

To clean your pan, fill it with water and simmer until the pan is clean. For large pots, you can pour in boiling water and cover the pot with plastic wrap; the condensation that collects on the plastic will drip down the sides of the pan and dissolve the cooked-on sugar. Or simply fill the pot with water and let stand until the sugar dissolves.

Note to Professionals: There are a few other steps you can take to prevent crystallization:

- Add glucose syrup (or corn syrup) in the ratio of 10 to 30 percent of the total weight of the sugar.
- Add 2 grams of cream of tartar per kilo of sugar.
- Add a few drops of tartaric acid per kilo of sugar.
- Add a few drops of white vinegar per kilo of sugar.

Vanilla Marshmallows

GUIMAUVE A LA VANILLE

Powdered sugar	58 grams	½ cup
Cornstarch	64 grams	½ cup
Silver leaf gelatin	9.6 grams	4 sheets
Egg whites	87 grams	¼ cup + 2 tablespoons
¼ vanilla bean, split lengthwise		
Granulated sugar	225 grams	1 cup + 2 tablespoons
Water	112 grams	½ cup
Light corn syrup	50 grams	2½ tablespoons

Marshmallows may seem mysterious and complex, but they're really easy—nothing more than meringue set with gelatin. If you can make a meringue, you can make your own marshmallows. They're playful and fun, and they can be made in different flavors. We make lemon, raspberry, and vanilla marshmallows, but you could add jams or pistachio paste for different flavors (add 15 to 20 percent of the weight of the egg whites and sugar).

You'll need an 8-inch-square baking pan, an 8-inch-square piece of acetate, and a Thermapen or other candy thermometer.

Mix the powdered sugar and cornstarch together. Line the baking pan with plastic wrap and sprinkle the plastic wrap generously with the powdered sugar mixture; set the remainder aside.

Place the gelatin in a bowl of ice water to soften.

Spray one side of the piece of acetate with nonstick spray; set aside.

Remove the gelatin from the water and squeeze out excess water. Place the gelatin in a small metal bowl set over a small pot of simmering water and melt it (do not let it simmer), then reduce the heat and keep it warm.

Meanwhile, place the egg whites in the bowl of a stand mixer fitted with the whisk attachment. Scrape the seeds from the vanilla bean and add the seeds to the egg whites.

Combine the granulated sugar, water, and corn syrup in a large saucepan and bring to a simmer over medium-high heat, stirring to dissolve the sugar, then simmer for about 5 minutes, until the syrup reaches 250°F/121.1°C.

Letting the syrup continue to cook, turn the mixer to medium speed. The goal is to have the whites at medium peaks when the syrup reaches 281° to 284°F/138° to 140°C. Should the whites reach stiff peaks before the syrup reaches the proper temperature, reduce the mixer speed to the lowest setting.

When the syrup reaches 281° to 284°F/138° to 140°C, remove it from the heat. Turn the mixer to medium speed and slowly add the syrup to the egg whites, pouring it between the side of the bowl and the whisk. Pour in the gelatin, increase the speed to medium-high, and mix for about 5 minutes, until the mixture is thickened, glossy, and warm but not hot.

Spray a spatula with nonstick spray. Spread the marshmallow evenly in the prepared pan. Top with the acetate, sprayed side down, and gently press it against the marshmallow to make the top perfectly smooth.

Set a piece of parchment paper larger than the marshmallow on a large cutting board.

Remove the sheet of acetate. Coat the top of the marshmallow with some of the reserved powdered sugar mixture. Flip the marshmallow onto the parchment paper, remove the plastic wrap, and sprinkle with more of the powdered sugar mixture as necessary.

It can be difficult to cut marshmallows evenly. Spray a large chef's knife with nonstick spray and trim the sides of the marshmallow square, then cut into 1-inch cubes (or other shapes), using a ruler as a guide (see Note to Professionals). Clean and respray the knife before each cut. If the marshmallows are sticky when you separate them, dust them lightly with additional powdered sugar mixture.

The marshmallows can be stored in a covered container at room temperature for up to 3 days.

MAKES ABOUT 4 DOZEN 1-INCH MARSHMALLOWS (250 GRAMS/8.8 OUNCES)

Note to Professionals: We use a guitar cutter for quick, uniform shapes.

Raspberry Marshmallows
GUIMAUVE A LA FRAMBOISE

Omit the vanilla bean. If desired, add 2 drops red food coloring, preferably Chefmaster Red Red, to the warm marshmallow mixture and mix just to combine. Remove the bowl from the mixer stand and gently whisk in 12 grams/2 tablespoons raspberry powder. Spread the marshmallow in the pan and proceed as directed.

Lemon Marshmallows
GUIMAUVE AU CITRON

Omit the vanilla bean. If desired, add 6 drops yellow food coloring, preferably Chefmaster Lemon Yellow, to the warm marshmallow mixture and mix just to combine. Add the grated zest of 2 lemons (12 grams/2 tablespoons) and mix to combine, then spread the marshmallow in the pan and proceed as directed.

Witches' Hats

½ recipe Speculoos dough
(page 48)

Mixture for Vanilla Marshmallows
(page 350), just made

Brune pâte à glacer (see Note,   400 grams | 4 ounces
page 120) or tempered
chocolate (see page 370), warm

Pâtisserie is noted for precision and exactitude, but it's also a craft that lends itself to whimsy and fun, one that can connect us immediately to the delights and wonders of childhood. These witches' hats are a perfect example. They combine some of my favorite things: cookies, marshmallows, and chocolate. It's hard to go wrong with that.

We make witches' hats in 3 sizes: 1½, 2, and 2½ inches in diameter. For the best proportions of cookie to marshmallow, we never make them bigger than 3 inches.

We use Cacao Barry pâte à glacer. ● *You'll need a 1½-, 2-, or 2½-inch round cutter and a pastry bag with a ½-inch plain tip.*

Preheat the oven to 325°F. Line a sheet pan with a Silpat or parchment paper.

Roll out the speculoos dough as directed (see page 48). Cut the dough into rounds, arrange on the prepared sheet pan, leaving about ¾ inch between them, and bake as directed, 12 to 14 minutes, depending on the size of the rounds. Set the pan on a cooling rack and cool for 5 to 10 minutes, then transfer the cookies to the rack to cool completely. (The cookies can be stored in a covered container for up to 3 days.)

Line a sheet pan with parchment paper and place the cooled cookies on another cooling rack, leaving at least 1 inch between them. Transfer the marshmallow to the pastry bag. Holding the bag vertically about ¼ inch above the center of a cookie, pipe the marshmallow so it covers the cookie to within ½ inch from the edges, then pull up on the pastry bag to form a cone. You will use about 5 grams for small cookies, 10 grams for medium ones, and 15 grams for large ones. Repeat with the remaining cookies and marshmallow. (Depending on the size of the hats, you may have extra marshmallow.)

Spoon some of the pâte à glacer or tempered chocolate over each hat to coat the marshmallow and cookie evenly. Let stand at room temperature until the chocolate sets.

The witches' hats are best served the day they are made.

MAKES TWENTY-FOUR 1½-INCH, SIXTEEN 2-INCH, OR FOURTEEN 2½-INCH COOKIES

So tasty it's scary!

Layered Fruit Marshmallows

Ingredients for Vanilla, Raspberry,
and Lemon Marshmallows
(pages 350–51), including the
optional food coloring

FOR PLAIN MARSHMALLOWS

Powdered sugar	58 grams	½ cup
Cornstarch	64 grams	½ cup

FOR CHOCOLATE-ENROBED MARSHMALLOWS

64% chocolate, tempered	300 grams	10.5 ounces
(optional; see page 370)	800 grams	28 ounces

This is a fairly elaborate recipe, but it results in a fabulous confection. Three layers of different colored and flavored marshmallows—vanilla, raspberry, and lemon—are spread between confectionery rulers, then cut and dusted with powdered sugar and cornstarch or cut into bars or squares and enrobed in chocolate.

You'll need four 12-by-18-inch pieces of acetate and six 24-by-½-inch-square confectionery rulers. ● *For this recipe, we use Valrhona Manjari 64% chocolate.*

Lightly spray the work surface or a cutting board (longer than 18 inches) with nonstick spray and wipe off any excess with a paper towel. Cover with one piece of acetate. Lightly spray and wipe the top of the acetate. Position two of the confectionery rulers 7 inches apart, running lengthwise on the acetate. Tape the ends of the rulers to the work surface to prevent them from shifting.

Prepare the vanilla marshmallow mixture and pour it onto the acetate. Spray a spatula with nonstick spray and spread the marshmallows over the acetate between the rulers, reaching the sides of the rulers. The mixture should be just slightly higher than the rulers; the length of the marshmallow doesn't matter at this point. Spray a second piece of acetate, wipe off any excess, and put it over the marshmallow, sprayed side down. Using a rolling pin, roll over the acetate to spread the marshmallow evenly and smooth the top.

The finished rectangle should be 7 inches by 14 inches. Remove the acetate.

Spread a little of the marshmallow mixture left in the bowl or on the spatula over the tops of both rulers to act as glue. Set two more rulers over the first set and press them together to adhere. Let the marshmallow set for 1 hour.

Prepare the raspberry marshmallow mixture, pour it over the vanilla layer, and repeat the spreading and rolling process, using the third sheet of acetate and matching the size of the vanilla layer as much as possible. Secure the final set of rulers and let the marshmallow sit at room temperature for 1 hour.

Prepare the lemon marshmallow mixture and repeat the process, leaving the final sheet of acetate in place on top. Let the marshmallow sit overnight.

FOR PLAIN MARSHMALLOWS: Lay a piece of parchment paper larger than the marshmallow on a large cutting board. Mix the powdered sugar and cornstarch together.

Remove the sheet of acetate and remove the rulers. Coat the top of the marshmallow with some of the powdered sugar mixture. Flip the marshmallow onto the parchment paper and sprinkle with more of the mixture.

Spray a large chef's knife with nonstick spray and cut through the layers, using a ruler as a guide. Cut the marshmallows into 1½-inch squares, 1½-by-3-inch rectangles, or any size you like. Clean and respray the knife before each cut. If the marshmallows are sticky when you separate them, dust them lightly with more of the powdered sugar mixture.

The marshmallows can be stored in a covered container for up to 3 days.

FOR CHOCOLATE-ENROBED MARSHMALLOWS: Remove the sheet of acetate, leaving the rulers in place. Spread the 300 grams/10.5 ounces tempered chocolate in a very thin layer over the top. Let sit for about 15 minutes, or until set.

Remove the rulers and flip the rectangle of marshmallow over. Trim the edges to straighten them. Note that if you try to cut through the chocolate with a cold knife, it will shatter. Run very hot water over the longest slicing knife you have, dry it well with a towel, and place it on the spot where you want to make your first cut. Cut through the marshmallow layers and then let the heat of the knife guide it through the layer of chocolate. Clean the knife (any chocolate on the knife would streak the marshmallows) and repeat the process to cut the marshmallows into strips, using a ruler as a guide, then turn the board 90 degrees and repeat in the other direction (see Note to Professionals). At the bakery, we typically cut these marshmallows into $1\frac{1}{2}$-by-3-inch bars or $1\frac{1}{2}$-inch squares.

Using the remaining 800 grams/28 ounces tempered chocolate, enrobe the marshmallows in chocolate (see Enrobing Candies in Chocolate, page 371). The marshmallows are delicate, so instead of rubbing any pooled chocolate from the bottoms using parchment paper, trim it with a hot paring knife.

Serve the marshmallows whole or, if you'd like, cut them in half to expose the layers.

The marshmallows can be stored in a covered container at room temperature for up to 3 days.

MAKES 3 TO 4 DOZEN MARSHMALLOWS

Note to Professionals: We use a guitar cutter for quick, uniform shapes.

YOU RULE

Professional kitchens rely on confectionery rulers or plastic guides to form perfectly even layers and smooth sides. The number of rulers you need varies with the number of layers you are making. Professional confectionery rulers can be very costly, so we use plastic ones that are cut 22 inches long by $\frac{1}{4}$ or $\frac{1}{2}$ inch square. Plastic fabricators (such as Tap Plastics) are a great source for buying inexpensive food-safe plastic guides cut to your specifications.

Marshmallow Eggs

Marshmallows (pages 350–51;
    any flavor), just mixed
    and still warm

White or colored decorating sugar, store-bought or homemade (recipe follows)	90 grams	¼ cup + 1 tablespoon

At Easter, the team loves to make marshmallow eggs. When you serve them in all kinds of colors, they're a joy to behold, especially for kids. We make different flavors and colors, coat them in various decorative sugars, and place them in egg cartons. For vanilla eggs, we use plain sugar, but for the raspberry we use our raspberry sugar and for the lemon, our lemon sugar. When people first open the carton, they think it's filled with dyed Easter eggs, not marshmallows. Be sure to buy sturdy plastic eggs to use as molds; the cheaper ones are really flimsy. Note that the marshmallows and decorating sugar should rest overnight before coating the eggs.

You'll need twelve two-piece plastic eggs, a clean egg carton, and a pastry bag with a ½-inch plain tip.

If the plastic eggs are new, open them, wash them, and dry thoroughly. Spray the inside of both halves of each egg with nonstick spray and set them in the egg carton.

Fill the pastry bag with the warm marshmallow mixture. Holding the tip close to the bottom of an egg half, slowly pull up as you fill the half completely; try not to leave any air pockets. Fill the other half and fit the top and bottom together—there will be some resistance, but they must be secure to form a perfectly shaped egg. Wipe off the excess marshmallow that oozes from the egg with a damp paper towel. Repeat with the remaining eggs. Stand the filled eggs in the egg carton and let them sit at room temperature overnight.

Put the decorating sugar in a small bowl. Remove the eggs from the molds. Toss the eggs in the sugar and then stand them in the egg carton.

If they will be served within a few hours, let the eggs sit at room temperature. For longer storage, place the egg carton in a large covered container for up to 2 weeks.

MAKES 12 EGGS

Colored Decorating Sugar

FOR RASPBERRY SUGAR

Large-crystal sparkling sugar	100 grams	¼ cup + 1½ tablespoons
6 drops diluted citric acid (see Note)		
Dehydrated raspberry powder, or as needed	1 gram	½ teaspoon
Powdered oil-soluble red food coloring		

FOR LEMON SUGAR

Large-crystal sparkling sugar	100 grams	¼ cup + 1½ tablespoons
6 drops diluted citric acid (see Note)		
Grated zest of ½ lemon (use a rasp grater)	1.5 grams	¾ teaspoon
Powdered oil-soluble yellow food coloring		

Don't be tempted to use liquid food coloring; it won't work here. If you'd like, wear a pair of plastic gloves to avoid staining your hands.

You'll need raspberry powder if making Raspberry Sugar and powdered oil-soluble red or yellow food coloring.

Place the sugar in a small bowl. Stir in the citric acid, raspberry powder or lemon zest, and just the amount of food coloring that fits on the tip of a small paring knife (less than a pinch), then use your hands to work the mixture together. If you'd like, add a little additional powder and/or food coloring. Spread the sugar on a baking sheet and let it dry overnight at room temperature.

NOTE: To make diluted citric acid, combine 2 grams/⅜ teaspoon citric acid and 2 grams/¾ teaspoon water in a small cup and stir to dissolve the citric acid.

Tweet, tweet treats!

Nougat aux Fruits

Egg whites	66 grams	¼ cup + 1½ teaspoons
Chestnut or lavender honey	333 grams	1¾ cups + 3½ tablespoons
Granulated sugar	553 grams	2¾ cups + ¾ teaspoon
	26 grams	2 tablespoons + ½ teaspoon
Water	166 grams	½ cup + 3 tablespoons
Glucose	120 grams	¼ cup + 1½ tablespoons
Cocoa butter, melted and still warm	20 grams	0.7 ounce
Skin-on whole almonds	233 grams	1½ cups
Shelled unsalted pistachios	82 grams	½ cup + 1 tablespoon
Dried cherries or cranberries, finely chopped	235 grams	2 cups

Classic nougat—honey, egg whites, and nuts—is usually made with almonds, but we like to make it our own by adding pistachios and dried cherries or cranberries. If you can find them, green pistachios from Sicily are the best. You can substitute other nuts or fruits for the pistachios and dried cherries or cranberries, using the same weight. Use a good honey, since it is the primary flavoring agent. We also include a chocolate version and a "Toblerone" variation that makes use of the nougat trimmings. And, if you like, you can enrobe the nougat in chocolate; see page 371.

Timing is important here, so have all of the components measured and ready to go before starting the syrup (see Note on Timing).

The recipe makes a large batch, but the nougat keeps for a long time and is great to give as a gift.

You'll need a Thermapen or other candy thermometer, two 24-by-½-inch-square confectionery rulers, two 11-by-18-inch pieces (preferably) of rice paper or six 8½-by-11-inch pieces, and cellophane. ● For this recipe, we use Cacao Barry cocoa butter.

Preheat the oven to 350°F (standard). Lay a 16-by-24-inch piece of parchment paper on the work surface or a large cutting board. Tape the edges of the paper to the surface or board. Place a large piece of the rice paper in the center, or arrange 3 smaller pieces, overlapping them, so they cover an 11-by-18-inch area. Position two confectionery rulers on each of the longer sides of the rice papers, leaving an 11-inch space between them, and tape the ends of the rulers to the parchment paper to prevent them from shifting.

Place the egg whites in the bowl of a stand mixer fitted with the whisk attachment.

Pour the honey into a medium saucepan and heat to 257°F/125°C over medium heat; lower or raise the heat as necessary so that the honey reaches the proper temperature when the egg whites reach stiff peaks.

Meanwhile, place the 553 grams/2¾ cups plus ¾ teaspoon sugar in a large saucepan and stir in the water to moisten it. Stir in the glucose and bring to a boil over medium-high heat, then lower the heat to medium.

After 4 to 5 minutes, when the syrup has reached 225°F/107°C, turn the mixer speed to medium-low. When the whites are full of bubbles and fluffy, but before they form soft peaks, gradually add the 26 grams/ 2 tablespoons plus ½ teaspoon sugar, then increase the speed to medium to medium-high and whip to stiff peaks.

Meanwhile, as the egg whites whip, check the temperature of the honey and increase the heat if necessary to reach 257°F/125°C. Should the whites reach stiff peaks before the honey reaches the proper temperature, reduce the speed of the mixer to the lowest setting.

As soon as the honey comes to the correct temperature, turn the mixer speed to medium-low and carefully pour in the honey between the side of the bowl and the whisk. Increase the speed to medium-high and whip until the mixture is thickened and glossy, about 4 minutes.

Meanwhile, bring the syrup to 298.4°F/148°C. Turn the mixer speed to medium-low and carefully pour in the syrup, then increase the speed to medium-high and mix for about 16 minutes, until thickened and warm, not hot. Reduce the speed to low, pour in the cocoa butter, and mix for about 1 minute.

Meanwhile, toast the almonds on a small baking sheet in the oven for 10 minutes, or until golden brown: break one open to check the color. Place in a bowl, toss with the pistachios and cherries, and keep warm.

When the nougat is thickened and holds a shape, stop the mixer, switch to the paddle attachment, and add the nuts and cherries, mixing only enough to incorporate them.

Spray a spatula with nonstick spray and spread the nougat on the rice paper between the rulers, reaching the sides of the rulers; the mixture should be just slightly higher than the rulers. Don't worry if the surface is uneven. Position the second large sheet or 3 smaller sheets of rice paper over the nougat. Using a rolling pin, roll over the nougat to spread evenly and smooth the top. The finished rectangle should be about 11 inches by 15 inches.

It is best to let the nougat set up in a cool room (60° to 65°F/15.5° to 18°C); let sit overnight. (The nougat would set up in the refrigerator, but there would be condensation.)

Remove the rulers from the sides and move the nougat, still in the rice paper, to a cutting board. Trim away any uneven edges; these trimmings can be finely chopped and used in ice cream or mousse or to make our version of Toblerone (see Note to Professionals). Cut the nougat into 11-by-¾-inch strips. Using a ruler, score a long side every ¾ inch. Spray a large chef's knife with nonstick spray and cut through the nougat, using the ruler as a guide for a straight edge; clean and respray the knife as necessary.

It is best to store the cut nougat wrapped individually in cellophane. Cut twenty 14-by-6-inch pieces of cellophane. Wrap each piece of nougat in a sheet and twist the ends of the cellophane in opposite directions to seal.

The nougat can be stored in a covered container at room temperature for up to 1 month.

PHOTOGRAPHS ON PAGES 360 AND 361   MAKES TWENTY 11-BY-¾-INCH PIECES

NOTE ON TIMING: The timing of the three preparations—whites, honey, and sugar—is critical to the success of the nougat. You can control the temperature of the honey and the sugar by adjusting the heat level or moving them off the heat when they are close to the final temperature and returning them to the heat when you are ready to use them. Here is a summary of the steps and temperatures: Heat the honey to 257°F/125°C. Cook the sugar and glucose to 298.4°F/148°C. Whip the whites to stiff peaks, add the honey, and whip for about 4 minutes. Add the sugar mixture.

Note to Professionals: To make our version of Toblerone, cut the nougat trimmings into small pieces (pull off any extra rice paper, but don't worry about what clings to the nougat). Pulse it in the food processor to break it up, then process into very fine pieces. We use 4 parts tempered milk chocolate to 3 parts nougat. Fold them together and let them set in a mold of your choice.

Chocolate Nougat

Just before the nougat is ready, slowly stir together 100 grams/ 3.5 ounces unsweetened (preferably Michel Cluizel 100%) chocolate, melted, with the 20 grams/0.7 ounce cocoa butter.

When the nougat is thickened, mix in the chocolate mixture. Then add the nuts and cherries and proceed as directed.

NOTE ON COCOA BUTTER: Cocoa butter is the vegetable fat extracted from cocoa beans during chocolate processing. It's a pale, neutral fat that is solid at room temperature. The reason good chocolate starts to melt immediately in your mouth is because the melting point of cocoa butter is just under body temperature. The cocoa butter gives the chocolate nougat a pleasing texture.

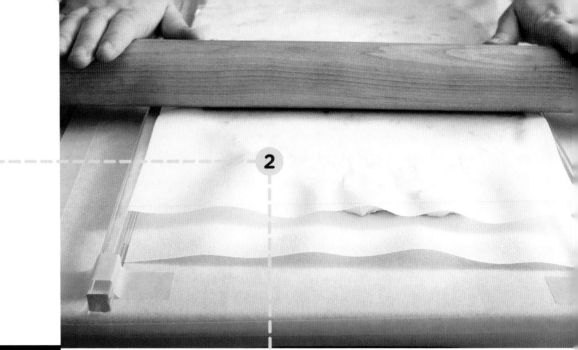

Pâtes de Fruits

Black Currant Pâte de Fruit

Granulated sugar	72 grams	¼ cup + 2 tablespoons
	650 grams	3¼ cups
Apple pectin	14 grams	2 tablespoons
Glucose	120 grams	⅓ cup
Black currant puree (see Notes to Professionals)	500 grams	17.6 ounces
Fresh Granny Smith apple juice or unsweetened, unfiltered apple juice	225 grams	¾ cup + 2½ tablespoons
Tartaric acid or cream of tartar	10 grams	2½ teaspoons
Granulated sugar for coating	200 grams	1 cup

I love these fruit jellies so much I used to stay up to work with our pastry chef into the early morning hours after service at The French Laundry, when the kitchen was cool, quiet, and empty, so we could offer them on our mignardises tray.

Tartaric acid is similar in texture to granulated sugar, while cream of tartar is powdery; either will provide the necessary acid to help set the pectin and add some acidic balance. White peaches have less acidity than black currants, so we use more tartaric acid and less pectin in that recipe.

For variety, other berry purees can be substituted for the black currant.

You'll need four 24-by-½-inch-square confectionery rulers or a 9-by-13-inch baking pan and a Thermapen or other candy thermometer.

• *For this recipe, we use Boiron or Perfect Puree black currant puree.*

Combine the 72 grams/¼ cup plus 2 tablespoons sugar and pectin in a small bowl. Place the remaining 650 grams/3¼ cups sugar in another bowl. It's difficult to transfer glucose from one container to the other because it is so sticky; you often lose some in the process. So weigh (or measure) the glucose directly over the bowl of sugar and pour it in, avoiding the edges of the bowl. Combining it with the sugar this way allows you to pour it cleanly when you transfer it to the saucepan.

If using confectionery rulers, line the work surface with a piece of parchment or aluminum foil larger than a Silpat. Place a Silpat over the center. (The overhang of parchment will help keep the work surface clean.) Position the rulers so they form a 9½-by-12-inch rectangle. Tape the ends of the rulers to the work surface to prevent them from shifting. If using a baking pan, line the pan with a double layer of plastic wrap.

Mix the puree, sugar-pectin mixture, and apple juice in a large saucepan and bring to a boil over medium-high heat, stirring with a heatproof spatula and skimming off any impurities that rise to the surface. Stir in the sugar and glucose and continue to boil, stirring and scraping the sides and bottom often and reducing the heat as necessary to prevent scorching, until the temperature reaches 225°F/107°C (see Notes to Professionals). To check the consistency, drop a small amount of the mixture onto a cold plate. It should firm quickly, not spread; lift easily from the plate; and not feel sticky to the touch.

Remove from the heat, stir in the tartaric acid or cream of tartar, and quickly pour the mixture between the rulers or into the prepared pan in an even layer. Let sit at room temperature for 30 minutes to firm completely.

Remove the rulers or lift the plastic wrap to remove the candy from the pan. Once the pâte de fruit is cut and coated in sugar, it is best eaten within 2 hours, but at this point the full sheet of candy can be wrapped in plastic wrap and stored at room temperature for up to 2 weeks or frozen for up to 1 month.

continued

TO CUT THE PATE DE FRUIT: Place 150 grams/¾ cup of the coating sugar on a sheet pan, and shake the pan to distribute it evenly. Place the sheet of candy on the sugar, then flip it over to coat the second side with sugar. (This initial coating of sugar makes it easier to cut the candy into squares.) Using a long slicing knife, trim any uneven edges. If at any point the candy sticks to the knife, rinse the knife under hot water, dry, and continue to cut. Cut into 1-inch-wide strips, then cut crosswise into 1-inch squares (see Note to Professionals).

Place the remaining 50 grams/¼ cup sugar in a small bowl. Dip all sides of the pâte de fruit squares in the sugar to coat them evenly. If they will be held for longer than 2 hours, store them in a covered container at room temperature for up to 5 days. If the sugar dissolves, toss them in additional sugar just before serving.

MAKES ABOUT 8 DOZEN PIECES

Notes to Professionals: We prefer Boiron and Perfect Puree fruit purees, but if they are unavailable, choose another puree with a 10 percent sugar content, like Ravi Fruit or Cap Fruit. Using purees with the same percentage of sugar gives consistency from batch to batch. Fresh fruit purees can be used, but we would suggest making a small batch first to determine the amounts of pectin, citric acid, and sugar needed. Particularly with fresh fruit, as the fruit mixture cooks impurities rise, and they should be skimmed off.

When working with fruit purees, we like to use a refractometer, a tool used in winemaking to measure the amount of sugar, or Brix, in the fruit. For this recipe, it should register 78° Brix.

We use a guitar cutter for quick, uniform shapes.

White Peach Pâte de Fruit

Granulated sugar	62 grams	¼ cup + 1 tablespoon
	550 grams	2¾ cups
Apple pectin	12 grams	1 tablespoon + 2 teaspoons
Glucose	120 grams	⅓ cup
White peach puree (see Notes to Professionals, left)	500 grams	17.6 ounces
Fresh Granny Smith apple juice or unsweetened, unfiltered apple juice	125 grams	½ cup
Tartaric acid or cream of tartar	15 grams	1 tablespoon + 1 teaspoon
Granulated sugar for coating	200 grams	1 cup

You'll need four 24-by-½-inch square confectionery rulers or a 10-inch-square baking pan and a Thermapen or other candy thermometer.

● *For this recipe, we use Boiron or Perfect Puree white peach puree.*

Combine the 62 grams/¼ cup plus 1 tablespoon sugar with the pectin. Place the remaining 550 grams/2¾ cups sugar in a bowl.

If using confectionery rulers, position them on the Silpat (see method above) so they form an 8-by-12-inch rectangle; line the baking pan with a double layer of plastic wrap. Proceed as directed for Black Currant Pâte de Fruit.

MAKES ABOUT 7 DOZEN PIECES

Fuhgeddaboudits

Unsalted butter	100 grams	3.5 ounces
Store-bought marshmallows	225 grams	4 cups
Kellogg's Rice Krispies	127 grams	4 cups
Caramel Jam (page 380)	128 grams	¼ cup + 3 tablespoons
50% milk chocolate, tempered (see page 370)	260 grams	9 ounces
Fleur de sel for sprinkling		

Often our inspiration comes from trying to make what we loved as kids even better. These are a direct knock-off of Rice Krispies Treats. We didn't really change the treats part at all, and commercial marshmallows work best (both for consistency and because that's what people expect), but we enhance them by adding a layer of caramel and coating them in milk chocolate. (And you can even use store-bought caramels instead of our caramel jam; see the Note.) When we were looking for a name, one that was catchy and said "New York," Sebastien's longtime colleague and friend Richard Capizzi, an Italian-American New Yorker, came up with the perfect suggestion.

You'll need a quarter sheet pan, a silicone mold with eight 2½-by-½-inch-deep round cavities, and a 2¼-inch round cutter. ● For this recipe, we use Michel Cluizel Mangaro 50% milk chocolate.

Spray the quarter sheet pan with nonstick spray. Line the bottom with parchment paper and spray the parchment.

Melt the butter in a medium saucepan over low heat. Add the marshmallows and stir until completely melted.

Place the cereal in a large bowl. Spray a spatula with nonstick spray and scrape the marshmallow mixture into the bowl of cereal.

Spray an offset spatula and spread the mixture evenly in the prepared pan. Cool for 15 to 20 minutes.

Place the silicone mold on the work surface. If the caramel jam is liquefied, pour 16 grams into each cavity. If the caramel is hard, spoon 16 grams into each cavity and place the mold in the microwave to heat and melt the caramel; the caramel should soften enough to spread to the edges of the cavities, but it does not have to liquefy. Set the mold on a sheet pan.

Using the cutter, cut 8 rounds of the cereal mixture. (What remains makes a great snack or can be used to make additional Fuhgeddaboudits.) Place a cereal round over the caramel in each mold. Refrigerate for 15 minutes or freeze for 5 minutes to harden the caramel.

TO ENROBE THE ROUNDS: Unmold the rounds and bring them to room temperature. Place a Silpat on the work surface.

Enrobe the candies with the chocolate; see page 371. Sprinkle the top of each with a pinch of fleur de sel.

The Fuhgeddaboudits can be stored in a covered container at room temperature for up to 1 month.

PHOTOGRAPH ON PAGE 343   MAKES 8 ROUNDS

NOTE: You can substitute 8 Kraft caramels (16 grams/about ½ ounce each) for the caramel jam. Melt the caramels as directed in that recipe.

Peppermint Patties

Granulated sugar	272 grams	1¼ cups + 2 tablespoons
Water	100 grams	¼ cup + 3 tablespoons
Pouring/icing fondant	272 grams	¾ cup + 1 tablespoon
Trimoline (invert sugar; see Note)	24 grams	1 tablespoon
Fondax (optional; see Note to Professionals)	16 grams	0.5 ounce
Peppermint oil	4 drops	
Invertase (optional)	1 gram	⅛ teaspoon
64% chocolate, tempered (see page 370), or brune pâte à glacer	320 grams	11 ounces

Peppermint patties are another classic American confection. For our version, we use invertase, an ingredient you may not be familiar with. It's an enzyme, usually commercially derived from yeast, that converts sucrose into an invert sugar. That means that if it is added to the peppermint filling, it will break the mixture down over time, making it smooth and creamy instead of a stiff paste. You don't have to use invertase, but the resulting contrasting textures are part of the pleasure of eating the peppermint patty. As the invertase changes the texture over time, try these at various stages to see which texture you like best; we prefer them after a week or two.

This recipe is somewhat difficult in that the filling must be piped while it's hot; wear heatproof gloves or a double layer of latex gloves, and keep a tall container, such as a large glass measuring cup, handy in case the pastry bag gets too hot and you want to set it down.

You'll need a silicone mold with eight 2½-by-½-inch round cavities, two disposable pastry bags, a pair of heatproof gloves or two pairs of latex gloves, a 3-pronged dipping fork (optional), and colored foil (optional).

● *For this recipe, we use Caullet pouring fondant, Erstein Trimoline, and Valrhona Manjari 64% chocolate.*

Set out the silicone mold, a large liquid measuring cup, the pastry bags, and the gloves on the work surface.

Place the sugar and water in a large saucepan and stir to moisten the sugar. Set the pan over high heat and, stirring until the sugar dissolves and checking the temperature often, bring to 240.8°F/116°C, 7 to 8 minutes.

Meanwhile, warm the fondant in a double boiler just to soften it. Set up another double boiler and heat over medium-high heat until the water is very hot; keep it at just below a simmer.

Remove the syrup from the heat and add the fondant, Trimoline, and Fondax, if using, stirring until melted and well combined. Return to the heat only if necessary to melt the ingredients. Stir in the peppermint oil, followed by the invertase, if using.

Put on the heatproof gloves or both pairs of latex gloves. Working quickly, transfer one-third of the mixture to the top of the double boiler to keep warm. Stand a pastry bag in the measuring cup and fill it with the remaining mixture. Lift out the bag and cut ¼ inch from the tip; keep the measuring cup nearby in case the bag becomes too hot to hold.

Pipe enough filling into each cavity to reach the top (47 to 50 grams). Let harden completely and cool to room temperature, about 15 minutes.

Remove the candies from the mold and set aside. Fill the second pastry bag as you did the first, and pipe the remaining filling into 4 of the cavities of the mold.

If you did not use invertase, the candies can sit at room temperature overnight before enrobing, but if you used it, they must be enrobed the same day, because the filling will begin to soften.

Place a Silpat on the work surface. Enrobe the candies in the chocolate; see page 371. As you place each dipped candy on the Silpat, lay the dipping fork on the top of it and then lift it up, leaving a decorative imprint in the chocolate. (If you don't have a dipping fork, use the back of a table knife and mark with a single line.) Let stand until the chocolate has set.

Wrap the patties individually in colored foil, if desired (we wrap them in green foil with a sticker in the center). Or wrap individually in plastic wrap. Store in a covered container at room temperature.

If the patties were made without invertase, they can be eaten right away. If you used the invertase, let them sit for about 1 week, giving the filling time to soften, before serving. Wrapped peppermint patties can be kept for up to 1 month.

PHOTOGRAPHS ON PAGES 368 AND 369 **MAKES 12 PATTIES**

NOTE ON INVERT SUGAR: Invert sugar (Trimoline is a widely available brand) is a mixture of glucose and fructose. It is often used in candy-making, as it produces a smoother result.

Note to Professionals: We add White Stokes Fondax to the peppermint patties to enhance the smooth texture of the filling; if it is unavailable, it can be omitted. We prefer to use dark tempered chocolate for enrobing the candy, but you can use white or milk chocolate as well.

IT'S ALL IN THE NUMBERS

Today most artisanal chocolates, and many commercial brands, list a percentage number on the label. This number refers to the percentage of the cacao solids and cocoa butter in the chocolate. Unsweetened chocolate and cocoa powder are 100% pure cacao, without any sugar added, and the percentage moves downward from there. For example, a bar marked 75% is three-quarters pure cacao; the other 25% is primarily sugar, along with flavorings such as vanilla. So, if you prefer sweeter chocolate, you'll be drawn to the flavors of a lower-percentage chocolate. If you are unable to find the type recommended in a specific recipe, look for another chocolate with the same percentages.

1

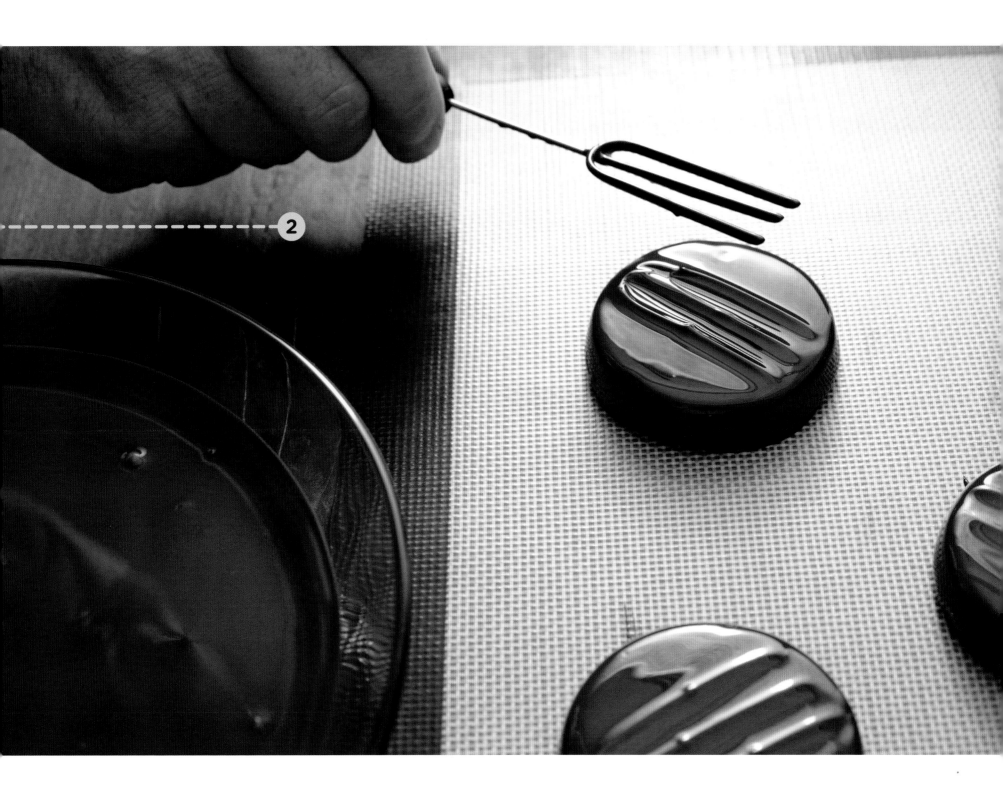

Tempering Chocolate

Chocolate is tempered to give it a smooth, shiny appearance and a better snap when it is broken or bitten into. When you purchase chocolate it is tempered, but when it is melted, the cocoa butter crystallizes, causing the surface of the chocolate to become dull and lose its beautiful sheen and snap. Returning it to "temper" matters when you are using the chocolate as a coating. It is not important if the melted chocolate is incorporated with other ingredients in baking.

We like to use the seeding method (adding tempered chocolate to the melted chocolate) because it works well for any type or amount of chocolate. All of the chocolate is chopped. A portion (about two-thirds) of it is melted to a specific temperature, depending on the type of chocolate being used, and the remaining chocolate is added to bring the chocolate "to temper" or the working temperature. Once the chocolate is set, it will maintain the desired shine.

A laser thermometer works well for accurate readings when tempering chocolate. To read the temperature, position the thermometer a few inches from the surface of the chocolate and shoot the laser eye into the middle of the surface area.

TO TEMPER: You start by chopping the chocolate, then melting two-thirds of it in the top of a double boiler over medium heat. Once the chocolate reaches the appropriate temperature (see chart at left), remove the top of the double boiler and set it on the work surface. Add the remaining chocolate, pushing it beneath the surface.

Allow the chocolate to rest for a few minutes to melt the chopped chocolate, then use an immersion blender or a spoon to recombine the chocolates. Check the temperature: it will be higher than the temperature for crystallization. Let the chocolate stand at room temperature, stirring from time to time, until it has reached the crystallization temperature.

Return the bowl to the double boiler and heat slowly until the chocolate reaches the working temperature. It is now ready to use for enrobing candy.

TEMPERATURES

	MILK CHOCOLATE	DARK CHOCOLATE
MELTING	113–118°F/45–47.7°C	131–136°F/55–57.7°C
CRYSTALLIZATION	81–82°F/27.2–27.7°C	82°–84°F/27.7–28.8°C
WORKING	84–86°F/28.8–30°C	88°–90°F/31.1–32.2°C

Enrobing Candies in Chocolate

The Layered Fruit Marshmallows (page 354), Fuhgeddaboudits (page 365), and Peppermint Patties (page 366) can all be enrobed in chocolate by dipping them. The Fuhgeddaboudits and Peppermint Patties can also be enrobed by the pouring method (see below). You'll need a dipping fork and tempered chocolate as specified in each individual recipe.

TO ENROBE CHOCOLATE BY DIPPING: Before you dip the candy in the tempered chocolate, the bottoms should be coated with chocolate. This layer of hardened chocolate will prevent any gaps from forming when the dipping fork is pulled out from the enrobed candy. The marshmallows will already have a bottom coating of chocolate, but you'll need to coat any of the other candies.

Place a Silpat on the work surface. Pour the tempered chocolate into a small deep bowl that is large enough to hold a piece of the candy easily. The deeper the chocolate, the easier it will be to enrobe the candy. Brush a coating of chocolate over the bottom of each candy (if you are making Fuhgeddaboudits, brush the cereal side and place them on the Silpat, chocolate side down). Let sit at room temperature for about 10 minutes, until the chocolate is completely hardened.

One at a time, using the dipping fork, lift a candy from the Silpat and lower it into the chocolate, completely submerging it. Check to make sure there are no holes or gaps in the coating. Lift the candy out of the chocolate and tap the fork against the side of the bowl, allowing any excess chocolate to drip back into the bowl, then carefully place the candy on a clean area of the Silpat and slide out the fork.

Repeat with the remaining candies.

It is best to let the chocolate set up in a cool room (60° to 65°F/15.5° to 18°C) overnight. (The chocolate would set up in the refrigerator, but there would be condensation.)

Once the candies are set, check to see if any chocolate has pooled at the bottom of the pieces. It can be removed by rubbing the pooled chocolate against a piece of parchment paper, for a more finished edge.

TO ENROBE CHOCOLATE BY POURING: Pour the tempered chocolate into a spouted measuring cup. Brush the bottoms of Fuhgeddaboudits and Peppermint Patties with chocolate as described above. Let set until completely hardened.

Place a Silpat on a sheet pan and top with a cooling rack. Place the candies, chocolate side down, on the rack.

Pour the tempered chocolate over the candy one piece at a time, making sure to cover the top and sides completely (excess chocolate will flow through the rack to the Silpat). With a small offset spatula, move the candies, allowing the grates of the rack to knock off any excess chocolate. Finish the candies as described in the individual recipes.

The candies can be wrapped individually in colored foil, cellophane, or plastic wrap. Store in a covered container at room temperature.

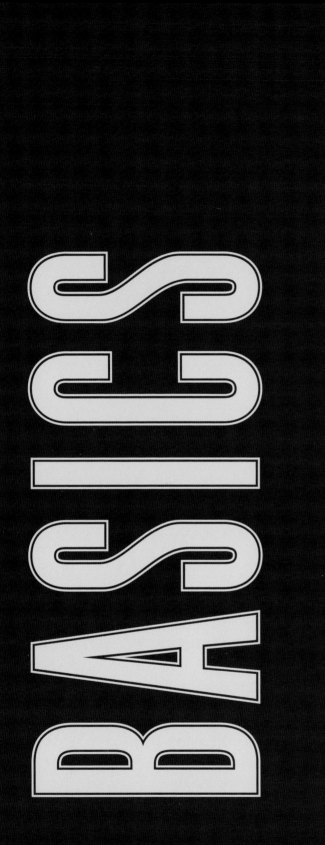

BASICS

CREAMS AND CURDS

Pastry cream, one of the pastry kitchen's foundation preparations, is easily varied and built on to make other creams. Very simple to make, it's a milk-based custard thickened with custard powder or all-purpose flour and enriched with butter. Once everything is mixed, Sebastien puts it into a pot cold, brings it to a simmer, cooks to thicken, then strains before adding the butter. Our chocolate pastry cream includes cocoa powder as well as melted chocolate, which is whisked in after the butter. That's it—so simple; no tempering of the eggs required. (He does the same for crème anglaise and ice cream bases.)

Pastry cream is very thick; when we want to lighten it, we often add whipped cream. If we want to lighten it but also create a cream that has enough body to hold its shape, we combine it with whipped cream and gelatin, which makes Diplomat Cream (page 374).

Buttercream (page 375) is another basic. Our buttercream is made with an Italian meringue. We use buttercream often as a building device; the butterfat sets up when cold and gives us a solid surface to work with. It also will give body to other creams. The mousseline cream we use in the Strawberry Parfait (page 111) is buttercream mixed with pastry cream.

Another cream we like is Almond Cream (page 376). Almond flour gives the cream flavor and adds richness to the pastry. We also use Frangipane (page 376), a mixture of almond cream and pastry cream, which is used in the Pithiviers (page 223).

Citrus curds add creamy flavor and acidity to any number of pastries, tarts, and cakes. I've always preferred the traditional method of whipping them over a water bath. Sebastien prefers to start the eggs, sugar, and citrus juice on the stovetop, then use the Vitamix to blend in the butter. To ensure that these curds have enough body, we add gelatin. Citrus curd is a simple preparation that can become a versatile part of your dessert repertoire.

Pastry Cream

CREME PATISSIERE

SMALL BATCH · MAKES 680 GRAMS/3 CUPS

Egg yolks	132 grams	½ cup + 1 tablespoon
½ vanilla bean, split lengthwise		
Granulated sugar	110 grams	½ cup + 1 tablespoon
Custard powder or all-purpose flour (see Note on Custard Powder)	83 grams	½ cup + 1½ tablespoons
Whole milk	550 grams	2 cups + 3 tablespoons
Unsalted butter, cut into ½-inch pieces, at room temperature	27 grams	1 ounce

LARGE BATCH · MAKES 810 GRAMS/3⅔ CUPS

Egg yolks	160 grams	½ cup + 2½ tablespoons
1 vanilla bean, split lengthwise		
Granulated sugar	133 grams	½ cup + 2½ tablespoons
Custard powder or all-purpose flour	100 grams	½ cup + 3½ tablespoons
Whole milk	666 grams	2½ cups + 2½ tablespoons
Unsalted butter, cut into ½-inch pieces, at room temperature	33 grams	1.2 ounces

For this recipe, we use Bird's custard powder.

Set up an ice bath. Place a medium bowl in the ice water and set a fine-mesh strainer over the bowl.

Put the yolks in the bowl of a stand mixer fitted with the whisk attachment. Scrape the seeds from the vanilla bean, add them to the yolks, and mix on medium-low speed for about 30 seconds. Reduce the speed to low and slowly pour in the sugar, then whisk on medium speed until lighter in color, about 1½ minutes. Scrape down the sides and bottom of the bowl, then whisk on medium-high speed for about 3 minutes, until the mixture is pale yellow and thick. When the whisk is lifted, the mixture should form a slowly dissolving ribbon.

Reduce the speed to low, add the custard powder or flour, and mix for 30 seconds. Scrape down the sides and bottom of the bowl. With the mixer running on the lowest speed, slowly pour in the milk. Scrape the bowl again and mix on low speed for another minute, or until combined.

Pour the mixture into a large saucepan, set over medium heat, and stir gently until it begins to thicken. Switch to a whisk and whisk as the cream comes to a simmer, rotating the whisk around the bottom to keep the cream from scorching. Once you see bubbles breaking the surface, cook for about 5 minutes longer, whisking constantly, until the pastry cream has thickened.

Pour the pastry cream through the strainer, pressing gently on it to push the thickened cream through. Whisk for about 1 minute to cool slightly, then whisk in the butter in 2 additions.

Pour into a covered container and press a piece of plastic wrap against the surface to prevent a skin from forming. Refrigerate for at least 1 hour. The cream can be refrigerated for up to 4 days.

When ready to use the cream, transfer to a bowl and stir gently until it has a creamy consistency.

NOTE ON CUSTARD POWDER: We like to use Bird's custard powder instead of the flour for a richer pastry cream with a brighter color.

Chocolate Pastry Cream

CREME PATISSIERE AU CHOCOLAT

70% chocolate, coarsely chopped	167 grams	5.8 ounces
100% unsweetened chocolate, coarsely chopped	25 grams	0.8 ounce
Custard powder or all-purpose flour (see Note on Custard Powder)	25 grams	2 tablespoons + 2 teaspoons
Unsweetened alkalized cocoa powder	25 grams	¼ cup + 1 tablespoon
Egg yolks	60 grams	¼ cup
Granulated sugar	87 grams	¼ cup + 3 tablespoons
Whole milk	500 grams	2 cups
Unsalted butter, cut into ½-inch pieces, at room temperature	52 grams	1.8 ounces

For this recipe, we use Valrhona Guanaja 70% chocolate, Valrhona Pure Pâte de Cacao 100%, Bird's custard powder, and Valrhona cocoa powder.

Melt the two chocolates together.

Combine the custard powder or all-purpose flour and the cocoa powder in a small bowl.

Set up an ice bath. Place a medium bowl in the ice water and set a fine-mesh strainer over the bowl.

Put the yolks in the bowl of a stand mixer fitted with the whisk attachment and mix on medium-low speed for about 30 seconds. Reduce the speed to low and slowly pour in the sugar, then whisk on medium speed until lighter in color, about 1½ minutes. Scrape down the sides and bottom of the bowl, then whisk on medium-high speed for about 3 minutes, until the mixture is pale yellow and thick. When the whisk is lifted, the mixture should form a slowly dissolving ribbon.

Reduce the speed to low, add the custard powder or flour mixture, and mix for 30 seconds. Scrape down the sides and bottom of the bowl. With the mixer running on low speed, slowly pour in the milk. Scrape the bowl again and mix for another minute, or until combined.

Pour the mixture into a large saucepan, set over medium heat, and stir gently until it begins to thicken. Switch to a whisk and whisk as the cream comes to a simmer, rotating the whisk around the bottom to keep the cream from scorching. Once you see bubbles breaking the surface, cook for about 5 minutes longer, whisking constantly, until the pastry cream has thickened.

Pour the pastry cream through the strainer, pressing gently to push the thickened cream through. Whisk for about 1 minute to cool slightly, then whisk in the butter in 2 additions. Scrape down the sides and bottom of the bowl. Add the chocolate in 2 additions, whisking until incorporated.

Pour into a covered container and press a piece of plastic wrap against the surface to prevent a skin from forming. Refrigerate for at least 1 hour. (The cream can be refrigerated for up to 4 days.)

When ready to use the cream, transfer to a bowl and stir gently until it has a creamy consistency.

MAKES 775 GRAMS/3½ CUPS

NOTE ON CUSTARD POWDER: We like to use Bird's custard powder instead of the flour for a richer pastry cream with a brighter color.

Orange Pastry Cream

Make a large batch of Pastry Cream (page 373), strain it, and whisk in the grated zest of 2 medium oranges. Whisk for about 1 minute, then add the butter as directed.

Diplomat Cream
CREME DIPLOMATE

Silver leaf gelatin	2 grams	⅘ sheet
Pastry Cream (page 373)	610 grams	2¾ cups
Heavy cream, whipped to medium peaks	200 grams	¾ cup + 1½ tablespoons

Place the gelatin in a bowl of ice water to soften.

Transfer one-third of the pastry cream to a medium microwave-safe bowl or a small saucepan. Remove the gelatin from the water, squeezing out excess water, and add to the bowl or pan. Heat, gently stirring, to loosen the pastry cream and dissolve the gelatin.

Meanwhile, transfer the remaining pastry cream to the bowl of a stand mixer fitted with the paddle attachment or to a medium bowl and mix or stir until smooth.

Strain the warm pastry cream through a fine-mesh strainer into the bowl with the rest of the pastry cream and mix or stir until smooth. Remove the bowl from the mixer stand and fold in the whipped cream one-third at a time.

Press a piece of plastic wrap against the surface to prevent a skin from forming and refrigerate until firm, at least 4 hours. (The cream can be refrigerated for up to 4 days.)

When ready to use the cream, transfer to a bowl and stir gently until it has a creamy consistency.

MAKES 750 GRAMS/3½ CUPS

Orange Diplomat Cream

Use 2.7 grams/1⅛ gelatin sheets and increase the heavy cream to 267 grams/1 cup plus 2 tablespoons. Substitute 810 grams/3⅔ cups Orange Pastry Cream (opposite) for the plain pastry cream.

MAKES 1 KILOGRAM/4⅔ CUPS

Basic Buttercream

Egg whites	75 grams	¼ cup + 1 tablespoon
Granulated sugar	150 grams	¾ cup
	33 grams	2 tablespoons + 2¼ teaspoons
Water	42 grams	3 tablespoons + 1 teaspoon
Unsalted butter, cut into ½-inch pieces, at room temperature	227 grams	8 ounces

Buttercream is one of the most important basics in the pastry kitchen. It's not essential that you use a high-fat butter, just the best quality butter you have access to.

Place the egg whites in the bowl of a stand mixer fitted with the whisk attachment.

Place the 150 grams/¾ cup sugar in a small saucepan, add the water, and stir to moisten the sugar. Bring to a simmer over medium-high heat, stirring occasionally, and simmer until the syrup reaches 230°/100°C.

Letting the syrup continue to cook, turn the mixer to medium speed, gradually pour in the remaining 33 grams/2 tablespoons plus 2¼ teaspoons sugar into the whites, and whip until the whites are beginning to form very loose peaks. If the whites are ready before the syrup reaches 248°F/120°C, turn the mixer to the lowest setting just to keep them moving.

When the syrup reaches 248°F/120°C, remove the pan from the heat. Turn the mixer to medium-low speed and slowly add the syrup to the whites, pouring it between the side of the bowl and the whisk. Increase the speed to medium-high and whisk for 15 minutes, or until the bottom of the bowl is at room temperature and the whites hold stiff peaks. (If the mixture is warm, it will melt the butter.)

Reduce the speed to medium and add the butter, a few pieces at a time. If at any point the mixture looks broken, increase the speed and beat to re-emulsify it, then reduce the speed and continue adding the butter. Check the consistency: if the buttercream is too loose to hold its shape, it should be refrigerated for up to a few hours to harden, then beaten again to return it to the proper consistency.

The buttercream can be stored in a covered container in the refrigerator for up to 5 days or frozen for up to 1 month; defrost frozen buttercream in the refrigerator overnight before using. Thirty minutes before using the buttercream, place it in the bowl of a mixer fitted with the paddle attachment and allow to soften. Then mix on low speed to return the buttercream to the proper consistency for piping or spreading.

MAKES 450 GRAMS/3 CUPS

French Buttercream

Granulated sugar	38 grams	3 tablespoons + ½ teaspoon
	38 grams	3 tablespoons + ½ teaspoon
Egg yolks	63 grams	¼ cup + ½ teaspoon
Whole milk	75 grams	¼ cup + 2¼ teaspoons
Unsalted butter, cut into ½-inch pieces, at room temperature	250 grams	8.8 ounces

Whisk 38 grams/3 tablespoons plus ½ teaspoon sugar and the yolks together in a medium bowl; set aside.

Combine the milk and the remaining 38 grams/3 tablespoons plus ½ teaspoon sugar in a medium saucepan, set over medium heat, and stir to dissolve the sugar. When the milk is at just below a simmer, remove the pan from the heat and, whisking constantly, pour it into the egg mixture. Return the mixture to the pan and place over medium heat. Whisking constantly, bring to a gentle simmer and simmer for 1 minute, lowering the heat if necessary to prevent the mixture from curdling; it should be very thick.

Strain the mixture through a fine-mesh strainer into the bowl of a stand mixer. Fit the mixer with the whisk attachment, turn the mixer to medium, and whisk for about 8 minutes, until the mixture is completely cool.

Add the butter, a few pieces at a time, to the egg yolk mixture. If at any point the mixture looks broken, increase the speed to re-emulsify it, then reduce the speed and continue adding the butter. Check the consistency: if the buttercream is too loose to hold its shape, it should be refrigerated for a few hours to harden, then beaten again to return it to the proper consistency.

The buttercream can be stored in a covered container in the refrigerator for up to 5 days or frozen for up to 1 month; defrost frozen buttercream in the refrigerator overnight before using. Thirty minutes before using the buttercream, place it in the bowl of a mixer fitted with the paddle attachment and allow it to soften. Then mix on low speed to return the buttercream to the proper consistency for piping or spreading.

MAKES 365 GRAMS/1⅔ CUPS

Almond Cream

SMALL BATCH		MAKES 275 GRAMS/1⅓ CUPS
Almond flour/meal	73 grams	½ cup + 2½ tablespoons
All-purpose flour	7 grams	2¼ teaspoons
Unsalted butter, at room temperature	73 grams	2.5 ounces
Powdered sugar	73 grams	½ cup + 2 tablespoons
Eggs	44 grams	2 tablespoons + 2 teaspoons

LARGE BATCH		MAKES 430 GRAMS/2 CUPS
Almond flour/meal	125 grams	1 cup + 1½ tablespoons
All-purpose flour	12 grams	1 tablespoon + 1 teaspoon
Unsalted butter, at room temperature	125 grams	4.4 ounces
Powdered sugar	125 grams	1 cup + 1½ tablespoons
Eggs	75 grams	¼ cup + 2 teaspoons

Sift the almond flour into a medium bowl; break up any lumps remaining in the sieve and add to the bowl. Add the all-purpose flour and whisk together.

Place the butter in the bowl of a stand mixer fitted with the paddle attachment and mix on medium-low, warming the bowl as needed (see Pommade, page 190), until the butter is the consistency of mayonnaise

and holds a peak when the paddle is lifted. Sift in the powdered sugar and mix on the lowest setting until incorporated, then increase the speed to low and mix until fluffy, 2 to 3 minutes. Scrape down the sides and bottom of the bowl. Add the almond mixture in 2 additions, pulsing to combine and then mixing on low speed for 15 to 30 seconds after each one. Scrape the bottom of the bowl to incorporate any dry ingredients that may have settled there.

Add the eggs and mix on low speed until combined and smooth, about 30 seconds. Transfer to a covered container. Press a piece of plastic wrap against the surface to prevent a skin from forming. Refrigerate until cold, about 2 hours. (The cream can be refrigerated for up to 4 days.)

Unless you are using the almond cream for the frangipane or Almond Croissants (page 249), it is best to warm it slightly in the microwave and then mix it by hand or slowly in a stand mixer fitted with the paddle attachment, increasing the speed as necessary, until it has a creamy consistency, before using.

Frangipane

Almond Cream (left)	200 grams	¾ cup + 3 tablespoons
Pastry Cream (page 373)	100 grams	¼ cup + 3 tablespoons

Frangipane is a combination of almond cream and pastry cream. Ours uses two parts almond cream and one part pastry cream. Pithiviers (page 223) are typically made with almond cream; we like the extra moisture frangipane brings to the dessert.

Place the two creams in the bowl of a stand mixer fitted with the paddle attachment and mix on low speed until well combined and smooth.

The frangipane can be used at this point or stored in a covered container. Press a piece of plastic wrap against the surface to keep a skin from forming and refrigerate for up to 4 days (depending on how long the two creams have been held separately).

If the frangipane has stiffened in the refrigerator, place it in the bowl of a stand mixer fitted with the paddle attachment and mix on low speed to loosen it, then increase the speed as necessary and mix until it has a creamy consistency.

MAKES 300 GRAMS/1¼ CUPS PLUS 1 TABLESPOON

Lemon or Lime Curd

CREME AU CITRON OU CITRON VERT

SMALL BATCH   MAKES 400 GRAMS/GENEROUS 1¾ CUPS

Silver leaf gelatin	1.8 grams	¾ sheet
Eggs	108 grams	¼ cup + 3 tablespoons
Granulated sugar	108 grams	½ cup + 2 teaspoons
Strained fresh lemon or lime juice	108 grams	¼ cup + 3 tablespoons
Unsalted butter, cut into ½-inch pieces, at room temperature	140 grams	5 ounces
Grated zest of ½ small lemon or ½ lime (optional)		

LARGE BATCH   MAKES 800 GRAMS/3½ CUPS

Silver leaf gelatin	3.6 grams	1½ sheets
Eggs	216 grams	¾ cup + 1½ tablespoons
Granulated sugar	216 grams	1 cup + 1½ tablespoons
Strained fresh lemon or lime juice	216 grams	¾ cup + 2 tablespoons
Unsalted butter, cut into ½-inch pieces, at room temperature	280 grams	9.9 ounces
Grated zest of ½ lemon or 1 lime (optional)		

Place the gelatin in a bowl of ice water to soften.

Meanwhile, whisk the eggs and sugar together in a medium saucepan. Slowly whisk in the lemon or lime juice. Place the pan over medium heat and whisk slowly, until the mixture begins to simmer. Simmer for 3 to 5 minutes, whisking constantly, until thickened. Remove the pan from the heat and whisk gently for 1 to 2 minutes to release steam and cool the curd slightly.

Remove the gelatin from the water, squeezing out excess water, and whisk it into the hot curd. Strain the curd through a fine-mesh strainer set over the container of a Vitamix and blend on low speed for a few seconds, then add the butter 2 or 3 pieces at a time, blending until incorporated. Add the zest, if using, and blend to incorporate. Let the curd cool to room temperature.

The curd can be used at this point or transferred to a covered container. Press a piece of plastic wrap against the surface to prevent a skin from forming and refrigerate for up to 4 days.

If the curd has been refrigerated and has stiffened, transfer it to the bowl of a stand mixer fitted with the paddle attachment and mix slowly until it reaches a creamy consistency.

Chocolate Glaze

GLACAGE AU CHOCOLAT

70% chocolate, coarsely chopped	110 grams	3.8 ounces
100% unsweetened chocolate, coarsely chopped	10 grams	0.4 ounce
Neutral glaze	300 grams	1 cup
Heavy cream	112 grams	¼ cup + 3½ tablespoons

We use this glaze for our chocolate éclairs instead of the typical chocolate fondant. Fondant is difficult to use and overly sweet, and it tends to crack if it sits too long on the éclair. We wanted a chocolate glaze that was intensely chocolaty but that set up smooth and shiny. So we created this one, a rich ganache to which we add a product called neutral glaze, which gives the ganache its sheen.

You'll need a Thermapen or other candy thermometer. ● *For this recipe, we use Valrhona Guanaja 70% chocolate, Valrhona Pure Pâte de Cacao 100%, and Caullet neutral glaze.*

Melt the chocolates together.

Warm the neutral glaze in a small saucepan over medium heat, stirring as it melts, then simmer for about 4 minutes, until it reaches 140°F/60°C.

Meanwhile, warm the cream in a second small saucepan.

Slowly pour the cream over the chocolate, stirring with a spatula (a whisk would aerate the mixture and make unwanted bubbles) until the mixture is smooth.

Set a fine-mesh strainer over a spouted measuring cup and strain the neutral glaze, then slowly stir the glaze into the chocolate mixture.

Press a piece of plastic wrap against the surface to prevent a skin from forming and cool to room temperature, about 1 hour, before using. The glaze should be fluid but not warm when used.

The glaze can be transferred to a covered container and refrigerated for up to 1 week. To use, heat the glaze in the top of a double boiler or in a medium bowl set over a saucepan of barely simmering water, stirring until melted and smooth but not hot.

MAKES 460 GRAMS/1¾ CUPS

Cream Cheese Frosting

Cream cheese, at room temperature	453 grams	1 pound
Powdered sugar	152 grams	1¼ cups + 1 tablespoon
¼ vanilla bean, split lengthwise		

Place the cream cheese in the bowl of a stand mixer fitted with the paddle attachment and mix on low speed until smooth, about 2 minutes. Scrape down the sides and bottom of the bowl, add the sugar, and pulse on the lowest speed to combine. Scrape the seeds from the vanilla bean, add them to the mixture, and mix for 2 to 3 minutes, until completely smooth.

The frosting can be used at this point or refrigerated for up to 3 days. If it has been refrigerated, let it sit at room temperature until just cool to the touch, then transfer to a mixer fitted with the paddle attachment and beat until smooth.

MAKES 572 GRAMS/2½ CUPS

Royal Icing

Powdered sugar	200 grams	1¾ cups
Fresh lemon juice	2 grams	¼ teaspoon
Egg whites	about 50 grams	3½ tablespoons

Royal icing is an easy powdered-sugar glaze. The lemon juice balances the sweetness of the powdered sugar and stabilizes the egg whites.

Sift the powdered sugar into the bowl of a stand mixer fitted with the paddle attachment. Add the lemon juice and mix on low speed. With the mixer running, slowly add just over half of the egg whites and mix until smooth. The icing should be loose enough to use as a glaze (much like the consistency of Elmer's glue). Add additional egg whites if needed.

MAKES 225 GRAMS/¾ CUP

Royal Icing for Allumettes

Reduce the powdered sugar to 120 grams/1 cup plus 2 teaspoons. Use 10 drops lemon juice, and reduce the egg whites to 25 grams/ 1 tablespoon plus 2 teaspoons.

MAKES 130 GRAMS/½ CUP

Sweetened Whipped Cream

SMALL BATCH		MAKES 150 GRAMS/1½ CUPS
Heavy cream	150 grams	½ cup + 2 tablespoons
Powdered sugar	5 grams	2¼ teaspoons
½ vanilla bean, split lengthwise		

MEDIUM BATCH		MAKES 300 GRAMS/3 CUPS
Heavy cream	300 grams	1¼ cups + 2 teaspoons
Powdered sugar	10 grams	1½ tablespoons
1 vanilla bean, split lengthwise		

LARGE BATCH		MAKES 450 GRAMS/4½ CUPS
Heavy cream	450 grams	1¾ cups + 2 tablespoons
Powdered sugar	15 grams	2 tablespoons + ½ teaspoon
1½ vanilla beans, split lengthwise		

We like to use a high-fat cream (40%) for our whipped cream; do use it if it's available to you. Sebastien uses powdered sugar because it dissolves more easily than granulated sugar. It's best to whip the cream just before you need it; although you can whip it in advance, it tends to break down in the refrigerator. But taking cream from liquid to soft, silken peaks is a matter of less than a minute.

Place the cream and powdered sugar in the bowl of a stand mixer fitted with the whisk attachment. Scrape the seeds from the vanilla bean and add them to the cream. Whisk at medium speed until the cream holds a shape when you lift it on the whisk and, if you will be piping it, is just stiff enough to be piped through a pastry bag; do not overwhip. It is best to spread or pipe the cream immediately after whipping.

Simple Syrup

Granulated sugar	100 grams	½ cup
Water	117 grams	½ cup

Simple syrup is basically equal parts sugar and water, simmered just to dissolve the sugar. We flavor it with rum to brush on the Rum Cake (page 106). You can use it to make fondant more pliable. Or plump dried fruit in it. Think of simple syrup as a tool.

Combine the sugar and water in a small saucepan and bring to a simmer over medium heat, stirring to dissolve the sugar. Remove from the heat and let cool to room temperature, then store in the refrigerator. The syrup keeps indefinitely.

MAKES 265 GRAMS/1 CUP

Candied Orange Peel

3 medium oranges	about 650 grams	1.4 pounds
Granulated sugar	about 300 grams	1½ cups
Light corn syrup	about 30 grams	1½ tablespoons

Halve the oranges lengthwise. Cut around the fruit, working between the flesh and the pith, to loosen the flesh from the peel. Scoop out the fruit with a spoon and reserve for another use. Scrape away any remaining flesh from the soft white pith.

Place the rinds rounded side down in a medium saucepan that holds them in a single layer or just slightly overlapping. Pour enough cold water into the pan, filling the cavities of the rinds as you do so, to keep them submerged. Bring to a boil over medium-high heat, then drain and rinse the rinds. Repeat the entire process 3 times. The rinds should be tender but not too soft, as they will cook again in the syrup.

Cut the rinds into ¼-inch-wide strips.

Weigh them, and place them in a clean saucepan with an equal weight of sugar and 10 percent of their weight in corn syrup. Add just enough water to cover. Bring to a simmer, stirring to dissolve the sugar, then simmer for about 1½ hours, turning the peels from time to time, until they are soft when pierced with a paring knife, but still hold their shape.

Transfer the peels to a small covered container and pour the syrup over the top. Let cool to room temperature, then refrigerate overnight before using. (The peels can be refrigerated for up to 2 months.)

If the sugar crystallizes, place the peels and syrup in a saucepan and warm slowly over low heat to melt the sugar.

Before using, trim off the white pith.

MAKES ABOUT 390 GRAMS/14 OUNCES

Raspberry or Cherry Jam

Granulated sugar	62 grams	¼ cup + 1 tablespoon
	62 grams	¼ cup + 1 tablespoon
Apple pectin	10 grams	1 tablespoon + 1 teaspoon
Raspberry or cherry puree	500 grams	17.6 ounces

Raspberry is the pastry chef's go-to fruit. It has a perfect sweet-tart balance that works well in countless desserts. Raspberry jam can be spread on cookies or on croissants or used to add an extra dimension to a tart. And it's very easy to make: simply bring all the ingredients to a simmer long enough for the pectin—the gelling agent—to activate, and you're done. You can also make a cherry version.

For this recipe, we use Boiron or Perfect Puree fruit puree.

Line a sheet pan with a Silpat. Combine 62 grams/¼ cup plus 1 tablespoon sugar and the pectin in a small bowl.

Combine the fruit puree with the remaining 62 grams/¼ cup plus 1 tablespoons sugar in a nonreactive pot, preferably lined copper, and stir over medium-high heat until it comes to a rolling boil, skimming off any foam that rises to the top. Stir in the pectin mixture and continue to stir as it comes to a boil. Boil, stirring for 3 minutes to activate the pectin. Pour the jam onto the prepared pan and let cool to room temperature.

Transfer the jam to a covered container and refrigerate for up to 1 week.

MAKES 460 GRAMS/1¼ CUPS

Caramel Jam

Glucose	170 grams	½ cup
Granulated sugar	250 grams	1¼ cups
Unsalted butter	40 grams	1.4 ounces
Heavy cream, warm	200 grams	¾ cup + 1½ tablespoons
Additional heavy cream if using for the Caramel Nut Tart or caramel sauce, warm	60 grams	¼ cup

We think of this as "jam" in quotes because while it is very thick, it varies in thickness depending on how hot you get the sugar before adding the other ingredients. We use it for the Caramel Nut Tart (page 140), the Caramel Apples (page 341), and the Fuhgeddaboudits (page 365). You can also serve it as a caramel sauce (use the additional cream in that case).

You'll need a Thermapen or other candy thermometer.

Place the glucose in a large saucepan and bring to a boil over high heat. Reduce the heat to medium-high and add the sugar one-third at a time, stirring just enough to incorporate before adding the next batch. (Adding all the sugar at once could cause the sugar to caramelize too quickly and unevenly.) After about 3 minutes, when the sugar has dissolved, the bubbles are a rich amber color, and the temperature is 350°F/177°C, reduce the heat to medium. Working quickly, stir in the butter. Once the butter has melted, gradually stir in the 200 grams/¾ cup plus 1½ tablespoons cream. Continue to cook, stirring and scraping to keep the mixture from scorching, until it reaches 248°F/120°C. Remove from the heat. If using the caramel for the tart, stir in the additional 60 grams/¼ cup cream. Strain the caramel through a fine-mesh strainer into a container; let cool (or pour directly into the Fuhgeddaboudits mold).

The caramel jam is ready to use. It can be refrigerated in a covered container for up to 3 weeks; to liquefy it, warm it slowly in a microwave or the top of a double boiler over barely simmering water.

MAKES 450 GRAMS/1½ CUPS

Note to Professionals: When making a large batch of caramel jam, we add 4 grams of sorbitol when the jam reaches 248°F/120°C to help prevent crystallization.

Brown Butter

Unsalted butter	453 grams	1 pound

Line a fine-mesh strainer with a double layer of cheesecloth and set over a medium bowl.

Melt the butter in a large saucepan over medium heat. As soon as it is melted, begin whisking to keep it from separating. Once the butter begins to boil, stop whisking and increase the heat to medium-high. Continue to cook the butter, whisking occasionally to keep the solids that settle on the bottom of the pan from burning, for about 5 minutes. As the moisture evaporates and the butter browns, the bubbles will lessen. Lift some of the butter on a spoon to check the color: when the butter is caramel colored, remove it from the heat and strain it into the bowl.

Discard the cheesecloth, and pour the clear butter into a container, leaving the sediment behind.

Use immediately, or store in a covered container in the refrigerator for up to 1 week. Remelt the butter slowly in the microwave or over low heat before using.

PHOTOGRAPH ON PAGE 191   MAKES 315 GRAMS/1½ CUPS + 1 TABLESPOON

Clarified Butter

Unsalted butter	453 grams	1 pound

Melt the butter in a 1-quart saucepan over low heat, without stirring. When the butter has melted, it will have separated into three layers: Skim off and discard the foamy layer of milk solids on top. The clear liquid beneath it is the clarified butter. Carefully pour it into a container, leaving the milky residue behind. Use immediately, or cover and refrigerate or freeze.

MAKES 285 GRAMS/1¼ CUPS

Egg Wash

Break 1 or more eggs, as needed, into a small bowl and whip with a fork or small whisk to combine the white(s) and yolk(s) well. Strain through a fine-mesh strainer before using.

Garlic Confit and Oil

Peeled garlic cloves	75 grams	½ cup
Canola oil	about 280 grams	1¼ cups

Cut off and discard the root ends of the garlic cloves. Place the cloves in a small saucepan and add enough oil to cover them by about 1 inch—none of the garlic cloves should be poking through the oil.

Set the saucepan on a diffuser over medium-low heat. The garlic should cook gently: very small bubbles will come up through the oil, but the bubbles should not break the surface; adjust the heat as necessary or move the pan to one side of the diffuser if it is cooking too quickly. Cook the garlic for about 40 minutes, stirring every 5 minutes or so, until the cloves are completely tender when pierced with the tip of a knife. Remove the saucepan from the heat and allow the garlic to cool in the oil.

Refrigerate the garlic, submerged in the oil, in a covered container, for up to 1 week.

MAKES 35 GRAMS/¼ CUP CONFIT AND 275 GRAMS/1¼ CUPS OIL

Sources

EQUIPMENT

AMAZON
www.amazon.com
Plastic Easter eggs; World Cuisine silicone hemisphere molds; Ateco plain, star, and French star pastry tips; Wilton #789 tip; Water Sports TL-600 Stream Machine Super Soaker; Matfer vol-au-vent cutters

COPPER GIFTS
www.coppergifts.com
Assorted cookie cutters, including snowflakes, dog bones, and pears

COUNTRY KITCHEN SWEETART
www.countrykitchensa.com
Acetate sheets, candy apple sticks, colored foil, cardboard rounds, dipping forks, daisy marguerite plunger set

HOME DEPOT
www.homedepot.com
Plastic tile comb, propane torch

JB PRINCE
www.jbprince.com
Plain round, oval, and Matfer fluted round cutter sets; financier molds (nonstick rectangular molds, M296); Flexipan cylinder M370V; disposable pastry bags; St.-Honoré 20-mm pastry tip (one of a set of three tips); 16-by-4-by-4-inch (2-pound) Pullman loaf pan; nonstick savarin molds; 1½ inch (#40) and 2½ inch (#10) ice cream scoops (aka commercial dishers); tart rings (flan rings), square tart forms (ring molds) and cake rings; bench scrapers; laser thermometer

MY WEIGH SCALES
www.myweigh.com
Assorted scales, including palm scales

N.Y. CAKE & BAKING DISTRIBUTOR
www.nycake.com
Fondant and gum paste decorating kit, fondant rolling pin, assorted silicone molds (hemispheres and rounds)

PAPERMART
www.papermart.com
Cellopaper (cellophane) and decorative packaging

SAN FRANCISCO BAKING INSTITUTE
www.sfbi.com
Lame (baker's blade holder) and blades, dough docker, bicycle cutter (strip cutter, 5-blade), lattice bicycle cutter, oven gloves, wooden boards and peels, linen canvas (*couche*), dough scrapers, and a wide variety of bread-baking supplies

SUR LA TABLE
www.surlatable.com
Perforated baking sheets; Chicago Metallic 8½-by-4½-inch loaf pans; 2¾-inch panettone molds and 4½-inch round paper molds; melon baller; mini, standard, and jumbo muffin pans; quarter and half sheet pans; cooling racks

TAP PLASTICS
www.tapplastics.com
Plastic cut to size for confectionary guides

THERMOWORKS
www.thermoworks.com
Thermapens

WILLIAMS-SONOMA
www.williams-sonoma.com
Anniversary Bundt pans, Bouchon mold, Caso B5 baking scales (#3290), All-Clad 10-inch nonstick frying pans, nonstick madeleine pans, pizza wheels, mini springform pans

Opposite, clockwise from top left, cutters for cookies and pastry: pear-shaped, Matfer #95 fluted, vol-au-vent, lattice bicycle

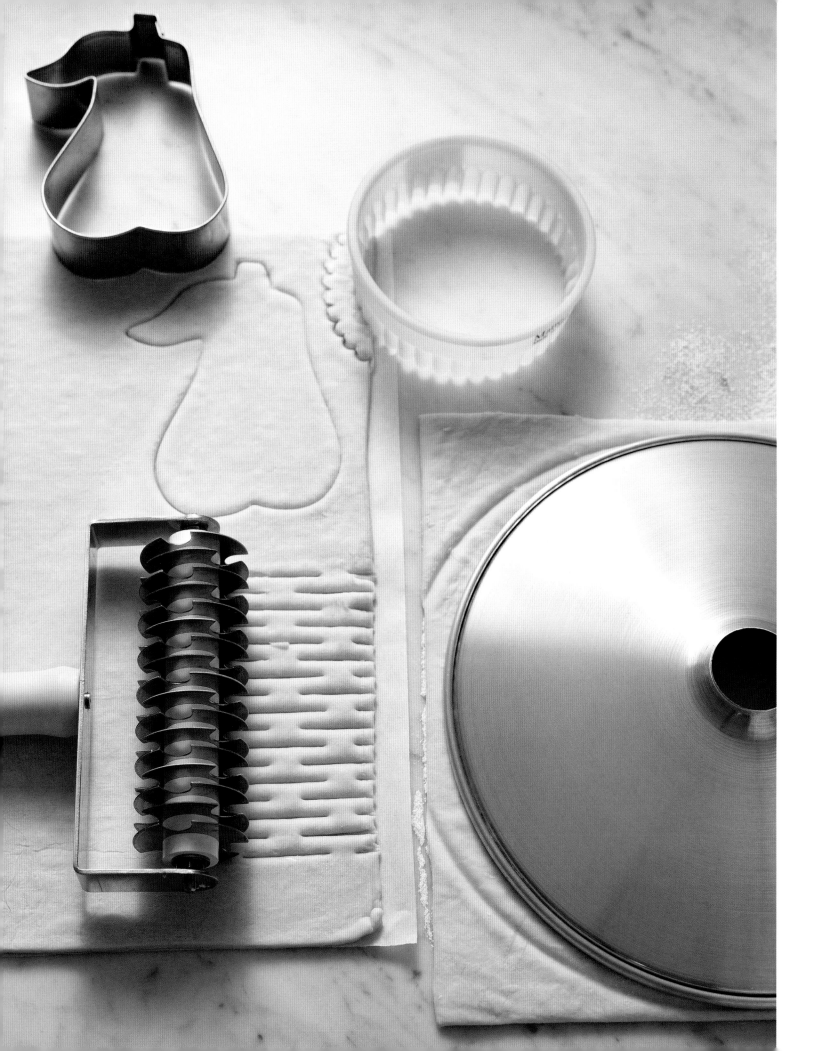

INGREDIENTS

ALBERT USTER
www.auiswiss.com
Yogurt powders

AMAZON
www.amazon.com
Bird's custard powder, diastatic malt powder, LorAnn Oils invertase, lemon and peppermint oils, Sicilian pistachios, SAF instant yeast, Virginia peanuts

THE BAKER'S KITCHEN
www.thebakerskitchen.net
ChefMaster gel food colorings

CHEF RUBBER
www.chefrubber.com
Colored cocoa butters

ESSENTIAL DEPOT
www.essentialdepot.com
Food-grade lye

KEITH GIUSTO BAKERY SUPPLY
www.centralmilling.com
Central Milling organic high-protein whole wheat flour and organic white rye flour

L'EPICERIE
www.lepicerie.com
Finely ground almond flour/meal; hazelnut flour/meal; apple pectin; Guittard Cocoa Rouge and Cocoa Noir; Valrhona cocoa powder; Guittard 72% chocolate, Valrhona 34% Caramélia, 35% Ivoire, 40% Jivara, 64% Manjari, 70% Guanja, and 100% Pure Pâte de Cacao chocolates; Cacao Barry 44% chocolate baking sticks; Cacao Barry cocoa butter; cocoa nibs; feuilletine; Caullet pouring fondant; Carma white rolling fondant; silver leaf gelatin; glucose; gold leaf; Erstein Trimoline (invert sugar); Caullet neutral glaze; Cacao Barry brune and ivoire pâte â glacer; pearl sugar; Cacao Barry white Crispearls and Valrhona 55% Les Perles; pistachio flour; Trablit pistachio paste; Cacao Barry praline paste; raspberry and strawberry powders; rice paper; vanilla beans and paste

N.Y. CAKE & BAKING DISTRIBUTOR
www.nycake.com
AmeriColor food coloring

THE PERFECT PUREE OF NAPA VALLEY
www.perfectpuree.com
Assorted fruit purees

WILLIAMS-SONOMA
www.williams-sonoma.com
Cup4Cup gluten-free flour

WORLD WIDE CHOCOLATE
www.worldwidechocolate.com
Michel Cluizel chocolates

Acknowledgments

SEBASTIEN

First and foremost, Matthew and I thank Thomas for all the opportunities he has given us, for how he has challenged us. We're forever grateful.

I'd also like to thank:

Nick Bonamico, for doing a great job at the Time Warner Center, for his help on the book, and for coming to Napa to work with Susie, Amy, and Deborah.

Richard Capizzi for his friendship, for our work in opening per se and the first Bouchon in Manhattan, and mostly for being there during both the tough and the good times.

Matthew McDonald for his invaluable participation in this book and his knowledge about bread (and also his stories about tattoos and HD bikes!).

Alessandra Altieri for helping me open Bouchon Rockefeller and steering the ship while I left to work on this book.

Scott Wheatfill from Bouchon Bistro and Bakery in Las Vegas for checking on me every week.

Gerald San Jose for helping with photography and assisting Deborah Jones while shooting in New York.

MATTHEW

My thanks go to:

Sebastien, for his limitless expertise.

Janine Weismann and Marie Betts from Bouchon Bistro and Bakery in Yountville for providing some of the last minute items we needed for the book, and for always going beyond what they needed to do.

Didier, Philippe, and Mitch for being great friends and mentors.

Derrick, Annarose, Maika, and Erik for helping me grow as a baker and a manager.

My parents for their impact on my life.

Our family of bakers in the company who make each other try harder every day.

And finally, we would like to thank our staffs at all the bakeries. They have been raising our expectations continually since the first day. We are enormously proud of this team.

THOMAS, SEBASTIEN, AND MATTHEW

Thanks to our team: Susie Heller for opening her home to us and for coordinating everything that was involved in the complex production of this book.

Amy Vogler for driving the bus and keeping us on our toes and on track. Her work, from overall conception of the book and its parts to her acute attention to detail in the recipes, is invaluable.

Deborah Jones for her care and for these amazing photos. We are grateful for the respect she gives to the food and to the chefs. We're also grateful to Josh Lewis, photo assistant and photo technician, who makes it possible for Deborah to do the work that she does.

Michael Ruhlman for listening to our stories and for bringing them to life with words only he can put together because of his knowledge about food. He makes you think twice before you answer him.

David and Joleen Hughes and their colleagues at Level for their extraordinary design work.

Special thanks to Ann Bramson and her team at Artisan, including Judith Sutton, who once again provided the copyediting that made the prose and the recipes a consistent and accurate whole; Sibylle Kazeroid, who brought all the elements together; and Nancy Murray, who got us to the end.

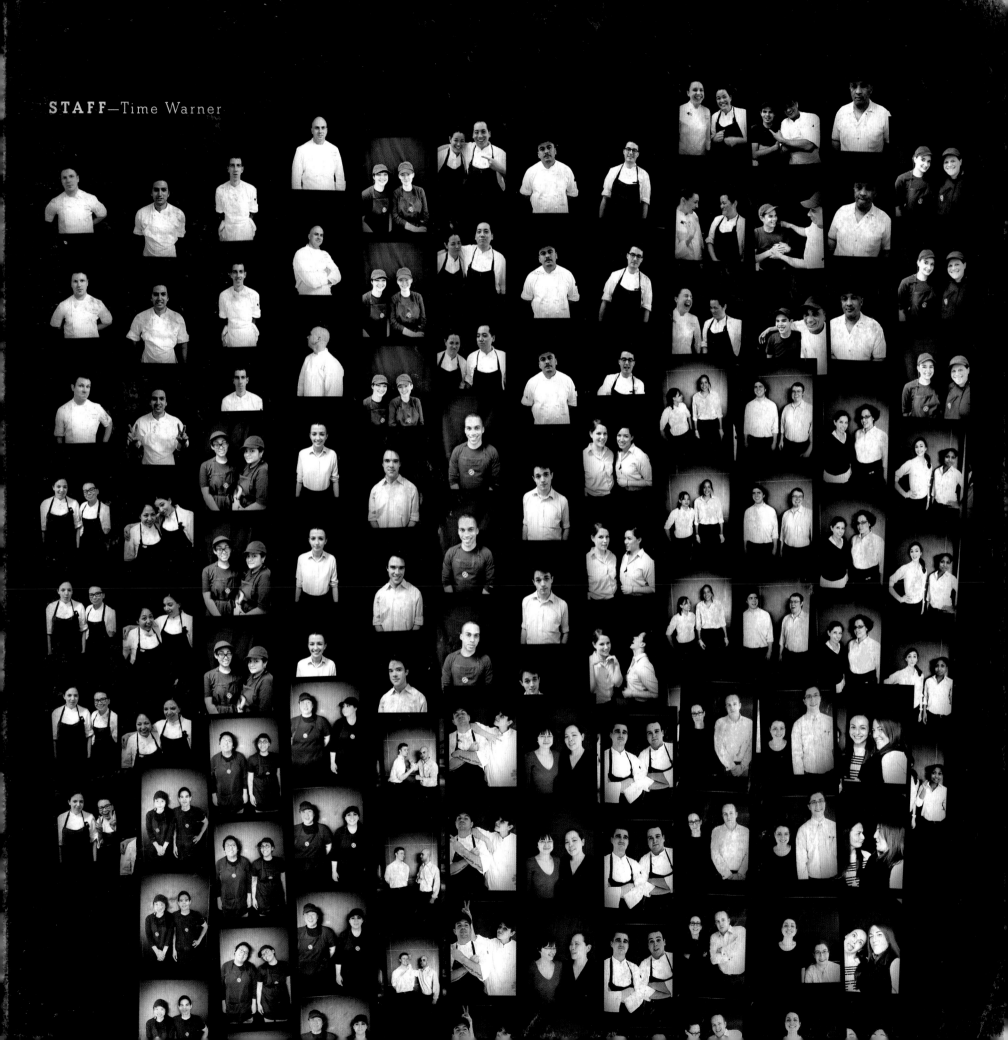

STAFF—Time Warner

STAFF—Las Vegas

Index